I0824325

Praise for *Attack from Within*

"McQuade recognizes that . . . we inhabit a single reality, one in which disinformation and violence are part of the same authoritarian playbook."

—NINA JANKOWICZ in *The Washington Post*

"A concise introduction to the threat to American democracy . . . for those curious about the past and future of political disinformation."

—*Publishers Weekly*

"A comprehensive guide to the dynamics of disinformation and a necessary call to the ethical commitment to truth that all democracies require."

—TIMOTHY SNYDER, author of the *New York Times* bestseller *On Tyranny*

"[McQuade's] writing and legal analysis are an antidote to both ignorance and political hysteria—at a time when we all need to be informed and vigilant about the threats posed by would-be authoritarians and their enablers."

—ARI MELBER, MS NOW Chief Legal Correspondent and host of *The Beat with Ari Melber*

"Meticulous, lucid, compelling. Spurred by the 'fierce urgency of now,' McQuade has laid out how we can recognize and then disarm the weapon of disinformation and, in the process, save American democracy."

—CAROL ANDERSON, author of *One Person, No Vote: How Voter Suppression is Destroying our Democracy* and the *New York Times* bestseller *White Rage*

"[McQuade's] message that we must make truth in democracy our national purpose could not come at a better moment."

—RUTH BEN-GHIAT, author of *Strongmen: From Mussolini to the Present*

"McQuade crystallizes the seriousness of what happened on January 6th and the ongoing threat to our country. Now more than ever, it's critical to read this profound book."

—PREET BHARARA, former United States Attorney for the Southern District of New York

"A compelling work about a challenge that—left unexamined and left unchecked—could undermine our democracy."

—ERIC H. HOLDER JR, 82nd Attorney General of the United States

The Fix

Saving America from the Corruption of a Mob-Style Government

Barbara McQuade

SEVEN STORIES PRESS
NEW YORK • OAKLAND • LONDON

Seven Stories Press
140 Watts Street
New York, NY 10013
www.sevenstories.com

College professors and high school and middle school teachers may order free examination copies of Seven Stories Press titles. Visit https://www.sevenstories.com/pg/resources-academics or email academic@sevenstories.com.

Library of Congress Cataloging-in-Publication Data is on file.

ISBN: 978-1-64421-555-5 (hardcover)
ISBN: 978-1-64421-556-2 (ebook)

Printed in the USA.

9 8 7 6 5 4 3 2 1

To Mom, who always looks on the bright side,
and Dad, who could fix anything.

CONTENTS

PART III: How We Take It Back

INTRODUCTION

THE FIX WAS IN

Five million and ten million.

Those were the dollar values of the contracts that Tom Hardiman lost for refusing to pay kickbacks in exchange for doing work for the City of Detroit.[1] Hardiman, the head of an infrastructure construction firm, was on the witness stand during the 2013 trial of former Detroit mayor Kwame Kilpatrick and his codefendants. A bright, charismatic politician, Kilpatrick had been indicted for using his office as a racketeering enterprise.[2] Among his codefendants was Bobby Ferguson, an excavation subcontractor and friend. The most serious charge against the men alleged a scheme commonly called "pay to play," in which individuals seeking to obtain contracts with the City of Detroit—some worth tens of millions of dollars—had to pay kickbacks to the mayor or his associates.

On this day, Hardiman testified that he had twice submitted bids on contracts to perform work for the City of Detroit.[3] While he was waiting to hear whether his bids would be accepted, Ferguson approached him and asked for a 25 percent cut. Hardiman declined. He later learned that he had lost both bids. The company that had won the work, it turned out, had included Ferguson's firm to perform excavation work in its bid. Hardiman learned the hard way that if he wanted to receive lucrative contracts from the Kilpatrick administration, he would have to hire the mayor's buddy and pay him a hefty portion of the proceeds. And so, he began including Ferguson in his contract bids.

Hardiman said he agreed to pay Ferguson because he was still haunted by the contracts he'd lost and feared Ferguson's sway over the mayor. Hardiman testified that once, Ferguson called and asked for twenty-five thousand dollars; Hardiman raced over to Ferguson's home with the money. Eventually, Hardiman was paying Ferguson to perform no work at all. As in most shakedowns, once Hardiman began paying extortion money, Ferguson kept coming back for more. The fix was in.

As the United States attorney in Detroit at the time, I oversaw our team's prosecution of the Kilpatrick enterprise, which resulted in convictions for multiple crimes, including racketeering conspiracy, bribery, wire fraud, extortion, and tax offenses.[4] Kilpatrick was sentenced to twenty-eight years in prison, though President Donald Trump later commuted his sentence. Despite Ferguson's lesser role in the case, he received no clemency from Trump; Ferguson was later granted compassionate release during the Covid-19 pandemic, in part because of the disparity caused by the break Trump had given to the more culpable Kilpatrick.[5] As the judge wrote at the time, Ferguson "was a single-minded crony of the mayor's, whose only apparent goal was to enrich himself at others' expense. He achieved that goal through threats and intimidation, primarily focused on the business expectations of his targets. But he was not the driver of the bus; that was Mr. Kilpatrick, where the power resided."[6]

Power

This is a book about power—how it is acquired, how it is abused, and how we, the people, can take it back. At the founding of our country, the framers of our Constitution sought to share power among three coequal branches of government, to prevent any one person or faction from accumulating too much. But we are now living through a time when a president has sought to become "where the power resides." Drawing on lessons about power and corruption from the world of criminal law, this book explores a pathway to fix what's wrong in our country in the same way I learned, as a federal prosecutor, to combat crime—through prevention, disruption, and deterrence.

Throughout history, we have seen political opportunists exploit the fragility of constitutional democracies. Once in power, corrupt leaders work to dismantle the very checks meant to constrain them: In 1930s Germany, democratic institutions were turned against the people to establish a regime of terror. In post-Soviet Russia, oligarchs and loyalists replaced public servants. Hungary and Turkey provide contemporary examples of democracies hollowed from within—not by military coups but by calculated political maneuvering and intimidation. We are seeing disturbingly similar patterns of events in the United States today.

These examples are intended not to alarm but to awaken. In each case above, leaders used raw power to dominate the political system—and, once in place, they silenced courts, weaponized agencies, vilified dissenters, and distorted laws with impunity. America is not immune to a descent into authoritarianism. Our system presumes that good-faith actors will steward power with humility and restraint—but what happens when power is claimed by someone who rejects those premises? What happens when the leader governs through mob-style corruption, cruelty, and chaos? When a president claims that our system of government is so broken, and that he is so all-powerful, that he alone can fix it?[7] This book—a follow-up to *Attack from Within*—is about the dangers of American autocracy and how we can stop it.

Corruption

In the Kilpatrick case and others, I have witnessed the corruption of power, in which individuals in positions of authority employ unscrupulous means to achieve their preferred outcomes. Corruption comes in many forms—threats, extortion, lies, self-dealing. But beyond the traditional concept of the word—official acts performed in exchange for monetary gain—corruption also entails abuse of the public trust in more subtle ways. Law professor Zephyr Teachout, who has studied how notions of corruption have evolved throughout our nation's history, writes:

> Corruption, in American tradition, does not just include blatant bribes and theft from the public till, but encompasses many situations where politicians and public institutions serve private interests at the public's expense. This idea of corruption jealously guards the public morality of the interactions between representatives of government and private parties, foreign parties, or other politicians.[8]

This expansive definition of corruption covers any government conduct that lacks integrity. During the Enlightenment, French philosopher Montesquieu argued that corruption was the opposite of virtue, which requires "love of equality."[9] Under this view, favoring the rich over the poor is a form of corruption. Gerrymandering voting districts constitutes corruption. Corruption also occurs when officials ignore institutional norms, act in bad faith, mislead the public, or abuse their lawful powers. Even allowing the appearance of bias is a type of corruption because it undermines public confidence in government. As Adlai Stevenson II once said, "Those who corrupt the public mind are just as evil as those who steal from the public purse."[10]

For example, in the early days of the republic, some members of Congress were outraged when Benjamin Franklin accepted a bejeweled snuff box from Louis XVI following his service as America's minister, or ambassador, to France. While some viewed the gift as a token of gratitude in line with the traditions of diplomacy, others saw it as a symbol of expectation and dependency that would compromise Franklin's unequivocal loyalty to the United States, since most people naturally feel goodwill toward someone who gives them a gift. At the very least, Franklin's acceptance of the snuff box created the *appearance* that he was now beholden to the French king. Unlike the political systems of Britain and France, in which displaying the trappings of power was commonplace, Teachout writes, the American political system was built on "civic virtues and a deep commitment to representative responsiveness at the core."[11] Americans have long favored the everyman politician, in the style of *Mr. Smith Goes to Washington*; leaders since George Washington have eschewed the pageantry of office, lest they appear to be wannabe kings.

Donald Trump has brought a very different approach to presidential politics, one that has corrupted our traditional expectation of public service that benefits the people. Trump has purged independent agencies of their leaders and installed lapdogs in their place, even when they appear to lack the skills and experience required for the job. He has pressured law firms, the media, and universities into accepting his demands for increased control over their activities in exchange for avoiding various forms of punishment. In the name of holding accountable public officials who engage in imagined "lawfare," Trump and his top officials at the Justice Department have themselves weaponized law enforcement to exact revenge on rivals. Trump has impounded congressional appropriations and deployed the National Guard to police American cities. He has ordered the deportation of immigrants without providing the due process they are guaranteed under the Constitution.[12] When judges rule against him, he has attacked them on social media or called for their impeachment.[13] Trump has used military force to oust a foreign leader, claim its oil resources, and stake out dominance over the Western Hemisphere, abandoning traditional allies and effectively carving up the world for each superpower to control its region, the way New York's crime families allocated the plundering of the city's five boroughs. Each of these acts has corrupted American values, ideals, norms, alliances, and traditions.

What these forms of corruption have in common is the abuse of public power for personal benefit. Extortion—a threat of harm unless a person accedes to demands—is a particularly insidious form of corruption because it creates a cycle of domination and submission. Most people who deal with an extortionist believe they will make a one-time payment, and then the pressure will be off. But just the opposite is true. It's like giving your lunch money to a bully: Once the extortionist knows you are an easy mark, they keep coming back for more. What's more, as Tom Hardiman learned, once you pay an extortionist, they own you. They know you won't complain, because to do so would be to admit your own guilt. That's called leverage. When a political system becomes corrupted, those who learn to play the game can reap the advantages, leading to a symbiotic relationship between the leader and wealthy business elites who benefit from a patronage relationship. Businesspeople support the leader's agenda with financial contributions and complicity, the leader rewards them with favorable financial opportunities and regulatory decisions, and the cycle continues, eventually leading to oligarchy, in which a government is controlled by a small number of individuals rather than by the people.

Trump has often been accused of operating like an authoritarian who seeks to maximize control. That may be true, but Trump's approach to power during his second term has also made him resemble something else—a mob boss. Trump exhibits many of the same characteristics as the corrupt defendants I encountered during my career as a federal prosecutor. Like the head of a crooked political machine or a criminal organization, Trump uses power not just to lead but to dominate. He makes threats or applies pain to his targets, forcing them to beg for mercy—and once they accede to his power, he controls them. In his farewell address, George Washington warned that laws without virtue could not protect us, and that "cunning, ambitious, and unprincipled men will be enabled to subvert the power of the people and to usurp for themselves the reins of government, destroying afterwards the very engines which have lifted them to unjust dominion."[14] While we have seen corruption and scandals in our government before, such as Boss Tweed's Tammany Hall Democratic Party machine in New York City and Richard Nixon's Watergate break-in and cover-up, we've never seen anything quite like Trump's open and public lust for power.

Trump's mastery of leverage no doubt reflects the influence of Roy Cohn, one of his early mentors. Cohn was a lawyer who served as chief counsel for Senator Joseph McCarthy's communist witch hunts of the 1950s and later represented members of New York's most notorious crime families.[15] A former Trump employee said that Cohn was the one who "tutored Trump to ignore the law."[16] Trump first met Cohn when he defended Trump and his father in a 1973 federal investigation into allegations of racial discrimination in their apartment rentals. The result was a settlement, but it went unenforced because of what a *Politico* profile called "Cohn's shameless, time-buying tactics."[17] During his career, Cohn was indicted four times but never convicted of any crime, prompting comparison to Harry Houdini,[18] though Cohn would eventually be disbarred for "dishonesty, fraud, deceit and misrepresentation."[19] Cohn once told *Penthouse* magazine, "I decided long ago to make my own rules."[20] Indeed, when Trump complained that his first attorney general, Jeff Sessions, had followed Department of Justice (DOJ) ethics protocols and recused himself from the Russia investigation in 2017, he asked aloud, "Where's my Roy Cohn?" As described by National Public Radio (NPR), "The clear implication was that Cohn, the advocate who stopped at nothing, would never have cowered before a few departmental rules or procedural niceties."[21] Don McGahn, who served as Trump's first White House counsel, told Special Counsel Robert Mueller that Trump complained about his habit of taking notes, a routine best practice of any ethical lawyer to document conduct and communications. According to McGahn, Trump told him, Roy Cohn "did not take notes."[22]

Cohn compared himself to Niccolò Machiavelli, the influential Renaissance political philosopher.[23] In his political treatise *The Prince,* Machiavelli argued that rulers could best succeed through deception, ruthlessness, and cruelty, and that it was better to be feared than loved.[24] It was essential, in Machiavelli's view, not to simply cross someone but to dominate them into submission: "If an injury has to be done to a man it should be so severe that his vengeance need not be feared."[25] According to Michael Franzese, a former member of the

Colombo crime family, Machiavelli was "kind of the patron saint of the mob." As interpreted by Franzese, Machiavelli's view was that "you can do anything you need to do to maintain power" because "the ends justify the means as long as you get what you want in the end."[26] Roy Cohn embraced these values. According to his biographer, "Cohn was known for pushing aggressive tactics to the limits and beyond, especially for filing lawsuits and countersuits to bully his adversaries."[27]

Cohn's influence can be seen in Trump's first book, *The Art of the Deal*. Trump writes, "The best thing you can do is deal from strength, and leverage is the biggest strength you have. Leverage is having something the other guy wants. Or better yet, needs. Or best of all, simply can't do without."[28] Sometimes, Trump writes, you have to manufacture your own leverage, noting that "leverage often requires imagination and salesmanship. In other words, you have to convince the other guy that it's in his interest to make the deal."[29]

With Cohn's training, perhaps it is no surprise that Trump was the first felon to serve in the White House, having been convicted in a New York state court in May 2024 of thirty-four counts of falsifying business records to conceal hush-money payments to an adult film star before the 2016 presidential election.[30] He managed to dodge the consequences of his conviction by regaining the presidency before he could be sentenced; in January 2025, the court granted Trump an "unconditional discharge," closing the case with no prison time required or fine assessed.[31]

In June 2023, Trump was also indicted by Special Counsel Jack Smith for unlawfully retaining sensitive government documents and obstructing the government's efforts to retrieve them.[32] Two months later, Smith indicted Trump again, this time in a case alleging fraudulent interference in the 2020 presidential election.[33] Later that month, Trump was indicted in Georgia alongside eighteen codefendants under the Racketeer Influenced and Corrupt Organizations (RICO) Act, alleging a scheme to interfere with the 2020 presidential election in that state.[34] Trump's lawyers managed to delay the trials for a variety of reasons unrelated to the merits of the charges:

disqualification of Fulton County district attorney Fani Willis over ethical concerns regarding a romantic relationship with a subordinate, a judicial finding that the federal special counsel regulations violated the Constitution's Appointments Clause, and a ruling by the US Supreme Court that a president is immune from criminal prosecution for conduct that occurs within the scope of his presidential duties.[35] As a result of the delays, Trump was able to avoid trials in all three cases by winning the 2024 election. Smith moved to dismiss, without prejudice, his federal cases against Trump for unlawfully retaining sensitive government documents and interfering with the 2020 presidential election, noting that his motion was based not on the merits of the charges but on the view of the Justice Department that a sitting president cannot be prosecuted.[36] The indictment in Georgia fizzled once Willis and her office were disqualified. Cohn—and Houdini—would have been proud.

Rather than be humbled by the indictments, Trump wore them as a badge of honor during the 2024 presidential campaign, often bragging that he had been indicted more times than "Alphonse Capone."[37] Capone, of course, was a notorious gangster who led the Chicago rackets during the Prohibition era, controlling illegal gambling, bootlegging, and prostitution.[38] He was said to be involved in bribery and murders, including the legendary gangland killing known as the Saint Valentine's Day Massacre, in which men dressed as police officers used machine guns to kill members of a rival gang.[39] Because of the fear that Capone sowed widely, prosecutors were unable to find witnesses to testify against him. Eventually, he was charged with and convicted of income tax evasion, a crime that can be prosecuted solely on the basis of documents.[40]

Trump repeated the comparison frequently, telling Fox News, "I've often said, Al Capone, he was one of the greatest of all time, if you like criminals. He was a mob boss, the likes of which—'Scarface,' they call him. And he got indicted once. I got indicted four times."[41] Trump told Iowa rallygoers that Capone "was seriously tough, right?" noting that "if you looked at him in the wrong way, he blew your brains out."[42] British journalist Samuel Earle argued that the frequency of the references made it clear that Trump relished the comparison to the dangerous mobster. According to Earle:

> Mr. Trump's eagerness to invoke Capone reflects an important shift in the image he wants to project to the world. In 2016, Mr. Trump played the reality TV star and businessman who would shake up politics, shock, and entertain. In 2020, Mr. Trump was the strongman, desperately trying to hold on to power by whatever means possible. In 2024, Mr. Trump is in his third act: the American gangster, heir to Al Capone—besieged by the authorities, charged with countless egregious felonies but surviving and thriving nonetheless, with an air of macho invincibility.[43]

The comparisons with Capone are abundant, given Trump's gangster-style assertions of power and his efforts to squeeze money from every opportunity. But Trump's leadership style goes beyond corruption in its narrow, criminal sense. Through his words and deeds, Trump has also corrupted our institutions, our foreign relations, our discourse, our values, and a system of government that had lasted 250 years.

Cruelty

Trump's taste for vengeance means that his power is used not just to advance his policy goals but to exact retribution, sometimes in cruel fashion. *New York Times* columnist Maureen Dowd wrote that, in contrast to the Founding Fathers, who spoke frequently of "virtue" to "help mold our anti-monarchical society," Trump "is not interested in virtue; only humiliation, conflict, enrichment, and revenge."[44] As a former prosecutor, I view respect for human dignity as a fundamental requirement for holding public office. The Trump administration, however, traffics in cruelty. Cuts by Trump's so-called Department of Government Efficiency (DOGE) to the United States Agency on International Development (USAID), which provides humanitarian aid such as food and medical treatment abroad, were expected to result in fourteen million deaths around the world over the next five years, with the most significant impact falling on children under the age of five.[45] Trump pushed through a budget bill that would harm some of America's most vulnerable citizens by cutting $1 trillion from Medicaid and $230 billion over ten years from the Supplemental Nutrition Assistance Program (SNAP), commonly referred to as "food stamps"[46]; he seems to reject the view of the nation, expressed by prior presidents of both parties, that "America is great because America is good."[47] When a Minnesota state legislator and her husband were shot and killed in their own home by an intruder in an act of apparent political violence, Trump offered no solace to the state's governor, Tim Walz, who had been Kamala Harris's running mate in the 2024 presidential election. When asked whether he had called Walz, Trump responded, "I think the governor of Minnesota is so whacked out, I'm not calling him. Why would I call him?"[48] Elon Musk, whom Trump appointed to serve as the head of DOGE, went so far as to say that "the fundamental weakness of Western civilization is empathy."[49]

Some of Trump's most cruel blows were leveled against immigrants, whom Trump has referred to as "animals" who "infest our country."[50] During a cabinet meeting tirade in December 2025, he referred to Somali immigrants as "garbage," as Vice President JD Vance banged the table in approval.[51] When the Trump administration sent planeloads of immigrants to a maximum-security prison for terrorists in El Salvador in March 2025, without prior notice or a hearing, the group included a Maryland man who became something of a cause célèbre. Kilmar Abrego Garcia, the federal government admitted, was deported in error—one of the hazards of failing to provide due process.[52] But despite court orders to "facilitate" his return, the Trump administration refused.[53] In May, federal prosecutors in Nashville indicted Abrego Garcia on charges of transporting undocumented immigrants[54]; it was only then that the government transported him back to the United States to face charges, even though it had the power to bring him back all along.[55] Upon his return, Deputy Attorney General Todd Blanche, a top official at the

US Department of Justice, posted a copy of the indictment against Abrego Garcia on X, along with the words, "Welcome back."[56] Then, rather than proceed with his trial, the government sought to deport Abrego Garcia to Uganda, a country half a world away to which he had no connection.[57] Courts intervened to prevent his immediate deportation.

Cruelty is contagious. It is not just Trump and Blanche who demonstrate a lack of common decency; other members of the administration and the Republican Party do, too. Mocking the misfortune of others has become the MAGA movement's calling card. In early July 2025, when the Supreme Court cleared the way for the administration to deport immigrants to a third country where they had no ties, Tricia McLaughlin, a spokeswoman for the Department of Homeland Security (DHS), posted on social media, "These sickos will be in South Sudan by Independence Day." The immigrants she called "sickos" were from Mexico, Vietnam, and other countries outside the continent of Africa, and some advocates feared they would face torture in South Sudan, a country plagued by violence and civil unrest. Yet they had received no notice or hearing to demonstrate the potential that they could be harmed—the basic elements of due process.[58] Homeland Security Secretary Kristi Noem posted the court's decision on social media with a video of Trump dancing.[59]

When I served in government, I was always taught not to "spike the football," referring to the way a running back might slam the pigskin into the turf in the end zone after scoring a touchdown. The metaphor suggests that government officials should not boast about victories in court, because the goal is not to "win" but to ensure that justice is served and the public is protected. Respect for the fair administration of justice merits a dignified response. And yet, when the court ruled in favor of the Trump administration, McLaughlin posted, "Fire up the deportation planes."[60]

How can you expect anything other than cruelty when the immigration program is driven by Stephen Miller, a top aide to Trump? In high school, Miller ran for student government on the platform of making the janitors work harder. During his campaign speech, he reportedly said, "Am I the only one who is sick and tired of being told to pick up my trash when we have plenty of janitors who are paid to *do it for us*?"[61]

The Trump White House and other executive branch agencies utilize social media to energize the MAGA base by expressing not just satisfaction but also glee over their enforcement actions.[62] In one post by the Department of Homeland Security, video footage described as an immigration raid was set to the Vanilla Ice rap song "Ice Ice Baby." The post said, "We're bringing ICE to the party."[63] The White House account posted similar memes, including a video of chained immigrants being loaded onto a deportation flight that was labeled as something that would bring pleasure to the viewer.[64] As Trump promised a surge of ICE agents in Chicago, he posted on his own Truth Social account a meme labeled "Chipocalypse Now," depicting himself as Robert Duvall's air cavalry commander in *Apocalypse Now*, with a caption evoking the Vietnam War film's famous line: "I love the smell of deportations in the morning."[65] During the nationwide "No Kings" rallies in October 2025, Trump posted on social media an AI-generated video depicting himself wearing a crown while flying a fighter jet labeled "King Trump" and dropping feces on protesters.[66] Nathan Taylor Pemberton, who writes about political extremism, called the administration's communications style "a new form of political propaganda, updating a dark art for the platform era." Pemberton described the communications style as "ruthless, inflammatory, and designed for maximum viral reach."[67] Welcome to Trump's America, the land of the free and the home of the troll.

Even Republicans outside the Trump administration have become infected with the virus of cruelty. In February 2025, GOP Congressman Mike Collins of Georgia used a tasteless joke to suggest an alternative way to remove an undocumented immigrant: "Or we could buy him a ticket on Pinochet Air for a free helicopter ride back."[68] (The former Chilean dictator was known for "death flights" during which dissidents were thrown to their deaths from airplanes and helicopters.)[69] In May 2025, Senator Joni Ernst, a Republican from Iowa, was confronted at a town hall in her home state by voters who opposed cuts to Medicaid in Trump's proposed budget bill.[70] When a member of the audience shouted, "People are going to die!" Ernst responded by saying, "We are all going to die." Ernst came under fire for the comment, but rather than express remorse, she doubled down on her callousness, recording a sarcastic video that she posted on social media.[71] In the video, Ernst looked earnestly into the camera and deadpanned: "I would like to take this opportunity to sincerely apologize for a statement that I made yesterday at my town hall"—a good start. But then she continued: "I made an incorrect assumption that everyone in the auditorium understood that yes, we are all going to perish from this Earth. So, I apologize." Her words made it clear that this was not an apology but rather an insult to her audience's intelligence. And then came the kicker: "And I'm really, really glad that I did not have to bring up the subject of the tooth fairy as well."[72]

The video may have earned the senator likes and shares from others who traffic in "owning the libs," but in creating it, she further debased our civil discourse and our respect for our fellow Americans, a growing trend on the far right. As Pemberton wrote, "These radicalized conservatives, some of whom are working as junior staff members and political operatives across the GOP, are showing us the future of conservatism, one demented post at a time." When a president and his party routinely mock their opponents, it normalizes their cruelty. According to Pemberton, the GOP's conduct has given permission to others "to defy social norms, float racial conspiracy theories, denigrate foreign cultures—to celebrate gruesome fantasies of barbarism, even permission to threaten select groups."[73]

Chaos

When your primary objectives are wealth and power, rather than effective government and sound policy, dysfunction is likely to ensue. Consequently, in addition to corruption and cruelty, chaos is also part of the Trump brand. By surrounding himself with advisers chosen primarily for fealty over ability, Trump has ensured his team is plagued by controversy and dysfunction. The early days of Trump's second term featured the use of the commercial messaging app Signal to communicate secret US attack plans in Yemen.[74] Among the Signal group's members were Vice President J. D. Vance, Secretary of State Marco Rubio, Secretary of Defense Pete Hegseth, and National Security Adviser Mike Waltz. Discussing secret military operations on an unsecure platform was bad enough, but Waltz exponentially compounded the problem when he accidentally added to the group chat a person who was not supposed to be there. Not only was Jeffrey Goldberg a civilian with no security clearance, he was also the editor in chief of *The Atlantic*.[75] The use of the Signal app to discuss the planned attack risked the lives of the airmen involved in the strike and possibly violated laws that protect national defense information from disclosure to unauthorized persons, but in the end, it was just another day in the Trump administration.

The Signal fiasco was also a harbinger of things to come: the hasty firing and rehiring of federal workers essential to maintaining the nation's nuclear stockpile, havoc in financial markets, uncertainty for businesses caused by on-again, off-again tariffs, and flip-flops on immigration raids targeting farm and hotel workers.[76] Six months into Trump's second term, half a dozen people were holding more than one high-level title.[77] Marco Rubio alone held four positions, serving simultaneously as secretary of state, acting national security advisor, acting administrator of USAID, and acting archivist of the United States—none of them small jobs.[78]

Perhaps as a result of this understaffing, members of the Trump administration have sometimes publicly failed to do the work of even their primary jobs. In May 2025, the Department of Health and Human Services issued a report titled "Make America Healthy Again"[79] that HHS secretary Robert F. Kennedy Jr. claimed adhered to "gold standard" science.[80] But the report contained errors in at least seven citations that experts attributed to the use of artificial intelligence.[81] Three of the problematic citations misstated the findings of the articles they referenced, and four of the papers cited did not exist at all.[82] A month later, with measles on the rise, Kennedy fired the members of the Centers for Disease Control's Advisory Committee for Immunization Practices and replaced them with vaccine skeptics.[83] Measles cases in the United States reached a thirty-three-year high in 2025, including the confirmed deaths of three people who were unvaccinated.[84] In August, Kennedy attempted to fire CDC director Susan Monarez, a Trump appointee, although the CDC director can be fired only by the president.[85] Trump fired her the next day, prompting four other senior officials to resign. One of the four, Dr. Demetre Daskalakis, director of the National Center for Immunization and Respiratory Diseases, wrote that he was leaving "because of the ongoing weaponizing of public health."[86] During Trump's August 2025 summit with Russian president Vladimir Putin in Alaska, State Department documents containing sensitive information about meeting times and locations, as well as US government employee phone numbers, were found left behind on a printer in the business center at the Hotel Captain Cook in Anchorage. National security law professor Jon Michaels said the gaffe was "evidence of the sloppiness and the incompetence of the administration."[87] As Maureen Dowd wrote in *The New York Times*, "Running government is harder than bloviating on Fox News and assorted podcasts."[88]

Meanwhile, at the Department of Homeland Security, Secretary Kristi Noem, entrusted with securing the nation, couldn't even secure her own purse. Within a few months on the job, she lost her DHS security badge, her passport, blank checks, three *thousand* dollars in cash, and the key to her apartment when a thief made off with the bag in a DC restaurant, even while under the watchful eye of her security detail.[89] Noem has made a show of cosplaying as an immigrant wrangler, patrolling the border on horseback, clad in cowboy hat and olive-green jacket. But when a tragic flood hit Texas in the summer of 2025, Noem's policy changes slowed the response of the Federal Emergency Management Administration (FEMA).[90] Noem's new policy required FEMA employees to obtain her personal approval before spending a hundred thousand dollars or more. Thus, when Noem did not provide the necessary approval until seventy-two hours after the floodwaters began to rise, the deployment of lifesaving assets was delayed. Noem's desire for maximum bureaucratic control prevented the nimble autonomy needed on the ground for local search-and-rescue crews to spring into action.[91] In the days following the flood, more than 80 percent of phone calls made to FEMA, numbering in the tens of thousands, went unanswered because hundreds of contractors at the agency's call centers had been fired.[92] The agency seemed even less prepared for hurricane season: FEMA director David Richardson, whose prior experience at DHS was in the Countering Weapons of Mass Destruction Office, told his staff shortly after taking office that he was unaware the United States had a hurricane season.[93]

Over at the Department of Government Efficiency, Elon Musk was leading cuts to the federal government without any apparent strategic plan in place. Musk's tenure lasted only 130 days, but in that time he slashed entire agencies, such as USAID, which provided humanitarian aid to developing nations and promoted American soft power around the world.[94] After his first month on the job, Musk appeared at the Conservative Political Action Conference wielding a chainsaw to revel in the ruthless cuts.[95] But reducing the federal workforce by 10 percent without careful consideration came at a cost. Some employees who were removed had to be rehired: After 2,000 employees were laid off at the Department of Energy, nearly 350 of them had to be recalled to their jobs at the National Nuclear Security Administration (NNSA), where they performed critical functions such as assembling nuclear warheads, managing radioactive waste sites, and preventing contamination of residential areas.[96] Rob Plonski, a deputy division director at the NNSA, posted a blunt assessment on social media: "Cutting the federal workforce responsible for these functions may be seen as reckless at best and adversarially opportunistic at worst."[97] The online magazine *Slate* called it "a mess, so farcical that it almost didn't feel real, except that it was."[98]

Trump's signature economic plan—"reciprocal tariffs" that would ostensibly balance the nation's trade deficit—was possibly even more chaotic. Announcing different tax rates for different countries, Trump referred to the day of his tariff decree in April as "Liberation Day."[99] Adverse reactions in the stock market, though, caused him to "pause" the blanket tariffs and then begin negotiating with individual countries for "deals" on rates.[100] Although the president lacked clear authority under constitutional and statutory law to impose tariffs, Trump did so seemingly at will, even for reasons beyond trade purposes, punishing Canada for alleged fentanyl smuggling and Brazil for the prosecution of its former president Jair Bolsonaro, a Trump ally.[101] When asked whether the tariff rate on Brazil was extortion, former Trump adviser Steve Bannon said, "It's MAGA, baby. It's a brave new world."[102]

According to *The New York Times*, after the first six months of Trump's second term, the tariffs were an "assault on global trade" without "any semblance of organization or structure." As the *Times* described it, "Trump has changed deadlines suddenly. He has blown up negotiations at the 11th hour, often raising unexpected issues." Airlangga Hartarto, the Indonesian minister for economic affairs, said that negotiating tariffs with Trump was like "going through a labyrinth" and arriving "back to Square 1."[103]

The Trump administration's combination of corruption, cruelty, and chaos is a triple threat to American democracy. And while Donald Trump will not be on the political stage forever, the MAGA movement will likely outlast his presidency. His relentless push for unchecked presidential power threatens not only to erode the norms of American democracy but also the very fabric of our society. If this trajectory continues, we risk becoming a democracy in name only, where power is controlled by the few, checks and balances are ignored, disparities in wealth grow wider, public confidence in government shrinks, information warfare prevails, and vigilante violence becomes ever more pervasive.

A Way Forward

To save America as we know it, we must first acknowledge the corruption, cruelty, and chaos that now exist all around us. Kwame Kilpatrick's criminal operation profited for years by using power to receive kickbacks, instill fear, and silence victims. It wasn't until individual victims found the courage to come forward and speak out that Kilpatrick and his accomplices were brought to justice. In the same way, other political leaders will continue to use leverage for personal gain over public virtue if we let them. But in a democracy, power belongs to the people. What we need is a clear plan and the political will to take it back.

This book offers ideas to reclaim power for the people. By looking to lessons from history and examples from other countries, we can identify methods for restoring the balance of authority in our country. We can implement structural changes to provide guardrails that can prevent this president or future leaders from abusing the power of the executive branch. It is not enough to resist the status quo: We must also lay out a vision for what comes next to address our problems, including economic issues, immigration, violent crime, climate change, and the impact of technology, with the hope and optimism that have always inspired the American spirit.

But we need not wait for future leaders to take action. There are a number of steps each of us can take to improve conditions in the United States right now. Importantly, we can choose right now to see ourselves and each other as individuals and resist divisive efforts to cast us as "the right" versus "the left." We must think for ourselves and see others not as our enemies, but as our fellow Americans seeking a common purpose of freedom and prosperity.

We, alone, can fix it.

PART I

The Playbook of Power—The New Authoritarianism

ONE

CARROTS AND STICKS

In the opening scene of *The Godfather*, a tuxedo-clad Vito Corleone is seated in a dark, shadowy room.[104] From an upstairs window, Corleone oversees revelers dancing to festive music in the bright sunshine at the wedding of his daughter. But the head of the Corleone crime family must attend to business. Amerigo Bonasera, a humble funeral director, has come to ask a favor from the crime don—an honorific title derived from the Latin term "dominus," meaning "lord."[105] Bonasera describes a brutal attack on his daughter and asks Corleone to arrange for the assailants to be beaten. Corleone first scolds Bonasera for failing to show him proper respect, for failing to develop a "friendship," for failing to call him "Godfather." Bonasera weeps and kisses Corleone's ring, submitting to the don's power. Ultimately, Corleone agrees to help. He asks for no monetary payment. Instead, he whispers these words to Bonasera: "Someday, and that day may never come, I'll call upon you to do a service for me."[106]

What Corleone demands is fealty: I will do you a favor, and then you will be beholden to me. Subservience is an essential component of any corrupt organization. The leader of a lawless political machine or the kingpin of a drug trafficking organization can't accomplish their goals alone. In fact, they would rather keep their own hands clean and use underlings to do their dirty work.

I know from my own work as a government manager that effective teams have members who feel safe speaking up and providing frank advice and candid feedback to the team's leader. But in a crime organization, the objectives are different. Loyalty to the boss—not to the mission or the cause—is essential to ensure that subordinates do not reveal corrupt plans or damaging secrets. When mob bosses speak in terms of loyalty, what they really mean is obedience. Leaders of criminal organizations use carrots and sticks to build this sort of loyalty and to punish betrayal. Underlings quickly learn what they must do to stay in the boss's good graces, and a breach of loyalty is met with swift retribution. In gang terms, "snitches get stitches."

Donald Trump has long prized this form of loyalty. Early in his first term, when the FBI was investigating Russia's efforts to interfere with the 2016 election, Trump invited the agency's director, James Comey, to dinner at the White House.[107] When Comey arrived, he was surprised to find that he was the only guest.[108] Comey surmised that the dinner was "an effort to have me ask for my job and create some sort of patronage relationship."[109] When Comey told Trump that he viewed the role of the FBI as apolitical and independent from the White House, Trump said, "I need loyalty. I expect loyalty."[110] Over the next two months, Trump would push Comey to "lift the cloud" the investigation was casting on his presidency, at one point stating, "Because I have been very loyal to you, very loyal; we had that thing you know."[111] Comey declined, and Trump fired him a few weeks later.[112]

The independence of the FBI director must have been a shock to Trump, who had learned how to develop loyal foot soldiers in the private sector. Michael Cohen, Trump's former lawyer and one-time fixer, said before going to prison for three years that he was motivated in his conduct by "blind loyalty to Donald Trump."[113] Among Cohen's crimes were violating campaign finance laws by making hush money payments for Trump and then lying about it to Congress.[114] Cohen later changed his views about Trump, testifying against him before Congress. Cohen said that Trump spoke in "code," running his organization "much like a mobster would do."[115]

Trump responded by calling Cohen "a rat," an underworld term for a law enforcement informant.[116]

In 2025, Trump was still living according to the mob ethos, viewing pardons as business transactions. He granted clemency for Democratic congressman Henry Cuellar of Texas, claiming without evidence that he and his wife had been indicted solely because he opposed the Biden administration on border issues.[117] Trump apparently expected Cuellar to switch parties for the 2026 midterm election in gratitude to Trump. When Cueller announced he would be running for re-election, as a Democrat, the president lambasted his "lack of LOYALTY"[118] Trump also sent a message to others seeking pardons to ensure they understood the expectation of payback, adding, "Oh' well, next time, no more Mr. Nice guy!"[119]

The Carrots

This form of loyalty also seemed to drive Trump's selections for appointees and advisers, many of whom lacked the qualifications typical for their jobs. Unlike his first term, when Trump surrounded himself with generals and veterans of prior administrations, his second term has featured appointees with very little experience in management or expertise in their fields. Until their nominations, it would have been astonishing to imagine former Fox News personality Pete Hegseth as secretary of defense, political flamethrower Kash Patel as FBI director, vaccine denier Robert F. Kennedy Jr. as secretary of health and human services, or former professional wrestling promoter Linda McMahon as secretary of education. Trump's first choice for attorney general, Matt Gaetz, was under investigation due to multiple allegations of criminal conduct, including sex trafficking and statutory rape, but Trump nominated the Florida congressman anyway, withdrawing the nomination only when it became clear that he lacked the votes for Senate confirmation.[120]

These appointments seemed absurd on their face. But when they are viewed through the lens of fealty rather than qualifications, they begin to make sense. The idea that Trump even considered Gaetz, described by NPR as "a conservative firebrand and loyal defender of Trump," for the nation's top law enforcement post demonstrated the president's desire for uncontested control above objective qualifications.[121] Trump's pick for ambassador to Malaysia, Nick Adams, a self-proclaimed "alpha male" social media influencer, was so grateful for his appointment that he posted on his Substack social media account a message of thanks to Trump, writing, "You are not only my favorite President, you are my favorite person."[122] Brendan Carr, though qualified on paper for his position as Trump's chairman of the Federal Communications Commission, began wearing a gold lapel pin with Trump's image, a startling shift from more commonplace American flag pins.[123] It was difficult to miss the symbolism—allegiance was now owed not to the nation but to its leader.

According to historian Ruth Ben-Ghiat, when individuals are placed in high office "without the credentials one would normally expect, they become dependent on and indebted to the leader."[124] This "engineered incompetence" has enormous value because it "makes those individuals more dependent on the leader and creates more space for the leader's powerful cronies to influence the institution to their own benefit."[125] In other words, a loyal pushover is easier to control than an independent expert. Hannah Arendt, a twentieth-century German American political theorist, described this concept in her seminal work, *The Origins of Totalitarianism*. "Totalitarianism in power invariably replaces all first-rate talents, regardless of their sympathies, with those crackpots and fools whose lack of intelligence and creativity is still the best guarantee of their loyalty."[126]

Take Hegseth: On the plus side, Trump's pick for secretary of defense was a Princeton graduate who had served in the military. He performed tours of duty with the Army National Guard in Guantanamo Bay, Iraq, and Afghanistan, earning two Bronze Stars for meritorious service. But honorable service in the armed forces alone does not qualify someone to lead the world's largest military organization, with three million active-duty service members, reservists, and civilian personnel stationed all over the world.[127]

According to retired lieutenant general Mark Hertling, a former Army commander, a defense secretary's duties include not only overseeing military commands around the globe but also providing advice on American capabilities and war plans when the president is considering a military operation, sometimes during a crisis. More than any other adviser to the president, the secretary of defense influences the president on whether to execute operations that could risk the lives of US troops or bring the country into war.[128] Hertling says that emotional intelligence is an essential trait for a secretary of defense, who must coordinate a unified national security and foreign policy strategy with the heads of departments of state, treasury, commerce, and homeland security; the director of national intelligence, and the national security advisor.[129] The secretary of defense, he notes, needs a "deep understanding of military strategy at the highest levels, operational logistics, the American way of war, and the unique (and at times competing) military cultures of the Army, Navy, Air Force, Marines, Space Force, and Coast Guard."[130] And through it all, he must foster "a culture of accountability, collaboration, and teamwork."[131]

And yet, Trump nominated Hegseth. Justin Higgins, a former Republican opposition researcher who vetted Hegseth for an undersecretary position during Trump's first administration, called him "perhaps one of the least qualified picks for secretary of defense that we've seen."[132] In addition to Hegseth's lack of significant management experience, his track record outside the military was deeply concerning. Hegseth had led two nonprofit organizations that advocated for veterans but resigned from both amid allegations of financial mismanagement or misconduct.[133] As the leader of Vets for Freedom, an organization with fewer than ten employees, Hegseth ran it into the ground; he racked up half a million dollars in debt and then left the organization to be folded into another entity.[134] Hegseth's experience as a financial manager did not bode well for overseeing the Pentagon's $1.3 billion budget.[135]

Hegseth later led another organization, Concerned Veterans for America, with an even more alarming record: A whistleblower report indicated that Hegseth was often so intoxicated while at work-related events that he sometimes had to be carried out.[136] According to the report, Hegseth once got so drunk at a strip club where he had taken members of his management team that he had to be physically restrained from jumping onstage to join the exotic dancers.[137] Substance abuse is a challenge for many Americans and is deserving of empathy and treatment, but it is a bright red flag for someone being considered to make decisions about whether to conduct air strikes or send troops into harm's way. The report also stated that Hegseth, who was married at the time, created a hostile work environment by repeatedly pursuing female staffers sexually.[138] In an email message, his own mother called him "an abuser of women" who "belittles, lies, cheats, sleeps around, and uses women for his own power and ego."[139] (She later apologized for writing the message and criticized *The New York Times* for publishing it.)[140] In the military, where sexual assault is a serious concern, a leader with a reputation for aggressive impropriety toward women is hardly the best role model.

Yet Hegseth was confirmed and, predictably, became embroiled in controversy almost immediately. In the incident that would become known as "Signalgate," Hegseth used a commercial messaging application to communicate with other cabinet officials about covert military operations in Yemen, demonstrating his dangerous combination of ignorance and arrogance. In the chat, Hegseth wrote, "We are currently clean on OPSEC," or operational security, ignoring the risks of using an unsecured commercial messaging application and apparently oblivious to the fact that a journalist had been inadvertently included in the group.[141] By April, reports indicated that his staff was in turmoil, leading to a headline in *The New York Times* reading, "Under Hegseth, Chaos Prevails at the Pentagon."[142]

If his incompetence could have been predicted so easily, why, then, would Trump select Hegseth to serve in such an important post in the first place? According to Higgins, the Republican vetter, Hegseth "was likely chosen because he seems willing to say and do anything Trump wants."[143] Hegseth demonstrated to the world his fawning submission to Trump during his confirmation hearing, when he told a senator that he had completed five sets of forty-seven pushups that morning, choosing the number to honor the nation's forty-seventh president.[144]

Indeed, when the time came, Hegseth did something a predecessor in Trump's first administration was unwilling to do—deploy military troops to confront civilians who were protesting on our own soil. Former Secretary of Defense Mark Esper had a more traditional résumé than Hegseth: undergraduate degree from West Point, master's degree in government from Harvard, and a doctorate in public policy from George Washington University; decorated combat commander; prior leadership positions at the Pentagon; adviser to congressional foreign relations and armed services committees; and defense industry executive.[145]

According to Esper, when racial justice protests erupted across the country in 2020 in response to the police killing of George Floyd, an unarmed Black civilian in Minneapolis, Trump wanted to deploy ten thousand troops on the streets of Washington, DC.[146] Esper wrote in his memoir that Trump asked Chairman of the Joint Chiefs of Staff General Mark Milley to attack the protestors.[147] As described by Esper, "We reached that point in the conversation where he looked frankly at Gen. Milley and said, 'Can't you just shoot them, just shoot them in the legs or something?' . . . . It was a suggestion and a formal question. And we were just all taken aback at that moment as this issue just hung very heavily in the air."[148] Esper publicly opposed Trump's push to deploy military troops on American soil to suppress protests, an act of insubordination that Trump viewed as unforgivable.[149] Shortly after the 2020 election, with only two months remaining in his administration, the president fired Esper via tweet.[150]

As he entered his second term, Trump was determined not to make the same mistake twice. During his confirmation hearing, when Hegseth was asked whether he would refuse an order from Trump to shoot protesters, he declined to answer.[151] Four months into Trump's second term, Hegseth defended Trump's deployment of five thousand members of the National Guard and marines to the streets of Los Angeles in response to immigration protests, calling them "a critical component of how we secure the homeland."[152] More troops would later be sent to Washington, DC, Chicago, and other American cities.[153] Within Hegseth's first few months on the job, GOP senator Thom Tillis of North Carolina, who had voted to confirm Hegseth, admitted that the secretary was "out of his depth as a manager of a large, complex organization."[154] Tillis made the concession only after announcing he would not seek reelection.[155] Qualifications like Esper's were once expected for the demanding job of leading the Pentagon, but credentials mean nothing to a corrupt leader who demands blind obedience over independent judgment.

Of course, the country suffers when its leaders are incompetent. Professor Brian Klaas, who studies global politics at University College London, writes that because tyrants "tend to be thin-skinned narcissists"[156] who surround themselves with sycophants, they "rarely get told that their stupid ideas are stupid, or that their ill-conceived wars are likely to be catastrophic." Klaas says, "Offering honest criticism is a deadly game and most advisers avoid doing so. Those who dare to gamble eventually lose and are purged. So over time, the advisers who remain are usually yes-men who act like bobbleheads, nodding along when the despot outlines some crackpot scheme."[157] So much for "the best and the brightest."

The Purge

While installing loyalists as agency heads, Trump also purged the independent experts in government whose fealty could not be presumed. Even before taking office, Trump announced that he would replace FBI director Christopher Wray, whom Trump himself had appointed to a ten-year term in 2017 but who had shown Trump no more loyalty than Comey had, permitting the 2022 search of Trump's Mar-a-Lago home to recover sensitive government documents that Trump had allegedly removed unlawfully from the White House.[158] Trump replaced Wray with Kash Patel, who has written books attacking the FBI as "a threat to the people."[159] During his first week in office in 2025, Trump fired seventeen inspectors general, the independent watchdogs who investigate misconduct within federal agencies.[160] Trump removed them without complying with the legal requirement to provide thirty days' notice to Congress, including a detailed rationale for the decisions.[161]

Trump also fired a Biden appointee from the National Labor Relations Board (NLRB) before the expiration of her term, despite statutory language that board members may be terminated only for "neglect of duty or malfeasance in office, but for no other cause."[162] The NLRB was left without a quorum, rendering it unable to perform its work of reviewing claims of unfair labor practices. Trump also fired the head of the Merit Systems Protection Board, which reviews claims brought by federal workers of unfair employment actions.[163] The Supreme Court granted Trump a temporary reprieve from court orders blocking the terminations and signaled that its approval may be permanent when the case comes back to the court on the merits.[164]

In August 2025, Trump fired Lisa Cook from her position on the Federal Reserve Board of Governors, well short of the expiration of her fourteen-year term. The president said he had found the statutorily required "cause" to fire her, citing allegations that Cook had made false statements on a mortgage application.[165] Cook sued, challenging her termination.[166] Her removal was a blow to the central bank's independence, which sets interest rates for the nation's lenders.[167] According to a spokesman for the Federal Reserve, "Long tenures and removal protections for governors serve as a vital safeguard, ensuring that monetary policy decisions are based on data, economic analysis, and the long-term interests of the American people."[168] Trump was constantly demanding that the Fed reduce interest rates and toying with the idea of firing its chair, Jerome Powell.[169] Lower interest rates were in Trump's short-term political interest because they would spark borrowing and investment, leading to a booming economy in time for the midterm elections, but they would also risk long-term harm to the economy by potentially triggering inflation.

The purge also extended to the Department of Justice, where Trump installed acting leaders who immediately fired more than a dozen prosecutors who had worked on the team of Special Counsel Jack Smith in the investigation of Trump.[170] They also fired FBI supervisors and demanded the names of agents who worked on the cases against defendants who participated in the January 6, 2021, attack at the US Capitol.[171] The interim US attorney in Washington, DC, Ed Martin, fired prosecutors hired during the Biden administration to work on the Capitol cases.[172] Later, seven senior supervisors were demoted because of their roles in cases against Capitol rioters and former Trump advisers Steve Bannon and Peter Navarro.[173] A former prosecutor in the office called the move "a vendetta against line prosecutors who were doing their job."[174] Scores of immigration judges, part of the Department of Justice, were fired without explanation and replaced with Trump appointees.[175]

Trump also removed Hampton Dellinger, a Biden appointee, as the head of the Office of Special Counsel (OSC), only one year into his statutory five-year term.[176] Not to be confused with Jack Smith's office, the OSC is an independent agency created by Congress following the Watergate scandal. Implemented as part of the Civil Service Reform Act, the OSC protects federal workers. Among its responsibilities are protecting whistleblowers and other federal workers from unlawful employment practices. It also enforces the Hatch Act, which prohibits political activity in federal workplaces.[177]

In Dellinger's place, Trump appointed Paul Ingrassia, who was then just three years out of law school.[178] Like Hegseth, Ingrassia's qualifications seemed to rest on his servility to Trump; he had been a fellow at Claremont Institute, the think tank home of John Eastman, the mastermind of the 2020 fake electors scheme.[179] Before his appointment, Ingrassia had called for pardoning individuals who were convicted of crimes committed during the January 6 attack at the US Capitol.[180] And he didn't stop there: He also urged reparations of one million dollars per family for those same convicts, demanded the resignation of any judge or prosecutor involved in "the J6 scam," and pressured Congress to "undertake impeachment proceedings against them if they do not cooperate." Ingrassia also advocated for Congress to make January 6 a national holiday, to place "the day's events in their proper historical context: as a peaceful protest against a great injustice affecting our electoral system."[181] In 2025, political independence was out, and blind obedience to Trump was in. Ingrassia would later withdraw himself from consideration after a group text chat was made public in which he told other Republicans that he had a "Nazi streak" and that Martin Luther King Day should be "tossed into the seventh circle of hell."[182]

In addition to replacing officials with sycophants, Trump created a new position at the Department of Homeland Security to oversee election integrity and then appointed an election denier to the job.[183] Heather Honey, a former private investigator with no experience running election systems, worked with Trump in an effort to overturn the 2020 presidential election results.[184] Arizona Secretary of State Adrian Fontes, a Democrat, said Honey had a "well-documented history of spreading election lies that have been debunked in court."[185] This fox would be making no pretense of guarding the henhouse.

The Sticks

Of course, with Trump, loyalty is a one-way street. Like Mark Esper and Michael Cohen, other former employees and appointees have learned that crossing Trump leads to punishment—and not just quietly, but cruelly. During Trump's first term, when Attorney General Jeff Sessions recused himself from the investigation into the Trump campaign's collusion with Russia, the president taunted him on social media and eventually fired him.[186] When Sessions's successor, William Barr, publicly contradicted Trump's claims that the 2020 election had been rigged, Trump demanded his resignation.[187]

Mike Pence, Trump's vice president in his first term, found himself not only insulted by his former boss but also targeted by an angry mob at the US Capitol when Trump publicly blamed him for failing to stop the certification of Joe Biden as president on January 6, 2021. According to Pence, "President Trump demanded that

I use my authority as vice president presiding over the count of the Electoral College to essentially overturn the election by returning or literally rejecting votes. I had no authority to do that."[188] After Pence issued his statement on the afternoon of January 6, indicating that he would proceed with the certification of Biden at the Capitol, Trump posted a tweet that endangered the life of the vice president—"Mike Pence didn't have the courage to do what should have been done"—prompting the crowd that had breached the Capitol to chant, "Hang Mike Pence!"[189] Some White House staffers later said the tweet prompted them to resign because it escalated the situation at the Capitol.[190]

These acts of vengeance were no one-offs; they were part of Trump's longtime strategy of what he calls "counter-punching."[191] The tactic is one he learned from his mentor, Roy Cohn.[192] As Trump wrote in *The Art of the Deal*, "When people treat me badly or unfairly or try to take advantage of me, my general attitude, all my life, has been to fight back very hard."[193] And according to his wife, Melania Trump, "When you attack Donald, he will punch back ten times harder."[194] Barbara Res, an engineer and lawyer who worked for Trump on construction projects in the 1980s, said of Trump, "He was always, 'Fire a gun at me, and I'll drop a nuclear bomb on your head,'" she said. "It was always, 'We're going to sue' whoever he thought was against him. He enjoyed it. He liked to make people suffer."[195] In August 2023, shortly after being indicted by Jack Smith for election interference, Trump posted on Truth Social, "IF YOU GO AFTER ME, I'M COMING AFTER YOU."[196]

During Trump's second term, when judges appointed by Trump ruled against him, he blamed Leonard Leo, the former chair of the conservative Federalist Society, which had provided recommendations for judicial appointments.[197] After a Trump appointee on the Court of International Trade joined a ruling to block Trump's tariffs, the centerpiece of his economic policy, Trump blasted Leo in a post on Truth Social, calling him "a sleazebag."[198] Trump also wrote that Leo "openly brags how he controls Judges, and even Justices of the United States Supreme Court," Trump wrote. "I hope that is not so, and don't believe it is!"[199] Trump seemed outraged that Leo had failed to deliver judges who, in exchange for being appointed by Trump, would always rule in Trump's favor—a warped, mob-style view of how the legal profession operates. Trump had a similar tantrum when the Supreme Court agreed that the tariffs were illegal.

The Fealty

By rewarding his appointees in advance, Trump was offering a sort of bribe: Once they accepted the title, they owed the boss their obedience in exchange. In addition, like new gang recruits who must perform an initiation rite to prove their fealty, Trump's cabinet officials were often put on the spot to perform in public to display their fawning loyalty to him. Cabinet meetings sometimes lasted for hours as Trump went around the table to extract compliments from each of his appointees. As described by *The New York Times*: "All of the president's men and women took their turns, each working a little bit harder than the last to offer Mr. Trump praise and to assure him that they were working to tackle his long list of grievances."[200]

In April 2025, Trump brought along his advisers as props when he met with President Nayib Bukele of El Salvador in the Oval Office to discuss the detention of immigrants from the United States at a maximum-security prison in his country, including the erroneous removal and imprisonment of Kilmar Abrego Garcia.[201] Trump and Bukele laughed callously about the detention of the immigrants, who received no due process before being transported to one of the world's most notorious prisons;[202] Trump even suggested sending "homegrown criminals"—American citizens—to the prison in El Salvador.[203] To lend his conduct a veneer of legitimacy, Trump trotted out Homeland Security Secretary Kristi Noem, Attorney General Pam Bondi, and Secretary of State Marco Rubio. It was time for them to earn their keep. As described by journalist Frank Bruni in *The New York Times*, the room was filled with "a gaggle of administration lackeys whom Trump had gathered around him in a perverse show of solidarity, by which I mean sycophancy."[204]

When Trump asked Noem to "say a few words about the border," she raved that it was "absolutely phenomenal what a great leader can do," ignoring the apparent legal and human rights violations that were occurring. Feigning ignorance about the public outcry over Abrego Garcia's removal from the United States without due process, his imprisonment in a foreign terrorist prison, and Trump's refusal to return him, Rubio said simply, "I don't understand what the confusion is."[205]

By then, Rubio had clearly made peace with his role as a Trump toady. In an earlier Oval Office meeting, the former Florida senator had sat silently by as Trump and Vice President J. D. Vance berated Ukrainian president Volodymyr Zelensky over Russia's war with his country.[206] Rubio had previously supported American aid for Ukraine. After the meeting, Rubio mocked Zelensky for "trying to Ukraine-splain on every issue" and posted on social media, "Thank you @POTUS for standing up for America in a way that no President has ever had the courage to do before. Thank you for putting America First. America is with you!"[207]

According to Bruni, such performances "underscore one of the most consequential dynamics of the second Trump administration: the enlistment and indoctrination of aides who will validate every fiction that Trump asks them to, obey all of his orders, and shield him from any accountability."[208] Of course, they must have known what they were signing up for: allegiance not to the public but to their leader.

"Someday, and that day may never come, I'll call upon you to do a service for me."

TWO

INVINCIBILITY THEATER

John Bravata had it all—a six-million-dollar home, ninety thousand dollars in jewelry, an expensive Maserati, and an even more expensive Ferrari. The ostentatious display of wealth gave the appearance of overwhelming success to the Michigan businessman, who led a group he called BBC Equities, also known as the "Billionaire Boys Club."[209] In fact, Bravata was a con artist, running a Ponzi scheme that would defraud investors out of fifty million dollars, robbing some of them of their life savings.[210] As I learned while supervising the case, the lavish display of wealth was a crucial element of the crime. The massive home, the flashy cars, and the expensive jewelry were all part of the charade that convinced investors that BBC Equities was a wild success.

That case highlighted the importance of dazzling imagery in fraud schemes. The trappings of success seduce potential victims to fall for the scam. The trick works in politics, too: Candidates want to look the part they are trying to project. Some lean into their backgrounds in the military or law enforcement to exude strength. Others seek to appear to be a person of the people, posing in rolled-up shirtsleeves or sitting at a kitchen table. Donald Trump, ever the showman, took the game to new heights, with no subtlety about his intentions. But visual imagery is not the only tool for conning victims or seizing power. In addition, corrupt politicians use disinformation to divide, distract, and punish. The consequence of these manipulations is to undermine public confidence in government and to normalize the use of political violence.

Invincibility Theater

Trump has long been a showman, a trait he has said he learned from his mother, who "had a flair for the dramatic and grand."[211] He has described her watching Queen Elizabeth II's 1952 coronation on television and being "enthralled with the pomp and circumstance, the whole idea of royalty and glamour."[212] He wrote that he once considered attending film school because he was "attracted to the glamour of the movies"; he admired Hollywood moguls like Samuel Goldwyn, Darryl Zanuck, and Louis B. Mayer because they were great showmen.[213]

Instead, Trump followed his father into the real estate business, where he used "bravado" and "hyperbole" to "play into people's fantasies."[214] In *The Art of the Deal*, Trump wrote, "People may not always think big themselves, but they can still get very excited by those who do. That's why a little hyperbole never hurts. People want to believe that something is the biggest and the greatest and the most spectacular." He called this "truthful hyperbole" "an innocent form of exaggeration—and a very effective form of promotion."[215]

In *The Art of the Deal*, Trump tells a story about one of his first real estate ventures. Setting up a meeting to discuss a deal in Manhattan in 1973, Trump wrote, "We had no formal name for the company . . . so I began to call it the Trump Organization. Somehow the word 'organization' made it sound bigger. Few people knew that the Trump Organization operated out of a couple of tiny offices on Avenue Z in Brooklyn."[216] Trump later decked out Trump Tower, his signature skyscraper on Fifth Avenue, with no smoke but plenty of mirrors. Trump wrote that "we used a lot of reflective glass, particularly on the sides of escalators. That was critical, because it made a fairly small core space look far larger and more dramatic."[217] In 2015, he would ride down that same escalator to announce his candidacy for president of the United States.[218] *A little hyperbole never hurts.*

Trump no doubt learned even more about the power of imagery while working on his reality television show, *The Apprentice*,[219] which *New York Times* writers Russ Buettner and Susanne Craig called "The Star-Making Machine That Made 'Donald Trump.'"[220] Each week from 2003 to 2017, viewers saw what appeared to be a wealthy businessman decisively wielding power from a large leather chair in a mahogany-paneled boardroom. Ivy League graduates competed with cutthroat ambition for an internship with the Trump Organization and the privilege of learning at the feet of a wealthy tycoon. But the show, Buettner and Craig wrote, would "test the bounds of reality television magic." In fact, the boardroom was created by set designers because producers found the real offices at Trump Tower too shabby, with chipped desks and musty carpet odors. And it was not just the office that needed a makeover. As Buettner and Craig wrote, "The producers would also need to invent a version of Donald Trump that did not actually exist—measured, thoughtful and endlessly wealthy—a complete rehabilitation of his public image."

At the time, Trump had been through four bankruptcies due to the failure of his casinos and hotels.[221] His Trump Shuttle airline had failed when his loans went into default, and he lost ownership to his creditors.[222] To stay afloat, he directed his siblings to sell, for less than market value, properties in a trust fund that his father had intended to keep in the family;[223] Trump would continue to develop his brand by putting his name on products ranging from steaks and vodka to bottled water.[224] He would eventually pay twenty-five million dollars to settle allegations of fraud made by students of his now-defunct Trump University; they claimed he failed to deliver on promises to provide education in the workings of the real estate business.[225] When *The Apprentice* was launched, Trump was well-known, but 58 percent of Americans had an unfavorable opinion of him. Over time, however, the show transformed his public image. The magic of television made him appear to be something he was not: a fabulously successful businessman.

Glitter and Gold

That illusion of success helped propel Trump to the White House in 2016. During his second term, Trump doubled down on imagery to create a sort of invincibility theater. Let's start with the décor: In 2025, Trump redecorated the Oval Office, adding ornate gold fixtures that would look at home at the Palace of Versailles.[226] The walls were adorned with gilded appliqués and gold-framed mirrors, and the mantel was replete with golden urns, vases, and decorative figurines.[227] Gold coasters stacked on end tables bore the name not of the United States or of the White House but of Trump.[228] He also redecorated the Cabinet Room, adding gold leaf to the ceiling trim and hanging more portraits, while admitting that he selected them based less on the subject and more on the size of the frame. "Look at those frames. You know, I'm a frame person. Sometimes I like frames more than I like the pictures."[229]

In mid-2025, Trump announced plans to add a ninety-thousand-square-foot ballroom to the White House, at a cost of two hundred million dollars. He had already bulldozed over and paved the Rose Garden, the better to accommodate large crowds for his speeches. The ballroom, he said, would be his legacy.[230] Some presidents are renowned for their honesty during times of crisis, and others for their leadership. Trump wanted to be remembered for glitz. He would tack on to the once modest, tasteful People's House an addition nearly the size of two football fields, the cost of which soon escalated to four hundred million dollars.[231] The staggering sum was raised through private donations from companies like Apple, Google, Lockheed Martin, and Palantir Technologies, many of which routinely bid for government contracts or were subject to regulatory action, thereby raising significant ethical concerns.[232] Additionally, contrary to Trump's initial assurances that the history of the building would be preserved, the entire East Wing of the White House was demolished in the construction process. After demolition began, Trump fired all six members of the Commission of Fine Arts, the independent agency that reviews construction plans for federal buildings to "preserve the dignity of the nation's capital."[233]

The ballroom's garish look reflected the same taste Trump displayed at his lavish apartment in Trump Tower in Manhattan and at his home at the Mar-a-Lago Resort in Florida, a style that author Peter York has referred to as "dictator chic."[234] York is the author of a book examining the homes of despots, such as Mu'ammar Gaddhafi and Saddam Hussein. According to York, the look is "an architectural and artistic means of establishing the power of the occupants, of intimidating and impressing any visitor."[235] As Trump said while admiring the Cabinet Room during a meeting, "This is a very important room. Very powerful room, great room."[236]

Trump's love of gold goes beyond White House décor, permeating much of his rhetoric and stagecraft. In his second inaugural address, he pledged that the next four years would be known as the "Golden Age of America."[237] He proposed an immigration "gold card," an expensive shortcut to a green card that would grant lawful permanent residence in the United States to anyone willing to pay five million dollars.[238] In December 2025, Trump announced plans to build a new series of battleships, to be called the "Trump class," part of a "Golden fleet" of twenty to twenty-five Navy vessels.[239] The *US Naval Institute News* estimated the cost of the ships at ten-to-fifteen billion dollars *each*.[240] Experts criticized the behemoth ships as ill-suited for modern warfare.[241] Trump's proposed $175 billion missile-defense system, the lucrative contract for which was expected to go to Elon Musk or some other wealthy Trump supporter, would be called, naturally, the "Golden Dome."[242]

Show of Force

The investment in imagery does not end there. Long on Trump's wish list, a military parade finally made its way down Pennsylvania Avenue in 2025. The purported purpose of the parade was to commemorate the army's 250th anniversary, but it also happened to coincide with Trump's seventy-ninth birthday. Appropriately enough, Trump was born on June 14, Flag Day. While many presidents pander to patriotism, Trump took it to a new level, physically hugging and kissing the flag on stage at the Conservative Political Action Committee convention in 2020.[243] During his second term, Trump had an eighty-eight-foot flagpole erected at the White House.[244] He even proposed prosecuting protesters who burn the American flag, even though the Supreme Court declared such conduct protected by the First Amendment in 1989.[245]

Waving the flag at every opportunity seems to be simply one more branding opportunity: If you listen to Trump, his supporters are "patriots" and his critics hate America.[246] The marketing pitch seems to be that if you love America, you should love Trump, because they are one and the same. According to White House spokeswoman Taylor Rogers, "The American flag has always been important to the President's identity—from the day he was born, on Flag Day, it was clear that his DNA is USA." With his standard uniform of a navy-blue suit, white shirt, and red tie—the same colors as the Stars and Stripes—Trump has quite literally wrapped himself in the flag.

The estimated cost of Trump's military parade was twenty-five to forty-five million dollars, spent at the same time he was slashing grant funding, firing federal workers, and pushing for cuts to the budget of the Veterans Administration.[247] But, to Trump, this didn't matter: If you want the world to think you are invincible, you must invest in *appearing* invincible. Tanks, planes, helicopters, and even a robot dog made their way past the reviewing stand of America's commander in chief, who repeatedly rose to salute soldiers marching by as fawning Fox News announcers provided live television coverage.

Donald Trump, of course, never served in the military; during the Vietnam War, he avoided the draft by obtaining a medical exemption due to bone spurs.[248] Nonetheless, Trump had fantasized about hosting a military parade ever since witnessing an extravagant Bastille Day procession down the Champs-Élysées in France during his first term.[249] As Trump explained, a parade was an opportunity to show off America's military power: "We have the greatest missiles in the world. We have the greatest submarines in the world. We have the greatest army tanks in the world. We have the greatest weapons in the world. And we're going to celebrate it."[250] Later in 2025, Trump proposed the construction of a victory arch in Washington, DC, to commemorate the nation's 250th birthday;[251] some critics called the structure the "Arc de Trump."[252] It was all a flex of America's—and Trump's—military might. As Machiavelli wrote, it is better to be feared than loved.

Use of Force

In addition to *showing* force, the Trump administration has also *used* force against immigrants, protesters, and ships at sea. In so doing, Trump often focuses on the substantive goal of public safety, one that most people certainly would consider desirable, rather than on the havoc he wreaks on the rule of law. But of course, the Constitution protects states' rights to manage their own affairs and guarantees individuals the rights to free speech, due process, and freedom from unreasonable searches and seizures. Those rights also apply to undocumented immigrants who are present in the territorial jurisdiction of the United States. In repeatedly overrunning the law, Trump seems to be betting that his supporters do not appreciate the nuances of complex statutes and constitutional doctrine—so much for fulfilling his constitutional duty to take care that the laws be faithfully executed.

This substance-over-process strategy is one Trump has employed repeatedly. For instance, Trump has used military troops to support immigration enforcement, although the military is never supposed to be deployed within the United States in this fashion. Over the objection of California governor Gavin Newsom and Los Angeles mayor Karen Bass, in June 2025, Trump deployed four thousand National Guard troops and seven hundred marines to Los Angeles—ostensibly to protect federal property, but really to suppress protests over immigration raids in the area.[253] While some protesters committed acts of violence and attacked federal buildings, the governor and mayor objected to the presence of military troops in a situation that local law enforcement could comfortably handle. A federal judge later ruled that Trump's use of troops to perform law enforcement activities violated the federal Posse Comitatus Act.[254]

In July, federal agents visited MacArthur Park, located in an area of Los Angeles with a large concentration of Latino residents. Accompanied by eighty members of the California National Guard, dozens of agents in military attire marched through the park, along with more agents on horseback.[255] A helicopter flew overhead, while military-style vehicles parked nearby. According to internal army documents, the objective of Operation Excalibur, as it was called, was "to demonstrate, through a show of presence, the capacity and freedom of maneuver of federal law enforcement within the Los Angeles Joint Operations Area."[256] The operations plan indicated that the park was surrounded by four schools and a retirement community, noting: "High density of civilians in complex urban terrain, moderate to high potential for collateral damage if threat activity requires use of lethal force in a kinetic engagement." Translation: *If we provoke trouble, innocent people may die.* Mayor Bass said the scene looked like "a city under siege, an armed occupation."[257] Yet according to Gregory Bovino, a Customs and Border Protection official in California, "Better get used to us now, cause this is going to be normal very soon. We will go anywhere, anytime we want in Los Angeles."[258] In other words, the operation was all about power. He would later bring aggressive immigration enforcement tactics to Minneapolis.

Trump would later send National Guard troops to Washington, DC, declaring that violent crime constituted an "emergency" in the city that justified a federal takeover of the municipal police department.[259] In so doing, Trump was using an aggressive reading of the statute that allows the president to utilize the DC municipal police during a federal emergency. In fact, he was doing just the opposite—using federal personnel to perform local police work.

Trump claimed that crime in the nation's capital was "out of control," even though statistics showed the rate to be at a thirty-year low.[260] He would later deploy National Guard troops in other cities, such as Portland, Oregon, Chicago, Memphis, Charlotte, and New Orleans, withdrawing them where they were unwanted only after the Supreme Court intervened.[261] During a September 2025 speech in Washington before America's active-duty generals, Trump compared Portland to a "war zone" and told them they should consider American cities their "training grounds," where they could "handle" "the enemy from within."[262]

In fact, it seemed that Trump was creating chaos to justify imposing order. His plans threatened to provoke civil unrest across the country as Americans demonstrated against a federal takeover of local law enforcement.[263] As columnist Michelle Goldberg wrote at the time, "In a post-reality environment, it turns out, the president didn't need to wait for a crisis to launch an authoritarian crackdown. Instead, he can simply invent one."[264] While crime and violence should be condemned, she wrote, "the idea that Trump needed to put soldiers on the streets of the city because riots were spinning out of control is pure fantasy."[265]

I know from my experience in law enforcement that surges of officers and zero-tolerance programs can be effective—but only for a short time. If Trump were really interested in reducing violent crime in American cities, he would have provided local police departments with more resources, assigned officers to high-crime neighborhoods, or bolstered grant funds for agencies that provide crime prevention programs. Instead, he cut such grant funding and deployed federal troops in visible tourist areas, such as on the National Mall. His tactics seemed more a show of force than a crime-reduction strategy. Trump revealed his own thinking when he predicted that violent crime would be a "big subject" in the 2026 midterm elections.[266] In fact, Trump seemed to be working to *make* it a significant issue by engaging in the kind of show that captures the public's attention, without delivering any tangible results. Trump said that he would "rescue" Washington from "crime, bloodshed, bedlam and squalor and worse."[267] Within a few weeks, he falsely claimed that crime in the nation's capital had been completely eliminated: "Washington, DC is a totally safe city. You're not reporting any crime because there is none."[268] He also posted this claim on social media: "DC IS NOW A CRIME FREE ZONE."[269] Trump suggested that assaults that "take place in the home" should not be counted in crime statistics, referring to the serious crime of domestic violence as "a little fight with the wife."[270] In fact, violent crime was not gone, though it was down 7 percent.[271] Perhaps the decrease was due to the visible presence of officers on the streets, which can deter crime. Or the single-digit drop might simply have reflected the statistical margin of error from one data-gathering period to the next.

At the same time that Trump was using troops to purportedly address crime on American streets, he rebranded the Department of Defense as the "Department of War." (Although only Congress can officially change the name of a cabinet department created by legislation, Trump used an executive order to give the department the "secondary title.")[272] The order made it clear that this directive was no mere empty gesture, directing department personnel to use the new name in all correspondence, communications, ceremonies, and "non-statutory documents."[273] After more than a decade as the central character in a television reality show, Trump understood the importance of branding. The executive order explained that the change would "signal to adversaries America's readiness to wage war to secure its interests."[274] No one seemed happier about the move than Pete Hegseth, who would henceforth be known as the "Secretary of War." He used a sports metaphor to gush over his new title: "As the president has said, we're not just defense, we're offense."[275] Hegseth later embellished upon the point to a room full of generals: "We also don't fight with stupid rules of engagement. We untie the hands of our warfighters to intimidate, demoralize, hunt, and kill the enemies of our country. No more politically correct and overbearing rules of engagement, just common sense, maximum lethality and authority for warfighters. . . . You kill people and break things for a living."[276] As Trump prepared to escalate federal law enforcement operations in Chicago, he posted a meme online, complete with helicopter emojis: "Chicago about to find out why it's called the Department of War."[277]

The rebranding was a stark change from the department's desired image for the past eight decades. Following World War II, Congress changed the department's name from War to Defense to emphasize its goal of peace over conquest; as the Cold War dawned, the United States emphasized deterrence over provocation.[278] Since that time, the country has grown into a superpower through its strategic use of soft power, providing humanitarian relief, engaging in diplomacy, and modeling democratic freedom. But Trump prefers hard power—exorbitant tariffs, isolation from allies, embrace of authoritarians, and the new name to signal military aggression. David E. Sanger, foreign policy and national security correspondent for *The New York Times*, wrote that the new nomenclature came at a particularly fraught time—"a moment when deterrence is more critical than ever—in cyberspace, outer space and a world where Russia and China are celebrating an uneasy partnership to challenge American pre-eminence." Of course, Trump has lacked any consistency in his chaotic presidency, also lobbying for the Nobel Peace Prize by bragging that he had "ended seven wars," a dubious claim that caused some foreign allies to bristle.[279]

The department's new name was more than symbolic. In 2025, Trump repeatedly directed military strikes in international waters at ships that he claimed were transporting illegal drugs into the United States.[280] These attacks killed scores of people that the Trump regime claimed were "narco-terrorists" who were "poisoning Americans."[281] Pete Hegseth gleefully posted on social media videos of the target boats bursting into flames.[282] "There will be no refuge or forgiveness," he wrote, "only justice."[283] No doubt, most Americans support the goal of reducing the flow of fentanyl and cocaine into the United States, but Trump's method—use of lethal force—had no apparent authorization under criminal, international, or military law.[284] In addition, some questioned the factual predication that all of the boats were, indeed, operated by members of a drug cartel.[285] Even though only Congress has the constitutional authority to declare war, Trump was going it alone: "I don't think we're going necessarily to ask for a declaration of war," he said. "I think we're just going to kill people that are bringing drugs into our country. OK. We're going to kill them. They're going to be, like, dead."[286] In one instance, when two men survived an initial strike on their boat, a second shot was fired to ensure their deaths, an act that was condemned even by John Yoo, the DOJ lawyer who authorized the CIA to engage in "enhanced interrogation" after the attacks of September 11, 2001.[287] The use of military force sent a message to the world that Trump felt unconstrained by the law to impose his will. *New York Times* national security writer Charlie Savage wrote that Trump was flaunting indifference to the law with "audacious transparency."[288] It was like a mob hit in broad daylight: Everyone knew what had happened, and no one was going to do anything about it.

The boat strikes presaged a breathtaking military operation in January 2026 to abduct Venezuela's president, Nicolás Maduro, and his wife, and transport them to the United States to face criminal charges of narco-terrorism.[289] The operation, in which eighty people in Venezuela were reported killed, almost certainly violated the United Nations Charter, which prohibits unprovoked attacks on sovereign nations.[290] Congress's 1945 ratification of the Charter made it "the supreme law of the land," under the US Constitution,[291] making Trump's operation an apparent violation of American law as well. In an interview after the operation, Stephen Miller, Trump's deputy chief of staff, scoffed at the idea of complying with laws. "We live in a world in which you can talk all you want about international niceties and everything else. But we live in a world, in the real world . . . that is governed by strength, that is governed by force, that is governed by power. These are the iron laws of the world."[292]

During a press conference to discuss the operation, Trump made it clear that the arrest was about far more than drug trafficking. The president announced that the United States would be seizing oil assets and "running" the government of Venezuela until "a proper transition" could take place.[293] John Feeley, a former US ambassador to Panama, said, "When Donald Trump says, 'We're going to run the place,' I want you to think of the Gambino family taking over the Colombo family's business out in Queens. They don't actually go out and run it. They just get an envelope."[294] For Trump, the payment in his envelope would contain Venezuela's rich oil assets and obedience to the United States.

Monkey See, Monkey Do

Trump's cabinet appointees also got in on the use of showmanship, using public appearances to cosplay as tough enforcers. Secretary of Homeland Security Kristi Noem wore a cowboy hat and ICE jacket as she patrolled the southern border on horseback.[295] Pete Hegseth lifted weights with soldiers, whom he referred to as "the warriors."[296] Alina Habba, who had served as Trump's personal lawyer in civil litigation and who had no prosecutorial experience, was installed as US attorney in New Jersey, where she quickly donned raid gear and participated in the arrest of a teenager for the cameras.[297] This stunt risked making her a witness and requiring her office to recuse itself from the case, but who cares about what might happen in the future when the cameras are rolling right now? Cabinet officials used social media to create the impression of daily accomplishments. As the *Wall Street Journal* described it, "Like figures in an action movie, they are constantly on-screen and in motion, using social-media platforms and friendly news outlets not only to amplify Trump's political messages but also to create a more intimate connection with supporters."[298]

In addition to room décor, parades, and costume parties, Trump's showboat presidency has also included staged televised signing ceremonies, with the president seated front and center. Surrounded by aides while signing executive orders at a rapid pace, Trump created the impression of an energetic president getting things done. He would hold up the order for the cameras to capture the image, replete with his signature, signed boldly in thick black Sharpie. When Trump's proposed budget, dubbed "One Big Beautiful Bill," was passed in Congress with only Republican support, he signed it on the Fourth of July, outdoors on the White House grounds, as military planes soared overhead. As reported by NBC News, Trump was "merging politics with patriotism."[299]

Mostly, Trump's executive orders were creating havoc—redefining birthright citizenship, withdrawing the United States from the World Health Organization, suspending the ban Congress had placed on TikTok unless it was sold by its Chinese-owned parent company, pardoning insurrectionists, and denouncing the "weaponization" of the law by former government officials.[300] An executive order freezing federal loans and grants was rescinded two days after it was issued due to the legal challenges and political backlash it immediately ignited.[301] Rather than accept responsibility for the chaos, White House spokeswoman Karoline Leavitt blamed the courts and the media.[302] A number of his executive orders would invite lawsuits, but Trump was playing with house money, and for him, the bet was a win-win proposition: If his orders succeeded in court, he would amass more power. If they failed, he could just blame "radical, leftist" judges for refusing to allow him to fulfill the "mandate" his voters had given him.[303] And regardless of outcome, all of the cases would be litigated by government lawyers at taxpayer expense. The entire exercise created the impression of an unstoppable force.

Controlling Culture

It wasn't enough for Trump to redecorate his own residence; he wants to impose his taste on the rest of America, too. In August 2025, he entered an executive order directing that all federal buildings be designed in a "classical" architectural style.[304] Among the reasons Trump cited were to "honor tradition," "command public respect," and "return to the magnificent classical style of Western civilization."[305]

Trump also dictated that America's cultural institutions of art and history embrace political orthodoxy. After accusing the John F. Kennedy Center for the Performing Arts of being "woke," he fired several of its board members and replaced them with Fox News personalities.[306] He then added his own name to the center's building, ahead of Kennedy's.[307] In a subsequent social media post, Trump posted pictures of marble he said he planned to use for armrests at the center.[308] Trump also issued directives dissolving the President's

Committee on Arts and Humanities, established by President Ronald Reagan to promote arts education; terminating federal funding for diversity, equity, and inclusion (DEI) initiatives; and restricting the National Endowment for the Arts and the National Endowment for the Humanities from issuing any grants "promoting" DEI.[309] At the Defense Department, books regarding race and gender identity were banned from school libraries on military bases.[310] The president fired National Portrait Gallery director Kim Sajet, calling her "a highly partisan person, and a strong supporter of DEI, which is totally inappropriate for her position."[311]

While US history offers much to celebrate, it also contains mistakes, injustices, and tragedies from which we can learn. Instead, the Trump administration revises the record of America's story to reflect his preferences. He has sought to scrub troubling facts in order to offer a glorified view of the past. In March 2025, he ordered a review of the exhibits at national parks, museums, and education centers.[312] The executive order, entitled "Restoring Truth and Sanity to American History," directed the removal of "divisive narratives" to instead focus on "the greatness of achievements and progress of the American people," aimed at "instilling pride in the hearts of all Americans."[313] Among the items earmarked for removal were signs at Cape Hatteras National Seashore noting rising sea levels as a result of climate change.[314] Another item criticized the "Lost Cause" narrative of the Civil War, a view that glorified the Confederacy and downplayed the role of slavery in the war's inception.[315] On the webpage for the Stonewall National Monument, which commemorates the gay rights movement, references to transgender Americans were removed, in line with Trump's executive order to recognize only two sexes, male and female.[316] The National Park Service took down a memorial to the nine people enslaved by George Washington. The exhibit explained that the president's house in Philadelphia "was a mirror of the young republic, reflecting both the ideals and contradictions of the new nation." The home stood in the shadow of Independence Hall, where the words "All men are created equal" were adopted, but not applied to all Americans.[317] Rather than confront the realities of history, Trump has sought to comfort Americans with images of a more romantic past. It's hard to miss the undertones of white supremacy in his efforts.

Trump also used his bully pulpit to try to erase the stain of racism from our nation's past, accusing the Smithsonian Institution of devoting too much focus to "how bad slavery was," complaining on Juneteenth that the country has too many holidays, and calling for the return of statues of Confederate leaders.[318] In addition, his administration erased references to the contributions of Black heroes, such as the Tuskegee Airmen, Harriet Tubman, and Jackie Robinson, whose page on the Defense Department's website was restored in the face of criticism.[319] Trump even pressured the restaurant chain Cracker Barrel to resurrect its original logo after the restaurant chain launched a new design, which conservative podcaster Isabel Brown called "part of a much larger, sinister undertow of our culture led by the radical Marxist left."[320] The new logo was a simple oval featuring the company's name, removing the character known as "Old Timer," a white man sitting next to a barrel. Cracker Barrel ultimately reverted to its old logo.[321] Even sports came within Trump's purview, as the felon president successfully pressured Major League Baseball to reinstate the late Pete Rose, banned for life for betting on baseball while managing the Cincinnati Reds.[322] MLB commissioner Rob Manfred admitted that Trump's input influenced his decision, which made Rose eligible for induction into baseball's Hall of Fame.[323] Betting on baseball is the sport's cardinal sin, in light of past scandals and the risk it poses to the integrity of the game. With that move, Trump was not only demonstrating his sway but also normalizing corruption.

Trump's efforts to control American arts and leisure echoed Mao Tse-tung's Cultural Revolution, in which historical artifacts were destroyed and cultural and religious sites demolished. According to Joe M. Pierre, a professor in the Department of Psychiatry and Behavioral Science at the University of California, San Francisco, authoritarians deliberately kindle a longing for the past. In the United States, that yearning is shared by some who feel threatened by today's multicultural society.[324] Pierre writes that Trump panders to this segment of the population with his "Make America Great Again" slogan by tapping into their "deep sense of nostalgia for a past" when the United States was dominated by a "common racial, religious, ideological, and moral identity." Trump exploits their "longing for the old days (e.g., 'Make America Great Again') based on the conclusion that their country has descended into moral depravity and that immigrants and other 'enemies from within' are trying to destroy the American Way."[325] He also fuels the grievances of Americans who resent the demise of white supremacy. All of it makes for a nation that is more openly divided.

In addition to seeking favor with their supporters, controlling arts and culture also allows an authoritarian leader to censor resistance by replacing works that are critical of their regime with propaganda that promotes their agenda.[326] For example, in Nazi Germany, the "Office of Culture" purged visual art depictions and theater productions of anything that did not meet "Aryan standards."[327] In recent times, Hungary's Viktor Orbán conditioned funding for the nation's cultural institutions on government approval of senior leaders.[328] In the United States, our Founding Fathers recognized that free speech is an essential component of democracy; artistic expression allows people to voice their views about their communities and their government. Presidential control of the arts and culture is a dangerous trend toward tyranny.

Illusions of Power

John Bravata was convicted at trial of mail and wire fraud and sentenced to prison. His glitz and glamor could get him only so far. In the same way, Trump's con games may have been an effective way to campaign and to capture public attention, "winning" the daily news cycle with one outrageous stunt after another, but they are a dangerous way to govern. Trump learned how to wow people from his years on a TV reality show, but his record in business, pocked with multiple bankruptcies and a civil judgment for fraud, demonstrates that his showmanship enriched himself alone. As president, Trump has used the same kinds of gimmicks to instill fear and maximize his own power—a distortion of democracy, where power belongs to the people.

THREE

DISINFORMATION WARFARE

Adarus Mazio Black was a cocaine kingpin who operated in Detroit in the 1990s. After hiring a hit man to kill two informants, Black went on the run. He obtained fake IDs, used aliases, and traveled to California and Arizona to lie low.[329] But Black was determined to avoid getting caught, so he took a drastic step: He went to Mexico and hired a surgeon to reshape his forehead and cheekbones.[330] And Black didn't stop there. Concerned that his fingerprints could give him away if he were ever arrested, he considered having his prints removed, just as John Dillinger used acid to obliterate his. But of course, the absence of fingerprints could also raise suspicion, so he went one step further, having his toe prints removed and grafted onto his fingers, and vice versa.[331] Nonetheless, after many years, Drug Enforcement Administration agents ultimately amassed sufficient evidence to identify Black and bring him to trial, including the testimony of the surgeon who had performed the print swap. Black was convicted and sentenced to life in prison. The key exhibit in the case was a photo of a DEA agent obtaining Black's fingerprints by inking and rolling his toes.

According to Machiavelli, rulers can best succeed through deception, ruthlessness, and cruelty—methods Donald Trump has often used to seize power and consolidate it.[332] Disinformation—the strategic use of false claims to advance an agenda—has long been one of Trump's favorite Machiavellian tools. In his second term, Trump continued to maintain that the 2020 presidential election, which he lost to Joe Biden, was "totally rigged."[333] He called Ukrainian president Volodymyr Zelensky "a dictator" one week and denied saying so the next.[334] Trump uses disinformation to distract, divide, punish, and even rewrite history. As described in the chapters that follow, he has made false or misleading claims against universities, law firms, the media, courts, the military, and foreign leaders, in an apparent effort to undermine their credibility and, consequently, their ability to check his own power. For example, he withheld federal funding from Harvard University under spurious claims of antisemitism sparked by protests against Israeli military action in Gaza, a devious move that deepened divisions between Jewish and Muslim students and their supporters.[335]

Distraction

One way Trump uses disinformation is as a form of distraction. When public opinion becomes unfavorable, Trump strategically makes outrageous claims to bump unfavorable news stories out of the headlines. As Trump wrote in *The Art of the Deal*, "One thing I've learned about the press is that they're always hungry for a good story, and the more sensational the better. It's in the nature of the job, and I understand that. The point is that if you are a little different or a little outrageous, or if you do things that are bold or controversial, the press is going to write about you."[336] When the news focused on the high price of eggs or the adverse stock market reaction to his tariffs, Trump would muse out loud about a third presidential term, igniting debates by legal scholars about whether a candidate could evade the language of the Constitution by running for vice president and then taking over when the president announced his preplanned resignation.[337] Similarly, when Trump's poll numbers dropped in response to unpopular cuts to government programs,[338] he talked of annexing Canada and making it the fifty-first state, or taking over Greenland.[339] When many in America—including Trump's MAGA supporters—demanded the release of the investigative files in the case of alleged child sex trafficker Jeffrey Epstein, which contained references to Trump, he sent National Guard troops to the streets of Washington, DC.[340] The chattering classes consistently took the bait. Trump could play the press like a matador, flinging his red cape at will to attract and divert attention when he was most vulnerable. When the Epstein files were released in December 2025, Trump distracted public attention by posting portraits of former presidents along the White House colonnade, including plaques for Barack Obama and Joe Biden containing disparaging descriptions.[341] The image for Biden was not even the forty-sixth president's portrait, but a picture of an auto-pen, mocking him for allegedly using the device to sign official documents, a common practice that bears no effect on the legality of the signature, despite Trump's claims to the contrary.

It is easy to blame the media for chasing Trump's latest outrageous claims, but ignoring him poses the danger of leaving his efforts to expand his power unchecked. One dynamic that makes his communication style so unsettling is his tendency to say things seemingly for shock value; it may be impossible to determine whether his statements are intended solely to distract or constitute a serious threat. For example, shortly after taking office for the second time, Trump posted on social media, "He who saves his Country does not violate any Law."[342] Was this just Trump being Trump, or was this a warning of things to come?

Punishment

During the 2024 campaign, Trump also used disinformation to accuse Democrats of "weaponizing" law enforcement to target him for political reasons. He and his supporters transformed what could have been a fatal political liability—criminal charges and convictions—into a political asset by accusing his opponents of "lawfare."[343] Upon returning to office in 2025, Trump used this unfounded lie to punish the officials he deemed responsible.

As a former prosecutor, I view the charges against Trump for election interference and unlawful retention of government documents as a reasonable exercise of prosecutorial discretion. The DOJ's Principles of Federal Prosecution provide guidance to help prosecutors make charging decisions.[344] First, prosecutors must determine whether they *can* bring charges; this test is satisfied if the evidence is sufficient to obtain and sustain a conviction. The superseding indictment against Trump in the election subversion case spelled out the facts over thirty-six pages, detailing evidence sufficient to obtain and sustain a conviction. Next, prosecutors must consider whether they *should* file charges. That's where prosecutorial discretion comes in: The Justice Department lacks the resources to file charges in every case where the evidence supports it, and criminal prosecution is not always in the best interests of justice. The Principles of Federal Prosecution provide a list of factors for prosecutors to consider in making this second decision. Among these factors is whether charges would advance a substantial federal interest. It is difficult to imagine an interest more substantial than the fairness of a presidential election. In the election interference case, Special Counsel Jack Smith charged Trump with conspiracy to defraud the United States by interfering in the lawful transfer of presidential power, obstructing an official proceeding by submitting false slates of electors for certification at a joint session of Congress, and conspiring to violate the voting rights of the American people. Frankly, in my view, a failure to file charges in light of such alleged egregious misconduct would have been a breach of duty by the Justice Department.

Prosecuting the government documents case also seemed warranted under the DOJ principles. The evidence seemed strong, given that the documents were found at Trump's Mar-a-Lago home after he had left the Oval Office, with some located in a ballroom, a bathroom, and Trump's private office.[345] According to the superseding indictment, the documents were highly sensitive and included information regarding the defense and weapons capabilities of both the United States and foreign countries; United States nuclear programs; potential vulnerabilities of the United States and its allies to military attack; and plans for possible retaliation in response to a foreign attack.[346] These are among our nation's most sensitive secrets, and yet Trump stored them like old high school yearbooks. In addition, Trump was charged not only with retaining the documents—which the National Archives had tried to retrieve from Trump for months—but also with obstructing the investigation by instructing associates to move the boxes when DOJ officials came to inspect them. Again, this case reflected a substantial federal interest in protecting national security.

A jury was never able to hear the evidence, and so Trump is still presumed innocent of all of these charges. But there is nothing to suggest the charges were improper. Both indictments were brought by a special counsel—an outside attorney appointed by the attorney general to avoid the appearance of bias—and both were returned by federal grand juries based on detailed evidence that the crimes had been committed. Yet Trump baselessly claimed that the charges were fabricated as a political attack against him.

After the Supreme Court's July 2024 decision that former presidents are immune from criminal prosecution for acts committed within the scope of their official duties, Smith obtained a superseding indictment to exclude any conduct that might be covered by the opinion. He dismissed the charges only after Trump's reelection, based on DOJ's judgment that a sitting president cannot be prosecuted for a crime.[347] Smith was careful to note, "This outcome is not based on the merits or strength of the case against the defendant."[348] At Smith's request, the court dismissed the case "without prejudice," meaning that it can be brought again. The classified documents case was also derailed on procedural grounds when district court judge Aileen Cannon found the special counsel regulations unconstitutional under the Appointments Clause and dismissed the indictment as void because Smith lacked the authority to file it.[349] Smith had appealed the order but, again, moved to dismiss the appeal when Trump was elected president in 2024, resulting in the indictment being dismissed without prejudice.[350] To this day, no judge or jury has ever ruled on the merits of the cases, though the possibility remains after Trump leaves office.

After returning to office in 2025, even though the charges had been dismissed, Trump continued to hammer home claims that the machinery of government had been used against him illegally. On his first day in office, he issued an executive order entitled "Ending the Weaponization of Government."[351] The order detailed baseless claims that the Biden administration had "engaged in an unprecedented, third-world weaponization of prosecutorial power to upend the democratic process." The president's missive included broad allegations of abuse against not just himself but also ordinary Americans. His order alleged, without evidence, that the prior administration had "targeted individuals who voiced opposition to the prior administration's policies," including "parents protesting at school board meetings, Americans who spoke out against the previous administration's actions, and other Americans who were simply exercising constitutionally protected rights." It compared the January 6 rioters, whom it said the Department of Justice "ruthlessly prosecuted," to Black Lives Matter protesters, whose cases were "dropped." This argument is, of course, like comparing apples and oranges. While a small percentage of otherwise peaceful Black Lives Matter protests resulted in violence and property damage, the suggestion that wrongdoers faced no consequences is false.[352] Many protesters were charged with crimes in state and federal courts.[353] But all of these claims created the false impression that the Biden administration had abused its power not only to advance its political agenda but also to infringe upon the civil liberties of ordinary Americans. It was a bit of jujitsu by official decree: gin up outrage to justify punishing former government actors for their imaginary misdeeds.

The executive order directed several agency heads, including the attorney general and the director of national intelligence, to review the government's actions for "appropriate remedial action." In response, Attorney General Pam Bondi issued a memo on her first day in office establishing a "Weaponization Working Group" to "restore integrity and credibility with the public."[354] Contrary to DOJ policy, the memo listed targets for investigation, including Special Counsel Smith and his staff; unspecified "improper investigative tactics and unethical prosecutions" relating to the "events" at the US Capitol on January 6, 2021; and federal cooperation with the "weaponization" to target

Trump by Manhattan district attorney Alvin Bragg and New York attorney general Letitia James. Bragg's sin was obtaining guilty verdicts in 2024 from a jury that found guilt beyond a reasonable doubt on all thirty-four counts of an indictment against Trump for falsifying business records to conceal hush-money payments to a pornographic film actress before the 2016 presidential election.[355] James fell into the crosshairs by securing a civil verdict against Trump in 2024 for fraudulent business practices.[356] An appeals court would later affirm Trump's liability in the civil case but overturn the disgorgement order of almost five hundred million dollars as excessive under the Eighth Amendment, prompting Trump to proclaim "total victory" and calling the case "a Political Witch Hunt, in a business sense, the likes of which no one has ever seen before."[357] Bondi's memo was a breathtaking piece of disinformation, bringing full circle one of Trump's biggest lies—the idea that he had been targeted by various law enforcement officials not because he was corrupt but because they were. And now it was time to turn the tables by investigating them, to "restore" the government's integrity and credibility. In fact, it was Trump who was weaponizing law enforcement by accusing his rivals of doing the same thing. These narratives were followed by indictments against James and former FBI Director James Comey, cases that failed in court. It seemed to be an effort to rewrite history.

Of course, the consequence of this kind of disinformation is the erosion of public trust in government. As a former federal prosecutor who spent more than twenty years in government, I find this loss of public trust painful and harmful. I know from my work that most federal law enforcement officials are scrupulously apolitical. While their decisions are not perfect, prosecutors are bound by the prohibition in the Principles of Federal Prosecution from making decisions based on partisan political considerations. Trump's personal vendettas risk eroding the public trust that is essential to effective law enforcement. Officials must have this trust before they can secure victims' cooperation, receive tips from witnesses, and gain credibility in court so that jurors will believe their testimony. But a large number of Americans now seem to buy the lies that law enforcement officials targeted Trump during the Biden administration. And that the special counsel did so, too. And the Manhattan district attorney. And the New York attorney general. Some Americans no doubt believe Trump's claims that they were all crooks. Others likely don't care because in the MAGA movement's us-versus-them worldview, all that matters is winning. Many others, however, likely saw Trump's attorney general as promoting his lies and concluded that she lacked integrity. Regardless of which view people take, they all lead down a path toward cynicism, which tends to cause citizens to tune out of politics altogether—one of the ultimate goals of an authoritarian.

Normalizing Violence

In addition to punishing his enemies, Trump has also used disinformation to rewrite history and exercise power. One consequence was to normalize political violence. Part of the false narrative of Trump's 2020 defeat was his claim of a rigged election. And if Trump rightfully won that election, then the people who responded to his call to rally at the US Capitol to protest the certification of Joe Biden as president were not villains but heroes. To complete the revision of that story, Trump issued a sweeping order of clemency to the defendants who attacked the Capitol on January 6, 2021.[358] On his first day in office, Trump signed the order commuting the prison sentences of fourteen men, members of the paramilitary groups known as the Proud Boys and Oath Keepers. They had been convicted of seditious conspiracy, the unlawful use of force to oppose the authority of the US government in administering the transfer of presidential power, and sentenced to lengthy prison terms. Trump released them. As for the other 1,500 defendants, Trump issued outright pardons—"full, complete, and unconditional"—for their crimes, which included assaulting police officers and damaging federal property to the tune of $2.7 billion. Trump further directed federal prosecutors to dismiss all charges that were still pending against any of the January 6 attackers. Later in 2025, Trump pardoned his lawyers, Rudy Giuliani, John Eastman, Sidney Powell, and others involved in the effort to overturn the 2020 election results.[359] Like a crime boss, Trump took care of those who got caught doing his bidding.

Of course, it was Trump who had urged protesters to come to Washington in the first place, tweeting an invitation once it had become clear that his legal efforts to overturn the outcome of the 2020 election had been futile. Instead, his focus would be on January 6, the day that Congress would convene to certify the election. Linking to a report prepared by adviser Peter Navarro, Trump posted that it was "statistically impossible to have lost the 2020 Election. Big protest in DC on January 6. Be there, will be wild!"[360] When his supporters assembled on January 6 as instructed, Trump gave a fiery speech, alleging that his "election victory," which he had won "by a landslide," had been "stolen by emboldened radical-left Democrats" and "the fake news media."[361] Urging them to "stop the steal," Trump proclaimed, "We fight like hell. And if you don't fight like hell, you're not going to have a country anymore."[362] He ended by saying they would "walk down Pennsylvania Avenue" to the Capitol.[363] Although Trump had instructed the crowd to protest "peacefully" and "patriotically," when the mob used brute force to enter the Capitol, assaulting and injuring police officers while waving Trump and Confederate flags, the president sat and watched on television for almost three hours before asking the protesters to leave. Liz Cheney, then the GOP congresswoman from Wyoming, said during the congressional investigation into the attack, "Donald Trump summoned the mob, assembled the mob, and lit the fuse of this attack."[364] Mitch McConnell, the GOP Senate leader at the time, said that Trump was "practically and morally responsible for provoking the events of the day."[365]

Since 2021, Trump has successfully indoctrinated many Americans to believe a different narrative. He has referred to January 6 not as an attack on American democracy but as a "day of love";[366] he describes the defendants not as attackers or vandals but as "hostages"[367] and "warriors."[368] "All they were doing," he told rallygoers in 2024, was "protesting a rigged election."[369] He has amplified claims that the attack was a "false flag" operation organized by government agents, falsely claiming that police officers urged the rioters into the Capitol. "What a setup that was," Trump said. "What a horrible, horrible thing."[370]

Trump used rhetoric and even music to convert the rioters into heroes, recording a recitation of the Pledge of Allegiance, dubbed over "The Star-Spangled Banner," sung by a group of January 6 defendants who called themselves the "J6 Prison Choir."[371] At his first rally for the 2024 presidential campaign, Trump stood with his hand over his heart as the recording played.[372] Once in office, Trump used his pardon power to create the impression that he was simply correcting an injustice by providing relief to patriotic Americans who had been the victims of corrupt prosecutions.

A few months later, the Department of Justice took another step to revise the events of January 6 when it paid a settlement of almost five million dollars to the estate of Ashli Babbitt, the woman who was shot and killed on January 6 while attempting to climb through a broken window into the Speaker's Lobby.[373] The window was the last barrier between the violent mob and members of Congress. At the time of the shooting, GOP House Speaker Kevin McCarthy praised the officer involved for protecting him and the nation's other lawmakers, stating, "I think the police officer did his job."[374] No judge or jury found that the shooting was improper; in fact, in 2021, the officer was cleared of any wrongdoing.[375] But in 2025, now led by Trump appointees, the Department of Justice entered into the settlement agreement to use tax dollars to compensate Babbitt's family for her death. In August 2025, the Air Force also approved full military funeral honors for Babbitt, which the Biden administration had denied.[376] Like the pardons and commutations, the payment helped to rewrite history.

To mark the fifth anniversary of the attack, the White House website posted a page that grossly distorted the facts.[377] According to the website:

> The Democrats masterfully reversed reality after January 6, branding peaceful patriotic protesters as "insurrectionists" and

> framing the event as a violent coup attempt orchestrated by Trump—despite no evidence of armed rebellion or intent to overthrow the government. In truth, it was the Democrats who staged the real insurrection by certifying a fraud-ridden election, ignoring widespread irregularities, and weaponizing federal agencies to hunt down dissenters, all while [Nancy] Pelosi's own security lapses invited the chaos they later exploited to seize and consolidate power. This gaslighting narrative allowed them to persecute innocent Americans, silence opposition, and distract from their own role in undermining democracy.[378]

Even for a liar like Trump, the revision of history was astonishing. On the official White House website, Trump was manipulating the American people into believing that the violent rioters were simply peaceful protesters advocating for a just cause.

In addition to rewriting history, the January 6 pardons, commutations, and Babbitt settlement did something else—they normalized violence. Like a crime boss, Trump sent a message that crimes committed on his behalf would be not only tolerated but celebrated. Loyalists would be rewarded. If the message were not clear by deed alone, Trump's pardon attorney, Ed Martin, would later post on X, "No MAGA left behind."[379]

While those who subscribe to the MAGA doctrine cheer on Trump's actions, many others see a green light for more violence—the antithesis of a country governed by the rule of law. In 2025, political violence continued to rise, yielding assassinations, threats, and harassment against public figures at every level.[380] Attacks were directed at targets on both the political left and the right. One particularly noteworthy tragedy occurred when conservative political activist Charlie Kirk was shot and killed during a speaking event on a college campus. That attack occurred a few months after a man disguised as a police officer killed Melissa Hortman, a Democratic Minnesota legislator, and her husband in their own home, after completing a nonfatal shooting of a state senator and his wife at their nearby house.[381] The alleged perpetrator in Kirk's murder was apprehended after a two-day manhunt.[382]

Earlier in the year, an arsonist set fire to the residence of Pennsylvania governor Josh Shapiro, a Democrat, while he and his family slept. The Shapiro family was lucky to escape unharmed, but the governor's mansion sustained substantial damage.[383] During the 2024 election, Trump survived two assassination attempts, one at a rally in Pennsylvania and another at his own golf course in Florida.[384]

In this new climate of might making right, targets of political violence extended beyond government leaders; other targets of death and destruction included a health care executive, a fertility clinic, and Tesla dealerships.[385] In 2025, safety concerns grew so grave at the University of Michigan that top executives and all members of the board of regents were assigned 24-7 security protection in response to death threats, harassing communications, and vandalism at their private homes.[386] True to form, Trump condemned political violence committed by those he deemed to be members of the "radical left" but pardoned those who engaged in violence on his behalf.[387]

According to Shuki Cohen, a psychology professor at John Jay College of Criminal Justice in New York, one of the driving factors behind political violence is nihilism, "just a vague doomsday mentality of burn it all down and go out in a blaze of glory."[388] Cohen said a common trait among perpetrators of political violence is "learned helplessness"—a sense that our government is unable to address their concerns, whether that concern is the moral failings of society, changing demographics, wealth disparity, or some other grievance.[389] When the deck of government feels stacked against ordinary people, some feel compelled to take drastic action. Violent extremists obeying this logic may identify with any part of the political spectrum. Trump's no-holds-barred speaking style, focusing on resentment, victimhood, and rigged political systems, only added fuel to the fire.

Trump's coarse language also gives license to others to engage in hate speech. After Trump began disparaging immigrants as "rapists" and "animals" during his 2016 campaign for president, language that was once taboo entered the mainstream. Republicans began frequently referring to migration as an "invasion."[390] During the 2024 campaign season, researchers reported a 50 percent uptick from the 2020 election in hate speech directed against minority groups.[391] Laura Loomer, a MAGA influencer and informal Trump adviser, disparaged Kamala Harris during the 2024 race for her Indian heritage; Loomer posted on X that if Harris became president, the White House would "smell like curry."

While Trump's divisive rhetoric is certainly not the sole cause of political violence, someone with a "doomsday" mentality could easily be triggered by his rants about an out-of-control flow of immigrants, an education system that teaches our children "to hate our country," and the "crisis of trust" created by "a radical and corrupt establishment" that "has extracted power and wealth from our citizens while the pillars of our society lay broken and seemingly in complete disrepair."[392] Most of us roll our eyes at that kind of over-the-top language, but for someone who is already mentally unstable, such words can sound like a call to action. A person in that condition may take the pardons of the January 6 attackers as an invitation to use brute force to achieve political objectives.

Election Interference

In 2025, Trump seemed to begin laying the groundwork for a disinformation campaign to influence the 2026 midterm elections by posting online that he would "lead a movement to get rid of MAIL-IN BALLOTS," which he claimed, without evidence, led to "MASSIVE VOTER FRAUD."[393] His post also falsely stated that the United States was the only country to use mail-in ballots; in fact, twenty-two other countries use them. In addition, he said, "Remember, the States are merely an 'agent' for the Federal Government in counting and tabulating the votes. They must do what the Federal Government, as represented by the President of the United States, tells them, FOR THE GOOD OF OUR COUNTRY, to do." Actually, just the opposite is true: The Constitution authorizes states to run elections, with oversight from Congress, and establishes no role at all for the president.[394] Trump's post also made accusations about voting machines, which he called "Highly Inaccurate, Very Expensive, and Seriously Controversial." According to FactCheck.org, there is no evidence of inaccuracies caused by voting machines, which are backed up by paper ballots for audits.[395] In fact, Fox News agreed to pay a $787.5-million-dollar settlement to Dominion Voting Systems for promulgating false claims that its voting machines were used to rig the 2020 election.[396] Newsmax and Trump lawyer Rudy Giuliani also reached settlements with Dominion for making similar claims.[397]

The Truth Social post came after Trump's March 2025 executive order to "Protect the Integrity of American Elections,"[398] which seemed to be another bit of political propaganda. The order requires voters to provide proof of citizenship and prohibits states from counting ballots received after Election Day, despite the Constitution's allocation of power to the states to set the "time, place, and manner" of their own elections unless overridden by Congress.[399] Despite the order's dubious legal authority, it tended to undermine public confidence in current voting processes. By making these statements in 2025, Trump seemed to be aiming to plant seeds of doubt in the public's mind about the accuracy of the nation's elections, perhaps to justify challenges if the results of future campaigns were not to his liking.

Eventually Exposed

We should all take comfort in the fact that Adarus Mazio Black was ultimately caught and brought to justice. And beyond legal punishment for his crimes, Black will always live with a physical reminder of his desperate bid to hide the truth: His surgically altered hands became what are called "drumstick fingers," bloated, curled, and disfigured. Corruption can do that to a person.

With time, Trump's tricks and lies will also be exposed as long as we, the people, work to reveal them. The real question is whether any of his supporters will care.

FOUR

ABOVE THE LAW

John Gotti, head of the Gambino crime family in New York during the 1980s and '90s, was known in the tabloids as the "Teflon Don" because no criminal charges ever seemed to stick to him.[400] With Gotti at the helm, the Gambino family is believed to have raked in five hundred million dollars from illegal activities, including drug trafficking and extortion.[401] Though he would eventually be convicted of racketeering and die in prison, for a time, Gotti seemed impervious to the law. According to his 2002 obituary in *The New York Times*, Gotti "flaunted his power during his reign as a mafia boss," wearing expensive designer suits and silk ties. In contrast to most organized crime leaders, who operated in the shadows, Gotti "reveled in media attention as the boss of the nation's largest and most influential organized crime group. He cut a colorful figure in New York City, wining and dining in elegant restaurants and nightspots surrounded by a coterie of bodyguards."[402] In fact, the *Times* reported, "Gotti's swagger and seeming immunity from punishment earned him mythic gangster status." Once represented by Roy Cohn, Gotti was also an avid reader of Machiavelli's *The Prince*.[403] Gotti showed that breaking the rules with impunity made him appear untouchable: The more someone can get away with, the more powerful they can seem to others.

Donald Trump, too, was sometimes referred to as "Teflon Don" for escaping accountability—and even winning reelection—despite his thirty-four felony convictions "for falsifying New York business records in order to conceal his illegal scheme to corrupt the 2016 election."[404] As a fellow denizen of New York in the 1980s, Trump most certainly was aware of Gotti's brazen style. Trump has followed a similar script in his second term as president: He uses executive orders to expand his own power, openly ignores ethical norms, and monetizes his office for personal gain. He takes what he wants, and he does it out in the open. His self-aggrandizing approach to political power is a dangerous affront to a democracy.

In their book *How Democracies Die*, political scientists Steven Levitsky and Daniel Ziblatt write that systems of self-governance survive when leaders obey "unwritten democratic norms";[405] among these norms are "mutual tolerance" and "forbearance."[406] Mutual tolerance means respecting other institutions of democracy, including coequal branches of government. This concept also requires acceptance of the opposing party as a legitimate part of the political system reflecting the preferences of a portion of the electorate. In the view of mutual tolerance, the tug and pull of debate lead to compromise that helps the nation advance. Forbearance means using power with restraint: A president who cares about preserving the strength of our democracy would not assert maximum power at the expense of other considerations simply because he can. As I learned from my work as a federal prosecutor, just because a government official has the authority to do something does not mean that it is wise or just to do so.

Instead of complying with these norms, Trump has pushed the limits of what he could get away with. He seems to subscribe to what former Supreme Court justice Oliver Wendell Holmes Jr. called the "bad man" theory of the law.[407] According to Holmes, law is best understood by viewing it the way a bad man would. A good man would comply with the law because it is morally and ethically proper to do so and because it helps bring order to society. A bad man does not care about morality and social order. He is self-concerned with the law only to the extent that he seeks to avoid the consequences of violating it—fines, prison, money damages, or other penalties. The bad man has no qualms about breaching a contract even after giving his word; instead, he calculates whether he would be better off simply paying any damages that might follow a breach. For the bad man, the law is not to be obeyed but to be navigated to his advantage. The bad man seeks not to follow the law but to exploit its loopholes. Trump seems to view our constitutional democracy in the same way. But, as University of Michigan constitutional law professor Richard Primus writes, "Presidents are not supposed to treat the Constitution the way a private lawyer treats the tax code—that is, as an adverse force to be defeated."[408] The president takes an oath to support and defend the Constitution, which, in turn, requires him to take care that the laws be faithfully executed. Instead, Trump's modus operandi seems to be to increase his executive power until someone stops him.

Seizing Power

During the four years Trump spent out of office after 2020, the Heritage Foundation worked with conservative thought leaders to develop Project 2025, a blueprint for advancing a far-right agenda during the next presidential administration. Though Trump tried to distance himself from the document during the campaign, owing to its extreme unpopularity with the American public, upon returning to office, he was all in on many of its agenda items, including making it easier to fire federal employees, declaring the existence of only two sexes, and prohibiting the FBI from investigating threats related to disinformation.[409] Thanks in part to Project 2025, Trump was ready to go on day one, with twenty-six executive orders lined up for his signature.[410] Instead of proposing a legislative agenda for Congress, as most presidents do, Trump went it alone.

Many of Trump's executive orders expanded his own power. Once again, Trump was exploiting the law. In its 2024 decision finding former presidents immune from criminal prosecution for conduct committed within the scope of official duties, the Supreme Court showed itself to be a friendly forum for broad executive authority. In that decision, the majority prioritized the president's ability to "boldly and fearlessly carry out his duties."[411] They were creating a monster.

One executive order, signed in February 2025, had a benign enough title: "Ensuring Accountability for All Agencies."[412] The content of the order, however, was astonishing. Noting that "previous administrations have allowed so-called 'independent regulatory agencies' to operate with minimal Presidential supervision," the order stated, "it shall be the policy of the executive branch to ensure Presidential supervision and control of the entire executive branch."[413] Agencies such as the Federal Trade Commission (FTC), the Federal Communications Commission (FCC), and the Securities and Exchange Commission (SEC) were created by Congress to be "deliberately insulated from political interference";[414] these agencies have long acted independently to serve the public interest, insulated from the shifting winds of politics.[415] With Trump's order, they would all be under the president's thumb. The order was based on what is known as the "unitary executive theory," that is, the once-fringe view that the Constitution's vesting clause gives the president *all* executive power. In one order, Trump sought to blow up the independent civil service, which he had long assailed as "the deep state."

The order embraced one of the ideas found in Project 2025: delegating to the director of the Office of Management and Budget the power to "review independent regulatory agencies' obligations for consistency with the President's policies and priorities" and to "adjust" spending of funds appropriated by Congress "as necessary and appropriate, to advance the President's policies and priorities."[416] The director of OMB was Russell Vought, one of the authors of Project 2025. The order included other provisions that allowed the White House to closely oversee the activities of independent agencies and the attorney general to provide binding legal advice. Under this order, Trump would not be simply setting priorities and allowing agencies to execute them as prior presidents had but, rather, tightly controlling his underlings.

In another order, Trump followed the advice of Project 2025 to restore Schedule F to the civil service regulations.[417] Schedule F, issued by

Trump late in his first term but never implemented, gave the president and his designees the ability to fire federal employees in policymaking roles. President Joe Biden had rescinded Schedule F in the interim. On the day he signed the order, Trump posted on social media, "If these government workers refuse to advance the policy interests of the President, or are engaging in corrupt behavior, they should no longer have a job. This is common sense, and will allow the federal government to finally be 'run like a business.' We must root out corruption and implement accountability in our Federal Workforce!"[418]

Of course, it was corruption that Congress sought to erase when it enacted the Pendleton Act in 1883.[419] The statute ended the spoils system, in which presidents would clean house every four years and replace federal employees with loyalists. The Pendleton Act required civil servants to be hired free from partisanship and fired only for just cause; merit protections enabled civil servants to develop experience and expertise in their fields so they could effectively perform important work. Those protections gave us nonpartisan experts to do things like operate the power grid, guide the space program, and safeguard the stockpile of nuclear weapons.

The concern with Schedule F is that it would bring politics back into the civil service. Everett Kelley, the president of the American Federation of Government Employees, said Schedule F was an effort to "corrupt the federal government and replace qualified public servants with political cronies."[420] Schedule F provided that federal workers in policymaking roles must "faithfully implement administration policies to the best of their ability, consistent with their constitutional oath and the vesting of executive authority solely in the President. Failure to do so is grounds for dismissal."[421] Civil servants serve the people, not the president. As I learned as a federal employee, the public is best served when civil servants provide their candid advice, whether their field is law, science, or any other. The order's demand for loyalty to the president could deter federal employees from doing their jobs, fearing that independence would be seen as insubordination. In that scenario, the silence of government experts would work against the public's best interests. And if those experts were not on board with Trump's agenda, his administration would drive them out. During a 2024 speech, Vought discussed his goal of putting federal employees "in trauma." As Vought imagined, "When they wake up in the morning, we want them to not want to go to work because they are increasingly viewed as the villains."[422]

Schedule F, which permits their firing, was part of a one-two punch directed at federal workers with Trump's "Merit Hiring Plan" in his second administration. Applicants were required to write an essay identifying one or two of Trump's "relevant executive orders or policy initiatives that are significant to you and explain[ing] how you would help implement them if hired."[423] The responses would, in most instances, reveal the employee's political views, permitting hiring on an otherwise impermissible basis. Both Schedule F and the Merit Hiring Plan appeared to be designed to fulfill a MAGA desire expressed by Vice President J. D. Vance in 2021, when he suggested that Trump should purge the federal government of career professionals. According to Vance, Trump should "fire every single mid-level bureaucrat, every civil servant in the administrative state. Replace them with our people."[424]

Trump and his enablers have imposed their will on federal agencies, muzzling or compelling speech according to their liking. For example, the administration prohibited the Department of Energy from using the phrases "green," "sustainable," and "climate change."[425] During the government shutdown in 2025 over a budget impasse, federal agency websites blamed Democrats in Congress for the lapse in funding. Visitors to the website of the Department of Housing and Urban Development were greeted with a banner reading, "The Radical Left in Congress shut down the government. HUD will use available resources to help Americans in need."[426] A similar banner at the Justice Department's website accused the opposition party by name, stating, "Democrats have shut down the government."[427] The Small Business Administration sent employees "suggested language" for their out-of-office email response during the shutdown, stating in part, "I am out of office for the foreseeable future because Senate Democrats voted to block a clean federal funding bill (H.R. 5371), leading to a government shutdown."[428] At airport security checkpoints across the country, travelers were unable to avoid video messages from DHS Secretary Kristi Noem stating that "Democrats in Congress refuse to fund the federal government," so "most of our TSA employees are working without pay."[429] These apparent violations of the Hatch Act, which prohibit federal employees from engaging in partisan politics on the job, went uncontested. At the time, the Office of Special Counsel, which investigates Hatch Act violations, was without a permanent leader after Trump had fired Special Counsel Hampton Dellinger and failed to get a replacement confirmed.[430] In any case, Hatch Act violations seemed not only tolerated but encouraged.

Seizing all executive authority by presidential decree was a significant power grab, enabling the president to use the bureaucracy of government to advance his own agenda instead of allowing career civil servants to exercise their best professional judgment. It was a tactic that moved America another step closer to authoritarianism. And Trump was daring anyone to do anything about it.

Government Ethics

Trump didn't just take power from other parts of the executive branch: He also defied acts of Congress. By impounding congressionally appropriated funds, firing inspectors general, dismantling independent agencies, and disregarding the merit protection system, Trump undermined guardrails established by Congress in the Watergate era to help the legislative branch balance the executive. In that scandal, Richard Nixon had authorized the break-in of the Democratic Party headquarters at the eponymous office complex, spied on his political opponents, and used his official power to conceal it.[431] As White House Counsel John Dean described it, Nixon sought to "use the available federal machinery to screw our political enemies."[432]

Nixon, of course, resigned to avoid impeachment and removal from office, but his misconduct seems almost quaint today. "Nixon was essentially a criminal, but an ordinary criminal who accepted the fact that the laws applied to him and that if he tried to violate them, he would be subject to punishment," said David Dorsen, one of the lawyers for the Senate's Watergate Committee. "Trump considers himself above the law, so that the system is to be rejected by him when he feels like it should be."[433] Congress responded to the Watergate scandal by enacting safeguards that Trump is now dismantling. In Trump's view, the courts can't restrict his power, and Congress can't either.

In addition to laws, ethical norms also went by the wayside. Presidents are not constrained by the same conflict-of-interest rules that apply to federal employees, but political considerations often rein them in.[434] In 2017, for example, the Trump Organization agreed to refrain from entering into any foreign business deals while Trump was in office.[435] This time around, even that norm was jettisoned.[436] By 2025, Trump had launched his Trump Media and Technology Group, which operates the Truth Social platform. It is a publicly traded company that accepts foreign investments.[437] Eric Trump, the president's son who leads the Trump Organization while his father is in the Oval Office, has entered into real estate deals in numerous foreign countries;[438] among the lucrative projects were Trump Towers in Jeddah and Dubai, a luxury resort in Qatar, and a Trump International Hotel in Oman.[439] A few months later, Trump met with Crown Prince Mohammed bin Salman (known as "MBS") in Riyadh, where he received a royal welcome featuring Arabian horses and Saudi F-15s that were made in the USA.[440] At an address in the Saudi capital, Trump broke with decades of foreign policy, telling the audience that the United States would no longer be "giving you lectures on how to live."[441] Instead, he urged them to seek "your own destinies in your own way."[442] Trump praised MBS as an "incredible man," despite the view of the CIA that he was responsible for the imprisonment of dissidents and human rights violations, including the torture, killing, and dismembering of Jamal Khashoggi, a journalist for *The Washington Post*.[443] Befitting his transactional nature, Trump's focus was on deals. He was all too willing to shrug off details like human rights violations and even murder. During a White House visit in November 2025, when MBS faced a question from a journalist about his role in the killing, Trump interjected and said, "Things happen."[444]

One deal Trump couldn't refuse was a gift from Qatar of a four-hundred-million-dollar jet, described as a "palace in the sky."[445] When asked whether he would accept the 747, Trump said, "I would never be one to turn down that kind of an offer."[446] The jet was to replace Air Force One, the plane used to transport the president, but following Trump's term in office, the new jet would be sent to his presidential library.[447] The plane would also require extensive work—projected to cost at least as much again as the value of the jet itself, if not far more—to check for listening devices and to outfit it with the complex security and communications features needed to transport a president of the United States.[448]

Democrats in Congress blasted the gift as a violation of the Constitution's prohibition on foreign gifts, or "emoluments." The foreign emoluments clause provides that "no Person holding any Office . . . shall, without the Consent of the Congress, accept of any present, Emolument, Office, or Title, of any kind whatever," from any foreign government or leader.[449] As Alexander Hamilton explained in Federalist 68, "nothing was more to be desired" than to oppose "cabal, intrigue and corruption. These most deadly adversaries of republican government might naturally have been expected to make their approaches from more than one quarter, but chiefly from the desire in foreign powers to gain an improper ascendant in our councils."[450] In other words, foreign adversaries might attempt to infiltrate the American government by bribing officials. One way to avoid that risk is to prohibit the president and other officeholders from accepting gifts from foreign dignitaries who might seek to curry favor. Accepting such gifts might compromise a president's independent judgment about serving the best interests of the United States. But for Trump, refusing the jet was a nonstarter. He mocked even the possibility: "I could be a stupid person, saying, 'No, we don't want a free, very expensive airplane.'"[451] Trump made it clear that he planned to take the gift and dared anyone to do anything about it. It was another mob-style flex that added to his self-aggrandizing aura of invincibility.

Trump also used private donors to bypass congressional funding for his pet projects, an apparent violation of the Constitution's allocation of the power of the purse to the legislative branch. The Antideficiency Act bars federal agencies from spending more money than is appropriated by Congress.[452] Nonetheless, in addition to soliciting private donations from large corporations to fund construction of the new, obscenely large White House ballroom, Trump also found a private donor during the 2025 government shutdown to make good on his promise to pay members of the military. *The New York Times* reported that Tim Mellon, heir to a Gilded Age banking and railroad fortune, paid $130 million to back Trump's boast.[453] The gift would provide only about $100 per member of the armed services,[454] but it allowed Trump to portray himself as their champion.

Not only does accepting private donations for government projects violate federal law, it also undermines democracy. Members of Congress approve funding for various government functions on behalf of their constituents, who, in turn, are able to hold their representatives accountable at the ballot box. Gifts from private donors circumvent that political process, allowing the wealthy few to bypass the will of the people. Additionally, private donations raise conflict-of-interest concerns. Government ethics laws include prohibitions on gifts to federal employees, with limited exceptions.[455] But Trump has exploited a loophole—the ban on gifts does not apply to the president.

The Crypto President

Perhaps the most significant conflict of interest came from Trump's venture into cryptocurrency. Cryptocurrencies are highly speculative, volatile assets.[456] As a result, they are susceptible to fraud schemes, such as the eight-billion-dollar conspiracy that landed FTX CEO Sam Bankman-Fried in prison in 2025.[457] Just four years earlier, Trump called cryptocurrency "a scam" and "potentially a disaster waiting to happen."[458] But he made a complete U-turn during the 2024 presidential campaign, when crypto firms became huge election donors.[459] According to Robert Weissman of Public Citizen, a nonprofit consumer advocacy organization, "There's millions of losers for every few winners in the crypto game. Trump is rigging the rules to make sure he's on the winning side, but regular people are going to be hurt."[460]

During the Biden administration, the Securities and Exchange Commission brought almost one hundred enforcement actions against the crypto industry, and crypto financiers wanted a president who would loosen the reins.[461] A *New York Times* exposé revealed that Trump's epiphany came after lobbying efforts by leaders of BTC Inc., a company that invests in and promotes Bitcoin, the original and most successful cryptocurrency. During a meeting with Trump in the summer of 2024, the BTC executives asked Trump to post a message on social media promoting the cryptocurrency. That night, using the precise language the executives proposed, Trump posted on Truth Social, "We want all the remaining Bitcoin to be MADE IN THE USA!!! It will help us be ENERGY DOMINANT!!!"[462] According to the *Times* piece, "the post was one of the earliest successes in a high-stakes lobbying campaign by the crypto industry that has put huge sums of money behind Mr. Trump and reaped enormous rewards." Bitcoin's value was soon soaring.[463] At a campaign event later that summer, Trump told industry leaders he would make the United States "the crypto capital of the planet" by relaxing regulations and decreasing enforcement actions.[464] Following his conversion to crypto, Trump secured endorsements and received millions in donations from the industry.[465] Events surrounding Trump's second inauguration even featured a "Crypto Ball," a gala held near the White House.[466]

Upon taking office, Trump quickly turned down the dial on efforts to regulate cryptocurrency and called for legislation to boost the industry.[467] Deputy Attorney General Todd Blanche, one of Trump's former defense attorneys, disbanded DOJ's National Cryptocurrency Enforcement Team, noting Trump's intention "to end the regulatory weaponization against digital assets."[468] The SEC dropped enforcement actions, including a case against a crypto issuer and his three crypto companies for market manipulation of his digital securities, Tron (TRX), BitTorrent (BTT), and Sun Token (SUN).[469]

China-born Justin Sun had been charged with "fraudulently manipulating the secondary market for TRX through extensive wash trading, which involves the simultaneous or near-simultaneous purchase and sale of a security to make it appear actively traded without an actual change in beneficial ownership, and for orchestrating a scheme to pay celebrities to tout TRX and BTT without disclosing their compensation."[470] The case was dismissed without a shrug. Trump's about-face on crypto was precisely the kind of you-scratch-my-back-I'll-scratch-yours arrangement that corrupts good government. But who was going to stop him? According to Weissman, the consumer advocate, Trump's embrace of the cryptocurrency industry was part of an "oligarchy and authoritarian move" to allow wealthy cryptocurrency dealers to slide money to Trump in order to be excused from enforcement actions, while he simultaneously ramped up his use of the law and law enforcement to crack down on immigrants and free speech.[471]

Trump and his sons even launched their own crypto company, World Liberty Financial, which earned fifty-seven million dollars in income for the Trumps in 2024.[472] Even after Trump took office, his image still covered the home page of the World Liberty Financial website,[473] the very picture of a conflict of interest: As president, Trump has significant influence over the regulation of the industry. As a crypto issuer, he would be eager to see the sector grow untethered. It is a fair question to ask whether his private investments in crypto influenced his official actions as president, such as his executive order creating a federal Bitcoin reserve and cryptocurrency stockpile, akin to the gold stockpile at Fort Knox.[474] His announcement led to a spike in World Liberty Financial's stock price.[475]

In addition to the conflict of interest it created, World Liberty Financial also became another vehicle for foreign influence. Investors in Trump's cryptocurrency came from all over the world, including Israel and Hong Kong.[476] In 2025, a Chinese entrepreneur invested in World Liberty Financial in a deal that was expected to provide up to twenty-two million dollars in payouts to the Trump family.[477] Did that count as a foreign emolument in violation of the Constitution? Trump seemed impervious to any criticism about his apparent ethical breaches, deflecting conflict-of-interest concerns by noting that his children control his businesses.[478] But, as Timothy P. Carney of the American Enterprise Institute has pointed out, even if the president himself is not running the Trump Organization, he profits when the company does well. According to Carney, "When he leaves the White House, the company is worth more, his personal wealth goes up."

In the fall of 2025, *The New York Times* reported financial connections between the Trump family's cryptocurrency firm and the United Arab Emirates.[479] In May, Sheikh Tahnoon bin Zayed Al Nahyan, a member of the ruling family that controls $1.5 trillion of the UAE's sovereign wealth, invested $2 billion into World Liberty Financial. Two weeks later, the Trump administration agreed to give the UAE access to AI computer chips, many of which were to be provided to Sheikh Tahnoon's own technology company, despite national security concerns that the chips could be shared with China.[480] According to the reporting, the two deals were negotiated simultaneously, in violation of government ethics rules.[481] As the *Times* put it, "While there is no evidence that one deal was explicitly offered in return for the other, the confluence of the two agreements is itself extraordinary. Taken together, they blurred the lines between personal and government business and raised questions about whether US interests were served."[482]

The appearance of pay-to-play opportunities with the administration extended even to the president's power of pardon. In October 2025, Trump pardoned Changpeng Zhou, founder of the cryptocurrency firm Binance.[483] Zhou was convicted of money laundering and had served four months in prison.[484] While Zhou was seeking a pardon, Binance entered into a business deal with World Liberty Financial that would generate tens of millions of dollars a year for the Trump family and Steve Witkoff, the president's adviser on the Middle East.[485]

Clemency for Zhou came after Trump had pardoned another man, Paul Walczak, who had been convicted of withholding $7.5

million from his employees and keeping the funds for himself instead of paying them to the IRS.[486] Three weeks earlier, Walczak's mother had attended a Trump fundraiser that cost one million dollars per person.[487] As a result of the pardon, Walczak would never serve a day of his eighteen-month sentence or repay the four million dollars in restitution that had been ordered by a court.[488] While there was no evidence of an overt quid pro quo, Walczak's sins appeared to have been washed away with a cash payoff. The presidency could be quite profitable for someone who knows how to make deals—and is unbothered by rewarding lawbreakers.

Pandering to Trump could also lead to clemency. In October 2025, Trump commuted the sentence of George Santos, the disgraced former GOP congressman from New York who was convicted of wire fraud and aggravated identity fraud.[489] In the spring of 2025, Santos was sentenced to more than seven years in prison and the payment of $373,000 in restitution.[490] His sentence reflected the seriousness of his crimes, which included defrauding campaign donors and using the funds to buy himself luxury goods and Botox injections.[491] Santos fawned over Trump, hitting on some of the president's favorite themes; on social media and in the press, Santos argued that his sentence was "politically influenced" and that he was the victim of "the weaponized justice system."[492] Before granting the commutation, Trump disclosed another factor in Santos's favor: Although the president claimed he did not know him, Trump also said Santos was "100 percent for Trump."[493] On October 13, 2025, Santos wrote a direct appeal to Trump in a local newspaper column: "A lifelong Republican and a proud believer in your America First vision, I never wavered," Santos gushed. "Supporting you wasn't just a political decision—it was personal. It was rooted in my conviction that you were the only leader who truly put this nation, and her people, first."[494] Four days later, the president ordered Santos's release, after he had served only three months of his sentence.[495] Santos clearly understood the power of publicly kissing the boss's ring.

Raking It In

Ever the huckster, Trump also monetized his presidency by marketing almost every product imaginable: Proceeds from Trump watches, digital trading cards, guitars, Bibles, and sneakers (available in high-top or low) brought in more than seven million dollars in 2024. Donald Trump Jr. founded an exclusive club in Washington that he called the Executive Branch, with a membership fee of five hundred thousand dollars.[496] Administration officials, CEOs, tech entrepreneurs, and other ambitious people hoping to curry favor with the president clambered to join, and the club had a waiting list even before its opening night.[497] In 2025, the president launched Victory 45-47, fragrances for men and women named after the numbers corresponding to his two presidential terms.[498] The 3.3-ounce bottle, which cost $250, was topped with a golden figurine of Trump himself on a pedestal bearing his signature.[499] The online "Trump Store" hawks everything from Trump pickleball paddles to Trump spa wear, including a Trump-branded terrycloth robe and slippers.[500] The Trump Organization also launched Trump Mobile, which offered cell phones and data plans.[501] The color of the phone, of course, was gold.

Trump even offered his own meme coin,[502] a type of cryptocurrency that is based on images or jokes.[503] In Trump's case, the meme coin was promoted with a depiction of a slimmed-down Trump with his fist raised, emblazoned with the words "FIGHT, FIGHT, FIGHT," the phrase he uttered after surviving a 2024 assassination attempt. Just days before his inauguration, the president-elect launched the $TRUMP meme coin at a value of $6.50 per coin. That day, he posted on X, "My NEW Official Trump Meme [coin] is HERE! It's time to celebrate everything we stand for: WINNING!"[504] The coin's value rose to $73 the night before he was sworn in.[505] First Lady Melania Trump also got in on the act, selling a $MELANIA meme coin as well. Even though the coin's value eventually declined, Trump still reaped fees from the trading of each coin, generating one hundred million dollars for him in a matter of weeks.[506] After

Trump took office, the SEC announced it would no longer regulate meme coins, prompting a former regulator to characterize the move as "making the pay-to-play deal explicit."[507]

When the price of Trump's meme coin plummeted, thousands of people who bought in lost their money. In response to the embarrassing plunge, Trump incentivized donors to purchase more by hosting a private dinner for the top 220 investors in the coin.[508] The invitation offered an "EXCLUSIVE INVITATION in the World": a White House tour, along with "an intimate private dinner" with Trump at his private golf club in Virginia.[509] Promoting sales, the invitation read, "The more $TRUMP you hold—and the longer you hold it—the higher Your Ranking will be."[510] At the dinner in May 2025, which a White House spokeswoman said Trump would be attending "in his personal time," Trump spoke from a lectern bearing the presidential seal, lauding the virtues of digital currency. The largest holder of $TRUMP in the room was Justin Sun, the crypto dealer whose case was later dismissed by the SEC.[511]

Laughing All the Way to the Bank

Trump was making deals to enrich himself and his family without regard to conflicts of interest or the appearance of corrupt patronage. And just like John Gotti, he was doing it in broad daylight. Trump seemed to know that, like a mob boss, the more he got away with, the more untouchable he appeared to be.

PART II

Capturing Centers of Power

FIVE

SILENCING CRITICS

For some time, the Detroit-area teenage girl had been chatting online with a sixteen-year-old boy—or so she thought. They had never met in person, but they had developed a relationship online, not uncommon in today's digital age. After gaining her trust, he asked her to send him pictures of herself. She did so, agreeing to requests that grew progressively more explicit. Eventually, she even agreed to perform sex acts on a webcam for him. Then things turned darker: He escalated his demands and threatened to send the sexually explicit photos to the girl's mother, school, and church. In fact, the "boy" was fifty-eight-year-old Anthony Fontana of Ontario, a "sextortionist" who had victimized at least four other teens by similar means—assuming a false identity, befriending the victims online, enticing them to send nude photos, and then using the photos as leverage to coerce more from them.[512] Sex offenders like Fontana, of course, are not just lonely hearts looking for love. They are predators with a lust for power and control.

The lesson to be drawn from cases of sextortion, or any kind of extortion, really, is the role of manipulation: The initial payment makes the victim immediately vulnerable. Once compromised, victims feel shame in their complicity, helping assure their silence. An extortionist uses this leverage to continually manipulate the victim.

During Donald Trump's second term as president, his efforts to silence civic institutions reminded me of cases of extortion I have seen in my career as a prosecutor. Trump used his favored tool—leverage—to manipulate law firms, the media, and universities by falsely accusing them of wrongdoing and then demanding restitution. For law firms, Trump alleged that their lawyers had engaged in "lawfare" against him or illegal hiring practices. Trump attacked the media with frivolous claims of defamation (essentially, punishment for refusing to serve as his mouthpiece), including a fifteen-billion-dollar lawsuit against *The New York Times* for questioning his success.[513] When it came to universities, Trump claimed that antisemitism was rampant on campuses and declared their diversity, equity, and inclusion programs illegal. Trump's use of disinformation seemed designed to bring these institutions to the table to negotiate their own punishment. Their admissions of guilt would undermine their credibility and, consequently, diminish their ability to counter his power.

For Trump, these pillars of liberal democracy—sources of power with progressive leanings—were the perfect prey. Like most victims of extortion, once targeted, law firms, media outlets, and universities had nothing but bad options: They could fight back, giving Trump a battle that would benefit him politically with his base—Trump's MAGA supporters had been told for years that members of the "elite" establishment looked down on them, and now they relished the payback.[514] Or, on the other hand, they could agree with Trump's demands to avoid losing federal funding and other punishments, expanding his power by bringing them to their knees.

Legal Infirmity

Trump used executive orders to attack law firms—essentially extorting almost one billion dollars in pro bono legal services from some of the nation's largest and most prominent legal entities, coercing eight of them to accede to his demands to free themselves from baseless accusations of wrongdoing. Trump used agreements with the firms to even the score against some of his legal enemies and to tarnish the reputations of diversity, equity, and inclusion programs. But his most significant reward from his deals with law firms was his intimidating display of power. By accepting punishment for spurious allegations in order to avoid negative consequences, the firms demonstrated how easy it would be for Trump to dominate adversaries in his second term. Every firm that caved helped the strongman grow stronger.

The assault on the legal profession began in March 2025, when Trump issued an executive order "Addressing Risks from Perkins Coie, LLC," a global law firm with twenty-one offices worldwide.[515] According to Trump's order, the firm had engaged in "dishonest and dangerous activity"; the order cited as an example its representation of the 2016 campaign of "failed Presidential candidate Hillary Clinton." The order further alleged that Perkins Coie had hired the research firm Fusion GPS, "which then manufactured a false 'dossier' designed to steal an election."

The mention of a dossier was an apparent reference to the largely debunked Steele Dossier, compiled by British former intelligence officer Christopher Steele, a collection of raw intelligence reports indicating that Russia held disparaging information about Trump.[516] The executive order appeared to be Trump's effort not only to exact revenge but to rewrite the history of the Russia investigation from 2016, when Special Counsel Robert Mueller found no criminal conspiracy but "identified numerous links between the Russian government and the Trump Campaign" and "established that the Russian government perceived it would benefit from a Trump presidency and worked to secure that outcome, and that the Campaign perceived that it would benefit electorally from information stolen and released through Russian efforts."[517] Trump spun the Mueller report as having "cleared" him, when, in fact, it revealed the Trump campaign's breathtaking betrayal of loyalty to America when it failed to alert the FBI to Russia's efforts to influence the election.[518]

Trump's executive order against Perkins Coie included all the greatest hits: In addition to regurgitating Trump's grievances about Hillary Clinton, the Steele Dossier, and the Russia investigation, it also accused the firm of "a pattern" of "egregious activity," such as working "with activist donors including George Soros to judicially overturn popular, necessary, and democratically enacted election laws, including those requiring voter identification." Soros, a wealthy Jewish donor to Democratic candidates and progressive causes, is a favorite bogeyman of the far right. The firm had previously employed attorney Marc Elias, who had represented the Biden campaign in 2020 and successfully fended off Trump's frivolous legal challenges to the election results in court. Elias has also filed numerous lawsuits challenging election laws that could suppress voter turnout;[519] voter ID laws, which have a disparate impact on low-income voters, are touted in MAGA circles as necessary to prevent imagined election fraud.

Trump's executive order also alleged that Perkins Coie engaged in discriminatory hiring practices through its commitment to diversity, equity, and inclusion. Of course, there is nothing per se illegal about DEI programs; many law firms aspire to build the kind of diversity in their ranks that their clients prefer by offering summer jobs to students from underrepresented communities in the legal profession, such as veterans, first-generation law students, and minorities. I learned as a manager that groups with diverse viewpoints and experiences make better decisions. Further, no court has found that such programs within business entities violate the law. Nonetheless, the Trump administration seemed to have adopted the Project 2025 view that "entities across the private and public sectors in the United States have been besieged in recent years by an unholy alliance of special interests, radicals in government, and the far Left," resulting in "(DEI) offices that have become the vehicles for this unlawful discrimination."[520] Apparently, the Trump administration's views on the merits of free enterprise go only so far: Even when a private law firm believes that it is in its best business interests for its lawyers to have diverse backgrounds and experiences, it nonetheless must yield to a president who thinks he knows better. Trump's order demonstrated that he had decided he was in charge, demanding that firms bend to his will, while feeding the narrative that he was ending "reverse" discrimination, a ploy that was certain to appeal to the MAGA right.

As a consequence of its alleged misconduct, the executive order meted out Perkins Coie's punishment: suspension of the security clearance of any lawyer in the firm who held one, termination of any government contract with the firm, limits on its access to government buildings, and a ban on hiring any of the firm's lawyers for government jobs.

Perkins Coie challenged the order in court and quickly obtained a temporary restraining order, blocking the Trump administration from enforcing it during the pendency of the lawsuit. In a 102-page opinion, District Judge Beryl Howell castigated the administration for its action, calling out Trump's power grab for what it was.[521] "Eliminating lawyers as the guardians of the rule of law," she wrote, "removes a major impediment to the path to more power." According to Howell, "the importance of independent lawyers to ensuring the American judicial system's fair and impartial administration of justice has been recognized in this country since its founding era." She called the executive order "an unprecedented attack on these foundational principles." Judge Howell cited Alexis de Tocqueville, the nineteenth-century French political philosopher, who wrote in his book *Democracy in America*, "the authority . . . intrusted to members of the legal profession . . . is the most powerful existing security against the excesses of democracy."[522] Destroying that security seemed to be the point of Trump's order.

In May 2025, Judge Howell declared that Trump's executive order violated Perkins Coie's First Amendment rights of free speech and free association, as well as its Fifth Amendment right to due process and its clients' Sixth Amendment right to counsel of their choice.[523] The Trump administration, not going away easily, appealed the decision.[524] Three other law firms—Jenner & Block, WilmerHale, and Susman Godfrey—would face similar executive orders against them and likewise defeat them in court.[525] As Judge Howell wrote in the Perkins Coie case, "If the founding history of this country is any guide, those who stood up in court to vindicate constitutional rights and, by so doing, served to promote the rule of law, will be the models lauded when this period of American history is written."[526]

But even as all four law firms that fought back easily won their legal challenges, more firms chose the path of least resistance. Rather than take on the Trump administration in court, eight prominent law firms entered into agreements to avoid the risks of further retribution against them and their clients. And once one firm took the easy way out, others followed. Paul, Weiss, Rifkind, Wharton & Garrison, a highly regarded global law firm based in New York, stunned the legal community when it entered into the first of these agreements to resolve spurious allegations made in an executive order similar to the one directed at Perkins Coie. Trump's order, "Addressing Risks from Paul Weiss," made the same claims about DEI that it had made against the other firms; the order also cited one Paul, Weiss lawyer for working on Mueller's team. What's more, the order castigated that same lawyer for representing the District of Columbia pro bono in a case against "individuals alleged to have participated in the events at or near the United States Capitol on January 6, 2021."[527] In other words, the lawyer had agreed to waive his fee to help the municipality recover from damages perpetrated by the insurrectionists. For that, his firm would be punished.

The executive order also singled out another Paul, Weiss attorney, Mark Pomerantz, who had taken a leave of absence from the firm to help investigate the criminal case in the Manhattan district attorney's office that resulted in the conviction of Trump for thirty-four counts of falsifying business records to conceal hush-money payments. In the order, Trump accused Pomerantz of joining the DA's office "to manufacture a prosecution against me" and alleged that he had "unethically led witnesses in ways designed to implicate me." The penalties to be assessed against Paul, Weiss were similar to those imposed on Perkins, Coie, relating to security clearances, government contracts, access to government buildings, and hiring.[528] Like a crime boss, Trump was seeking vengeance against those who had crossed him.

But rather than bring to trial what likely would have been another slam-dunk victory in court, Paul, Weiss chose appeasement. In light of the firm's reputation for performing pro bono work on behalf of social justice causes, the news was particularly shocking. Brad Karp, the firm's managing partner, said the agreement was necessary to save the firm from an "existential crisis."[529] Perhaps Karp was concerned about protecting the firm's clients, some of whom likely were involved in negotiations with the federal government for contracts or for plea deals in criminal cases. But one also wonders whether that "crisis" was simply the concern that the firm's partners would risk losing profitable work from clients who might choose to take their business to other firms where the lawyers were not subject to Trump's wrath. In light of the potential harm to the independence of the legal profession, though, Karp's choice seemed shortsighted. Loss of revenue seems like a small price to pay to stand up to a president who was using half-truths to amass political power. In 2024, the firm's average pay per equity partner was $7.5 million, with some earning up to $20 million a year.[530] Surely, it seemed that if any law firm could afford to mount a fight, Paul, Weiss could. Whatever Paul, Weiss saved in revenues, it lost in the value of its reputation.

While it is hard to imagine that a lawyer as accomplished as Karp would agree to any deal with Trump on just a handshake, no written agreement has been made public to date. As a result, the details are a bit sketchy, and Trump's account of the agreement differed from Karp's. An email from Karp to the firm stated that he had pledged $40 million in pro bono legal services for "various initiatives."[531] Trump's statement about the agreement instead used the phrase "*Administration* initiatives,"[532] which could refer to a very different set of projects. In both versions, these initiatives were described as serving the "Nation's veterans, fairness in our justice system, the President's Task Force to Combat Antisemitism, and other mutually agreed projects."[533] Trump claimed Karp had also "acknowledged the wrongdoing of former Paul, Weiss partner, Mark Pomerantz, the grave dangers of Weaponization, and the vital need to restore our System of Justice," concessions that were not included in Karp's email.[534] In addition, the firm committed to employing "mutually agreed upon" experts to audit its employment practices, as well as to implementing merit-based hiring, promotion, and retention policies. But in his description of the deal, Trump claimed that Paul, Weiss had further agreed that it "will not adopt, use, or pursue any DEI policies."[535] That language was absent from Karp's email. Without seeing a copy of the agreement, it was difficult to assess whether Karp was downplaying his concessions or Trump was embellishing them. Regardless, landing a trophy like Paul, Weiss had the predictable domino effect on other firms.

Seven firms followed Paul, Weiss's lead, promising pro bono legal services regarding unspecified matters.[536] Within a few months, they, too, suffered reputational damage among law students contemplating their future careers, and some clients began to look for alternative firms to handle their legal work.[537] Some of the capitulating firms agreed to provide pro bono services even *before* any order was entered, violating the warning historian Timothy Snyder has issued as the cardinal rule in facing authoritarians: Do not obey in advance.[538] All told, the firms that entered into agreements with Trump promised to provide almost a billion dollars' worth of legal services for free to Trump's pet causes.[539] Trump has suggested that those hours might be used to help the coal industry or to negotiate tariffs.[540]

Sometimes, business deals require a compromise of short-term interests for long-term gains. Firm leaders at these companies, including transactional lawyers who close some of the world's biggest deals, may have thought they were getting a good bargain. Perhaps they thought that their firms would be providing pro bono legal services anyway, so it cost them nothing more to direct their efforts to a cause favored by the president. But the real harm of their capitulation, of course, was to inflate Trump's sense of empowerment, both to him and the public.

According to Elizabeth Grossman, a former Paul, Weiss attorney who now leads Common Cause Illinois, the firm was "thinking about their bottom line . . . I think what we've seen is that they made the wrong decision." Indeed, within a few months, ten lawyers had left the firm, and its reputation was scarred in legal recruiting at law schools. One of the lawyers to part ways with Paul, Weiss was former Manhattan US attorney Damian Williams. His destination? Jenner & Block, one of the firms that fought an executive order.[541] Moreover, a group of lawyers who left Paul, Weiss and started their own firm took along with them Meta and Google as their clients, likely the sources of highly lucrative legal fees.[542] In the end, not only was the deal detrimental to the independence of the legal profession, it was also bad for the firm. As posted on social media by Neera Tanden, head of the Center for American Progress, a Democratic think tank, "Paul Weiss's actions will live in infamy."[543]

I have learned from extortion cases I have seen that it is important not to blame the victim. While one would hope that those who have suffered would have the courage to speak out to expose the extortionist and stop the escalating harm to themselves and others, it is essential to remember that the real wrongdoer is the extortionist who is pressuring potential victims to pay up. But appeasing the extortionist rarely makes them stop squeezing. In fact, it usually just leads to more demands.

Trump reaped multiple benefits from his mob-style treatment of law firms that had crossed him. Chief among them was their silence. As Michael S. Schmidt, an investigative reporter with *The New York Times* noted, a marked change from Trump's first administration to his second was the reluctance of legal experts to criticize Trump's increasing lawlessness in the media. According to Schmidt, he and his colleagues had seen a chilling effect that they attributed to Trump's punishment of law firms, universities, and other institutions. "The reluctance that we've seen suggests that even people not yet within the administration's direct sightlines are becoming worried about speaking freely."[544] Schmidt further observed:

> It can be hard to show the tangible effects of a vengeful government, particularly because concerns about retribution often spur people *not* to do something they normally would. But the quiet in Washington is noticeable, and meaningful. Silence, particularly around something fairly innocuous like explaining the law, reflects a level of fear that feels new.

Using power to muzzle experts creates a dangerous feedback loop: As public awareness of the threat diminishes, the power of those imposing silence only grows.

Another benefit Trump obtained by coercing law firms into "deals" was to remove them from the playing field in lawsuits against him and his administration. In his first term, Big Law, as the large firms are known collectively, threw its considerable weight behind challenges to government actions:[545] During Trump's first term, large law firms filed cases in 75 percent of the lawsuits challenging Trump's executive orders.[546] During the first ten months of his second term, they filed only 15 percent of those kinds of cases, leaving small- and medium-sized firms, state attorneys general, and nonprofit organizations with fewer resources to do the heavy lifting.[547] For instance, in Trump's first term, Paul, Weiss and other large firms provided pro bono legal services to help reunite immigrants affected by Trump's family separation program. Brad Karp even coauthored a 2018 opinion piece in *The New York Times* blasting the initiative as "unlawful and immoral," writing, "The world is watching, and the private bar is mobilizing to serve the thousands who have been imperiled by the Trump administration—and to ensure that the rule of law is protected as well."[548] In 2025, with deals with the Trump administration in place, not only were some of the nation's most prominent law firms sidelined from these battles, they were now potentially available for Trump's use to advance his agenda. What a difference four years makes.

Media

In addition to law firms, the media also found themselves in a new, compromised posture in Trump's second term. In authoritarian regimes, controlling the media is a crucial step in seizing and maintaining power. According to Princeton professor Kim Lane Scheppele, who spent a decade in Hungary watching the rise of Viktor Orbán, by punishing the press for coverage he disliked, Orbán drove independent media out of business—not overnight, but in plain sight.[549] Orbán used audits, investigations, and regulations to neutralize the industry. If the press cedes its watchdog role by writing only fawning praise for the leader, the public loses awareness of official misconduct, self-serving transactions, and the national protest movements that often rise up to confront them. Using extortion tactics to squeeze the press helps a ruler control the narrative and manipulate public perception.

Trump has long referred to the press as "the enemy of the people."[550] During Trump's first term, the mainstream media seemed undeterred, plowing ahead with hard-hitting journalism critical of Trump's norm-bending style. *The Washington Post* and *The New York Times* uncovered stories about national security advisor Michael Flynn's contacts with the Russian ambassador that led to Flynn's resignation after just weeks on the job.[551] A 2020 *Times* exposé revealed Trump's troubled finances and minuscule income tax payments, providing at least one explanation for the president's refusal to make his income tax returns public.[552] The *Post* leaned into its reputation for investigative reporting, adding a tagline: "Democracy Dies in Darkness."[553] In 2017, *Post* columnist Dana Milbank wrote that Trump "took on the institution of a free press—and it fought back. Trump came into office after intimidating publishers, barring journalists from covering him, and threatening to rewrite press laws. He has continued to discredit the 'fake news' media at every opportunity. Instead of driving out independent media, he wound up inspiring a new golden age in American journalism."[554]

But in the 2024 election cycle, some members of the press started hedging their bets—none more so than *The Washington Post,* which killed its endorsement of Kamala Harris for president at the direction of its owner, Jeff Bezos.[555] The *Post*'s publisher denied any effort to favor Trump, stating that the paper had simply decided to stop endorsing candidates altogether so readers could make up their own minds.[556] In response to the move, hundreds of thousands of readers canceled their subscriptions, and multiple staff members resigned.[557] The day after Trump was elected, Bezos posted on X, "Big congratulations to our 45th and now 47th President on an extraordinary political comeback and decisive victory. No nation has bigger opportunities. Wishing @realDonaldTrump all success in leading and uniting the America we all love."[558]

This was a remarkable change of heart for Bezos, a multibillionaire who also owns the retail giant Amazon, as well as MGM Studios, Whole Foods, Zappos, and Blue Origin—a pioneer in private space travel. During the 2016 election, Bezos was quick to defend the *Post* from Trump's attacks. Trump had used Twitter to call the *Post* a "fake news" outlet that Bezos had bought just so that he could take business-loss deductions "to screw public on low taxation of @Amazon! Big tax shelter."[559] Bezos responded by tweeting that he would "reserve him a seat on the Blue Origin rocket. #sendDonaldtospace."[560]

But by the 2024 election, Bezos's business strategy had apparently changed since the first Trump administration, when Amazon lost a ten-billion-dollar bid to provide cloud computing at the Pentagon, prompting the tech giant to sue the Trump administration for the president's alleged improper influence in an effort to "screw Amazon."[561] Bezos also may have been influenced by a pending civil lawsuit against Amazon filed during the Biden administration by the Federal Trade Commission, alleging antitrust violations.[562] Perhaps by seeking better treatment from the federal government, Bezos was violating Snyder's rule, obeying in advance. Not only did Bezos congratulate Trump on his electoral victory, Amazon also donated one million dollars to the incoming president's inaugural fund.[563] Moreover, in December 2024, Amazon paid forty million dollars for the rights to a documentary about Melania Trump that would generate twenty-eight million dollars for the First Lady, and began airing reruns of *The Apprentice*.[564]

Other news outlets also appeared to be obeying in advance: In December 2024, ABC agreed to pay the president-elect fifteen million dollars to settle a defamation lawsuit that seemed eminently defensible. Trump had alleged that news host George Stephanopoulos had harmed his reputation by stating on air that Trump had been found liable for raping writer E. Jean Carroll. In fact, a jury in a civil suit brought by Carroll had found that Trump was guilty of defaming and sexually abusing her, but had not raped her.[565] Still, many thought that the claim was meritless in light of a statement on the record by the judge in the case that it was accurate to refer to Trump's conduct as rape "in common modern parlance."[566] According to CNN, critics said that ABC and its parent company, the Walt Disney Company, were "bowing to Trump for craven political purposes."[567]

Paramount Global, the parent company of CBS News, may not have obeyed in advance, but it seemed willing to appease Trump when it paid sixteen million dollars to settle a lawsuit. Trump had sued CBS over the editing of a 2024 interview with Kamala Harris on its *60 Minutes* news show. CBS had used one part of Harris's answer to a question on Israel and Palestine for *60 Minutes*, and another portion for its *Face the Nation* program. CBS's conduct seemed to be a routine exercise of editorial discretion, but Trump characterized it as election interference. In addition to the payment, the media company also agreed that in the future *60 Minutes* would release full transcripts of interviews with presidential candidates. In February, after CBS released the full transcript of Harris's interview, Trump blasted the network on social media, posting: "CBS should lose its license, and the cheaters at 60 Minutes should all be thrown out, and this disreputable 'NEWS' show should be immediately terminated."[568]

Northwestern University law professor Heidi Kitrosser called the lawsuit "laughable" and "an affront to the First Amendment," suggesting that Trump's "concern first and foremost is to intimidate the press."[569] The chief executive of CBS News and its local stations, Wendy McMahon, and *60 Minutes* executive producer Bill Owens, who opposed settling the case, resigned from the company in the spring of 2025, perhaps clearing the way for the settlement. One factor that may have motivated Paramount in its decision was its proposed merger with Skydance Media, which required approval from Trump's FCC.[570] It had all the hallmarks of a pay-to-play arrangement; according to Kitrosser, the payment of the legal settlement was, in fact, "protection money."[571] Stephen Colbert, host of *The Late Show* on CBS, mocked the settlement as a "big fat bribe."[572] One week later, the network canceled Colbert's show, calling it "purely a financial decision."[573]

Those who did not obey in advance learned how quickly Trump could punish them. After winning the presidency in 2024, Trump promptly sued *The Des Moines Register* and pollster J. Ann Selzer for publishing a poll showing Trump three points behind Harris in Iowa the day before the November election.[574] In fact, Trump won the state by fourteen points. Trump made a novel claim that publishing the poll was consumer fraud.[575] Although the polling data did not match the ultimate election results, *The Des Moines Register* stood by its reporting. Experts criticized the aggressive court filing, noting that political polling that fails to accurately predict the actual election outcome is not a deceptive business practice, and some viewed the suit as part of a broader attack on the media.[576] According to Sharon Moshavi, president of the International Center for Journalists, authoritarian leaders like Orbán have silenced dissent not by eliminating the free press, which would be impossible to do, but by attacking it every chance they get. "It's death by a thousand cuts," she said. "It's attacks from multiple angles."[577]

One of those cuts was suffered by the Associated Press, which was removed from the White House press pool after it failed to change its influential stylebook to conform to Trump's preference for the term "Gulf of America" to refer to the body of water west of Florida rather than its longstanding name, "Gulf of Mexico."[578] Even though the wire service had participated in the press pool for more than a century, it was purged in apparent retaliation for editorial decisions the president didn't like. AP executive editor Julie Pace said, "For anyone who thinks the Associated Press's lawsuit against President Trump's White House is about the name of a body of water, think bigger. It's really about whether the government can control what you say."[579] The AP sued the Trump administration for violating its First Amendment rights. After a lower court issued a temporarily blocking the administration's order, the Court of Appeals for the District of Columbia reversed. The two judges ruling in favor of the administration were appointed by Trump.[580] The one dissenting judge, a Barack Obama appointee, wrote that "if the White House were privileged to exclude journalists based on viewpoint, each and every member of the White House press corps would hesitate to publish anything an incumbent administration might dislike."[581] This, of course, was the point.

In addition to purging the AP from the Oval Office, the Trump regime also ousted other media outlets from workspaces inside the Pentagon, where they enjoyed access to Defense Department leaders. Out were mainstream media outlets such as NBC News, CNN, NPR, *The New York Times*, *The Washington Post*, and *Politico*. In were right-wing media companies like *Breitbart*, One America News Network, the *New York Post*, Newsmax, the *Daily Caller*, and *Washington Examiner*.[582] While the progressive-leaning *HuffPost* was added to the Pentagon workspace, it is a far smaller publication than the media giants that were removed. The move seemed to reward and amplify favorable news coverage for the Trump Defense Department while punishing critics. The value of replacing independent reporters with toadies became apparent when Trump and Vice President J. D. Vance met Ukraine's president, Volodymyr Zelensky, in the Oval Office in February. Zelensky, whose nation was at war with Russia, was wearing modest black clothing and combat boots.[583] During a confrontation that grew hostile, Brian Glenn, a reporter with Real America's Voice, piled on by asking the leader of the war-torn country why he was not wearing a suit to visit the president. Glenn then added, "A lot of Americans have problems with you respecting this office."[584] Far from being an objective journalist, Glenn was the boyfriend of Marjorie Taylor Greene, a former MAGA Congresswoman from Georgia.[585]

Other members of the media also found themselves under attack. Trump issued an executive order cutting funding for the Corporation for Public Broadcasting, alleging bias in the coverage provided by NPR and PBS.[586] In addition, Brendan Carr, Trump's Federal Communications Commission chair, initiated investigations against NPR and PBS, citing concerns that they were violating the law by airing commercial advertising by announcing underwriting donations.[587] Media lawyer Andrew Jay Schwartzman called the probe "more of a scare tactic than the identification of a genuine problem."[588] Carr also opened investigations against ABC and NBC over their DEI programs, to ensure they were not "promoting invidious forms of discrimination in violation of FCC and civil rights laws."[589] Perhaps deciding that the fight was not worth the risk, PBS announced it would voluntarily shut down its DEI programs under pressure from the administration.[590]

Carr would take his intimidation tactics to new heights when late-night comedian Jimmy Kimmel criticized the Trump administration's response to the shocking murder of right-wing political activist Charlie Kirk. Kimmel called Kirk's death itself a "senseless murder."[591] But Kimmel also said, "The MAGA gang" is "desperately trying to characterize this kid who murdered Charlie Kirk as anything other than one of them and doing everything they can to score political points from it."[592] If the "MAGA gang" comment was a joke, it was not particularly funny, and not necessarily accurate, but it was pointed at political opportunists, not Kirk or his killer. More importantly, the comment was clearly protected from government retaliation under the First Amendment. During a podcast interview, Carr suggested that ABC could lose its broadcast license for airing Kimmel's show. "We can do this the easy way or the hard way," he said. "These companies can find ways to change conduct, to take action, frankly, on Kimmel, or, you know, there's going to be additional work for the FCC ahead."[593] Within hours, ABC had suspended Kimmel indefinitely.[594] Trump applauded ABC on social media for "finally having the courage to do what had to be done." The network seemed to be bowing to the pressure of Carr's threat.[595]

The rest of the nation, however, was not pleased by the network's decision. Even Ted Cruz, the conservative GOP senator from Texas, blasted the intrusion on protected speech. Calling Carr's comments "dangerous as hell," Cruz said they were "right out of *Goodfellas*," the famous mob movie.[596] Cruz compared Carr to "a mafioso coming into a bar, going, 'Nice bar you have here; it'd be a shame if something happened to it.'"[597] A week after the suspension, ABC put Kimmel back on the air. The Walt Disney Company, which owns ABC, explained that it had decided to suspend Kimmel for his "ill-timed" and "insensitive" comments "to avoid further inflaming a tense situation at an emotional moment for our country" and had decided to reinstate Kimmel after "having thoughtful conversations with Jimmy."[598] Perhaps another reason for Kimmel's return was the public outcry from critics, ranging from citizen protesters to Hollywood celebrities and former President Barack Obama—or the $6.4 billion dollars in market capitalization that Disney lost within the week as outraged customers canceled subscriptions to its services.[599]

Trump also used an executive order to gut international radio broadcaster Voice of America (VOA) and urged Congress to shut it down altogether, on the grounds that it was the "Voice of Radical America" and a "TOTAL LEFTWING DISASTER."[600] In fact, Voice of America was founded during World War II to provide information to people in countries where governments censor news media.[601] Providing news in forty-eight languages, VOA fulfilled a valuable national security mission by countering propaganda and disinformation from Russia, Iran, China, and other hostile foreign adversaries. VOA executive director Michael Abramowitz denied any political bias in the broadcaster's coverage, noting that unlike other news organizations, VOA is still required by law to be fair and balanced. (Other broadcasters were freed from this requirement in 1987, when Ronald Reagan's FCC repealed the rule known as the Fairness Doctrine.) He noted that VOA's charter requires the outlet to present the "full spectrum of American political opinion." Consequently, it airs shows featuring both Democrats and Republicans.[602] Still, Trump's move seemed to be motivated at least in part by the same purpose as his crackdown on the mainstream media: to squelch opposing viewpoints.

Universities

In addition to law firms and the media, universities also found themselves targeted by the Trump administration. The assault seemed similar to the extortionate attacks on the other institutions—spurious claims of misconduct used to coerce victims to negotiate their own punishment. For universities, their transgressions seem to vary depending on the day of the week—excessive government spending on federal grants, DEI programs, antisemitism, too many international students. Like Orbán's treatment of the media, it was an effort to silence critics through death by a thousand cuts.

But why would the Trump administration target higher education? Research universities are the crown jewel of American success, incubators of scientific discovery, life-saving research, and academic inquiry. The innovations achieved at universities enhance our national security and propel our economy. Universities also benefit individuals by encouraging self-discovery; by developing critical thinking that empowers them to solve some of the world's most complex problems; by exposing them to other people and perspectives that enable them to thrive in a pluralistic society; by teaching appreciation of history, literature, languages, and culture; by improving earnings potential; and by generating upward mobility.

According to Jason Stanley, a philosophy professor who studies fascism, authoritarian regimes see universities as a significant threat to their power. Because universities promote critical thought and free speech, they counter the authoritarian's goal of "complete subservience."[603] Stanley also notes that bright young students "have always been the source of resistance against authoritarianism and unjust war."[604] As a result, he says, authoritarians seek to delegitimize universities.[605] For example, in Italy in 1931, every university professor was required to sign a loyalty oath to dictator Benito Mussolini. Those who refused—only twelve did so—were fired.[606] Some were jailed or forced into exile.[607] The loyalty oath was important, another scholar writes, because "it signaled to the rest of the country that there would be no resistance in the world of Italian ideas."[608] Compelling universities to bow before the leader paves the way for subjugating the entire populace.

Attacking universities was also popular with Trump's MAGA base. In an interview with Fox News, GOP congresswoman Elise Stefanik of New York said, "If you look at the faculty, the tenured faculty of all these schools, they are so out of touch with American values. Ninety-seven percent of the faculty are self-identified Democrats or progressives. They are propping up these radical, far-left ideas and really teaching anti-Americanism."[609] Stefanik earned praise from her party in December 2023 by aggressively questioning the presidents of the University of Pennsylvania, Harvard University, and the Massachusetts Institute of Technology during a congressional hearing.[610] In response, Claudine Gay, Harvard's first Black woman president, gave nuanced but politically damaging answers about free speech and antisemitism on campus, leaving the impression of an out-of-touch academic. The hearing would lead to her resignation less than a month later.[611]

Trump has used MAGA's resentment of higher education to his advantage, referring to university faculties as "Marxist maniacs," even though he himself is a graduate of the Ivy League University of Pennsylvania. In 2021, J. D. Vance, a Yale Law School alumnus, called universities "very hostile institutions," telling the audience at a conservative conference, "If any of us want to do the things we want to do for our country and the people who live in it—we have to honestly and aggressively attack the universities in this country."[612]

Just as he had done with law firms, Trump targeted the biggest names in academia. He went after Columbia University, the scene of vigorous protests over Israel's war in Gaza; the University of Virginia, whose DEI programs Trump opposed, and the University of Pennsylvania, where a transgender woman competed on the swim team. The president scored some quick wins, with Columbia capitulating in March 2025 after Trump accused the university of failing to protect Jewish students during protests and stripped it of four hundred million dollars in federal grants. National Institutes of Health grants awarded to its scientists and doctors were suddenly canceled on the basis of "unsafe antisemitic actions,"[613] putting the university in a difficult spot.

Targeting universities for antisemitism was a devious ploy. No doubt there is plenty of antisemitism in America, on college campuses and elsewhere, just as there is anti-Muslim bias. But it seemed ludicrous to assert that antisemitism was the true basis for Trump to single out Harvard for harsh treatment: This is the man who, just a few months later in July 2025, would refer to bankers as "Shylocks" while boasting about the passage of a budget bill.[614] The Anti-Defamation League denounced Trump's use of the term, which it said "evokes a centuries-old antisemitic trope about Jews and greed that is extremely offensive and dangerous."[615] And this was not the first time Trump had shown indifference toward antisemitism. In 2017, he failed to strongly denounce the racist and antisemitic "Unite the Right" rally in Charlottesville, Virginia, where protesters chanted "Jews will not replace us" and "Blood and soil"—a Nazi slogan.[616] Trump also drew criticism from Jewish leaders in 2022 when he dined with rap artist Kanye West, who had tweeted that he would "go death con 3 ON JEWISH PEOPLE," and Nick Fuentes, an outspoken Holocaust denier.[617] The leader of the Anti-Defamation League blasted Trump's conduct as "the normalization of antisemitism."[618] Yet when it came to Harvard, Trump conveniently used antisemitism as a basis for harsh treatment, simultaneously deepening rifts between Jewish and Muslim students and sympathizers on each side of the Israel/Palestine conflict.

Many were able to see through the charade. "It's self-evident it's not about antisemitism," said Yehuda Kurtzer, the president of Shalom Hartman Institute, a research center based in Jerusalem that studies Jewish life.[619] "Why would that have anything to do with cutting funding for research? It's about conservative fears of higher education, and antisemitism is an excuse."[620] Harvard Law School professor Andrew Manuel Crespo saw the motive as control: "It's a transparent effort to change what is taught, what we say in our classrooms, what we teach our students, to make sure that the only things that are actually said on university campuses are things that the Trump administration wants to hear and wants to be said."[621] Trump was fomenting social discord to develop leverage against the university. And while Trump's critics opposed his extortion of Harvard, most did not want to be seen as defending antisemitism or denying that it exists.

Eventually, Columbia agreed to Trump's demands to ban face masks on campus, permit security officers to make arrests, and, most alarmingly, to move control from university faculty to a new official who would oversee its Middle Eastern, South Asian, and African

Studies Department.[622] The new official would also review curriculum changes and control the hiring process for nontenured faculty. Overtaking academic freedom was an ominous stride toward authoritarianism. "Imagine if newspapers were told: 'We're going to monitor your journalism to make sure that you hire Trump-friendly journalists and opinion writers.' You would know you're not living in a democracy anymore," Stanley said. "It's no different with universities."[623]

The University of Virginia similarly caved to Trump's pressure. University president James Ryan was forced to resign amid pressure from Trump's Justice Department over its DEI programs.[624] In his resignation letter, Ryan wrote that he was inclined to fight for what he believed in but did not want to save his own job at the expense of "the hundreds of employees who would lose their jobs, the researchers who would lose their funding, and the hundreds of students who could lose financial aid or have their visas withheld."[625] The Justice Department had been investigating the university to determine whether it had violated civil rights laws that prohibit recipients of federal funds from engaging in discrimination.[626] After Ryan's resignation, Harmeet Dhillon, the assistant attorney general of DOJ's Civil Rights Division, said, "Jim Ryan has built his entire career on what was the academic vogue, which is DEI. Now it isn't. So I think it is time for new leadership that's willing to comply with federal law."[627]

After a similar attack on Northwestern University, its president, Michael H. Schill, resigned in September 2025.[628] In November, Northwestern agreed to pay $75 million to resolve allegations of antisemitism and other forms of discrimination.[629] The settlement restored $800 million in federal research funds.[630]

The University of Pennsylvania also agreed to demands by the Trump administration regarding transgender athletes. The Department of Education had accused the university of violating civil rights laws by permitting Lia Thomas, a transgender woman, to swim on its women's team after she met the National Collegiate Athletic Association's hormone requirements.[631] Under the terms of the agreement, transgender women would be banned from the school's women's teams and Thomas would be stripped of her accomplishments. Secretary of Education Linda McMahon said that the agreement was "yet another example of the Trump effect in action. Thanks to the leadership of President Trump, Penn has agreed both to apologize for its past Title IX violations and to ensure that women's sports are protected at the University for future generations of female athletes."[632]

One university decided to fight back: Harvard, the nation's oldest and perhaps most prominent university, refused to bow to Trump's demands. In April 2025, the administration accused Harvard University of "ideological capture" and antisemitism.[633] Government officials sent a letter threatening to withhold federal funding unless Harvard met its demands—changes in governance, hiring practices, and diversity, equity, and inclusion programs, as well as "audits" to ensure "viewpoint diversity."[634] When Harvard rejected Trump's demands and filed a lawsuit challenging the threats, Trump's squeeze tightened. He froze $2.2 billion in federal funds, rescinded the university's ability to issue visas to international students (who make up 27 percent of the university's student body), and threatened to withdraw the university's accreditation.[635] Without accreditation, students cannot obtain loans to attend an institution and are likely to choose to enroll in other schools.[636]

While Harvard was winning favorable court rulings against Trump's demands and retaliation, the pressure continued to mount.[637] Trump ally Jim Jordan, a far-right congressman from Ohio, joined in the attack by opening an oversight investigation into Harvard and other Ivy League universities for potential antitrust violations in setting tuition rates.[638] In July 2025, Harvard showed a crack in its armor when web pages for centers serving Harvard's minority, women, and LGBTQ students suddenly disappeared from the university's website.[639] Harvard also announced that its diversity office for the Faculty of Arts and Sciences would be replaced by a new Office of Culture and Community, a sign that the Trump administration called "good news."[640] Like a crime boss, Trump was creating his own leverage to coerce Harvard into submission.

M. Gessen, a columnist for *The New York Times* and author of books on totalitarianism and autocracy, wrote that Trump's attacks on universities were like mobster shakedowns of victims for protection money.[641] Gessen argued that Trump was motivated to target universities by "anti-intellectualism and greed, and the fact that Trump is building a mafia state . . . in which one person, the patron, the don, distributes money and power. And so in order to build a mafia state, such an aspiring patron needs to strip other agents of their money and power. Some universities are actually quite wealthy, so they are to some extent independent financial centers, and they are centers of independent, intellectual and political power. And that's what Trump is really going after."[642]

Regardless of motive, the potential harm to democracy from the capture of these institutions was alarming. Lee Bollinger, former president of Columbia University, pulled no punches in assessing the danger:

> We're in the midst of an authoritarian takeover of the US government. It's been coming and coming, and not everybody is prepared to read it that way. The characters regarded as people to emulate, like Orbán and Putin and so on, all indicate that the strategy is to create an illiberal democracy or an authoritarian democracy or a strongman democracy. That's what we're experiencing. Our problem in part is a failure of imagination. We cannot get ourselves to see how this is going to unfold in its most frightening versions. You neutralize the branches of government; you neutralize the media; you neutralize universities, and you're on your way.[643]

The universities that gave in to Trump's demands may have thought they were buying relief for themselves, but it was likely only temporary. And by acceding to the government's demands, they empowered Trump to squeeze more universities to fall in line with his increasingly authoritarian dictates. As Gessen wrote, "[T]here's no such thing as negotiating with this administration. It is always going to demand more concessions until nothing is left of the institution that Trump has targeted."[644]

The Power of Speech

Anthony Fontana was eventually brought to justice. He was arrested, prosecuted, convicted, and sentenced to thirty years in prison—but only because one teenage girl had the courage to speak out.[645] Had she remained silent, he would have continued to prey on her and countless other victims. Silence is the hidden accomplice of the extortionist.

We have seen the effects of silence on democracy in Orbán's Hungary. According to David Pressman, a former US ambassador to Hungary, as the country's prime minister, Orbán slowly suffocated his nation's democracy. Pressman watched as institutions and businesses made "deals" with Orbán to keep "peace with the strongman, in exchange for subjugation and humiliation."[646] But, as Pressman wrote, capitulation was a grave mistake. "*Going along* is what did them in. Those best positioned to uphold democratic norms chose the comfort of an illusion over the courage of action. They were and are invisible by choice—and that choice disfigured them and ultimately their country. The lesson of Hungary is this: We cannot claim to care about democracy only when it costs nothing."

SIX

DOING INJUSTICE

New York City mayor Eric Adams, a former police officer, was charged with betraying the public trust by accepting bribes.[647] In September 2024, the US attorney's office in Manhattan announced an indictment, alleging that Adams had accepted illegal campaign contributions and luxury overseas travel from foreign nationals in Turkey during a five-year span while serving first as Brooklyn borough president and then as mayor. In exchange, Adams allegedly arranged for Turkey's consulate in New York to open without passing a fire inspection, even after a fire official had deemed it unsafe to occupy. Adams also allegedly acquiesced to a Turkish official's request to refrain from issuing a statement recognizing the Armenian genocide—perpetrated by Ottoman Turks during World War I—on its annual remembrance day.

But in a stunning turn of events, in the first days of the second Trump administration, news broke that Justice Department leaders wanted to dismiss all charges. The reason for the change of heart? A deal. But not a typical plea deal: The government offered to drop all charges against Adams if he agreed to obey President Donald Trump and help enforce his new immigration laws.[648] In addition to directing the dismissal, acting Deputy Attorney General Emil Bove, a former Trump defense attorney, also proposed doing so "without prejudice"—meaning that the charges could be coercively dangled over Adams's head and reinstated if he failed to fulfill his end of the deal.[649] Danielle Sassoon, the interim US attorney in the Southern District of New York, where the charges had been filed, resigned over "an improper offer of immigration enforcement assistance in exchange for a dismissal of his case," calling it "what amounted to a *quid pro quo*."[650] In Latin, "quid pro quo" means "this for that," a term that in bribery prosecutions indicates a thing of value traded for the performance of an official duty.

Sassoon was no bleeding-heart liberal. She was a member of the conservative Federalist Society and a former law clerk to the late US Supreme Court justice Antonin Scalia—a darling of the right.[651] Trump himself had appointed her to her position as interim US attorney.[652] Six additional federal prosecutors in New York and Washington refused to obey the demands of their Trump-aligned superiors and immediately resigned over the deal.[653] Three more later resigned rather than falsely admit to improper conduct in the Adams case, a demand made by Deputy Attorney General Todd Blanche, another former Trump defense attorney.[654] In defiance, the three attorneys wrote, "We will not confess wrongdoing when there was none. . . . Now, the Department has decided that obedience supersedes all else, requiring us to abdicate our legal and ethical obligations in favor of directions from Washington."[655]

While denying any illegal quid pro quo, Tom Homan, Trump's border czar, appeared alongside Adams for a television interview and essentially confirmed that the arrangement was just that, saying that Adams would now be allowing federal immigration agents into the Rikers Island jail. "If he doesn't come through," Homan said, "I'll be back in New York City, and we won't be sitting on the couch. I'll be in his office, up his butt saying, 'Where the hell is the agreement we came to?'"[656] The judge assigned to the case saw through the deal, though he was powerless to force the Justice Department to prosecute the charges. He ultimately dismissed the case, but *with* prejudice, so that DOJ could not use the threat of reinstatement of charges to control Adams.[657] Otherwise, the judge wrote, the potential to refile the indictment would hang "like the proverbial Sword of Damocles over the Mayor."[658]

There was a certain irony in using what could be characterized as bribery to dismiss a case charging bribery. The convicted felon who was found guilty of paying hush money to sway his election was remolding the Department of Justice in his own image—brash, defiant, dedicated to serving his interests instead of upholding the rule of law. Paul Rosenzweig, who served as a senior official in the George W. Bush administration, said that Trump was "transmuting DOJ into his personal law firm," which he called "a rejection of the founding principle of the rule of law."[659]

As someone who spent almost twenty years of my professional life as a federal prosecutor, the corruption of the Justice Department was painful to watch. Certainly, DOJ was never perfect, but most of us who took the oath to serve believed the department was a vehicle for seeking justice, protecting victims, and serving our country through the even-handed administration of the law. People were drawn to the work not for the compensation, which was modest, but for the opportunity to do meaningful and impactful work. The Department of Justice, as we often reminded ourselves, is the only cabinet agency named for a virtue.

During my time at DOJ, we were reminded that since Watergate, policy limiting communications between the White House and the Justice Department—as well as DOJ's Principles of Federal Prosecution—made it clear that partisan politics was never to play a role in case decisions. [660] We lauded people like Robert H. Jackson, the Nuremberg prosecutor and Supreme Court justice who once served as our nation's attorney general. In 1940, Jackson gave an often-quoted speech at DOJ's Great Hall, reminding the nation's US attorneys of the importance of "the spirit of fair play and decency that should animate the federal prosecutor."[661] In addition, many federal prosecutors frame and hang the famous quote from the case of *Berger v. United States*, in which the Supreme Court wrote:

> The United States Attorney is the representative not of an ordinary party to a controversy, but of a sovereignty whose obligation

> to govern impartially is as compelling as its obligation to govern at all, and whose interest, therefore, in a criminal prosecution is not that it shall win a case, but that justice shall be done. As such, he is in a peculiar and very definite sense the servant of the law, the two-fold aim of which is that guilt shall not escape or innocence suffer. He may prosecute with earnestness and vigor—indeed, he should do so. But, while he may strike hard blows, he is not at liberty to strike foul ones. It is as much his duty to refrain from improper methods calculated to produce a wrongful conviction as it is to use every legitimate means to bring about a just one.[662]

Maybe it seems naive in today's cynical world, but we took those words seriously. As US attorney, I would meet with every new prosecutor on their first day on the job to explain that they were now stewards of the Department of Justice, whose integrity was more important than winning any case.

Trump complained about his lack of control over DOJ during his first term, when investigations probed his campaign's contacts with Russia. When Trump tried to intervene, he was investigated for obstruction of justice. But in his second term, as Brookings Institution fellow Quinta Jurecic wrote, those guardrails were gone.[663] Between Trump's two terms, a Supreme Court opinion had given him immunity from criminal prosecution for conduct committed at the outer perimeter of his official duties.[664] According to Chief Justice John Roberts, the president has "exclusive authority over the investigative and prosecutorial functions of the Justice Department and its officials." As a result, Jurecic wrote, Trump's second administration was "barely bothering to hide its actions or justify them as anything other than an effort to turn the Justice Department into Trump's personal gang of enforcers."[665]

Perhaps signaling that Trump would take a different approach to the Justice Department during his second term, he delivered a highly partisan political speech in March 2025, in the very same Great Hall where Robert H. Jackson had once spoken so eloquently. But instead of uplifting inspiring notions of justice, Trump used the occasion to air his grievances about "a corrupt group of hacks and radicals" who had prosecuted him during the Biden administration, "to prevent me from becoming the president of the United States."[666] Making no pretense of an independent Justice Department, Trump declared he was now "the chief law enforcement officer in our country."[667] By 2026, an enormous banner bearing Trump's image would deface DOJ's Washington headquarters symbolizing the capture of its independence.

Bondi on Board

The Adams case signaled that political corruption would no longer be a priority of the Department of Justice during Trump's mob-style rule. That prophecy was soon fulfilled when Pam Bondi took office as attorney general. Bondi was a former attorney general of Florida who had been a media surrogate for Trump. During the 2016 Republican National Convention, as Bondi delivered remarks, the crowd began chanting "Lock her up," referring to Hillary Clinton, who had not been convicted of any crime—an appalling affront to the rule of law. Rather than chasten the crowd or simply ignore the chant, Bondi instead joined in, saying, "Lock her up. I love that!"[668] During her confirmation hearings, Bondi pledged to "restore integrity to that department," reinforcing Trump's false narrative that DOJ had lost its way during the Biden administration. As attorney general, she was prepared to obey the boss and carry out the vendettas he had promised during the campaign.[669]

According to Democratic senator Sheldon Whitehouse of Rhode Island, a former US attorney, Trump was ushering America into "a golden age of public corruption."[670] Indeed, shortly after taking office, the president issued executive orders "pausing" enforcement of the Foreign Corrupt Practices Act, which criminalizes bribery by American companies in foreign countries,[671] and "ending the weaponization of law enforcement,"[672] an effort to rewrite the history of his own criminal prosecutions.

Now, Bondi appeared ready to do her part. On her first day on the job, she issued fourteen memoranda. In addition to creating the Weaponization Working Group, Bondi's memos shifted priorities toward immigration cases and away from corruption. She limited enforcement of the Foreign Corrupt Practices Act to cases involving drug cartels and transnational criminal organizations,[673] effectively giving the green light to bribery by American business operators overseas. Bondi disbanded the FBI's Foreign Influence Task Force and limited enforcement of the Foreign Agents Registration Act, both of which are used to protect US politics from hostile foreign powers.[674] She also dismantled DOJ units targeting kleptocracy, which seized the assets of Russian oligarchs.[675] And soon, Bondi and her top aides would gut the Public Integrity Section, the DOJ component that specializes in corruption cases.[676] Todd Blanche, Bondi's deputy, dissolved the National Cryptocurrency Enforcement Team just as Trump was expanding his own financial interests in the industry.[677] Paul Rosenzweig, the senior official in the Bush administration, said that the Trump administration was "dismantling all the means of oversight of public corruption," noting, "The law is only for his enemies now."[678]

Kashing In

No one seemed more poised to exact retribution on Trump's enemies than Kash Patel, the president's nominee for FBI director. Trump had already busted one norm when he announced that he would replace Christopher Wray, whom Trump had appointed to the post in 2017 after firing James Comey in the midst of the Russia investigation. By law, FBI directors serve ten-year terms. Trump had terminated Comey short of his full term and was prepared to do the same to Wray, who stepped down voluntarily after Trump's announcement.

FBI director is a powerful position, overseeing 38,000 agents, lawyers, analysts, scientists, language specialists, and support personnel.[679] The bureau has broad investigative jurisdiction and the ability to initiate surveillance against targets of investigation. Patel would be an FBI director with a background like no other: He had served in Trump's first administration in various roles but was primarily known for his provocative defense of the president. It was Patel who claimed that Trump had declassified the government documents that the former president was charged with unlawfully retaining.[680] And it was Patel who had produced the "Justice for All" recording featuring the voices of Trump and jailed January 6 defendants.[681] Patel also authored a book called *Government Gangsters: The Deep State, the Truth, and the Battle for Our Democracy*.[682] The book includes a list of sixty government officials Patel said were part of the so-called "deep state," which he described as "a cabal of unelected tyrants" who pose "the most dangerous threat to our democracy."[683] Some of the names you would expect were on the list—Trump rivals like Kamala Harris, Barack Obama, and Hillary Clinton.[684] But also included were former Trump appointees like Attorney General William Barr, who resigned at the end of Trump's first term rather than advance false claims about election fraud; John Bolton, the former national security adviser who wrote a book that was unflattering to Trump; and Mark Esper, who served as Trump's secretary of defense and refused to go along with a military response to protesters.[685] Before joining the FBI, Patel had even authored a children's book entitled *The Plot Against the King*, as well as two sequels. The story involved a conspiracy against "King Donald" and "Keeper Komey's spying slugs," who falsely accuse the good king of cheating to win an election. The hero of the story is a loyal wizard whose name is—you guessed it—"Kash."

In addition to Patel's obsequious fealty to Trump, he had made troubling statements about the FBI and Trump's goals for a second administration. In November 2024, after Trump was elected, Patel said that he would "shut down the FBI Hoover Building on day one and reopen it the next day as a museum of the deep state."[686] During a podcast interview, Patel also proposed using the law "criminally or civilly" against Trump's political rivals: "We will go out and find the conspirators not just in government, but in the media."[687] Patel appeared ready and able to serve as Trump's personal police force for seeking revenge.

During his confirmation hearings, Patel pledged that he would not engage in "retributive actions."[688] He also assured the 14,000-member FBI Agents Association that he would appoint a career FBI agent with operational expertise as deputy director to counter his own lack of experience.[689] Instead, he tapped Dan Bongino, a far-right podcast host. Though Bongino had once been a police officer and a Secret Service agent, he had never worked for the nation's premier law enforcement agency, which has its own high standards and unique culture. Bongino had even called the agency "irredeemably corrupt."[690] By August 2025, after Bongino clashed with Pam Bondi over the failure to release the Epstein files, she would appoint a "co-deputy director" to share Bongino's job. But former Missouri attorney general Andrew Bailey was a politician who also lacked FBI experience and operational expertise. Lest anyone believe Bailey was brought in to restore integrity to bureau leadership, Todd Blanche welcomed him with these words: "As Missouri's attorney general, he took on the swamp, fought weaponized government, and defended the Constitution. Now he is bringing that fight to DOJ."[691]

Upon taking office, Patel confirmed some of his critics' fears. He suspended an analyst, Brian Auten, whose name appeared on the list in *Government Gangsters*.[692] Auten had worked on the investigation into Russian interference in the 2016 presidential election and Russia's interactions with the Trump campaign.[693] Patel, in line with MAGA doctrine, had pushed false claims to delegitimize the investigation.[694] Patel also fired agents who had been photographed kneeling with protestors during Black Lives Matter demonstrations in the District of Columbia.[695] Reports indicated that Patel used polygraph tests to question dozens of agents about their trustworthiness and leaks, even inquiring whether agents had ever said anything negative about Patel himself.[696] If criticizing the boss from time to time were legitimate grounds for firing, most Americans would be out of a job.

Eagle Ed Martin

"Name and shame" was a technique Ed Martin touted when he became head of Bondi's Weaponization Working Group.[697] Traditionally, "name and shame" at the Department of Justice meant something very different: naming in *indictments* individuals, often foreign nationals located overseas, who had committed serious crimes, even though they likely could not be extradited to the United States to be put on trial. For example, in 2014, five Chinese military hackers were indicted for economic espionage against the US steel industry.[698] Similarly, in 2018, Special Counsel Robert Mueller indicted members of the Russia-based Internet Research Agency.[699] While arrests of the defendants in either case were unlikely given their locations, naming them and exposing their conduct was valuable to US national security and foreign policy.

But Martin had an altogether different definition of name and shame, stating that even if the Justice Department were unable to assemble sufficient evidence to prosecute individuals whom he believed had "weaponized" government—likely those involved in criminal cases against Trump or the January 6 cases—he would publicly disclose adverse information about them. Such a move would violate the longstanding DOJ policy of refraining from disparaging individuals except as required in court filings and open court hearings.[700] At a press conference announcing his new jobs, Martin said, "There are some really bad actors, some people that did some really bad things to the American people. And if they can be charged, we'll charge them. But if they can't be charged, we will name them. . . . In a culture that respects shame, they should be people that are ashamed."[701]

In his social media biography, Martin would refer to himself as "Trump's Weaponization Czar." He would occupy that role while also serving as DOJ's pardon attorney, where he would dole out pardons for those in good standing with Trump.[702] Martin landed the dual roles after failing to secure sufficient support in the Senate for confirmation as US attorney for the District of Columbia; Trump had installed Martin as the interim US attorney in the nation's capital in

January 2025 and later nominated him to the permanent post. Martin was a "Stop the Steal" election denier who was present at the Capitol on January 6, 2021.[703] He served as a lawyer for January 6 defendants and raised money for some of them.[704] During his four months on the job as interim US attorney, Martin served as Trump's hatchet man, purging the office of prosecutors who worked on the Capitol cases. He also dismissed the pending cases, even though he was still the attorney of record for the defendant on one of them—a blatant conflict of interest and ethical lapse.[705]

By traditional standards, Martin was a poor fit for US attorney. As a former US attorney myself, I am aware that most appointees have backgrounds as prosecutors with little to no partisan political activity; in a job that requires delicate deliberations about criminal charges, US attorneys without political baggage are best situated to make independent decisions based on the facts and the law. Moreover, non-partisan US attorneys are better able to earn and maintain public trust when they take action that sometimes runs counter to the interests of political parties and sitting government officials.

Martin, who had never served as a prosecutor at any level, was a political actor from Missouri, where he had once served as chair of the state Republican Party and later led Phyllis Schlafly's Eagle Forum, a conservative political activist group.[706] He used the moniker "Eagle" in his social media handle even after assuming the role of interim US attorney.[707] Martin made an early impression by generating a flurry of letters that seemed to advance Trump's political interests. For instance, in February, Martin made public a letter he had sent to Elon Musk, who was then slashing government programs and jobs at the Department of Government Efficiency.[708] Addressing Musk as "Elon," the letter stated that Martin had learned that some members of the DOGE team had received online threats, and so he wanted to assure Musk "that we will pursue any and all legal action against anyone who impedes your work or threatens your people."[709] A few days later, Martin posted another letter, stating, "If people are discovered to have broken the law or even acted simply unethically, we will investigate them," adding in bold letters, "we will chase them to the end of the Earth to hold them accountable."[710] While online threats are certainly appropriate matters for federal investigation and prosecution, Martin's letters were more than just unusual. First, a US attorney lacks the authority to investigate someone for acting "simply unethically." Second, the letters suggested that Musk was receiving special treatment. And third, the letters violated the usual DOJ policy of refraining from confirming even the existence of an investigation unless and until charges were filed, so as to avoid compromising the investigation and harming the reputation of an individual who may not ultimately be charged with any crime.

Martin did not stop with letters to Trump's allies—he also wrote to the president's rivals. In a project he called "Operation Whirlwind," Martin would use his US attorney letterhead to write to a wide range of politicians, institutions, and others in a campaign likely intended to intimidate them and chill free speech. Among the recipients of the letters were Democratic Senate minority leader Chuck Schumer of New York and Democratic congressman Robert Garcia of California. Martin wrote that he was seeking "information and clarification" about their public statements.[711] The name of Martin's operation appears to have come from a statement Schumer made in 2020 at a pro-choice rally, barely within the five-year statute of limitations when Martin launched his letter-writing campaign. Schumer had told the crowd that Supreme Court Justices Neil Gorsuch and Brett Kavanaugh "have released the whirlwind and you will pay the price. You won't know what hit you if you go forward with these awful decisions."[712] His words may have shown poor judgment in an era of rising political violence, and Schumer apologized the next day. But his statement fell far short of the legal standard required to charge a crime. Martin followed up with two more letters demanding a response from Schumer.[713]

Martin's letter to Garcia also sought "clarification" regarding statements the congressman had made during a television interview in which he disparaged Trump. Garcia said, "What the American public wants is for us to bring actual weapons to this bar fight. This is an actual fight for democracy."[714] Like Schumer, Garcia showed bad judgment in his choice of words. Still, the remarks did not rise to the level of prosecutable "true threats," defined as "serious expressions conveying that a speaker means to commit an unlawful act of violence."[715] Protecting victims from true threats is crucial because they put people in fear of violence and cause corresponding disruption in their lives. Still, no reasonable person would conclude that Schumer or Garcia had communicated true threats.

In addition to Schumer and Garcia, other recipients of Martin's letters included Georgetown University Law Center and four medical journals. In his letter to the dean at Georgetown, Martin demanded an end to diversity, equity, and inclusion programs and stated that he would not hire graduates from these programs.[716] Earning accolades in the media, Dean William M. Treanor responded to Martin's letter with a stern rebuke in which he refused to be silenced. Treanor, a constitutional law scholar, wrote, "Given the First Amendment's protection of a university's freedom to determine its own curriculum and how to deliver it, the constitutional violation behind this threat is clear, as is the attack on the University's mission as a Jesuit and Catholic institution."[717] The letters to the medical journals—which mentioned their tax-exempt status in what may have been a thinly veiled threat—expressed concerns that they were "partisans in various scientific debates," without citing any specific examples. They further inquired about topics such as misinformation, the journals' practices regarding competing viewpoints, and the role of advertisers in determining content. J. T. Morris, a lawyer for a free speech advocacy group, expressed concern that officials like Martin might "abuse their authority and try to use the legal process and abuse the court system into compelling scientific journals and medical professionals and anybody else they disagree with into silence."[718]

Despite the controversy surrounding the letters, or perhaps because of them, Trump nominated Martin for the permanent position of DC US attorney. In light of Trump's vows of retribution against his political opponents, a fair inference is that Martin's letters were an effort to help the president fulfill those promises.[719] Given that he published the letters on his social media account, Martin seems to have been more interested in intimidating the recipients than in investigating crimes, while ideally also deterring would-be critics from speaking out about actions taken by the Trump administration. It was all too much for Senator Thom Tillis, a Republican from North Carolina, who refused to support Martin because of his involvement in the events of January 6, leaving Martin without sufficient votes for confirmation.[720] Undeterred, the Trump administration simply shifted Martin over to another job at DOJ, as head of the Weaponization Working Group and the Office of the Pardon Attorney, where he would need no Senate confirmation. He promptly hired Jared L. Wise as an adviser for the group. Wise was a former FBI employee who had been a January 6 defendant.[721]

The name-and-shame strategy may also have been at work when Trump's DOJ filed criminal charges against James Comey and New York attorney general Letitia James. Both cases, filed two weeks apart in fall 2025, appeared legally flimsy, but even more concerning was the procedural lead-up. In late September, Trump had posted to Truth Social a message to "Pam" (presumably Bondi) demanding charges against Comey, James, and Senator Adam Schiff.[722] All three had investigated Trump—Comey in the Russia probe, James in a state civil fraud case, and Schiff in Trump's two impeachment inquiries. Trump wrote that all three were "guilty as hell."[723] His post made clear that his motive was revenge: "They impeached me twice, and indicted me (5 times!), OVER NOTHING," he wrote. "JUSTICE MUST BE SERVED, NOW!!!"[724] His post also disparaged his own appointee as US attorney in the Eastern District of Virginia, Erik Siebert, calling him "[a] Woke RINO, who was never going to do his job."[725] Seibert resigned and was replaced with Lindsey Halligan, a former insurance lawyer who was then working as a White House aide.[726] Despite her complete lack of experience as a prosecutor, Trump installed Halligan to lead one of the nation's most important US attorneys' offices, with jurisdiction over cases arising out of the CIA, the Pentagon, and Dulles International Airport, where international terrorists and spies are often first brought to the United States. She showed up for work on a Monday and, three days later, filed the Comey indictment, charging him with making false statements during a congressional hearing almost five years earlier.[727] Apparently unable to find any career prosecutor to sign the indictment or present the case to the grand jury, she did so herself, a highly unusual occurrence.[728] She repeated the exercise the following week to obtain an indictment against James for mortgage fraud. In both cases, career prosecutors who had led the investigations had concluded that the evidence was insufficient to support any charges.[729] When a judge found Halligan's appointment invalid, the James and Comey cases were both dismissed.[730] Engineered incompetence had struck again.

The two indictments were a blow to the independence of US Attorney's Offices, which pride themselves on acting without fear or favor. Since the Watergate era, limits on communications between the White House and DOJ have sought to protect case decisions from political taint or even its appearance. DOJ's Principles of Federal Prosecution, the policies that guide the exercise of discretion, prohibit consideration of "political associations, activities, or beliefs" in bringing a case.[731] Under Trump, those policies suddenly seemed like relics of the past. Following Comey's indictment, Trump was asked by reporters who was next on his "retribution" list. "It's not a list, but I think there'll be others," Trump said. "I mean, they're corrupt. These were corrupt radical left Democrats, but Comey, essentially was, he was worse than a Democrat. I would say the Democrats are better than Comey. But no, there'll be others."[732] True to his word, in late 2025, a "grand conspiracy" investigation appeared to be taking shape, as the US attorney in Miami began issuing grand jury subpoenas to officials who had led the 2016 investigation into Russia's efforts to interfere with the presidential election, despite completed investigations by DOJ's inspector general and two special counsels.[733] In an extraordinary letter to the chief judge of the Southern District of Florida, Ken Wainstein, a former DOJ official now serving as attorney for former CIA director John Brennan, wrote, "We are no longer in a normal time. We are now in a time when the Justice Department has surrendered much of its independence and the president is directly commanding his attorney general and her leadership team to use their prosecutorial authorities against his perceived political adversaries."[734]

Former New Jersey governor Chris Christie, who also served as US attorney in that state under President George W. Bush, compared the management of the Justice Department to that of an organized crime enterprise. "Here's the difference between Trump II and Trump I," Christie said in a television interview.[735] "The Department of Justice is no longer the premier prosecuting office in America. What it is now is a capo regime who goes out and executes hits when directed by the Don to do so. That's what it is."[736]

What is the point of filing an indictment that will almost certainly lead to acquittal or pretrial dismissal for selective or vindictive prosecution—or even on the grounds that the US attorney was illegally appointed? Humiliation, revenge, cruelty—in other words, name and shame.

Pirro-ette

Trump's replacement for Ed Martin as the nominee for US attorney in Washington, DC, was another devoted follower, Jeanine Pirro. Like Pete Hegseth and other members of the Trump regime, Pirro was a former Fox News personality. Unlike Martin, Pirro had significant experience as a prosecutor and a judge, having been elected district attorney for Westchester County, New York, three times. That was almost twenty years earlier, however, before she stepped down as district attorney to run against Hillary Clinton for a Senate seat in 2006.

Now, Pirro shared with Martin what was perhaps the most important qualification for the job: obedience to Trump. Pirro had been aligned with Trump for a long time; her ex-husband, Albert J. Pirro Jr., had once served as Trump's lawyer and received a pardon from Trump in 2017 for a tax-evasion conviction. On Fox News, Pirro was a reliable voice of support.[737] In 2016, she defended Trump during the *Access Hollywood* controversy, in which Trump could be heard in a recording discussing women in vulgar terms. Following the 2020 election, Pirro joined the chorus of false claims about Dominion Voting Systems, which named her as a defendant in its defamation lawsuit against Fox News. (The media company eventually settled the case for $787.5 million.) She also downplayed the January 6 attack on the US Capitol as a political "narrative" and called for a probe of DOJ investigators and a Capitol police officer.[738] On her radio show, she advocated for criminal investigations into Trump's rivals, including prosecutors and judges assigned to his legal cases. While she seemed more qualified and perhaps less reckless than Martin, her subordination to Trump created the impression that she lacked the political impartiality required of a US attorney. Once confirmed, Pirro was a forceful advocate for Trump's use of National Guard troops on the streets of Washington, DC.[739]

Turn New Jersey Red

The situation was no better in New Jersey, where Trump installed one of his former attorneys, Alina Habba, as interim US attorney. Like Martin and Halligan, Habba had no prior experience as a prosecutor. Her theatrical participation in a camera-ready arrest was only the first indicator that she would be unlike most US attorneys.[740]

Just days after starting the job, Habba gave a podcast interview in which she said, "We could turn New Jersey red," eliminating any pretense of political neutrality. Habba continued her comments by saying, "Hopefully, while I'm there, I can help that cause."[741] While serving in a role that must shun even the appearance of bias, Habba expressly stated that she had political goals. In the days to come, she did nothing to calm her critics: She launched investigations into New Jersey's Democratic governor and attorney general over state policies that limited the ability of state officials to assist federal law enforcement agents in immigration cases.[742] Of course, there is a difference between obstructing federal law enforcement officers, which could constitute a crime, and refraining from providing active assistance, which is a lawful act of state sovereignty. Habba seemed uninterested in that difference. Habba also filed criminal charges against a

Democratic congresswoman over an incident that occurred during an oversight visit at an immigration detention facility.[743] After New Jersey's US senators refused to support Habba's nomination, and the judges of the district court declined to extend her interim appointment, Habba clung to her role as US attorney until an appeals court ruled that she was serving illegally.[744] She resigned in late 2025.[745]

The Purge

Part of building a team of obedient subordinates is eliminating anyone who might remain objective and independent. As a result, after Trump's second inauguration, DOJ leaders wasted no time removing prosecutors who worked on cases that challenged Trump—the 1,500 cases arising from the January 6, 2021, attack on the US Capitol and the special counsel's cases against him.

First to go were senior leaders at the FBI. In January, Emil Bove, then serving as acting deputy attorney general, sent a memo to the acting FBI director, Brian Driscoll. The memo, bearing the subject line "Terminations," directed Driscoll to fire eight senior FBI officials.[746] According to the memo, Bove said he did not "believe that the current leadership of the Justice Department can trust these FBI employees to assist in implementing the President's agenda faithfully."[747] Of course, FBI supervisors, like all federal employees, take an oath to support and defend the Constitution of the United States, not the president's agenda. Trump was substituting fealty to the boss for fidelity to the Constitution.

In addition, Bove directed Driscoll to collect the names of FBI personnel "assigned at any time to investigations" relating to the January 6, 2021, attack on the US Capitol. Trump had referred to the criminal prosecutions as "a grave national injustice."[748] Bove's memo indicated that he would be undertaking a "review process to determine whether additional personnel actions are needed."[749] The memo sent shockwaves through the federal government; firing FBI employees simply for doing their jobs would violate civil service laws that protect them from political reprisals.[750] It was bad enough that Trump had granted clemency to more than 1,500 defendants for crimes committed during the attack, signaling that vigilantes would be rewarded for their violence when acting in service to Trump. Now, it appeared that DOJ was considering punishing government employees who had investigated these cases, a move that would advance Trump's false narrative that they had done something wrong. While a subsequent memo from Bove stated that employees were not at risk if they "simply followed orders and carried out their duties in an ethical manner," he added that he was looking for "those who acted with corrupt or partisan intent, who blatantly defied orders from Department leadership, or who exercised discretion in weaponizing the FBI"—hardly reassuring words when the administration's view was that the entire January 6 operation was an act of "weaponization."[751] Driscoll himself was forced to leave a few months later.

The personnel shakeup was likely to further erode the public's respect for the law and those who enforce it. And it sent a terrible message to government employees that they could be at risk if they were to participate in investigations of powerful people. After serving as Trump's henchman at DOJ, Bove would be rewarded with a judgeship on the Third Circuit Court of Appeals, just one step below the US Supreme Court.[752] Driscoll and other senior leaders who were fired from their jobs at the FBI filed lawsuits alleging that they were dismissed as part of a "campaign of retribution" for their "failure to demonstrate sufficient political loyalty."[753] In their complaint, the former supervisors claimed that leadership "not only acted unlawfully but deliberately chose to prioritize politicizing the FBI over protecting the American people."[754]

Driscoll alleged that when interviewing for his job with Kash Patel, he was told he could have a top position at the FBI as long as he was "not prolific on social media, did not donate to the Democratic Party, and did not vote for Kamala Harris in the 2024 election," an appalling injection of partisan politics into the civil service.[755] Next, Driscoll claimed, he interviewed with Paul Ingrassia, who would later flame out as a nominee to head the Office of Special

Counsel over racist text messages; at this time, Ingrassia was serving as a transition liaison. According to the lawsuit, Ingrassia asked Driscoll whether he supported Trump and how he felt about diversity, equity, and inclusion initiatives.[756] Driscoll's lawsuit also alleged that his selection as acting director was the result of a clerical error: He was actually slated to be the acting deputy director, and another official, Robert Kissane, had been selected as the acting director. But someone at the White House mixed up the two men and their roles in a press release and was unwilling to admit the error. Instead of disclosing a mistake, the suit claimed, the administration preferred to permit the wrong man to lead the nation's premier law enforcement agency.[757] More incompetence, more chaos.

Next in the line of fire were the prosecutors who worked on cases Trump disliked. In the District of Columbia, Martin fired dozens of prosecutors at the US attorney's office who were hired to handle some of the January 6 prosecutions.[758] These were probationary employees, on the job for less than two years and entitled to fewer civil service protections than more senior lawyers; Martin's predecessor had hired them to handle the 1,500 cases that were taxing the office's resources.[759] Rather than reassigning them to other work, Martin removed them from the department. DOJ leaders fired other lawyers and staffers who worked on the special counsel's team.[760] More than twenty employees had been detailed to work on the investigations into Trump for election interference and unlawful retention of government documents.[761] Now they were gone, simply for doing their jobs.

By March, Pam Bondi had removed dozens of experienced senior career officials in the Civil Rights Division, the Executive Office for Immigration Review, the US Attorney's Office in Washington, DC, and the National Security Division.[762] The purpose of having career leaders in government is to build expertise and institutional knowledge and maintain continuity between administrations. Removing them at the president's whim reverted the nation to an earlier era when the spoils system meant that presidents would clean house after every administration and fill jobs with lackeys as rewards for their patronage. Any ability to do the job well was mere coincidence.

Elizabeth G. Oyer, the DOJ pardon attorney, said she was fired for refusing to restore the gun rights of actor Mel Gibson, a prominent supporter and personal friend of Trump.[763] She said her decision was consistent with DOJ practice to deny restoration to individuals like Gibson with convictions for domestic violence. She believed that she was fired for refusing to violate the department's integrity and put public safety at risk by performing a political favor for the president.[764] Her termination indicated that this was now Trump's DOJ, where mob-style machinations increasingly replaced legal and ethical principles.

In apparent violation of civil service protections, Bondi also began firing DOJ personnel without explanation, simply sending them an email with the subject line: "Notice of Removal from Federal Service."[765] The email stated bluntly: "Pursuant to Article II of the United States Constitution and the laws of the United States, you are removed from federal service effective immediately."[766] The seemingly random targeting of the removal notices sparked fear, rumors, and speculation about why Bondi had singled out certain individuals.[767] Whether by design or not, the emails caused other DOJ employees to retire or resign rather than risk termination or assignment to a task of questionable legality. One FBI agent said he was fired because of his friendship with Peter Strzok, a colleague at the FBI who had investigated the Russian interference case during Trump's first term.[768] Another employee who received one of Bondi's termination emails was Maurene Comey, a federal prosecutor in the Southern District of New York and the daughter of James Comey, the former FBI director and Trump's longtime nemesis. Maurene Comey filed a lawsuit challenging her dismissal, but many others did not.[769] Even though an employee terminated in this manner would likely win a legal challenge, many were not interested in fighting that battle only to return to a job where they were considered an enemy.

Some employees resigned from a DOJ that they no longer recognized. At the Federal Programs Branch, tasked with defending Trump's legally questionable executive orders, two thirds of its 110-member workforce had left by July.[770] The notion of defending orders redefining birthright citizenship or defunding Harvard—and doing so "zealously," as Bondi had directed—was likely repulsive to many of those who resigned.[771] As lawyers in the unit left, the workload of the others continued to increase. According to a Reuters report, one lawyer who left the unit said, "Many of these people came to work at Federal Programs to defend aspects of our constitutional system. How could they participate in the project of tearing it down?"[772] The response from the Trump administration likely confirmed to the departing lawyers that they had made the right decision in leaving. According to White House spokesperson Harrison Fields, "Any sanctimonious career bureaucrat expressing faux outrage over the President's policies while sitting idly by during the rank weaponization by the previous administration has no grounds to stand on."[773] In Trump's DOJ, up was down and down was up, and there was no place for those who disagreed.

Corrupting Processes

As Bondi and other DOJ leaders assembled their MAGA team, they began working to advance Trump's agenda, even if it meant corrupting the integrity of the department. The legal hardball began with immigration cases. The Justice Department was defending an aggressive interpretation of the Alien Enemies Act, which permits the president to remove noncitizens who "invade" the country. It was a stretch to argue that the act covered undocumented immigrants, and so Justice Department lawyers were preparing their strategy. According to a whistleblower, a former DOJ lawyer named Erez Reuveni, Emil Bove went so far as to suggest in a meeting that Justice Department lawyers ignore court orders blocking deportation flights. According to Reuveni, Bove had said during a meeting that the planes needed to take off "no matter what." Reuveni alleged that Bove then said that DOJ would need to consider telling the courts "f**k you" and ignore any such order—a stunning violation of the Constitution and the rule of law.[774] Reuveni, a fifteen-year DOJ veteran who had worked in Republican and Democratic administrations, would later be suspended and then fired for admitting in court that Kilmar Abrego Garcia had been deported to El Salvador in error and that Reuveni was unaware of any legal basis for his removal.[775] Former prosecutor Ty Cobb, who served as a White House lawyer during Trump's first term, said, "Never in history has DOJ broken so defiantly from respecting, as it's obligated to do, the decisions of federal courts. This is a war that Trump and Bondi are waging against the rule of law."[776]

Dismantling Civil Rights Protections

In addition to relaxing corruption enforcement, in May, the Justice Department also announced that it would abandon consent decrees with police departments around the country, including in Minneapolis, Louisville, Memphis, and Ferguson, Missouri, the locations of high-profile police killings.[777] The police departments had reached agreements with DOJ to resolve allegations of civil rights violations involving the use of excessive force by police officers.[778] Having participated in federal oversight of the Detroit Police Department (DPD) while serving as US attorney, I know that consent judgments can be transformational because they bring expert assistance and resources to the table. After investigative findings of the use of excessive force, arrests without probable cause, and deplorable conditions of confinement, DPD leadership implemented changes in policies, training, equipment, and management that turned its department around into one that was constitutionally compliant and high performing. In my experience, most chiefs desperately want to comply with constitutional policing requirements and yearn for sufficient resources to improve their often-underfunded departments.

According to Chuck Wexler, the executive director of the Police Executive Research Forum, DOJ's dismissals may have appeared to be pro-police, but only to outside onlookers. "The irony is that cities that most need help to update their policies and training would not get the resources without the federal consent decree."[779] While views on police investigations can vary across administrations, ending federal oversight of police practices eliminated one more check on the abuse of power.

In addition, the Justice Department dismissed voting-rights lawsuits filed during the Biden administration.[780] DOJ lawyers had filed complaints challenging new voting restrictions in Georgia and Arizona, purges of voter registrations in Virginia and Alabama, redistricting in Texas and Louisiana, and at-large districts that could dilute the voting power of communities of color in Pennsylvania and Georgia. While individual plaintiffs took up the causes, they lacked the expertise and heft of the Justice Department as an advocate against attacks on voting rights.

At the same time, reports indicated that DOJ was exploring charging election workers in the future if they failed to secure computers, which would conveniently advance the narrative that elections are vulnerable to fraud.[781] In addition, Trump directed the attorney general to investigate compliance with campaign finance law by online fundraising platforms, singling out ActBlue, an entity used exclusively by Democratic candidates.[782] His directive was a gross violation of DOJ norms requiring freedom from White House control. Although election security and clean campaigns are legitimate goals, Trump's motives were suspect in light of his baseless claims that the 2020 election had been stolen.

Targeting Enemies

Perhaps the greatest threat to the Justice Department's integrity was its use to target Trump's enemies. After baselessly accusing the Biden administration of "weaponizing" government, Trump's team seemed to do just that. Even before the indictments of James Comey and Letitia James, Trump issued presidential memoranda in April 2025 directing the investigations of Chris Krebs, the former director of the Cybersecurity and Infrastructure Security Agency (CISA) who had publicly stated that the 2020 election was "the most secure in history," and Miles Taylor, a former Trump official who had written an anonymous scathing opinion piece in *The New York Times* critical of Trump's presidency. (Taylor later revealed his identity.)[783] Now, he and Krebs were in Trump's crosshairs for speaking out against him.

In addition to charging Comey with lying to Congress, federal law enforcement authorities also investigated Comey for posting an image on social media of seashells spelling out the numbers "86" and "47." In restaurant parlance, to "86" something means to cancel it. Trump, of course, is the forty-seventh president, and so "86 47" had become a political statement opposing the president and his policies; the phrase even appeared on T-shirts at protests against Trump.[784] Others interpreted the post as a call to assassinate the president.[785] In my opinion, the post was beneath the dignity of a former FBI director, but protected by the First Amendment. Still, when Secret Service agents questioned Comey, he quickly deleted the post, apologized, and said he did not intend to communicate any threat and that he opposed "violence of any kind."[786]

Nonetheless, Trump's team pounced on Comey's gaffe. Trump called him "a dirty cop" and said, "He knew exactly what that meant. A child knows what that meant. If you're the FBI director and you don't know what that meant, that meant assassination. And it says it loud and clear."[787] Tulsi Gabbard, Trump's director of national intelligence, said Comey should be jailed for the post.[788] Reports indicated that federal law enforcement agents went so far as to tail Comey and his wife as they drove home from a vacation in North Carolina to their home in the Washington, DC, area. According to the report, Secret Service agents tracked Comey's phone, while others waited at his home to question him. While agents were likely simply performing their duties, the decision to go to such lengths in response to a Trump critic posting a picture of seashells seemed designed more to intimidate than to protect. Exploiting Comey's miscue was a harbinger of things to come.

In addition to approving criminal charges against Trump's perceived enemies, Bondi implemented a change that would permit prosecutors to obtain records from reporters. Reversing a policy by her predecessor, Merrick Garland, to allow the free press to engage in newsgathering activities without undue interference, Bondi rescinded regulations that protected communications records of members of the media. Now, investigators would be free to use search warrants and grand jury subpoenas to obtain reporters' phone and email records as well as live testimony.[789] Her move was lawful, but an aggressive policy choice in a nation that values the right to a free press. Bondi said the goal was to identify leaks by government employees, but compelling reporters to produce their communications records would likely have a chilling effect on their work. If investigators can obtain a reporter's call logs in the days and hours before the publication of a big story, they can potentially piece together the identity of an anonymous source.

Garland's approach had struck me as a sound process for protecting the First Amendment rights of the free press. It is one thing to obtain email and phone records from government employees, who must use proper channels to become whistleblowers and may not disclose sensitive government information to people not entitled to receive it, including reporters. It is quite another thing to compel the production of *reporters'* records, because that step could also reveal the identities of sources for other stories, making people less likely to speak to reporters about matters of public interest. Bondi's move was another way to silence critics and chill free speech.

Even the grantmaking component of the Justice Department got in on the act, canceling funds awarded to the American Bar Association (ABA) to serve victims of domestic violence and barring DOJ employees from participating in ABA events on official time.[790] Deputy Attorney General Todd Blanche explained, with remarkable candor, that the reason for the attendance ban was the ABA's participation in a lawsuit against the Trump administration for its freeze on humanitarian aid at USAID.[791] The ABA had also condemned Trump's attacks on law firms and statements by administration officials targeting judges and questioning the legitimacy of judicial review.[792] The world's largest association of legal professionals filed suit against the Justice Department, alleging unlawful retaliation for exercising its First Amendment right to petition the courts.[793] While a federal court issued an injunction blocking the department from implementing its proposed penalties on First Amendment grounds, DOJ officials had already sent a symbolic message that they were willing to retaliate against those who opposed them.[794]

Law Is King

The dismissal of the Adams case sent an astonishing message that political considerations would not only be tolerated in the second Trump administration, but that they would be its modus operandi. Politicizing the Department of Justice is not just a corruption of an American institution; it is also a move that makes America less safe. As Trump's legal thugs forced out career professionals who have developed expertise in complex areas like cybersecurity, terrorism, corruption, and counterespionage, they were replaced with new lawyers selected on the basis of obedience rather than competence. Trump's disregard for the rule of law means that those installed by him cannot be trusted in court. Under his mob-style regime, America is increasingly a country where people are investigated or fired for political revenge. As this practice becomes normalized, good people will no longer seek to serve in these important roles. Without lawyers of integrity to uphold the rule of law, the core principles of equal justice and due process are at risk. Perhaps Trump's election—despite being found guilty of multiple felonies—indicates that a majority of the voting public no longer cares about the rule of law. But I think Americans will miss it when it's gone. As Paul Rosenzweig, the former Bush official, noted, "Thomas Paine said: 'In America, the law is king.' Trump wants to make his word the law and himself the king."[795]

SEVEN

ENTER THE BROLIGARCHS

In 2015, Dr. Mona Hanna made a horrible discovery. After hearing reports of discolored drinking water from her patients, the Flint, Michigan, pediatrician began tracking her patients' health. Her data showed what she had feared: a spike in the number of children in her practice with elevated levels of lead in their blood.[796] The announcement of her findings would finally get the attention of government officials, who for more than a year had been ignoring residents' complaints about contaminated water.[797]

By 2011, the city of Flint had fallen on hard economic times. The industrial town had seen better days, when auto plants provided well-paying jobs to what was then a population of two hundred thousand residents. But by the second decade of the twenty-first century, Flint was half that size, with a withering tax base and 40 percent of its residents living in poverty. Without a robust revenue stream, the municipality once known as "Buick City" was on the brink of bankruptcy. Michigan governor Rick Snyder had a solution: He replaced the city's elected mayor with an emergency financial manager who would run its government like a business, slashing costs to balance the books.[798]

One way the emergency manager decided to save money was by switching the city's water source from Lake Huron to the nearby

Flint River in 2013.[799] But after making the change, no one treated the water to prevent corrosion from lead water pipes from leaching into the drinking water supply.[800] The result was a catastrophe: Lead seeped into the water of tens of thousands of Flint residents. Twelve people died after an outbreak of Legionnaires' disease.[801] Countless children were exposed to lead, which can damage the brain and nervous system.[802] Adults who drank or bathed in the water faced increased risk of kidney failure and cardiovascular problems.[803] But residents' complaints about the foul smell and the water's color went unheeded. Even after General Motors stopped using the local water supply because it was corroding its machinery, state officials insisted the water was safe.[804] It was only after Dr. Hanna provided concrete data that they acknowledged the problem.

At the time, I was serving as US attorney for the Eastern District of Michigan, which includes Flint. Federal agents and prosecutors in my office explored any basis for federal criminal charges and found none. The state attorney general charged a few state officials with neglect of duty, but the cases fizzled on procedural grounds.[805] There were no criminal laws on the books to address this scenario. While civil penalties were available and were pursued, the tragedy in Flint was not something that legislatures had contemplated when writing criminal statutes. But it is what happens when the government puts dollars and cents above public interest.

The concept of running government "like a business" has some superficial appeal. Businesses must compete with one another, satisfy their customers, and balance their books—all laudable goals. But business has a different mission from government. The mission of government is to protect and serve the people. In business, profits prevail over public virtue. And Donald Trump's approach to running the government like a business is all about leveraging others to increase his power as well as his personal profits. In turn, businesses understand that, in Trump's transactional world, they can make more money by providing favors to the president.

Front Row Billionaires

From the very beginning of Trump's second term, it was clear that this administration would have a new relationship with business leaders. As Trump was sworn in as the forty-seventh president of the United States in the Capitol Rotunda, prominent seats were filled by a who's who of America's tech billionaires—Jeff Bezos, Mark Zuckerberg, Elon Musk, Vivek Ramaswamy, and Tim Cook.[806] In the transactional world of Trump 2.0, they appeared ready to do whatever it took to reap financial rewards. On this day, they were all too willing to be showcased like trophies the president had collected and put on display for the world to see. The world's richest men were there to kiss the ring of the new boss.

Just as Bezos had changed his tune on Trump, so too had Zuckerberg. Just a few years earlier, the presence of the Meta CEO at Trump's inauguration would have been a surprise. Following the January 6, 2021, attack on the US Capitol, Facebook, a social media platform owned by Meta, suspended the president's account. In 2024, Trump accused Zuckerberg of "plotting" against him and of having "steered" Facebook to influence the 2020 election in Biden's favor.[807] "We are watching him closely," Trump wrote, "and if he does anything illegal this time, he will spend the rest of his life in prison—as will others who cheat in the 2024 Presidential Election."[808] Trump's election to a second term appeared to change Zuckerberg's view: A few weeks before the 2025 inauguration, Zuckerberg announced an end to Meta's use of third-party fact-checkers on Facebook, as well as the company's other social media platforms, Instagram and Threads.[809] Meta would instead adopt a "community notes" model similar to that used at X, the platform formerly known as Twitter that is owned by Elon Musk. Zuckerberg explained in a video the decision to scrap Meta's efforts to combat disinformation, calling Trump's second election "a cultural tipping point toward once again prioritizing speech."[810] The change came despite the Senate Intelligence Committee's conclusion that Russia had used fake Facebook accounts to post disinformation to influence the 2016 presidential election.[811]

Zuckerberg's change of perspective may also have been influenced by a desire for better treatment from government regulators. As Trump entered office in 2025, Meta was facing a lawsuit brought by the Federal Trade Commission for alleged violations of antitrust laws, putting Zuckerberg's fortunes in the hands of the incoming administration.[812] By then, not only had Zuckerberg announced his epiphany about fact-checking, Meta had reinstated Trump's Facebook account, paid Trump twenty-five million dollars to settle his lawsuit challenging the suspension, and donated one million dollars to Trump's 2025 inaugural committee.[813] The "cultural tipping point" seemed to have brought the Facebook CEO clarity about how deal-making would be done in the new administration.

Musk, the CEO of electric auto maker Tesla, the private space travel company SpaceX, and satellite-based telecommunications provider Starlink, had also shifted his views about Trump in recent years. Historically, Musk had supported both Republicans and Democrats, donating to the campaigns of Barack Obama and Hillary Clinton.[814] In 2022, Musk tweeted that Trump should "hang up his hat & sail into the sunset."[815] But in 2024, Musk poured $275 million into Trump's race, appearing alongside the candidate with his black "MAGA" baseball cap and literally leaping with excitement on a rally stage.[816] With billions of dollars in government contracts with the Department of Defense and NASA at stake, perhaps Musk believed he would benefit from friendly relations with a Trump White House.[817]

After Trump took office in 2025, Trump put Musk and Vivek Ramaswamy in charge of his new Department of Government Efficiency (DOGE)—ironically named after Musk's favorite meme and cryptocurrency.[818] According to Trump, DOGE would "dismantle Government Bureaucracy, slash excess regulations, cut wasteful expenditures, and restructure Federal Agencies."[819] Ramaswamy, a pharmaceutical entrepreneur, would quickly exit to campaign for governor of Ohio,[820] leaving the work to Musk, who wasted no time terminating government employees and shuttering federal agencies. Trump even allowed Musk to conduct briefings about his work in the Oval Office. Musk clearly understood the mob ethos of the Trump administration, appearing alongside the president while wearing a black T-shirt emblazoned with the words "The Dogefather," in the motif of the Mario Puzo book and Francis Ford Coppola movie trilogy about the Corleone crime family.[821]

But just a few months later, Musk would be out of his White House role after failing to sway a Supreme Court race in Wisconsin on which he had spent heavily and which he called "important for the future of civilization." Musk also clashed with Trump on tariffs and later criticized the president's "big, beautiful" budget bill as "a disgusting abomination."[822] He made the mistake of waging a war of words with Trump on his social media platform, X, even claiming that Trump's name appeared in the then-confidential law enforcement files of his one-time friend Jeffrey Epstein, the registered sex offender who allegedly committed suicide in jail while facing charges for sexually exploiting and abusing "dozens of underage girls." [823] It was then that Trump used his leverage, posting a threat to terminate government subsidies to and contracts with Musk's companies.[824] Musk backed down, expressing "regret" that his comments "went too far"—not quite an apology, but a humbling surrender for a man with Musk's hubris.[825] Roy Cohn's lessons in using mob-style leverage worked for Trump once again.

The Gilded Age Meets the Russian Oligarchy

Just days into his second term, Trump said, "We were our richest from 1870 to 1913."[826] The truth of that statement, of course, depends on who "we" are. Those years were profitable for business titans such as Cornelius Vanderbilt, John D. Rockefeller Sr., and Andrew Carnegie, who amassed enormous wealth in railroads, oil, and steel, respectively. Of course, those men also became known as "robber barons" for their exploitation of workers and consumers. Mark Twain called the era in which they dominated the American economy "the Gilded Age." It was a time of excess and ostentatious displays of wealth, but the riches were only a shiny veneer covering a society that was corroded by greed and stricken by poverty.[827] According to historian Richard White, in the Gilded Age, "corruption suffused government and the economy."[828] For example, he said, John D. Rockefeller ousted competitors to his Standard Oil by dropping prices in exchange for kickbacks from railroads.[829] Industrialists hired strikebreakers and bribed elected officials to crush organized labor.[830] For those without wealth and power, the Gilded Age brought what White described as "the decline of virtually every measure of well-being."[831] The word "slum" became part of the American lexicon in this era.[832]

Today, the names Vanderbilt, Rockefeller, and Carnegie have been replaced by Musk, Zuckerberg, and Bezos. According to history professor Edward T. O'Donnell, "troubling themes in the nineteenth century are almost identical, in different ways, to what we're experiencing right now." Architectural historian Rebekah Beaulieu notes that Trump's four-hundred-million-dollar White House addition is a reflection of America's growing wealth gap.[833] According to Beaulieu, "The optics of building a ballroom in a residential space in 2025 draws a very straight line to the socioeconomic stratification of late-nineteenth-century Gilded Age America. This is before the middle class existed, when there was a huge disparity between the haves and the have-nots. That's exactly what we are messaging with something like this."[834]

With massive wealth, O'Donnell says, comes "massive political power."[835] The political influence of the wealthy can lead to a symbiotic relationship with a corrupt government official, enabling him to amass ever more power. In today's Russia, for instance, Vladimir Putin has shown that a leader who controls the levers of power can even manipulate the wealthy to ensure their support. According to Sam Peach, a Russian studies scholar, "Putin built a system in which political loyalty is exchanged for economic privilege, ensuring that Russia's most powerful business figures remain bound to the presidency."[836] Following the collapse of the Soviet Union, Russia's emerging economy struggled.[837] When the government defaulted on loans, a small circle of ruthless businessmen collected collateral at drastically reduced rates and thereby amassed immense wealth.[838] This group of oligarchs operated freely during Boris Yeltsin's presidency, but when Putin took office, he asserted greater control over them.[839] For example, when one media mogul criticized the Russian government, he was charged with embezzlement and forced to sell his business empire. Another oligarch critical of Putin suddenly found himself investigated for tax fraud. Soon after, an embezzlement probe began into a business in which he was a shareholder; eventually, he fled the country.[840] The pattern would repeat itself with other prominent and rich critics. Putin was creating leverage to increase his power and control.

Eventually, Peach writes, "Putin shifted focus from confrontation to consolidation, building a new system in which economic privilege was tightly bound to personal loyalty."[841] Putin's new oligarchs "derived their positions entirely from his favor."[842] The Russian leader gave his cronies control over entire industries—railroads, energy, defense, and health care. Putin offered security and privilege in exchange for fealty.[843] Today's Russian oligarchs are not the robber barons of the Gilded Age; they enjoy wealth only in exchange for total obedience to Putin. Those who choose otherwise are at risk of mysteriously dying of what's been termed "sudden Russian death syndrome."[844]

Leverage, Not Philosophy

Just as Trump did with law firms, the media, and universities, he created leverage over businesses as well. His punishment of one signaled to others that he would manufacture misconduct to force appeasement. Conversely, if you wanted something for your company, like approval of a merger or favorable treatment from a regulator, it was best to be on Trump's good side. That uncomfortable truth meant business leaders were silenced from speaking out against the president, an unhealthy dynamic in a democracy.

For example, Trump allowed the social media giant TikTok to continue operating even after a congressionally imposed deadline for the company to be sold by its Chinese owner, ByteDance—a violation of a federal statute and the constitutional separation of powers.[845] While the platform enjoyed popularity in the United

States, it presented significant concerns about data privacy, malware dangers, disinformation campaigns, and espionage recruitment. Senator Mark Warner, a Democrat from Virginia and vice chair of the Senate Intelligence Committee, said the Trump administration was "flouting the law and ignoring its own national security findings about the risks" posed by TikTok.[846] Trump had previously expressed similar concerns about TikTok but reversed his position in 2024 after meeting with megadonor Jeff Yass, an investor in ByteDance.[847] Trump's repeated extensions of the statutory deadline for TikTok to be divested from ByteDance came after TikTok's CEO made fawning statements about Trump in January, just before the change in administration. "We are grateful and pleased to have the support of a president who truly understands our platform," CEO Shou Zi Chew said, "one who has used TikTok to express his own thoughts and perspectives, connecting with the world and generating more than sixty billion views of his content in the process."[848] In Trump's system, flattering the boss is the way to get ahead.

In addition, Trump became increasingly involved in a wide variety of private business interests in his second term, demonstrating that he was no conservative. "People come in and they need something," Trump explained.[849] Of course, Trump gave nothing without getting something in exchange. For example, he allowed the sale of US Steel to the Japanese Nippon Steel, over the objection of the United Steelworkers union, but maintained control of a "Golden Share" (again displaying his obsession with gold), which would give the president and his successors in office extraordinary and unusual control over a private business.[850] The president retained power over the company's board of directors and acquired the authority to veto certain corporate actions.[851] This arrangement put the power of a manufacturing component that is critical to national security into the hands not only of a foreign business but also of the president, whose decisions regarding its fate would be unchecked by other branches of government. Trump created leverage exclusively for himself that could be used in the future.

Trump also converted government funding under the CHIPS Act into an equity stake in Intel, the computer chip maker. The 2022 statute was intended to boost US semiconductor production, both to spur America's economy and to protect national security. Instead, Trump created leverage against Intel by calling for the resignation of its CEO, Lip-Bu Tan, a US citizen, based on what conservative columnist Bret Stephens of *The New York Times* called "vague allegations that he had invested in Chinese technology companies that US officials say have links to China's military."[852] Tan scrambled to meet with the president in an effort to save his job. Trump ultimately withdrew his demand, but only in exchange for a 10 percent stake in the company, making the US government Intel's largest shareholder.[853] Under the deal, the government would use almost nine billion dollars awarded to Intel under the CHIPS Act but not yet paid, to take its 10 percent share in the company—and at a discount, at that. By holding Tan's job over his head, Trump was able to pressure the CEO into agreeing to provide Trump with a significant share in the company. So much for free markets. Trump's team went on to strike "deals" with Nvidia and Advanced Micro Devices (AMD), in which the US government would take 15 percent of their proceeds from chip sales to China in exchange for permitting the exports.[854] When Trump threatened to send National Guard troops into San Francisco, as he had done in other cities, he said he had changed his mind after hearing from Nvidia's CEO, Jensen Huang, among others.[855] Trump also credited the city's mayor, Daniel Lurie, for the decision to refrain from deploying troops because, as Trump put it, "he asked, very nicely."[856] It was the verbal equivalent of kissing Trump's ring.

Experts sounded the alarm regarding the unstable business climate created by Trump's "dealmaking." Gautam Mukunda, a lecturer at the Yale University School of Management, said, "There's this Darth Vader aspect of the whole thing. If your situation with the administration can swing so radically in such a short span of time based on nothing more than a meeting, then it can always swing back."[857] Bret Stephens likened the deal to those cut by entities in other sectors: "Intel will now join the stable of other cowed and compliant corporations, universities, and law firms living in fear of the next Truth Social post, funding revocation, or regulatory obstruction.

And that's to say nothing of the FBI searches that could await those unlucky enough to have once served Trump with insufficient servility. . . . Trump's personalized control of ever-broader swaths of the economy based on ever-thinner pretexts is the beginning of a long trend with neither a political check nor a limiting principle."[858]

In the mid-2020s, some on the right were embracing new governing philosophies. For example, Vice President J. D. Vance stated that he was influenced by several "New Right" thinkers, including Patrick Deneen and Curtis Yarvin. Deneen, a Notre Dame political philosophy professor, is the author of *Regime Change*, a book that advocates replacing liberalism with a "postliberal order" that elevates conservative and religious values over individual rights.[859] Yarvin is a tech blogger who argues that American democracy is run by corrupt elites who prioritize their own interests over those of the people. He proposes the "liquidation" of the Constitution, democracy, and the rule of law, with a government headed by a monarch who leads like the CEO of a start-up.[860] Yarvin's plan would also eliminate public schools, universities, the press, and international relations and would implement a policy called "RAGE"—Retire All Government Employees.[861]

Trump, on the other hand, seems driven less by any moral philosophy than by an insatiable desire to grab power and hoard wealth by making "deals." His approach is likewise gaining popularity in other parts of the world. According to historian Anne Applebaum, author of *Autocracy, Inc.: The Dictators Who Want to Run the World*, "greed, nihilism, and transactionalism are reshaping" global politics. "As old rules and norms fall away," she writes, "they are not replaced by a new structure. They are replaced by nothing."[862]

Privatization

One shift in government policy during the second Trump administration has been to increase the privatization of government functions, including prisons, mail delivery, and even weather forecasting. While he was still leading the Department of Government Efficiency, Elon Musk said, "We should privatize anything that can reasonably be privatized."[863] The argument often advanced in favor of using private companies to provide public services is that efficiency drives commercial markets, so that taxpayers will receive the best services at the lowest cost. And often, for-profit companies that take over nonprofit public functions initially work well. Then, as they make money, they start cutting services and raising prices. One need only look at the consolidation of banks, hospitals, and the media, some bought by hedge funds or "turnaround artists" who squeeze every penny out of a business and leave behind a hollowed-out version of its predecessor. As I observed in Flint, it is consumers who suffer in this process.

One risk of putting public services in the hands of private actors is that they gain complete power over American capacity in that sector. For example, if we were to privatize space travel and eliminate NASA, then men like Musk and Bezos would control the industry. If they were to later decide that this line of business was no longer sufficiently profitable, they could stop engaging in it altogether. If so, then American progress in space exploration would halt, allowing hostile foreign adversaries to advance their capabilities beyond those of the United States. There are some functions the government performs not to make money or avoid expenses but to serve the best interests of the public.

Upon taking office in 2025, Trump immediately began privatizing government functions. He signed an executive order rescinding President Joe Biden's ban on using for-profit prisons to house federal inmates and detainees.[864] The private prison business is lucrative, with contracts valued in the tens of millions of dollars. Trump's election caused the stock prices of the two largest public companies that manage prisons and immigration detention centers to soar.[865] Biden's order, meanwhile, was a response to findings that for-profit prisons were incentivized to prolong an inmate's confinement to make more money. In addition, a 2016 DOJ inspector general report found that private prisons resulted in more safety and security incidents per capita than government-run facilities.[866] Perhaps that's because, with their focus on profit, private prisons tend to reduce costs by hiring fewer guards and paying them lower wages than public prisons; this tendency led to scandals involving understaffing and inadequate training in state prisons in Mississippi in 2014 and Idaho in 2015.[867]

In the Idaho case, the FBI opened a criminal investigation into the for-profit Corrections Corporation of America (CCA) for massively understaffing a prison and falsifying records to conceal it. In a civil lawsuit, the American Civil Liberties Union (ACLU) alleged that CCA had utilized prison gangs for staffing, which led to an attack on a group of inmates that left one badly injured.[868] The prison had become so violent that it had earned the nickname "Gladiator School."[869] While the federal government might save money by outsourcing prison administration to the private sector, the evidence clearly indicates this shift degrades the conditions of confinement. Perhaps Trump was betting on the fact that many Americans don't care about the treatment of people in prison or may even revel in their misfortune. Still, the way we treat the most vulnerable members of society reflects who we are as a people. A person does not lose all constitutional rights when they enter the prison gates, and ceding control to privateers increases the risk of a prisoner's mistreatment.

The US Postal Service was another popular target of privatization. In December 2024, Trump floated the idea of contracting out mail delivery, citing competition with FedEx, UPS, and Amazon. "It's an idea a lot of people have had for a long time. We're looking at it," he said.[870] While private firms could take over mail delivery, the concern would again be cost-cutting and service reductions. Union leaders warned that an estimated 51 million people living in rural areas would be most affected if postal service were contracted to a for-profit business, which for efficiency reasons would be incentivized to limit or even eliminate routes with low population density.[871] Private companies could even impose charges for mail delivery beyond the cost of postage or raise the price of stamps exponentially. Protesting postal union members carried numerous signs to this effect, including one that read, "The post office belongs to the people, not billionaires."[872] According to Brian L. Renfroe, the president of the National Association of Letter Carriers, "Private business is interested in doing things that are profitable, as they should be. But that is the distinction between private business and what we are, a public service, where we serve everyone, everywhere, no matter where they live, for the same price every day."[873]

One of the agencies Project 2025 targeted for private replacement was the National Weather Service (NWS). Arguing that the next administration should "fully commercialize its forecasting operations," the plan's authors seemed motivated as much by their disdain for environmental concerns as cost savings.[874] Project 2025 called NWS's parent organization, the National Oceanic and Atmospheric Administration (NOAA), "a colossal operation that has become one of the main drivers of the climate change alarm industry and, as such, is harmful to future US prosperity."[875] Since the 1880s, the government has provided weather forecasting services as a public good.[876] Farmers, crisis responders, construction workers, mining companies, and event planners all rely heavily on weather reports to plan their operations; even ordinary citizens plan their days by checking the weather. By delegating weather forecasting to for-profit companies, we risk price gouging that makes this information affordable to some people and not others. Rick Spinrad, who led NOAA during the Biden administration, described the problem with making weather a paid service: "Are we really talking about making weather products available only to those who can afford them? Basically, turning the weather service into a subscription streaming service? As a taxpayer, I don't want to be in the position of saying, 'I get a better weather forecast because I'm willing to pay for it.'"[877] Weather information would risk becoming like Netflix or Amazon Prime: a luxury good for those with disposable income.

Another consequence of privatizing government services is that some companies win out over others, creating incentives to support the politicians who award contracts. For example, software company Palantir Technologies, cofounded by Trump supporter Peter Thiel, obtained $322 million in government contracts during the first half of 2025.[878] Its stock price soared 600 percent in the twelve-month period ending in August 2025.[879] Palantir also provided sophisticated AI capabilities to the Defense Department, becoming so deeply embedded, *The Wall Street Journal* reported, that some Pentagon officials "worried about becoming overdependent on a single contractor for their data-processing needs."[880] In other words, a single contractor providing soldiers with the software they need to track enemies on the battlefield holds monopoly power over the Pentagon to continue its contracts, even as its asking prices increase. In addition, if Palantir were to go under, the Defense Department would be left without the necessary processing capabilities until it could find a new contractor. Palantir also raised concerns when it secured a government contract to develop software that compiled data for use in immigration enforcement.[881] In May 2025, thirteen former employees issued an open letter accusing Palantir of "normalizing authoritarianism."[882] According to the *Wall Street Journal*, Palantir was deepening its influence with the Trump administration, which tapped current and former Palantir employees for high-level jobs in government.[883] As in Putin's Russia, businesses were rewarded with money and power when they provided financial support for the boss, deepening the nation's descent into oligarchy.

In addition to creating disparities between the haves and have-nots, shifting government functions to for-profit contractors also creates opportunities for corruption. While leading DOGE, Musk led cuts to NOAA at the same time that his company SpaceX was poised to profit from sending weather satellites into space, posing an apparent conflict of interest.[884] In July 2025, the Associated Press reported that multiple Trump officials had ties to businesses that would profit from privatizing weather forecasting.[885] Trump's commerce secretary, Howard Lutnick, who oversaw NOAA and the National Weather Service, previously ran the financial firm Cantor Fitzgerald, which he left in the control of his adult sons while in office. Cantor has investments in weather and climate information: The firm owns a controlling interest in an entity that operates a "weather derivatives marketplace," in which investors essentially "bet" on climate events.[886] It also has an interest in Satellogic, a satellite company that provides natural disaster imagery, which now touts itself as an emerging federal contractor.[887] Another administration official, Neil Jacobs, served as acting NOAA administrator during Trump's first term and was appointed to the permanent position in his second. Jacobs previously worked as a scientist for Panasonic Weather Solutions, a division of the private electronics giant. Taylor Jordan, the president's nominee for another leadership position at NOAA, was a lobbyist who represented clients with interests in the weather and satellite industries.[888] Would their ties to companies that could benefit from their official acts compromise their loyalty to the United States? The Commerce Department responded to concerns with a statement that all would "follow the law and rely on the advice of the Department's ethics counsel."[889] But these apparent conflicts of interest allowed federal officials to make government decisions that could benefit their personal finances.

Wealth Disparities

When the rich get richer at the public trough, they erode democracy and equality. Ben Rhodes, who served as deputy national security advisor during the Obama administration, writes in his book *After the Fall* about the symbiotic relationship between authoritarians and oligarchs. An authoritarian leader can reward wealthy citizens with low taxes and favorable government policies, he writes, and they, in turn, will fund his campaigns.[890] Of course, such policies do nothing for the rest of the public. Laws made by the wealthy for the wealthy are unlikely to benefit the masses. According to Charles Murray, a political scientist at the conservative American Enterprise Institute, "The people who have so much influence on the course of the nation have little direct experience with the lives of ordinary Americans, and make their judgments about what's good for other people based on their own highly atypical lives."[891] For example, Trump demonstrated his lack of appreciation for the financial concerns of working-class families when he suggested that the only consequence of high tariffs would be a reasonable downscaling in the purchase of consumer goods. During a media interview, he said that he did not think a girl needed to have "thirty dolls."[892] He was describing an abundance of wealth inconsistent with reality for most families, seemingly oblivious to the inability of some parents to provide even the basic necessities for their children. Trump's indifference to the needs of the American people did not end there: On the night before a month-old government shutdown was due to cause a lapse in funding for food stamps, Trump hosted a party at his Mar-a-Lago club with a Great Gatsby theme, a perfect metaphor for Trump's careless disregard for ordinary people.[893]

Indeed, since the 1980s, the rich have become richer, the middle class has shrunk, and America's low-income population has grown.[894] As a child in Michigan in the 1970s, I lived in a middle-class neighborhood where a typical family had one parent working on an auto assembly line and the other staying home with the kids. Such a family's income was enough to afford a home, two cars, and maybe even a boat or a cottage up north. By the twenty-first century, that version of the American dream was no longer available. Since the Reagan administration, government policies and economic trends have bolstered the incomes of the wealthy at the expense of everyone else. For example, in 1980, taxpayers earning seven hundred thousand dollars or more per year were taxed at a rate of 70 percent. Today, the highest tax rate for any taxpayer is 37 percent.[895] Capital gains, dividend income, and inherited estates—income typically received by those who are already wealthy—are taxed at a fraction of the rate they were in the 1970s.[896] In fact, today, no taxes at all are assessed on inherited estates until after the first *eleven million* dollars.[897]

The promises of trickle-down benefits of tax cuts for the rich that create more jobs for the working class have been proven to be the "voodoo economics" that George H. W. Bush warned about in 1980.[898] At the same time, executive salaries have skyrocketed, regulations have been restructured in favor of corporate profits and against the public interest, overseas manufacturing has led to the shuttering of American factories, and automation has reduced the availability of blue-collar jobs. Before the 1980s, most Americans saw their earnings rise in step with the economy's growth. Since then, only families earning $180,000 to $450,000 have seen the same rate of increase, while 90 percent of Americans have seen their earnings grow more slowly than the economy. The winners? The top 1 percent, whose income has grown at a rate higher than the rate of overall economic growth.[899] This ever-widening wealth gap leaves many Americans frustrated and indignant.[900] The growing reliance on computer technology and artificial intelligence threatens to make the problem even worse.

But rather than acknowledging the true causes of wealth disparity, Trump and his cohorts convinced voters that the blame for their economic woes lay with "elites" in large cities, DEI, and immigrants. By blaming others for harms to the working class, Trump persuaded his supporters to vote against their own financial self-interest in order to "Make America Great Again." The slogan evokes a longing for a mythical past, a postwar period when the white middle class thrived. Of course, that was also a time when women were second-class citizens, people of color were excluded from parts of society, and members of the LGBTQ community were invisible. For many American communities, those times were not so great.

Trump's "One Big Beautiful Bill," a budget package signed into law on July 4, 2025, promised to make the wealth gap even wider. The bill cut Medicaid and other health care benefits by more than one trillion dollars.[901] The nonpartisan Congressional Budget Office estimated that the budget bill would result in twelve million people losing health care coverage and that patients in rural communities would experience a reduction in health care services.[902] SNAP, the food stamps program was cut by $230 billion over the next ten years.[903] Not only did the bill reduce spending in ways that would harm the most vulnerable Americans, it also cut taxes and increased spending for the Defense Department, immigration raids, mass arrests, detentions, and deportations, a move that promised to mortgage the nation's future.[904] The Congressional Budget Office concluded that the bill would increase America's deficit by $3.4 trillion over ten years.[905] But Trump was focused on doling out perks and bonuses for his wealthy cronies, without regard for the nation's future—all part of his transactional, self-serving agenda.

Why do lower- and middle-income Americans and their elected representatives vote against their economic self-interest? It is challenging to understand all the reasons, but part of the MAGA strategy appears to be to divide and conquer: If voters can be persuaded that they are less well off than their parents' generation because of immigrants and DEI, and not because of the influence of the wealthy, then Trump and his billionaire buddies can keep the wheels of profit churning. That motive would explain why Trump so frequently stokes grievance and resentment among working-class voters. It also explains J. D. Vance's post about the budget bill that cut taxes for the wealthy and slashed spending for the poor. Vance urged voters to focus on the bill's provisions to remove immigrants: "The thing that will bankrupt this country more than any other policy is flooding the country with illegal immigration and then giving those migrants generous benefits," Vance wrote. The bill "fixes this problem. . . . Everything else—the CBO score, the proper baseline, the minutiae of the Medicaid policy—is immaterial compared to the ICE money and immigration enforcement provisions."[906]

People over Profits

As the people of Flint learned, running government like a business rarely benefits anyone except those businesses or the government officials who reap their financial support. Cutting costs and improving efficiency are laudable goals for any organization, and we should continually assess how we spend taxpayer funds to ensure that we are maximizing value. But the reason we have public services is that the government does things that are more important than the bottom line. If the postal service loses money on mail delivery, we should explore ways to modernize and reduce costs, but we cannot simply close up shop, as a private business can just because it's unable to turn a profit. We don't ask the court system or the military to turn a profit because we recognize the value of the services they provide. We should not expect other essential parts of government to be profitable, either. Moreover, because privatizing government functions risks increasing corruption, we should recognize that we cannot put a price on everything.

EIGHT

SCAPEGOATS AND PAWNS

Chaka Castro was no ordinary thief. In 2014, she used online research to think big. Identifying her targets from her home in Texas, Castro would send robbery crews to neighborhoods all over the country, including Michigan.[907] The crews would surveil a target's home and, when the time was right, break a window to enter or walk in through an unlocked door. Sometimes, the crew would use one of its members as a decoy, having them stand on the front porch and ring the doorbell. When the homeowner answered, masked men with guns would jump from the bushes and rush into the house, where they would bind and gag the residents, including young children, at gunpoint and steal their money and belongings.[908] What was particularly clever about Castro's scheme was the way she targeted her victims: She would use data available online to identify just the right prey—ideally, the owner of a small cash business, such as a restaurant or dry cleaner. The owner should live in a high-end neighborhood, to make the venture worthwhile. And there was one more thing: The victim should be an immigrant from a country where the banking system is less than trustworthy. Castro calculated that such targets would be more likely than others to store cash at home, and she was often right.[909] Castro and her crew robbed more than twenty homes in this manner.[910]

Chaka Castro is not the only one who knows how to choose her victims carefully. Authoritarians and criminals do the same, looking for just the right quarry. In authoritarian regimes, leaders pick on scapegoats and pawns to build rapport with their populist base. Nothing unites like a common enemy. According to political scientists Russell Muirhead and Nancy L. Rosenblum in their book *A Lot of People Are Saying*, far-right political extremists depict their opponents as an "existential threat" whose "covert goal is to deny America as a Christian nation, depreciate America as a white nation," and cede it to a "new world order" of "Muslims, liberals, Jews, [and] African Americans" so that progressives can gain power.[911] When the correct targets are selected and blamed, the public will not just tolerate cruelty to the out-group, it will applaud it. For example, in Nazi Germany, historian Ruth Ben-Ghiat writes, "marginalizing those who threatened the people's purity and survival was also a form of care, since Nazi morality saw the persecution of enemies as a righteous and patriotic act."[912] According to Tom Pepinsky, a professor of government and public policy at Cornell University, in a deeply polarized society, some people "feel real pleasure in seeing the capital-O 'other' being put down and controlled."[913] Consequently, political power in such societies can be gained by persecuting members of disfavored groups.

Donald Trump and his far-right allies choose their victims carefully as well. People on the left, immigrants, and members of the transgender community, in particular, have been popular targets of MAGA policies. They are pawns in his political game, people whose well-being he readily sacrifices in the interest of gaining more power.

Immigration Enforcement

According to Ben-Ghiat, one tactic used by authoritarians is to create a crisis and then implement extreme measures to address it. That's because "[c]risis time justifies states of emergency and the scapegoating of enemies who endanger the country from inside the nation or across the border."[914] Sure enough, on Trump's first day in office in 2025, he declared a national emergency at the border.[915] Trump's declaration invoked the National Emergencies Act for possible deployment of military troops to the southwest border.[916] As described below, several other actions also targeted immigrants. The Trump regime even initially barred a youth baseball team from Venezuela from entering the United States to compete in the teen version of the Little League World Series, though they would later gain entry.[917] To Trump, they were simply more pawns to manipulate at will. Ben-Ghiat has written that "conjuring a 'dangerous invasion' to justify states of exception and crackdowns that involve state security forces is one of the oldest authoritarian tricks."[918] In Chile, for example, following the 1973 coup, the country's military dictatorship justified mass repression by falsely claiming they were protecting the public from "foreign agitators" and "extremists" who entered the country illegally.[919] According to Ben-Ghiat, the "massive and exaggerated deployment of state security personnel and the display of arms and uniforms" is designed to frighten not only immigrants but allies.[920] An intimidating show of force can cause would-be protesters to retreat into submission.

One of the ways Trump stoked fear and outrage about the nation's immigration challenges was by cynically exploiting the tragic 2024 death of Laken Riley, a nursing student at the University of Georgia who was murdered by an undocumented immigrant while she was out for a run. Riley's death was a horrific tragedy, but Trump used her murder for political advantage, announcing while campaigning for president that it was "time to secure our border, and remove these criminals and thugs from our Country, so nothing like this can happen again!"[921] The first bill Trump signed after taking office in 2025 was the "Laken Riley Act," which required federal authorities to detain any immigrant without legal status who is charged with a crime while their case is pending.[922] The bill merely reflected the current practice in most judicial districts, but it gave the impression that Trump was getting tough on immigration enforcement. Some of his supporters voiced their approval of Trump's tactics: During a pro-Trump rally in February 2025, Beatrice Richards, a self-identified two-time Trump voter who was selling Trump sweatshirts, hats, and mugs on tables near the Washington Monument, said Trump's crackdown on immigration was "very good, because those are bad people. Coming to harm people—good people here in America. They are criminals."[923]

Trump has long seized on anti-immigration sentiment in his political rhetoric, but not against just any immigrants—his focus has been on those who are Black and brown. When announcing his campaign for president in 2015, for example, Trump disparaged immigrants from Mexico: "When Mexico sends its people, they're not sending their best," he said. "They're sending people that have lots of problems, and they're bringing those problems. . . . They're bringing drugs. They're bringing crime. They're rapists. And some, I assume, are good people."[924] Trump tried to stoke anti-immigrant sentiment again in the 2024 presidential campaign, during an interview with the National Association of Black Journalists, when he said that immigrants were taking "Black jobs."[925]

To no one's surprise, Trump ramped up immigration enforcement upon taking office, as was his prerogative as president. But like so much of this administration's conduct, the concern was not so much *what* it was doing as *how* it was doing it—prioritizing quantity over quality, attempting to redefine birthright citizenship, declaring an invasion at the border, invoking wartime authority, arresting international students for speaking out on college campuses, and using masked agents to instill fear and intimidation. All of these tactics contributed to the cruelty and chaos of Trump's immigration enforcement machine.

Prioritizing Quantity over Quality

As a former federal prosecutor who focused on national security cases, I have prosecuted plenty of immigration cases, including schemes to smuggle foreign nationals into the country, visa- and marriage-fraud rings, worksite violations for hiring undocumented immigrants, and fraudulent procurement of citizenship. But one consideration that was always important in government work was the allocation of federal resources. We had the personnel to prosecute only a certain number of cases. Most years in the Eastern District of Michigan, we brought about a thousand cases, give or take. Our goal was to utilize the resources of the office to improve the quality of life for the people of our district by maximizing our impact on public safety. For this reason, we worked in sync with federal agencies, including ICE's Enforcement and Removal Operations, to prioritize the prosecution of immigrant suspects who posed a threat to national security or public safety. That meant agents might forgo devoting resources to looking for landscapers and construction workers who had overstayed their visas in favor of tracking down violent drug dealers or domestic abusers.

But in the Trump administration, the show of shock and awe seemed to take precedence over public safety. The administration frequently referred to undocumented immigrants as "criminals," a misleading term for people who had committed no crime other than being present in the United States without legal status.[926] In late May 2025, news reports indicated that DHS Secretary Kristi Noem and White House Deputy Chief of Staff Stephen Miller had issued quotas to Immigration and Customs Enforcement of three thousand arrests per day, three times the number of daily arrests that were occurring at the start of Trump's second term.[927] As reported in *The New Republic*, Miller "lit into ICE officials in a meeting . . . addressing them so aggressively that some felt they were at risk of being fired if they didn't meet the new quota."[928] Miller reportedly told the officials that they were no longer targeting just the "worst of the worst" criminals, but anyone without legal status to be in the country.[929] Miller even ordered ICE to go to Home Depot store parking lots, where undocumented immigrants sometimes congregate to obtain work as day laborers.[930]

An aggressive quota would undoubtedly mean that agents would now be required to prioritize volume over public safety, arresting parents as they dropped their children off at school or worshippers as they arrived at church, all without regard to whether they posed any danger. In fact, the Trump regime explicitly changed the prior administration's policy that precluded agents from making immigration arrests at schools, churches, and health care facilities—places that provide essential services to members of the public, which immigrants might now avoid for fear of arrest.[931] And while agents were busy padding their numbers, they had less capacity for the time-consuming investigative work needed to find the targets who really endangered public safety. The performative strategy was all about showcasing the boss's crackdown. In May 2025, Miller said the administration was even "actively looking at" suspending the writ of habeas corpus, the constitutional right that allows people to petition a court to challenge their detention. Miller called habeas corpus "a privilege" that can be suspended in a time of "invasion."[932] Twisting a right into a privilege, and distorting immigrant concerns into an "invasion," were semantic tricks without basis in law and a frightening affront to civil liberties.

Redefining Birthright Citizenship

Among Trump's most aggressive executive orders since taking office were two aimed at immigrants: one purporting to remove birthright citizenship and another declaring an "invasion" by Tren de Aragua, a Venezuelan drug cartel, in order to invoke the Alien Enemies Act to deport any of its alleged members over the age of fourteen.[933] Since the end of the Civil War, anyone born in the United States has been recognized as a US citizen. The Fourteenth Amendment provides, in part, that "all persons born or naturalized in the United States, and subject to the jurisdiction thereof, are citizens of the United States and of the State wherein they reside."[934] On his first day in office, Trump issued an executive order attempting to redefine what it meant to be "subject to the jurisdiction" of the United States, excluding from this definition a person whose "mother was unlawfully present in the United States" or whose "mother's presence in the United States at the time of said person's birth was lawful but temporary" (for example, visiting on a student, work, or tourist visa) "and the father was not a United States citizen or lawful permanent resident at the time of said person's birth."[935] This new definition threatened to strip citizenship from children born in the United States to undocumented parents, children whom immigration hawks sometimes disparage as "anchor babies."

But the Trump administration was not writing on a clean slate. The Supreme Court's 1898 decision in *United States v. Wong Kim Ark* had already ruled that this exclusion applied to only three groups of people: children of Native American tribes on reservations; children of foreign enemies occupying American territory during war; and children of diplomats. With the passage of the Indian Citizenship Act in 1924, the language would no longer apply to Native Americans. Anyone else born on US soil was a citizen, including the plaintiff in the case, who was born in San Francisco to parents who were immigrants from China, though they were lawful permanent residents in the United States, a fact that could potentially distinguish the case from Trump's order.[936] But as Georgetown law professor Stephen Vladeck has noted, the Supreme Court clarified in 1982 in *Plyler v. Doe* and reaffirmed three years later in *Immigration and Naturalization Service v. Rios-Peneda* that the Fourteenth Amendment's birthright citizenship clause applies even to the children of undocumented immigrants.[937] The illogic of the argument that children of undocumented immigrants are not "subject to the jurisdiction" of the United States would mean that they would be immune from federal law enforcement operations, a result the administration surely did not intend. Consequently, the law is quite clear that a president cannot erase citizenship with the stroke of a pen. Only a constitutional amendment can do that.

Trump's legal advisers had to know that the birthright citizenship order was an indefensible loser and that advocating for it was a cynical—and even corrupt—breach of the president's oath to support and defend the Constitution. So, what was the point of issuing it? Perhaps it was to take a flyer on finding a sympathetic judge who might rule in the administration's favor, using taxpayer-funded lawyers at the Department of Justice to litigate the case. Or maybe it was an effort to deter immigrants from giving birth in the United States, believing that their children would no longer reap the benefits of citizenship just because they were born here. But it seems to me that at least two other goals were at work. First, the order would help normalize the idea that undocumented immigrants are second-class citizens. Second, it would pander to Trump's base, whom he had convinced that immigrants were a threat to their way of life. Regardless of the outcome of legal challenges in court, Trump could claim victory by demonstrating to his voters that he was aggressively executing his deportation agenda and blame "leftist" judges for any legal defeats.

Invoking the Alien Enemies Act

Another of Trump's audacious executive orders was one issued in March, declaring an "invasion" by Tren de Aragua, a drug cartel that Trump claimed was linked to the government of Venezuela. He used the declaration to invoke the Alien Enemies Act, which permits the government to deport foreign nationals of an invading country.[938] However, the order distorted the language of the law, which limits its use to times of "a declared war between the United States and any foreign nation or government, or any invasion or predatory incursion [that] is perpetrated, attempted, or threatened against the territory of the United States by any foreign nation or government."[939] The Alien Enemies Act was passed in 1798 as part of the Alien and Sedition Acts, when the United States feared war with France and wanted the authority to expel potential foreign spies and saboteurs if necessary.[940] Even then, critics feared the abuse of these authorities. Thomas Jefferson warned that they could empower a president to be "the accuser, counsel, judge and jury, whose suspicions may be the evidence, his order the sentence, his officer the executioner and his breast the sole record of the transaction."[941]

The Alien Enemies Act was invoked during the War of 1812 and both world wars—notably, only during wartime. President Franklin D. Roosevelt used the Alien Enemies Act to intern Japanese, German, and Italian immigrants—including American citizens—during World War II based solely on fears about their loyalty that arose from their ancestry. This internment came to be seen as a civil liberties violation for which the US government later apologized.[942] The lack of a war or predatory incursion was not the only problem with Trump's executive order. By its terms, the Act applies only to nationals of an enemy foreign *government*, not members of a drug cartel.

In May 2025, a Trump-appointed judge in Texas blocked the enforcement of the order as to Venezuelan immigrants because it exceeded "the scope of the statute and is contrary to the plain, ordinary meaning of the statute's terms."[943] The Fifth Circuit Court of Appeals affirmed that decision in September.[944] But these court orders came only after some men had already been removed from the United States under Trump's directive. In March, three planeloads of men were sent to a prison in El Salvador, even as a federal judge heard oral argument challenging the administration's authority to do so.[945] Five Venezuelan men filed a petition for habeas corpus and certification of a class action, along with a motion for a temporary restraining order, alleging that deportation under the order violated the Alien Enemies Act as well as their Fifth Amendment right to due process. During an emergency hearing conducted online on a Saturday, District Judge James Boasberg blocked the removal of all Venezuelan immigrants in the United States pursuant to the order and even told the government that, if necessary, it should turn the planes around. That night, while the five named plaintiffs remained in the United States, the government removed about 250 other men to a terrorist prison in El Salvador, in apparent violation of the judge's order.[946] In a stunning breach of respect for a court order, DOJ official Abhishek Kambli claimed that the government was permitted to ignore the order because the judge had issued it orally. "An injunction is not ordered until it's in the written filing."[947] That view is utter nonsense. Attorney General Pam Bondi would later file a grievance against Boasberg for sharing his colleagues' criticisms of the Trump administration—part of his job requirements as the chief judge of his district.[948] Attacking the independence of the judiciary at every opportunity was part of Trump's full-court press for more power.

The morning after the men were sent to El Salvador, Salvadoran president Nayib Bukele posted a video on X showing their arrival. Set to dramatic music, the video depicted an overwhelming presence of police vehicles and guards dressed in tactical gear as men in shackles were roughly escorted from planes to buses and then to a building bearing a sign identifying it as "CECOT," the country's notorious terrorism confinement center. When the facility opened in 2023, El Salvador's security minister said that the only way out was "inside a coffin."[949] Upon arrival, the men were forced to their knees while guards shaved their heads and facial hair.[950] Some sat on the floor in their underwear, while others were herded into a large cell. In the online post, Bukele expressed his gratitude to the United States for paying a fee, "a high one for us," that would help make the prison system self-sustainable.[951] Secretary of State Marco Rubio called Bukele "a great friend to the United States" for taking the men, which he agreed to do only in exchange for a six-million-dollar payment.[952]

The cruel treatment of the prisoners was degrading not only to the men but also to the viewer. Publishing a video of their harsh confinement was consistent with the authoritarian strategy to dehumanize and scapegoat adversaries and undesirables. It was a grotesque indulgence in the misfortune of others. I imagine the video was intended to strike the same emotional response in the viewer evoked by distributing postcards of lynchings of Black men in the South, once a common practice.[953] Most people cringe in horror at the sight, but some are conditioned to delight in the dehumanizing abuse of those they view as other. Bukele later posted a screenshot of a *New York Post* headline indicating that a judge had ordered the Trump administration to return the flights to the United States, along with his own comment: "Oopsie . . . Too late" and a laughing emoji. White House spokesman Steven Cheung reposted Bukele's message, along with a GIF of Denzel Washington saying "Boom." The clip was taken from *Training Day*, a movie about corrupt police officers.[954]

Days later, Homeland Security Secretary Kristi Noem visited the Salvadoran prison for photo ops, posing in front of a cell packed with men with shaved heads wearing only underwear. In contrast, she wore a fifty-thousand-dollar Rolex watch.[955] She recorded and posted a video, warning people who enter the United States unlawfully that "this is one of the consequences you could face."[956] It was hard to miss the imagery—white supremacy, cruelty, fear, subordination of the poor immigrant by the wealthy American. When later asked at a congressional hearing to define habeas corpus, the right of prisoners to petition courts to review the legality of their detention, Noem gave an answer that was horrifying in either its ignorance or its willingness to subvert a bedrock constitutional right. She testified that habeas corpus was "a constitutional right that the president has to be able to remove people from this country."[957]

Trump and his allies revel in harsh treatment of immigrants, coming up with nicknames for detention facilities such as "Alligator Alcatraz," in Florida's Everglades, and the "Speedway Slammer" in Indiana.[958] A government social media post featured an ICE baseball cap on an ear of corn, promoting a new detention facility in Nebraska to be called the "Cornhusker Clink."[959] The president even joked that if any detainees were to escape from the Florida facility, they would need to learn the best way to run from an alligator.[960] Even if one were to agree with Trump's policy on immigration enforcement, the insensitivity to the plight of other human beings was breathtaking. *The New York Times* called it "government by troll."[961] Not only was Trump robbing the detainees of their humanity, he was robbing us of ours.

Jailing Foreign Students for Disfavored Speech

Outspoken international students were also targets of Trump's intolerance. Upon taking office, the president sought to fulfill his campaign promise to deport international students involved in campus protests.[962] Even lawful permanent resident status did not spare Mahmoud Khalil from arrest by immigration officials. Born to Palestinian refugees in Syria, Khalil had become a prominent voice in pro-Palestinian protests at Columbia University during the war in

Gaza before he was jailed and put into deportation proceedings in March 2025.[963]

The underlying events were tragic and sparked strong passions around the world. On October 7, 2023, Hamas operatives conducted a surprise terrorist attack, killing more than 1,200 Israelis and taking 251 hostages, many of whom died in captivity.[964] Israel responded by killing more than 67,000 Palestinians—at least 20,000 of whom were children.[965] The war triggered protests on college campuses throughout the country and allegations of harassment of both Jewish and Muslim students.[966]

Khalil's arrest at his university apartment, despite his green-card status, made headlines.[967] ICE agents also threatened to arrest his wife, who was present during Khalil's arrest and was eight months pregnant.[968] His lawyer, Samah Sisay, accused the Trump administration of making "an example of him to chill others from making similar speech. Not agreeing with your government's foreign policy decision to support Israel is not a reason for you to be in deportation proceedings."[969] Khalil's arrest came days after the Trump administration cut four hundred million dollars in federal funding to Columbia for allegedly failing to prevent antisemitism on its campus.[970] On the day of his arrest, the White House posted a photo of Mahmoud on social media with a mocking message that stated, "SHALOM, MAHMOUD!"—more cruelty.[971] It added, "ICE proudly apprehended and detained Mahmoud Khalil, a Radical Foreign Pro-Hamas Student on the campus of @Columbia University. This is the first arrest of many to come. –President Donald J. Trump."[972] Regardless of one's opinion of Khalil's views, the arrest seemed to be a blatant violation of his free speech rights—which apply to all persons present within the jurisdiction of the United States, regardless of their citizenship status—and an effort to intimidate and silence others from speaking out.

Khalil came to the United States in 2022 and earned a master's degree from Columbia's School of International and Public Affairs in 2024.[973] Since arriving, he had married a US citizen, who gave birth to their first child while Khalil was still in custody; an ICE official denied his request for a furlough to attend the birth of his child.[974] After Khalil's arrest, Secretary of State Marco Rubio said he was relying on a provision of the Immigration and Nationality Act to remove Khalil from the country.[975] That provision states, "An alien whose presence or activities in the United States the Secretary of State has reasonable ground to believe would have potentially serious adverse foreign policy consequences for the United States is deportable."[976] Homeland Security spokeswoman Tricia McLaughlin said in a statement that the administration had taken action against Khalil because he "led activities aligned to Hamas, a designated terrorist organization."[977] Trump press secretary Karoline Leavitt explained that "this administration is not going to tolerate individuals having the privilege of studying in our country and then siding with pro-terrorist organizations that have killed Americans."[978]

As a former terrorism prosecutor, I have learned to recognize words like "aligned" or "siding with" as signaling a lack of evidence of the kind of direct connection with a terrorist organization typically required to pursue legal remedies. No evidence was presented that Khalil was working under the direction or control of Hamas—a requirement for a criminal charge of providing material support to a foreign terrorist organization. Instead, the action against Khalil seemed to be a direct response to the expression of a viewpoint that the Trump administration disfavored. Donna Lieberman, president of the New York Civil Liberties Union, said Khalil's arrest and attempted deportation were "targeted retaliation and an extreme attack on the First Amendment."[979]

Khalil filed a habeas corpus petition challenging his detention. After Khalil was shipped to Louisiana, he successfully petitioned the courts to hear his case in New Jersey, the location of the first immigration facility where he was held after being arrested. The district court in New Jersey entered a temporary restraining order blocking Khalil's deportation, finding that Rubio's basis for detention was "likely unconstitutional" because of statutory vagueness—that is, the law failed to provide adequate notice of what it prohibits and lacked clarity that invited arbitrary enforcement, and it had a chilling effect on Khalil's free speech rights, in apparent violation of the First Amendment.[980] In addition, Rubio had failed to explain how Khalil's domestic statements on campus affected US foreign policy.[981] In June 2025, the court ruled against Trump and issued a preliminary injunction requiring Khalil's release, finding that he was suffering irreparable harm to his career, reputation, and free speech rights.[982]

Another Columbia University student, Mohsen Mahdawi, who was active in pro-Palestinian protests suffered a fate similar to that of Khalil.[983] Mahdawi, who was born in Gaza, was arrested in April 2025 when he arrived for an interview in support of his application for US citizenship. A judge later ordered his release.[984]

A few weeks after Mahmoud's arrest, six masked agents in plain clothes apprehended another foreign graduate student in apparent retaliation for exercising her free speech rights. In late March, Tufts doctoral student Rümeysa Öztürk was arrested outside her home in Somerville, Massachusetts. Although the agents verbally identified themselves as police, they reportedly gave the student from Turkey no reason for her arrest, though she, too, was a pro-Palestinian activist, having coauthored an opinion piece in the student newspaper a year earlier that was critical of the university's investments in Israel.[985] A spokeswoman for the Department of Homeland Security later told the Associated Press that Öztürk's student visa had been revoked because she "engaged in activities in support of Hamas, a foreign terrorist organization that relishes the killing of Americans. A visa is a privilege, not a right. Glorifying and supporting terrorists who kill Americans is grounds for visa issuance to be terminated. This is common sense security."[986]

Like Mahmoud, Öztürk filed a petition for a writ of habeas corpus, seeking her release and restoration of her visa. A federal district court judge found that she had made a "substantial claim" that she had been unlawfully detained in violation of her free speech and due process rights, and ordered her released from custody while her case proceeds.[987] The court found "credible evidence" that "her detention is punishment for her op-ed, and that her punishment is intended to serve as a warning to other non-citizens who are contemplating public speech on issues of the day."[988]

Regardless of the outcome of the Öztürk case, her arrest was a chilling episode. Bystander Michael Mathis, a neighbor whose security camera recorded her arrest, said, "It looked like a kidnapping. They approach her and start grabbing her with their faces covered. They're covering their faces. They're in unmarked vehicles."[989] The manner of the arrest seemed designed to maximize fear and intimidation to shut down dissent among international students, and to please members of the MAGA movement who cheered Trump's crackdown on immigrants.

ICE agents continued to wear masks and plain clothes during enforcement operations, adding to the intimidating nature of their seemingly random arrests.[990] By July 2025, the Associated Press called masked agents "a regular sight around the country" and "one of the most potent and contentious visuals of 2025."[991] The White House defended the practice on the grounds that agents were being harassed and needed protection from threats and doxing.[992] But state attorneys general argued that the masks provoked fear.[993] And a group of Democratic senators asked ICE to stop using masks because the practice represented "a clear attempt to compound that fear and chaos."[994] Indeed, Öztürk said that she had felt "terror" during her abduction.[995] In her petition, she said that she "screamed as a man in a hooded sweatshirt grabbed her" before she was encircled by several other masked men who handcuffed her and put her in an unmarked car.[996] In addition to instilling fear, the masks also removed a check on government misconduct: If agents were to engage in excessive force or other abuse, masks would make it difficult for a victim to identify the perpetrator.

Öztürk's petition also quoted Trump's comments at a 2024 campaign event, in which he stated: "One thing I do is, any student that protests, I throw them out of the country. You know, there are a lot of foreign students. As soon as they hear that, they're going to behave."[997] It was a clear indication of intent to abuse governmental power to retaliate against a person for exercising free speech rights, and a gross violation of the US Constitution. The lawless disdain for civil liberties is an alarming sign of tyranny. A federal district court judge would later rule in a scathing opinion that the deportation of pro-Palestinian student activists in retaliation for their speech violated the First Amendment. Judge William Young, appointed to the bench by President Ronald Reagan, wrote, "The President's palpable misunderstanding that the government simply cannot seek retribution for speech he disdains poses a great threat to Americans' freedom of speech."[998]

Transgender Americans

Immigrants are not the only political scapegoats in Trump's regime. Like many on the far right, Trump has repeatedly attacked transgender and nonbinary people, campaigning for president with an ad that proclaimed that Kamala Harris was for "they/them" and Trump was for "you."[999] Ground Media CEO David Rochkind said the ads "weaponize trans-identity to sow fear and division, making our country less safe for everyone."[1000] Trump also stoked transphobia with ludicrous disinformation that children were obtaining gender-affirming surgeries at school. At a Wisconsin rally, Trump told the crowd: "Can you imagine—you're a parent and your son leaves the house and you say, 'Jimmy, I love you so much, go have a good day in school,' and your son comes back with a brutal operation? Can you even imagine this? What the hell is wrong with our country?"[1001] Of course, no children were undergoing surgeries at their schools, let alone "brutal" ones. And it seems to be no coincidence that the nightmare scenario Trump evoked involved a boy transitioning to being a girl, rather than vice versa, relying on unspoken misogyny among Trump's supporters. According to NBC News, the habit of accusing members of the LGBTQ community of being "groomers" of children or "pedophiles" had been relegated to the margins of society for decades, but has been resuscitated as part of today's far-right politics.[1002] Such baseless claims might endanger the lives of people in those communities, but Trump was willing to gamble with their safety to score political points with the far right.

On Trump's first day in office in his second term, he issued an executive order rendering the transgender community invisible as far as the government was concerned. It required that government-issued identification documents, such as passports and visas, as well as the personnel records of federal employees, "accurately reflect the holder's sex," meaning they must match the person's sex assigned at birth as reflected on their birth certificate. The order further directed federal agencies to remove all references in government forms, policies, or communications that "inculcate gender ideology" and, where forms required indicating an individual's sex, that they must limit the options to "male" or "female," and "shall not request gender identity."[1003] After a transgender woman in Minneapolis killed two children in a mass shooting at a church in August 2025, the Trump administration considered banning all transgender people from possessing guns by declaring that they are all, categorically, mentally ill.[1004]

Later, Trump issued another executive order, this one banning transgender service members from the military.[1005] Entitled "Prioritizing Military Excellence and Readiness," the order referred to "the warrior ethos" and "unit cohesion." The order stated, "Adoption of a gender identity inconsistent with an individual's sex conflicts with a soldier's commitment to an honorable, truthful, and disciplined lifestyle, even in one's personal life. A man's assertion that he is a woman, and his requirement that others honor this falsehood, is not consistent with the humility and selflessness required of a service member."[1006] Again, the ultimate horror in Trump's mind involved male transition to female; trans men were apparently beneath his consideration. Declaring the military's high standards inconsistent with "the medical, surgical, and mental health constraints on individuals with gender dysphoria" and "shifting pronoun usage or use of pronouns that inaccurately reflect an individual's sex," the order directed the secretary of defense to revise enlistment standards within sixty days. Accordingly, Pete Hegseth issued a memo initiating discharge procedures for transgender troops. The memo stated that "the Department only recognizes two sexes: male and female. An individual's sex is immutable, unchanging during a person's life." Of course, that statement ignores the reality for many Americans. The memo went on to define the proper use of pronouns: "Pronoun usage when referring to Service members must reflect a Service member's sex. In keeping with good order and discipline, salutations (e.g., addressing a senior officer as "Sir" or "Ma'am") must also reflect an individual's sex."[1007]

An advocacy group for transgender service members and veterans issued a statement noting that transgender Americans had served in the US military "openly and honorably" for nearly a decade. "Thousands of transgender troops are currently serving, and are fully qualified for the positions in which they serve."[1008] Yet, as reported at Military.com, transgender service members "described their own process of leaving the military as full of indignities that ranged from evaporating support from leadership to forced administrative leave and being denied the right to wear a uniform at retirement."[1009] Logan Ireland, a master sergeant in the US Air Force, called the ban "absolutely heartbreaking" and "open cruelty."[1010] Other transgender military members forced to leave called the new policy "dehumanizing."[1011] In addition to degrading the dignity of service members who had made personal sacrifices to serve, the ban also deprived honorable public servants of their place in the military. Among the members forced out were those who had completed tours of duty in Iraq and Afghanistan, as well as those holding specialized positions, such as intelligence analysts, IT specialists, and aeronautical engineers.[1012] Their experience and expertise was needlessly lost to the nation's military, weakening its readiness. The ban seemed to be nothing more than a cruel way to score political points, while harming the very institution it purported to improve.

In addition to banning transgender troops, Hegseth also ordered the renaming of a naval ship named after former San Francisco city supervisor Harvey Milk.[1013] Milk, a noted gay-rights activist, served in the navy as a diver during the Korean War, until he was forced to resign because of his sexual orientation.[1014] Milk was assassinated in office in 1978.[1015] According to a Pentagon spokesman, "Secretary Hegseth is committed to ensuring that the names attached to all DOD installations and assets are reflective of the Commander-in-Chief's priorities, our nation's history, and the warrior ethos."[1016] Congresswoman Nancy Pelosi, who worked with Milk, called the move "a shameful, vindictive erasure of those who fought to break down barriers for all to chase the American Dream."[1017] Hegseth later said, "People want to be proud of the name of the ship they're sailing on," suggesting that Harvey Milk's name fell short of that standard.[1018]

Trump's declaration during his inauguration speech that "there are only two genders: male and female" excluded approximately two million transgender Americans solely for the sake of political advantage. In fact, the American Medical Association has stated that "empirical evidence has demonstrated that trans and non-binary gender identities are normal variations of human identity and expression."[1019] In addition, according to the Cleveland Clinic, one in one hundred Americans is intersex, meaning that they have "genitals, chromosomes, or reproductive organs that don't fit into a male/female sex binary."[1020] As Jill Lawrence wrote in a moving essay in *The Bulwark*, Trump's decree conflating "gender, a social and psychological concept, with terms for biological sex categories (male and female)," was a particularly cynical ploy for a politician who once supported transgender rights. In 2016, Trump had opposed a North Carolina bill requiring people to use the bathroom that matched the sex on their birth certificates, stating that his friend Caitlyn Jenner would be allowed to use any bathroom in Trump Tower.[1021] By 2025, Trump was willing to sacrifice her rights and those of other transgender Americans for his own political gain.

One way Trump and other far-right politicians have made the issue of trans rights relevant is to claim that they are protecting girls and women from "men" in women's sports. Trump's executive order recognizing only two sexes was titled "Defending Women from Gender Ideology Extremism and Restoring Biological Truth to the Federal Government."[1022] (Again, it always seems to be men transitioning to women who threaten Trump and his base.) The issue of transgender athletes in sports creates genuine tensions between inclusion and fairness, but one size does not need to fit all. The issues surrounding archery, for example, differ from those in boxing or powerlifting. Moreover, concerns for younger children who are merely participating in sports for social fulfillment are far different from the needs of those competing at elite levels. I know from my own experience playing youth and high school sports that most athletes participate for social, fitness, and mental wellness reasons; only a small percentage will go on to compete in college or beyond. For athletes at that elite level, perhaps different solutions are needed than are required for the rest of us who just enjoy throwing a ball around and spending time with our friends. For those competing at higher levels, Human Rights Watch has recommended that governing bodies of various sports work to find options that promote the important values at stake while protecting the dignity, privacy, and heath of athletes.[1023]

But instead of working to find solutions, Trump and his MAGA cohorts express extreme views to stoke fear. When South Carolina governor Nikki Haley was campaigning for president in 2023, rather than addressing issues of fairness and inclusion, she conjured imaginary threats to the safety of girls: "How are we supposed to get our girls used to the fact that biological boys are in their locker room?"[1024] As a former girl, now a woman, and a mother of a girl, I have to say that I am just not bothered by that idea. For one reason, cisgender students have been dressing alongside their LGBTQ classmates since the invention of gym class. In addition, the numbers just don't make this issue the enormous problem Haley suggests it is. In 2025, among the 175,000 students competing in high school sports in Michigan, the number of transgender athletes seeking to compete was . . . two.[1025] Perhaps the focus should be on discouraging sexual assault rather than on who is using which locker room. Haley nonetheless called transgender girls playing girls' sports "the women's issue of our time."

Some politicians portray the very existence of transgender people as a threat, but, as Lawrence wrote in her essay, our own "comfort or discomfort levels with someone else's life or what they want to be called" are "immaterial. All that matters is common courtesy, respect for fellow Americans, and horror at the attacks on them."[1026] Indeed, it seems that some politicians are always in search of some out-group they can demonize to fuel fear, but making any category of people second-class citizens is at odds with the American promise of equality.

Antifa

Following the murder of conservative political activist Charlie Kirk in September 2025, Trump had an opportunity to seek national unity. Instead, he used the tragedy to further stoke division. During Kirk's memorial service, his widow, Erika Kirk, publicly forgave her husband's murderer and said the best response to hate is not hate, but love.[1027] In shocking contrast, Trump followed her moment of grace by telling the crowd, "I hate my opponent, and I don't want the best for them."[1028] Trump would exploit Kirk's death by blaming "the radical left."[1029] A twenty-two-year-old man was charged with Kirk's murder, and his contemporaneous text messages indicated a political motive, stating he had "had enough" of Kirk's "hate," but all evidence indicated that he had acted alone.[1030] Ignoring recent attacks targeting Democrats, such as the murders two months before of Minnesota legislator Melissa Hortman and her husband, Trump fanned the flames of conspiracy by blaming political violence on organized networks of left-wing operatives and funders.

Vice President J. D. Vance and Deputy Chief of Staff Stephen Miller echoed and amplified these claims. Vance guest-hosted Kirk's podcast, blaming the "far left" for political violence and saying it was "not a both-sides problem."[1031] In fact, although left-wing politically motivated attacks outnumbered right-wing ones by a count of four to one in the first six months of 2025, Vance's statement provided a misleading snapshot of longer trends.[1032] For the *thirty years* preceding 2025, right-wing-inspired violence was more common.[1033] Of course, government leaders should condemn political violence regardless of who commits it. During the same podcast episode, Stephen Miller said the Trump administration planned to target "the actual organized cells that carry out and facilitate the violence." Miller then vowed, "With God as my witness, we are going to use every resource we have at the Department of Justice, Homeland Security, throughout this government to identify, disrupt, dismantle, and destroy these networks and make America safe again for the American people."[1034] Miller later posted a message on X that read: "There is a large and growing movement of leftwing terrorism in this country. It is well organized and funded. And it is shielded by far-left Democrat judges, prosecutors and attorneys general. The only remedy is to use legitimate state power to dismantle terrorism and terror networks."[1035]

Twelve days after Kirk's death, the White House made good on Miller's podcast promise, issuing an executive order designating "antifa" as a domestic terrorist organization, even though no legal authority exists to do so.[1036] In light of civil liberties concerns with investigating domestic groups over their political activity, Congress has limited the designation of terrorist organizations to foreign actors. "Antifa" is short for "antifascist," but it refers to an amorphous, unofficial network of protestors "who view themselves as part of a protest tradition that arcs back to opposition groups in Nazi Germany and fascist Italy prior to World War II."[1037] Antifa activists focuses their efforts against white supremacist groups, the KKK, and neo-Nazis, using tactics ranging from nonviolent civil disobedience and mutual aid to online hacking, violence, and property damage.[1038] But, according to former FBI director Christopher Wray, antifa isn't an organization with any structure akin to that of terrorism groups, such as the far-right transnational Terrorgram Collective.[1039] In a 2020 congressional hearing, Wray testified that antifa is "not a group or an organization. It's a movement or an ideology."[1040] Consequently, a president could no more designate antifa as a terrorist organization than he could designate feminism or "the patriarchy." Nonetheless, Trump's order directed "all relevant executive departments and agencies . . . to investigate, disrupt, and dismantle any and all illegal operations . . . conducted by Antifa . . . including those who fund such operations."[1041]

Three days later, Trump issued an even broader presidential memorandum on "countering domestic terrorism and organized political violence."[1042] Protecting public safety certainly is an important objective, but the memo further advanced the false narrative of a left-wing conspiracy. "This political violence is not a series of isolated incidents and does not emerge organically," the memo read. "Instead, it is a culmination of sophisticated, organized campaigns of targeted intimidation, radicalization, threats, and violence designed to silence opposing speech, limit political activity, change or direct policy outcomes, and prevent the functioning of a democratic society."[1043] Trump was employing a debater's trick known as the "part-whole fallacy": because something is true for part of a group (one person who opposed Kirk politically was a violent murderer), then the same thing must be true for the whole group (all people who disagree with Kirk's views must be violent extremists). Of course, the reason this tactic is called a *fallacy* is that it is far from the truth. In fact, a person could consider themselves both an antifascist and a pacificist, with no association whatsoever with any form of violent extremism. It is even fair to say that the heroes of World War II were antifascists.

Trump's memo directed the attorney general, the IRS, and the FBI-led Joint Terrorism Task Forces to investigate "all participants in these criminal and terroristic conspiracies—including the organized structures, networks, entities, organizations, funding sources, and predicate actions behind them."[1044] The president baselessly identified George Soros, the billionaire who funds progressive causes, as "a likely candidate" for prosecution; in fact, *The New York Times* reported that a DOJ official directed several US attorney's offices to develop plans to investigate Soros's Open Society Foundations, which provides grants for groups that work to promote human rights, equity, and democracy.[1045] Binaifer Nowrojee, president of the foundation, said the organization's activities were lawful and peaceful. "This is not about George Soros," she said. "This is about the United States slowly losing its democracy bit by bit in ways that we've seen elsewhere in the world."[1046]

As political activist Saul Alinsky once said, "Never let a crisis go to waste."[1047] Most presidents would have used Kirk's murder as an opportunity to call for nonviolence, but Trump exploited it to fuel outrage by falsely portraying "the left" as a monolithic threat to national security.

Equal Justice Under Law

Eventually, the law caught up to Chaka Castro when police officers responded to one of the robberies in progress and arrested suspects.[1048] Phone records led investigators to Castro, and searches of electronic devices uncovered evidence of her role in the crimes. She was ultimately convicted in federal court in Detroit and sent to prison for thirty-seven years.[1049] Her scheme to prey on vulnerable victims had been an initial success, but it was short-lived. It usually is.

Targeting specific groups for political purposes has been a consistent theme throughout American history. Whether it's Native Americans, African Americans, women, religious minorities, immigrants, communists, or the LGBTQ community, powerful figures have long used fear to divide Americans and advance their political agendas. But oppressing groups is inconsistent with our American values of equal justice under law. Trump's abuse of members of the American family to increase his own power defiles democracy and our individual rights of self-determination. The Declaration of Independence cites the "self-evident" truth that "all men are created equal" and that they have "unalienable rights" of "life, liberty, and the pursuit of happiness." Attacks on people because of their race, country of origin, political views, or gender identity are a blatant rejection of those principles. As Supreme Court justice Robert H. Jackson once wrote, "If there is any fixed star in our constitutional constellation, it is that no official, high or petty, can prescribe what shall be orthodox in politics, nationalism, religion, or other matters of opinion or force citizens to confess by word or act their faith therein."[1050]

NINE

SEPARATION OF PARTIES

In 2014, researchers at the University of West Virginia noticed something unusual: The new Volkswagen (VW) vehicles they were testing for compliance with emissions standards were failing repeatedly.[1051] The results seemed particularly curious for the diesel-powered VWs, which were marketed as environmentally friendly. The researchers alerted the Environmental Protection Agency (EPA), which had tested the vehicles in its Ann Arbor, Michigan, lab, where they had passed emissions tests. Further investigation by the EPA revealed that the cars had emitted only small amounts of pollutants during government testing while spewing much higher levels on the road. Hidden software—a "defeat device"—allowed the cars to run in "clean" mode when mounted on a dynamometer testing device and to switch to "performance" mode under other circumstances. In other words, Volkswagen was cheating on the test.

Volkswagen knew that its VW, Audi, and Porsche-branded vehicles could not be sold on the US market unless they met EPA standards, but they were unable to achieve their goals of fuel efficiency, price, and compliance simultaneously.[1052] So, the company engineered a solution to fool government regulators and American buyers into believing its "clean diesel" vehicles satisfied the EPA standards. In fact, it was all a fraud. Not only did Volkswagen pollute the air and dupe customers who thought they were buying cars that were good for the planet, it also gained an unfair competitive advantage over other carmakers who played by the rules. As regulators began asking questions about the discrepancy, some VW employees destroyed incriminating documents, further compounding their criminal culpability.[1053]

Because the false certifications were submitted from a VW office in Auburn Hills, Michigan, the case landed in my office. A team of dedicated investigators and prosecutors traveled to Germany to gather evidence, conducting interviews and analyzing documents. The assembled evidence led to an indictment for fraud and conspiracy.[1054] Volkswagen would ultimately enter a corporate guilty plea in a Detroit courtroom and pay a $2.8 billion fine.

Writing software to cheat emissions tests and covertly installing it on an entire fleet of vehicles is not something that anyone can achieve alone. In fact, many of the executives at Volkswagen who should have alerted others to the scheme had simply gone along with it. Perhaps they were complicit out of greed—or maybe it was fear. Whatever their motivation, the checks and balances in their compliance system failed. Volkswagen's CEO resigned, and two of its executives were convicted of crimes in the United States; four more were found guilty in German courts.[1055] As of this writing, charges against thirty-one employees, including former CEO Martin Winterkorn, remained pending.[1056] The business decision to cheat was an unmitigated disaster. If any of the VW employees in the know had objected to the company's illegal and unethical business tactics, they could have saved the company billions of dollars, incalculable damage to its reputation, and the freedom and careers of the individuals involved.

I think of the VW case when I see what is happening in America today. We are experiencing a similar failure of checks and balances in our constitutional system. Whether participants are motivated by fear, political ambition, or thirst for power, our legislative and judicial branches are not working as intended by the framers. During his second term, President Donald Trump has repeatedly shown disdain for the constitutional roles of Congress and the judiciary, usurping legislative power and ignoring court orders. What's more, Republicans in Congress and a conservative Supreme Court have passively allowed the president's power grab. And with a cowed Republican majority in both houses of Congress, impeachment no longer seems to be a realistic check on a president's misconduct.

When the Founding Fathers set out to draft a constitution, they had recently won their independence from the British monarchy. Preventing the tyranny of an overly powerful executive was a top priority for them. In forging a new blueprint for governing, they sought to limit future leaders' power so that they could not abridge the freedoms Americans had just declared and won. As James Madison wrote in Federalist 47, "The accumulation of all powers, legislative, executive, and judiciary, in the same hands, whether of one, a few, or many, and whether hereditary, self-appointed, or elective, may justly be pronounced the very definition of tyranny." The solution? A form of government with three separate and coequal branches. The first three articles of the Constitution describe the legislature, executive, and judiciary, in that order, with each branch able to check the others to prevent any one branch from asserting too much power. When Congress passes a law that the president deems unwise, the president has the power to veto it unless the veto is overridden by a two-thirds vote in the House and Senate. If the president commits a high crime or misdemeanor while in office, the House can impeach and the Senate can convict, and the president can even be barred from ever holding federal office again. Judges are appointed by the president but must be confirmed by the Senate. As Madison described in Federalist 51, in distributing power, "the constant aim is to divide and arrange the several offices in such a manner as that each may be a check on the other, that the private interest of every individual may be a sentinel over the public rights."[1057] The reason for these checks, according to Madison, was that "ambition must be made to counteract ambition." The premise for this structure was that each branch would favor its own powers. According to Carl Hulse of *The New York Times*, the Senate in particular was at one time "known for strong personalities and formidable politicians who were eager to assert their power and saw themselves as equal partners to the president, with the ability to shape legislation and the right to reject nominees they deemed unfit or unqualified. Over the past few decades, the Senate has become a much more partisan institution, and both parties have seen power shift to the White House."[1058] In the second Trump term, with Republicans paving the way, what was once a separation of powers had become a separation of parties.

Congress

It is noteworthy that the powers of Congress are listed in Article I of the Constitution—the first article. After all, it is our elected representatives who are empowered to make laws. The president is not mentioned until Article II of the document, where he is directed to "take care that the laws be faithfully executed."[1059] However, during his second term, Trump was determined not only to carry out the law but also to change it on his own, daring Congress or the courts to stop him. A president's executive orders cannot legally overrule statutes or the Constitution, but Trump issued presidential declarations on matters ranging from redefining birthright citizenship to declaring the existence of only two sexes.[1060] He quickly gutted agencies created by Congress in the public interest, such as the Consumer Financial Protection Bureau, which protects the public from fraud.[1061] He slashed spending at the Department of Education and promised to eliminate the department altogether, even though it was created by an act of Congress. Education Secretary Linda McMahon, the former CEO of World Wrestling Entertainment who lied on her résumé about having a degree in education,[1062] said the department's "final mission" would be "to send education back to the states."[1063] Trump fired inspectors general in violation of federal statutes that required he deliver thirty days' notice and a detailed rationale to Congress.[1064] He imposed tariffs, even though the Constitution gives the power to levy taxes to the legislative branch.[1065] In a lawsuit challenging the legality of the tariffs, the Supreme Court appeared skeptical of Trump's authority to impose them in light of that constitutional allocation of power.[1066] Rather than spend funds that had been appropriated by Congress, Trump withheld them from programs he disfavored, such as the Head Start child care program for families in poverty and charging stations for electric vehicles, in apparent violation of the Impoundment Control Act.[1067] Congress, and not the president, has the power of the purse to decide the nation's spending. The president must administer it "faithfully." Trump conducted all of this chaotic activity with nary a peep from GOP members of Congress.

Not Checks But Enablers

In fact, rather than serving as a check on executive power, most Republicans in Congress became servile enablers and sycophants. Senator Lindsey Graham of South Carolina seemed to shrug off the inspector general firings, saying, "Just tell them you need to follow the law next time."[1068] Even before Trump took office, the GOP-controlled Senate signaled its submission to Trump by confirming cabinet nominees with what journalist Gabriel Sherman, writing in *Vanity Fair,* called "only a faint whiff of pushback on some of their boundary-scorching backgrounds."[1069] In July 2025, at a time when a majority of Americans disapproved of Trump's performance in office, House Speaker Mike Johnson said in a television interview, "His approval ratings are skyrocketing."[1070] According to Johnson, Trump "was at a 90 percent approval rating. There's never been a president that high." In fact, approval for Trump wasn't that high either, hovering at around 42 percent.[1071] That same month, Congress approved what Trump called his "One Big Beautiful Bill," a budget that cut Medicaid and food stamps while maintaining tax cuts for wealthy Americans. The budget also added billions in spending on immigration enforcement, which would deepen the national debt by $3.4 trillion.[1072] Yet even the antidebt hawks caved in to Trump.[1073] Three weeks later, Congress approved Trump's proposed rescission bill to claw back nine billion dollars in funds already appropriated for foreign aid and public broadcasting—the first time approved funds had been rescinded in decades—despite the White House's failure to provide details Congress requested.[1074] Senator Roger Wicker, a Republican from Mississippi, said on the chamber floor that the Senate was "perhaps approaching a disregard for the constitutional responsibilities of the legislative branch under Article I" in what would "amount to the House and Senate basically saying, we cede that decision voluntarily to the executive branch."[1075] Nonetheless, he later voted in favor of the rescission.[1076]

In July 2025, when members of Congress began discussing legislative action requiring the Justice Department to release the Jeffrey Epstein investigative files, which Attorney General Pam Bondi had told Trump contained the president's name multiple times, Johnson rose to Trump's defense.[1077] Rather than allow the House to vote on the action, Johnson released members early for their summer recess.[1078] Ultimately, Congress enacted legislation requiring DOJ to disclose its files by December 19, 2025. DOJ produced some of the documents in installments, including benign photos of Trump, but failed to meet the deadline.[1079]

Fear

While some members of Congress were undoubtedly in sync with Trump politically, others appeared to succumb to pressure from the president. Reports indicated that Thom Tillis, a Republican from North Carolina, received "credible death threats" when he was considering voting against confirming Pete Hegseth as secretary of defense.[1080] Tillis ultimately voted in Hegseth's favor, but when he voted against advancing the president's budget bill, Trump said he would be seeking primary challengers for Tillis's seat.[1081] Shortly thereafter, Tillis announced he would retire from the Senate rather than seek reelection.[1082] Fear of the consequences for crossing Trump went even beyond primary elections: Liz Cheney, the former Republican congresswoman from Wyoming, told CNN that some of her GOP colleagues had declined to vote for Trump's second impeachment based on his role in the January 6, 2021, attack on the US Capitol because they were "afraid for their own security—afraid, in some instances, for their lives."[1083]

Alaska senator Lisa Murkowski, a Republican, admitted in April 2025 that she and her colleagues were "all afraid" to speak out in the political climate that existed during the second Trump administration.[1084] "I'm oftentimes very anxious myself about using my voice because retaliation is real. And that's not right." Murkowski, one of the few Republicans to speak out against Trump's treatment of Ukrainian president Volodymyr Zelensky and the ruthless cuts by DOGE, perhaps felt empowered to make those statements because she would not be up for reelection until 2028.[1085] In addition, Murkowski represents a state that uses ranked-choice voting, a method that tends to weed out extremists from either party, making it more difficult for Trump to find a primary opponent to challenge her.[1086] But she was in the minority in speaking out. Former senator Jeff Flake, a Republican who resigned during Trump's first term rather than seek reelection, said that in the Trump administration, there is no room for any good-faith debate over policy positions: "Any deviation from his dictates is treated as apostasy. It's no longer about ideas or governing philosophies. It's about personal allegiance to a single man, whose positions can shift by the day."[1087] The compromised principles in the Senate, according to Flake, harm not just the GOP but the public. "When a party's North Star is an individual, the direction of policy and the integrity of governance itself suffer."[1088]

Arrest

The fear of retribution became tangible when members of Congress began to be arrested and restrained by federal law enforcement officers. Although there was no direct evidence that these actions against them were purely retaliatory, the willingness of the executive branch to use law enforcement powers so audaciously against lawmakers nonetheless sent a message.

In May 2025, LaMonica McIver, a Democratic congresswoman from New Jersey, was arrested and later charged with felony offenses for "forcibly impeding and interfering" with federal agents and officers at an immigration detention facility in Newark.[1089] According to the indictment, McIver was at the facility to conduct congressional oversight that coincided with an immigration protest rally.[1090] When the gates to the facility opened to allow a vehicle to enter, McIver, along with Newark mayor Ras Baraka and other members of Congress, followed the car inside. Authorities told Baraka that he was not permitted inside and attempted to arrest him when he refused to leave. According to the indictment, McIver yelled "Circle the mayor" and "slammed her forearm into the body" of a federal agent.[1091]

Video of the incident showed McIver pushing through the scrum of people, but it seemed a stretch to say she "slammed" her forearm into anyone.[1092] Alina Habba, then Trump's US attorney in New Jersey, initially charged Baraka with a misdemeanor for trespassing—a charge that Habba later dismissed, earning her a stern rebuke from the magistrate judge assigned to the case. The judge called the arrest "hasty," "severe," and a "worrisome misstep" and the dismissal "an embarrassing retraction."[1093] Nonetheless, Habba proceeded with charges against McIver, stating, "No one is above the law—politicians or otherwise."[1094]

As a former federal prosecutor, I agree with Habba's sentiment that officeholders are not free to thwart the law, and that it is a crime to forcibly obstruct a law enforcement official in performing his duties. But I also know that charges against members of Congress are considered highly sensitive decisions that ought to be made only after careful review, so as not to encroach upon the work of a coequal branch of government. In this case, McIver was exercising her lawful oversight duty as a member of Congress and was authorized to visit the facility even without advance notice. McIver no doubt played a role in the conflict but as her attorney, Paul Fishman, noted, "Rather than facilitating [McIver's] inspection, ICE agents chose to escalate what should have been a peaceful situation into chaos."[1095]

Habba had the option to decline filing charges. Instead, she made a curious statement that she had "persistently made efforts to address these issues without bringing criminal charges, and [had] given Representative McIver every opportunity to come to a resolution, but she has unfortunately declined."[1096] What kind of offer does a prosecutor make to a putative defendant short of criminal charges? Criminal prosecution is not like a civil case, where a monetary award can resolve the dispute. Did Habba offer some sort of pretrial diversion in exchange for an admission of guilt? She did not say. But other members of Congress denounced the charges as overreach. Jamie Raskin, a Democrat from Maryland, described the indictment as an act of intimidation: "Charging Members of Congress for doing our jobs is a dangerous precedent to set," he said. "It reveals the increasingly authoritarian nature of this Administration and its relentless, illegal attempts to suppress any dissent or oversight, including from judges, Members of Congress, and the American people, which check lawless executive power."[1097]

McIver was not the only member of Congress to land in the crosshairs of federal law enforcement. When the Trump administration deployed the National Guard to respond to protests over immigration enforcement in Los Angeles, Senator Alex Padilla of California attended a press conference featuring Homeland Security Secretary Kristi Noem. When Padilla attempted to ask Noem a question, he was escorted out by federal agents, taken to the floor in the hallway, and handcuffed.[1098] Afterwards, Noem claimed not to have recognized Padilla because he was not wearing his Senate lapel pin. That might be true, but the senator had begun his question by stating, "I am Senator Alex Padilla. I have a question for the secretary."[1099] Even the Republican Senator Murkowski was disturbed by the arrest: "I've seen that one clip," Murkowski said. "It is horrible. It is shocking at every level. It's not the America I know."[1100]

The Courts

It wasn't just Congress that Trump sought to neutralize with fear and intimidation but also the courts. Article III of the Constitution vests the judicial power of the United States in "one supreme court, and in such inferior courts as the Congress may from time to time ordain and establish."[1101] In 1789, Congress passed the Judiciary Act, establishing the district and circuit courts.[1102] As the Supreme Court explained in 1803 in the landmark case of *Marbury v. Madison*, "It is emphatically the duty" of the courts "to say what the law is."[1103] But Trump's Justice Department has seen an independent judiciary not as a bulwark of democracy but as an obstacle blocking its agenda. During a 2025 speech to the Federalist Society, an organization of conservative lawyers and law students, Deputy Attorney General Todd Blanche went so far as to cast judges essentially as an enemy.[1104] Making a recruiting pitch for society members to join DOJ, Blanche told the audience, "We need you, because it is a war, and it's something we will not win unless we keep on fighting."[1105] Blanche bemoaned the public's failure to appreciate "what a travesty it is when you have an individual judge be able to stop an entire operation or an entire administrative policy that's constitutional and allowed just because he or she chooses to do so. So, it's a war."[1106] Of course, a judge is not just able but *required* to stop an administration operation when the judge disagrees with DOJ's assessment that the policy is constitutional. Blanche's comments suggested that the executive branch operates above the judiciary, a remarkable distortion of the Constitution's establishment of coequal branches of government.

Defying Court Orders

All of us in the United States, private individuals and public officials alike, are bound to comply with court orders. Indeed, that is the very essence of the concept of the rule of law. When President Dwight D. Eisenhower sent in federal troops to enforce court orders permitting Black students to attend the public high school in Little Rock, Arkansas, in 1957, he explained the imperative to obey court orders. "The very basis of our individual rights and freedoms rests upon the certainty that the President and the Executive Branch of Government will support and ensure the carrying out of the decisions of the Federal Courts, even, when necessary, with all the means at the President's command. Unless the President did so, anarchy would result. There would be no security for any except that which each one of us could provide for himself."[1107]

The constitutional command to comply with court orders remains in effect regardless of whether a president agrees with it. Yet the second Trump administration has sometimes played fast and loose with court orders. When the Justice Department failed to comply with the Supreme Court's order to "facilitate" the return of Kilmar Abrego Garcia from custody in El Salvador, Judge J. Harvie Wilkinson III, issued a blistering opinion, writing, "The government is asserting a right to stash away residents of this country in foreign prisons without the semblance of due process that is the foundation of our constitutional order. Further, it claims in essence that because it has rid itself of custody that there is nothing that can be done. This should be shocking not only to judges, but to the intuitive sense of liberty that Americans far removed from courthouses still hold dear."[1108] According to Wilkinson, "'Facilitate' is an active verb. It requires that steps be taken as the Supreme Court has made perfectly clear."[1109] The Reagan appointee went on:

> "Facilitation" does not permit the admittedly erroneous deportation of an individual to the one country's prisons that the withholding order forbids and, further, to do so in disregard of a court order that the government not so subtly spurns. "Facilitation" does not sanction the abrogation of habeas corpus through the transfer of custody to foreign detention centers in the manner attempted here. Allowing all this would "facilitate" foreign detention more than it would domestic return. It would reduce the rule of law to lawlessness and tarnish the very values for which Americans of diverse views and persuasions have always stood.[1110]

Judge Wilkinson noted the danger that flowed from the government's assertion of power: "If today the Executive claims the right to deport without due process and in disregard of court orders, what assurance will there be tomorrow that it will not deport American citizens and then disclaim responsibility to bring them home?"[111] The government finally brought Garcia back—but only, of course, after he was indicted on charges of harboring undocumented immigrants.

Even after the case returned to the district court for further proceedings, the Trump administration continued to drag its feet in complying with court orders. Judge Paula Xinis finally entered an order finding that the government was "not acting in good faith" in the discovery process.[112] "For weeks," Judge Xinis wrote, the government has "sought refuge behind vague and unsubstantiated assertions of privilege, using them as a shield to obstruct discovery and evade compliance with this Court's orders." She added that the government's objections to discovery requests "reflect a willful refusal to comply with this Court's Discovery Order and governing rules."[113] An administration that refuses to comply with court orders corrupts our constitutional system of checks and balances and threatens to upend the rule of law. Yet the Trump administration remained convinced of its right to do as it wished. Despite his Yale law degree, Vice President J. D. Vance, for one, had previewed his disdain for the authority of the judiciary as far back as 2021, when discussing his vision to fire civil servants: "When the courts stop you, stand before the country like Andrew Jackson did and say, 'The chief justice has made his ruling. Now let him enforce it.'"[114]

Loophole Appointments

In addition to evading court orders, the Trump administration brazenly undermined the checks provided by Congress and the courts in the appointment of US attorneys. Under the Judiciary Act of 1789, Congress directed the appointment of an attorney for the government in each judicial district, which now numbers ninety-four. Ordinarily, US attorneys are nominated by the president and must be confirmed by the Senate before they may take office. That's the process I went through to serve as US attorney for the Eastern District of Michigan during the Obama administration. Instead,

Trump worked to circumvent the Senate's check on his appointees by installing interim US attorneys. An 1863 federal statute permits the attorney general to fill vacancies with interim appointees for 120 days without Senate confirmation.[1115] Ed Martin in the District of Columbia, Alina Habba in the District of New Jersey, and Danielle Sassoon in the Southern District of New York were all interim appointees. After the 120 days expire, if no permanent US attorney has been appointed by the president and confirmed by the Senate, the statute says that the district court, and not the president or the attorney general, may appoint a lawyer to fill the vacancy. Sometimes, the courts simply extend the interim. However, the statute leaves this decision to the court's discretion. According to a 1986 DOJ memo written by government attorney Samuel Alito before he took the bench, the attorney general is entitled to appoint only one 120-day interim US attorney; the 120-day clock can't be restarted by appointing successive interims.[1116] Once the initial interim period expires, it is the court, and not the attorney general or the president, who may appoint the US Attorney. This interpretation of the statute prevents a president from doing an end run around the Senate's confirmation authority.

In 2025, the Trump administration blew past this statutory requirement in several districts, including the District of Columbia, Northern New York, and New Jersey. In May, when it became apparent that nominee Ed Martin lacked Senate support for confirmation as US attorney in DC and his 120 days had expired, the Trump administration simply appointed another interim, an authority not provided by the statutes.[1117] Rather than allowing the court to fill the vacancy, as the law requires, Trump installed his ally Jeanine Pirro, a former county prosecutor and judge known for her Fox News commentary.[1118] Senator Dick Durbin, an Illinois Democrat, said Trump's second interim appointment was a "daisy chain situation" and "a violation of what we were trying to achieve" with the 1863 statute.[1119] Trump later nominated Pirro to the permanent position, and she was confirmed by the Senate.[1120]

In Northern New York, the Trump administration found a work-around to install its choice without check. Attorney General Pam Bondi had appointed John A. Sarcone III as interim US attorney and, by June, 120 days had expired with no presidentially appointed and Senate-confirmed US attorney and no nominee pending. By statute, the decision to replace Sarcone fell to the judges. The court declined to renew Sarcone, who had caused controversy while in office: He had reported to police that an undocumented immigrant had "threatened his life," an accusation refuted by video. He had also listed a boarded-up building as his home address in an affidavit about an alleged threat, and, when a newspaper reported on the incident, had the publication removed from his office's media distribution list.[1121] Further, Sarcone falsely told a member of the media that the judges had voted to extend him when they had not.[1122] And before taking office, Sarcone had written that President Joe Biden was a "traitor," "the worst person to occupy the White House, and someone who should be charged with treason."[1123] Sarcone had also posted on social media that President Barack Obama should be "the first illegal alien to be deported."[1124]

Any one of those factors might have been enough to convince the judges that Sarcone was unfit for the job, and the court declined to extend his appointment past his initial 120 days. But the court also declined to appoint another lawyer to the role.[1125] Clearly, the judges were sending a message: We respect the administration's prerogative to choose a US attorney, as long as it isn't this guy. Instead of finding another lawyer to serve as US attorney, though, the Trump administration played the role of Oliver Wendell Holmes's "bad man" and looked for loopholes. First, Bondi named Sarcone a "special assistant to the Attorney General." Then, using a different statute, the 1998 Federal Vacancies Reform Act, which allows deputies or first assistants to serve as acting officials for 210 days, she installed Sarcone as the first assistant US attorney. Hence, presto chango, the president was able to designate him as the "acting" US attorney.[1126] Different title, same result; judges and democracy be damned.

The situation in New Jersey was even more tense when the court voted to replace Alina Habba after her 120 days expired as interim

US attorney. The judges instead selected Desiree Grace, a career prosecutor whom Habba herself had selected to serve as her first assistant.[1127] Calling members of the district court "rogue judges," Attorney General Bondi fired Grace and appointed Habba as first assistant. Then, like Sarcone, Habba was named "acting" US attorney, even though her nomination for the permanent position was pending—an apparent violation of the law.[1128] DOJ used similar work-arounds to install US attorneys in other districts. Judges would find Trump's appointments of US attorneys violated the law in New Jersey, Nevada, California, and Virginia, putting cases brought in those districts during their tenure in jeopardy.[1129] The appointments were a blend of chaos and hubris. Georgetown law professor Stephen Vladeck called the conduct "part of the broader, reprehensible pattern of this administration wrongly trying to undermine public faith in the judiciary."[1130]

Intimidating Judges

Not only did the Trump administration flout court orders and the laws governing appointments, the president also used his bully pulpit to attack the integrity of the judiciary, lashing out at judges who decided cases against him. In a post on social media, Trump went after Judge James Boasberg, the federal judge in the District of Columbia who blocked the deportation of Venezuelan men to El Salvador without due process. Trump called Boasberg a "Radical Left Lunatic of a Judge, a troublemaker and agitator,"[1131] writing, "this judge, like many of the Crooked Judges I am forced to appear before, should be IMPEACHED!!!"[1132] The post drew a rare rebuke from Supreme Court chief justice John Roberts, who stated, "For more than two centuries, it has been established that impeachment is not an appropriate response to disagreement concerning a judicial decision. The normal appellate review process exists for that purpose."[1133] When District Judge Allison Burroughs ruled against the administration in the Harvard case, Trump called her a "TOTAL DISASTER."[1134] And in a bizarre Memorial Day greeting on social media, Trump referred to "JUDGES WHO ARE ON A MISSION TO KEEP MURDERERS, DRUG DEALERS, RAPISTS, GANG MEMBERS, AND RELEASED PRISONERS FROM ALL OVER THE WORLD, IN OUR COUNTRY," calling them "USA HATING JUDGES WHO SUFFER FROM AN IDEOLOGY THAT IS SICK, AND VERY DANGEROUS FOR OUR COUNTRY" and "MONSTERS WHO WANT OUR COUNTRY TO GO TO HELL."[1135] The diatribe read like a fevered rant, but when a person's words can start wars and move markets, they cannot be taken lightly. When judges ruled against Trump's use of the National Guard in US cities, Deputy Chief of Staff Stephen Miller didn't just criticize their opinions, he also accused them of "legal insurrection."[1136]

During the spring of 2025, the US Marshals Service, which provides protection for the federal judiciary, announced a spike in threats against judges, with 162 judges receiving threats in a six-week period coinciding with some of Trump's harshest rhetoric.[1137] The attacks from the president and the threats from members of the public created a climate that threatened to undermine the independence of the federal judiciary, one of the pillars of our constitutional democracy. As Judge Wilkinson wrote in his opinion regarding Kilmar Abrego Garcia, "The Judiciary will lose much from the constant intimations of its illegitimacy, to which by dint of custom and detachment we can only sparingly reply. The Executive will lose much from a public perception of its lawlessness and all of its attendant contagions. The Executive may succeed for a time in weakening the courts, but over time history will script the tragic gap between what was and all that might have been, and law in time will sign its epitaph."[1138]

Prosecution of Judges

The Trump administration went even further than criticizing the courts when it used the legal system itself against judges. In March 2025, the Department of Justice filed criminal charges against a Wisconsin state court judge.[1139] According to an indictment, Judge

Hannah Dugan obstructed justice when she helped an undocumented immigrant evade arrest by federal agents by escorting him out a side entrance to her courtroom. The man was arrested outside the courthouse after a foot chase,[1140] and Dugan was convicted at trial. Like the McIver indictment, the charges against Dugan appeared to be an aggressive use of prosecutorial discretion. In discussing the case, Attorney General Pam Bondi said, "What's happening to our judiciary is beyond me."[1141] She then used the term "deranged."[1142] Clearly, the administration was sending a message that it would not tolerate pushback from other branches of government that crossed a legal line, no matter how slight.

In June 2025, the Trump administration sued all fifteen judges on the district court in Maryland. The suit challenged an order issued by the chief judge blocking the government from deporting any immigrant who filed a petition for habeas corpus until 4:00 p.m. the following business day.[1143] According to the language of the order, the goal was to temporarily maintain the status quo, to give each immigrant access to the courts and an attorney and to give the government a "fulsome opportunity to brief and present arguments in its defense."[1144] In other words, without a temporary pause, the government could whisk immigrants out of the country before they had the opportunity for the notice and hearing that due process requires. The lawsuit was a remarkable assertion of executive power against the judiciary, which is ordinarily afforded broad discretion to manage cases on its docket. A Trump-appointed judge, brought in from another district to handle the case, wrote a scathing opinion dismissing the administration's suit, calling it "novel and potentially calamitous."[1145] "Although some tension between the coordinate branches of government is a hallmark of our constitutional system," the judge wrote, "this concerted effort by the executive to smear and impugn individual judges who rule against it is both unprecedented and unfortunate."[1146]

Enabling Executive Abuse

At the same time that Trump was disparaging the judiciary, the Supreme Court's conservative majority morphed into a force that enabled Trump's mob-style use of power. During his first term, Trump appointed three justices, such that he enjoyed a conservative supermajority on the court. While I don't view the court as simply a rubber stamp for Trump, the majority of justices have issued numerous decisions consistent with his interests, enabling his power grab when they should have been checking it. Finding presidents immune from criminal prosecution, expanding the court's emergency docket, invalidating the power of courts to issue universal injunctions, and applying the "unitary executive theory" all advanced Trump's efforts to gain control.

First, in July 2024, the Supreme Court ruled in Trump's favor when he challenged the indictment against him for interfering with the 2020 presidential election on grounds of "presidential immunity." On behalf of the majority, Chief Justice John Roberts, wrote, "We conclude that under our constitutional structure of separated powers, the nature of Presidential power requires that a former President have some immunity from criminal prosecution for official acts during his tenure in office. At least with respect to the President's exercise of his core constitutional powers, this immunity must be absolute."[1147] To those of us who grew up during the Watergate era, the decision was a stunning departure from what we thought was an essential check on a president's abuse of power. President Gerald Ford's pardon of Richard Nixon would have been unnecessary if they had believed for an instant that a president was immune from criminal prosecution. The current court left it for another day to decide the full scope of immunity for exercising duties that are outside of a president's core constitutional powers, and, of course, the case against Trump was dismissed when he was elected to a second term.

In dissenting from the court's decision, Justice Sonia Sotomayor pointed out that the majority's opinion would insulate a president from criminal prosecution even for grave abuses of official power. If a president "[o]rders the Navy's SEAL Team 6 to assassinate a political rival? Immune. Organizes a military coup to hold onto power? Immune. Takes a bribe in exchange for a pardon? Immune. Immune, immune, immune."[1148] Rather than refute the dissent's argument, Chief Justice Roberts dismissed it as "striking a chilling doom," and concluded that it was more important to ensure that a president be able to perform his duties "boldly and fearlessly."[1149] It was not only a significant victory for Trump in his criminal case in 2024 but a license for lawlessness in his second term.

Unlike during his first term, when Trump was under investigation not only for his role in fomenting his campaign's connections with Russia but also for obstruction of the special counsel's investigation, during his second term, he was virtually free from risk of prosecution. Without fear of criminal consequences, Trump was at liberty to engage in mob-style tactics as long as he was acting in his official capacity. As the court intended, Trump was asserting his power "boldly and fearlessly."

The Shadow Docket

Besides protecting Trump from the risk of prosecution for actions taken in office, the court has made growing use of its emergency docket to provide quick relief to Trump when some of his aggressive new policies became mired in litigation. Also known as the "shadow docket" because of its diminished visibility compared to the court's ordinary work, the emergency docket allows the court to address issues that require immediate action; a typical emergency petition might be for a stay of execution to consider a new argument by a death row inmate. Hearing cases on the emergency docket is generally disfavored because of their truncated briefing schedules, expedited oral arguments (if they are held at all), and typically short orders that do not explain the court's reasoning. Yet the Roberts court repeatedly used the emergency docket to lift stays entered by district courts blocking some of Trump's drastic executive actions, such as mass terminations at the Department of Education,[1150] cancellation of National Institute of Health grants relating to DEI,[1151] and the use of racial profiling in immigration enforcement.[1152]

During Trump's second term, a number of the president's executive orders were met with legal challenges in which district court judges issued temporary restraining orders based on findings that the plaintiffs had shown a substantial likelihood of success on the legal merits and a risk of irreparable harm if the orders went into effect, among other factors. What's more, these orders often had nationwide application, to avoid the chaos that would result from having different policies in different parts of the country. The effect of these orders was to prevent the president's policies from going into effect while the lawsuit was pending. Nationwide injunctions frustrate presidents because they slow down their agenda, but they also serve as an important check on a president's power when a judge finds a substantial likelihood that the president's agenda or the means by which it is being implemented is illegal. Nationwide injunctions were implemented against other presidents' executive orders, including Barack Obama's repeal of the "Don't Ask, Don't Tell" policy in the military and President Joe Biden's plans to impose Covid vaccine mandates and provide student loan relief, among other initiatives.[1153] But Trump found them to be an intolerable impediment to his policy agenda, posting online: "Unlawful nationwide injunctions by Radical Left Judges could lead to the destruction of the country!"[1154]

In early 2025, the Trump administration sought emergency relief from the Supreme Court after several district courts had temporarily blocked Trump's executive order eliminating birthright citizenship for children born to undocumented parents.[1155] The administration, however, did not seek judicial review on the merits of those decisions, which were not yet ripe for adjudication. Instead, it sought review on the emergency docket by challenging the district courts' authority to enter universal injunctions at all. Rather than require the cases to run their course, the Supreme Court accepted the petition and then ruled in the administration's favor, holding that district courts lacked the power to issue injunctions that applied to anyone other than the parties to the case, unless a broader remedy was needed to provide the plaintiffs with complete relief.[1156] As a result, the court entered partial stays of the district courts' orders, limiting them to the plaintiffs in the individual cases.[1157]

In the history of the federal judiciary, this was the first time the Supreme Court had ruled that lower courts lacked the authority to issue universal injunctions, thereby removing one more check on a president's abuse of authority. Senate Minority Leader Chuck Schumer of New York called the court's decision "a terrifying step towards authoritarianism."[1158] According to J. Michael Luttig, a retired judge appointed by President George H. W. Bush, the majority's ruling on this matter showed that the Roberts court was "acquiescing in and accommodating the president's lawlessness. And it is doing so without briefing, without argument, without deliberation—and without even a single word of explanation of its decisions."[1159] Luttig, who served as a law clerk to justices Antonin Scalia and Warren Burger, explained, "The Supreme Court was never intended to function like this. Never before has it entertained such challenges from the president, and never before has it decided them so flippantly." At precisely the moment when the country needed a strong judicial branch to protect the public from overreach by the executive branch, a majority of the justices were weakening it.

Unitary Executive Theory

The Supreme Court has also been receptive to Trump's arguments in favor of the unitary executive theory. The theory is based on the Constitution's vesting clause, in Article II, which states, "The executive Power shall be vested in a President of the United States of America." Advocates for the unitary executive theory argue that the vesting clause implies that *all* executive power belongs to the president. Taken to its logical conclusion, the unitary executive theory means that the president controls all decisions and all employees in the executive branch, and that he may fire any of them at will, including administrative law judges, inspectors general, commissioners, and civil servants, regardless of legislation to the contrary because Congress cannot take away power granted to the president by the Constitution. For a president seeking to maximize his power, the unitary executive theory prevents members of the "deep state"—that is, the professional civil service—from getting in his way.

One instance where the shadow docket met the unitary executive theory was in a case challenging the firing of employees from the Department of Education. In July 2025, the Supreme Court granted the Trump administration's petition to block a lower court order that would have reinstated 1,400 employees who had been fired from the department.[1160] In an executive order issued in March 2025, Trump had directed Linda McMahon, the education secretary, to "take all necessary steps to facilitate the closure of the Department of Education and return authority over education to the States and local communities."[1161] Because an act of Congress created the Department of Education, the plaintiffs in the subsequent lawsuit argued that the president could not dismantle it. The administration responded that it had the authority to fire employees to achieve efficiency and its preferred allocation of resources.

The Supreme Court's majority decided, in a one-paragraph, unsigned order on the shadow docket, to stay the district court's order and allow the employees to be fired immediately while the case worked its way through the court system.[1162] Dissenting, Justice Sotomayor wrote that the court was handing the president "the power to repeal statutes by firing all those necessary to carry them out." She scolded the majority for failing to rein in the president: "When the Executive publicly announces its intent to break the law, and then executes on that promise, it is the Judiciary's duty to check that lawlessness, not expedite it."[1163] Luttig described the court's complicity in Trump's conduct in even starker terms: "The chief justice is presiding over the end of the rule of law in America."[1164]

Local Government Officials

In addition to members of Congress and judges, Trump also attacked governors, mayors, and cities. Though the Republican Party long advocated for states' rights, those values seemed to evaporate during the second Trump administration.

Maine governor Janet Mills found her state under investigation after she verbally sparred with Trump at the White House.[1165] In February 2025, Trump was addressing the nation's governors when he asked if Maine's chief executive was in the room. A video of a transgender runner winning a track event in Maine had recently been circulating on social media. When Mills acknowledged that she was present, Trump told her, "Your population doesn't want men playing in women's sports." He then admonished her to "comply" with his recent order directing states to ban transgender athletes in women's sports, "because otherwise, you're not getting any federal funding." Mills replied, "I'll see you in court."[1166] Trump may have been upstaged in the moment, but that would not be their last encounter. His administration soon launched three investigations into Maine under Title IX, which prohibits discrimination in education based on sex.[1167] In addition, Attorney General Pam Bondi threatened officials in Maine and two other states unless they complied with Trump's order to ban transgender athletes.[1168] The probes and threats had the odor of retribution.

On the other coast of the United States, California public officials were ignored in June 2025 when they asked the Trump administration not to send military troops to counter protestors in Los Angeles. Nonetheless, Trump deployed two thousand members of the California National Guard, disregarding the statutory language that mandates, "Orders for these purposes shall be issued through the governors of the States."[1169] Governor Gavin Newsom said Trump did not contact his office to issue the order.[1170] Instead, Newsom said, the "move is purposefully inflammatory and will only escalate tensions."[1171] Trump said he would support arresting Newsom if necessary, prompting Newsom to call Trump's remarks an "unmistakable step toward authoritarianism."[1172] Los Angeles mayor Karen Bass called it an "unnecessary deployment" that caused a "chaotic escalation."[1173]

Sanctuary Cities

Trump's efforts to aggressively enforce immigration laws did not end in Los Angeles. The administration also filed lawsuits against cities that had implemented policies preventing local law enforcement agencies from assisting the federal government in its enforcement efforts. In July 2025, New York became the seventh such so-called "sanctuary" city to be sued by Trump.[1174] The lawsuit, which named Mayor Eric Adams despite his prior deal with the Trump administration, alleged that the Constitution's Supremacy Clause gave the federal government "well-established, pre-eminent and pre-emptive authority to regulate immigration."[1175]

While it is true that the federal government controls the enforcement of immigration laws and that state and local governments cannot interfere with federal enforcement, the federal government cannot commandeer state or city officials to act as its agents. Accordingly, city ordinances that prohibit ICE agents from entering local jails to question inmates or limit communication between federal and local law enforcement agents are legally permissible. Moreover, some view these local ordinances as effective policies for public safety and welfare. These laws are designed to encourage undocumented immigrants to seek medical care or report when they are victims of or witnesses to a crime.[1176] Two days after the administration filed the suit against New York, a federal court dismissed a similar lawsuit against the City of Chicago.[1177] In light of the weakness of the legal theory behind the suits, perhaps the real goal was to intimidate cities into cooperating with the far-right MAGA agenda—another move to mute critics and neutralize checks on Trump's power.

Asleep at the Wheel

When Volkswagen's executives failed to check the company's dishonest ambitions, the result was firings, prosecutions, and a thirty-three-billion-dollar payout in criminal penalties and compensatory damages. It was a steep price to pay for cheating consumers and regulators. But when checks on power fail, decisionmakers' worst instincts can run free.

Congress has many tools at its disposal to check a president who abuses power. Aside from impeachment, Congress can reject or delay a vote on nominees, refuse to fund initiatives, conduct oversight hearings, and even sue a president. The Republican-controlled Congress at the outset of Trump's second term did none of those things, allowing Trump to run roughshod over the American people. While courts often blocked Trump's executive orders, the president aggressively attacked the judiciary to undermine public confidence in the justice system. Through it all, when it did not actively aid Trump's agenda, the Supreme Court was mainly a sleeping giant. As Justice Ketanji Brown Jackson wrote in a dissenting opinion, "[R]ight when the Judiciary should be hunkering down to do all it can to preserve the law's constraints, the Court opts instead to make vindicating the rule of law and preventing manifestly injurious Government action as difficult as possible."[1178]

TEN

STRONGMEN AND SOFT POWER

Umar Farouk Abdulmutallab was long past having any concern for the 289 passengers on Flight 253.[1179] The twenty-one-year-old graduate student had boarded the plane in Amsterdam. With only the cash in his pocket, he had tried booking flights to Houston, Chicago, and some other US cities, but the fares were too expensive. Finally, he asked the desk clerk if there were any flights available for four hundred dollars. The response? Non-stop to Detroit.

That's how Abdulmutallab came to be seated in Seat 19A on a 737 over Woodhaven, Michigan, not far from Detroit's Metropolitan Airport, on Christmas morning in 2009. He had smuggled aboard a bomb contained in a plastic test tube by concealing it in his underwear. Technology would soon evolve to detect more than just metal at security checkpoints, but those advanced machines had not yet come to Amsterdam's Schiphol Airport. And so, having completed a cleansing ritual in the plane's restroom to prepare himself to meet his maker, Abdulmutallab put a blanket over his head and pressed the plunger of the bomb's syringe, a step that would combine explosive powders in the test tube between his legs and spark a deadly explosion. But fate intervened: The powders did ignite as Abdulmutallab expected, creating a fireball in his window seat next to the plane's wing, where the plane's fuel is stored. But instead of detonating a massive explosion that would take the plane down, as he had anticipated, the bomb managed to injure no one except Abdulmutallab himself. Passengers seated nearby and flight attendants pulled him from his seat and put out the blaze with fire extinguishers and water. While many of the passengers onboard had feared the worst when they saw fire and smoke and felt the plane lurch toward an emergency landing, they were relieved to land in Detroit without significant physical injuries.

I had been confirmed as US attorney for the Eastern District of Michigan just the day before and, suddenly, I had my first case. We had been lucky all around. The bomb had failed, no one besides Abdulmutallab was injured, and he had confessed to attempting to blow up the plane on behalf of al-Qaeda. Unlike most criminal defendants I have dealt with, Abdulmutallab expressed no remorse and did nothing to minimize his own criminal culpability. An outstanding team of agents and prosecutors assembled a case that resulted in his conviction and a life sentence in prison, but he made it easy for us. He admitted that he had become radicalized online by the sermons of Anwar Al-Awlaki, a US citizen who had become an al-Qaeda cleric. Abdulmutallab said he had traveled to Yemen to meet Awlaki and join his cause. Upon learning that Abdulmutallab spoke flawless English and had a valid US visa, Al-Awlaki had assigned him the task of using the bomb to blow up a US airliner over American soil, a mission Abdulmutallab readily agreed to perform.

It was when investigators asked Abdulmutallab how he could be willing to kill so many innocent civilians, even children, who were on the flight, that he said he was long past having any concern for others. All that mattered was completing his mission for al-Qaeda. In other words, the innocent victims were mere collateral damage.

I think of Abdulmutallab sometimes when I see people so consumed by one goal that they become blind to the other consequences of their actions. While I do not equate Donald Trump with Abdulmutallab, I do see his foreign policy as being so myopically focused on his own power and the MAGA agenda that he is missing the bigger picture of the negative consequences that will befall our country as a consequence.

Subverting Allies

Perhaps one of Trump's most shocking moves after retaking the White House in 2025 was his betrayal of America's Western allies. Since World War II, the United States has been a steadfast supporter of the North Atlantic Treaty Organization (NATO). This strategic alliance aims to ensure the collective defense of its member nations in Europe and North America.[1180] An attack against one member is seen as an attack against all, providing security through deterrence on both sides of the Atlantic. Although Ukraine is not a member of NATO, the organization considers Russia's 2014 annexation of Crimea and its 2022 invasion of Ukraine to be acts of aggression that threaten the entire region.[1181]

That's why Trump's public moves that appeared to side with Russian President Vladimir Putin were so jarring. Perhaps frustrated by his inability to end the war in Ukraine on "Day One" of his second term in office, as he promised repeatedly on the 2024 campaign trail,[1182] Trump brought his mob tactics to the negotiating table. The war provided Trump with leverage, and he was ready to use it. Trump demanded that—in exchange for the military aid already provided to Ukraine over the past three years—the former Soviet Republic grant the United States rights to its rare-earth and other minerals, which Trump claimed were worth five hundred billion dollars.[1183] *The New York Times* called the move an "overtly transactional and mercantilist stance toward resolving a conflict."[1184] Ukraine balked at giving up its mineral rights when Trump refused to make specific commitments in exchange.[1185] And so, Trump applied more leverage, threatening to cut off the country's access to Starlink, the satellite internet system owned by Elon Musk, which provided the nation with crucial military and civilian communications.[1186] Trump ridiculed his predecessor, President Joe Biden, for protecting the national security of members of the NATO alliance without demanding anything in exchange, consistent with traditional practice: "Biden just gave them money—there was no loan, there was no security, was no anything," Trump said, vowing to do things differently.[1187]

Of course, the United States has become a global superpower over the past eighty years precisely *because* it offers security to other countries without expecting payment in return. By providing military aid to allies, the US government strengthens those alliances because it makes the cost of attacking any one allied nation too steep. But mutual aid and diplomacy seem inconsistent with Trump's worldview regarding how favors are done—even military aid must be given only in exchange for something tangible of value in return.

When Trump's demands alone did not cause Ukrainian president Volodymyr Zelensky to capitulate, Trump applied further pressure. He publicly disparaged Zelensky, falsely claiming that his approval rating in Ukraine was 4 percent when, in fact, it was 52 percent.[1188] Trump also belittled Zelensky in a Truth Social post: "Think of it, a modestly successful comedian, Volodymyr Zelenskyy, talked the United States of America into spending $350 Billion, to go into a War that couldn't be won, that never had to start, but a War that he, without the US and 'TRUMP,' will never be able to settle."[1189] Trump's post inflated the amount spent on aid by a factor of three, and also threatened to abandon America's European allies altogether: "This War is far more important to Europe than it is to us," he wrote. "We have a big, beautiful Ocean as separation."[1190]

Trump went so far as to call Zelensky a dictator, parroting Russian talking points to delegitimize his leadership.[1191] Trump's remarks appear to have been based on Zelensky's cancellation of the country's 2024 election, consistent with provisions in Ukraine's constitution that prohibit elections during periods of martial law, which has been in place since Russia's invasion on February 24, 2022.[1192] Trump's remarks about Zelensky as a dictator stirred strong criticism from leaders in Germany, the United Kingdom, and Sweden.[1193] Remarkably, Trump even falsely stated that it was Zelensky who had started the war, claiming that the Ukrainian president was spinning "a web of disinformation" by accusing Russia of invading his country.[1194] During a Fox News interview, Trump said he was "tired" of hearing that Russia was to blame for the war: "Every time I say, 'Oh, it's not Russia's fault,' I always get slammed by the fake news."[1195]

One disturbing display of Trump's mob tactics occurred during a White House meeting with Zelensky in February 2025 that can only be described as a shakedown. This was the same meeting where a reporter questioned Zelensky's attire, the modest black shirt, pants, and boots he had worn in solidarity with his people since the Russian invasion, a visual reminder that his country was at war.[1196] When the Ukrainian president arrived for the meeting, Trump mocked Zelensky's wardrobe choice, telling the press, "He's all dressed up today." *Atlantic* writer Jonathan Chait compared Trump's condescension to the scene in the mob movie *Goodfellas* in which a made member of the Gambino crime family belittles Joe Pesci's character with nearly identical language.[1197] It seemed like an intimidation tactic aimed at gaining the upper hand.

Tag-teaming with Vice President J. D. Vance, Trump publicly humiliated Zelensky in the Oval Office meeting as television cameras captured the confrontation for the world to see.[1198] *New York Times* columnist Peter Baker called the meeting a "verbal brawl" that "startled Washington, unnerved Europe, outraged Kyiv and delighted Moscow."[1199] Trump again falsely accused Ukraine of starting the war.[1200] Chiding Zelensky for showing insufficient gratitude to the United States for providing military aid, Trump tried to coerce Zelensky into negotiating a peace deal with Russia, even threatening to abandon Ukraine altogether if Zelensky did not accept his terms.[1201] Trump diminished Ukraine's power at the bargaining table, telling Zelensky, "You've allowed yourself to be in a very bad position," and "You don't have the cards right now. With us, you start having cards."[1202] Vice President J. D. Vance was only too happy to play the role of attack dog, having previously said he didn't "really care about what happens to Ukraine one way or the other."[1203] During the Oval Office meeting, Vance derided Zelensky for failing to sufficiently thank Trump for his assistance and called Zelensky "disrespectful" even as he interrupted the Ukrainian president.[1204] The visit would end early with the cancellation of a planned press event.[1205]

Was Trump creating his own leverage as part of his dealmaking process, or was he doing Putin's bidding? And if so, why? Was it pure revenge—retaliation against Zelensky for failing to do Trump "a favor" during his first term in the White House? In 2019, Trump had pressured Zelensky to announce a baseless corruption investigation into Joe Biden and his son Hunter in exchange for releasing military aid to Ukraine, leading to Trump's first impeachment.[1206] Regardless of the reasons, Trump's posture toward Zelensky seemed to be a complete betrayal of America's alliances, and one with tremendously harmful consequences—elevating Putin, demoralizing Ukraine, prolonging the war, and destabilizing Europe. Trump seemed so determined to bring Zelensky to heel that he was willing to risk disastrous collateral consequences.

Deep Love for Strongmen

Trump's siding with Putin was a bizarre posture for an American president, but it was consistent with his long admiration for—and even envy of—strongmen. In contrast to his treatment of Zelensky, Trump literally gave Putin a red-carpet greeting when they met in Alaska to discuss Ukraine's fate—without the Ukrainian president.[1207] Since World War II, American diplomacy has sought to foster democracies worldwide, based on the conviction that they promote US interests by enhancing political stability, securing peace, promoting economic development, and mitigating refugee crises.[1208] Previous US presidents from both parties denounced authoritarian leaders who violate democratic norms and human rights. By contrast, Trump has praised dictators and even emulated them by attacking pillars of democracy, such as the press, universities, law firms, and the judiciary.

Trump has long expressed admiration for authoritarian leaders. In 2016, he publicly praised former Iraqi dictator Saddam Hussein, saying, "You know what he did well? He killed terrorists. He did that so good. They didn't read 'em the rights, they didn't talk. They were a terrorist; it was over."[1209] Of course, Husseins's regime was also a state sponsor of terrorism and killed civilians, including the gassing of five thousand Iraqi Kurdish men, women, and children.[1210] During Trump's first term, after Republican senators called North Korean dictator Kim Jong Un a "nut job," "tyrannical, and "a lunatic," Trump revealed that the two had exchanged "beautiful" letters and "fell in love."[1211] In 2018, Trump fawned over Chinese president Xi Jinping. According to Human Rights Watch, China has "no independent civil society, no freedom of expression, association, assembly or religion, and human rights defenders and other perceived critics of the government are persecuted."[1212] In addition, ethnic minorities are mistreated,[1213] the government controls the media, and "the Great Firewall" blocks access to information routinely searched on the internet.[1214] Yet Trump complimented Xi as a "strong man," a "King," and "president for life" who "controls 1.4 billion people with an iron fist." Trump added, "I think it's great. Maybe we'll give that a shot someday."[1215]

Perhaps the most significant similarities to the United States in democratic backsliding are found in Turkey and Hungary. In 2025, Trump raised eyebrows when he praised President Recep Tayyip Erdoğan of Turkey as "a good leader," without mentioning the recent arrest of the mayor of Istanbul—Erdoğan's political rival—and the resulting protests in Turkey.[1216] Since first being elected in 2003, Erdoğan has gradually evolved from a democratic leader into one who used his power as president to attack the media, the courts, and other democratic institutions.[1217] Erdoğan amended Turkey's constitution to weaken the judiciary. He purged government employees he labeled members of the "deep state" and replaced them with loyalists. He characterized his presidency as representing "the people's will" and refused to recognize checks on his power.[1218] The parallels to Trump are obvious.

In Hungary, Prime Minister Viktor Orbán has worked to undermine democracy since regaining power in 2010. According to former US ambassador to Hungary David Pressman, Orbán has weakened the independence of the judiciary, attacked the free press, and opened the door to corruption.[1219] Silencing critics has been essential to his power grab. For example, when Orbán dismantled the civil service, his supporters relentlessly attacked a young woman who spoke out against the move.[1220] According to Pressman, the Orbán regime sent "a clear message to anyone that the costs of disagreeing, the cost of engaging is so high. And as a result of that, a lot of people choose just not to."[1221]

Orbán has become something of a darling among MAGA supporters because of his embrace of far-right values. Orbán brags of his country's "illiberal democracy," in which he has cracked down on immigrants and the LGBT community.[1222] But Hungary offers a vital warning to the United States. Pressman has said that Hungary portrays itself as a "bulwark of conservatism" simply as a cover for corrupt politicians to grab more power.[1223] Orbán's government, Pressman says, claims to be "standing up for important values on issues that resonate with a lot of Americans, whether it's gays or guns or migration. But in fact, what's happening in Hungary isn't conservatism, it's corruption. And it's a system that's designed to enrich a clique of elites to take public assets and put them in private pockets while talking about standing up for conservative values."[1224] According to Pressman, Orbán seized power by transferring public assets to oligarchs, who have rewarded him by keeping him in power.[1225] During the 2024 presidential campaign, Trump hosted Orbán at his Mar-a-Lago home, heaping praise on the Hungarian prime minister, "There's nobody that's better, smarter, or a better leader than Viktor Orbán. He's fantastic . . . He's a non-controversial figure because he says, 'This is the way it's going to be,' and that's the end of it. Right? He's the boss."[1226]

In contrast to the regimes of these leaders, American democracy was founded on the idea of a chief executive with limited authority, with other branches of government having the power to hold him in check. Mimicking Erdoğan and Orbán is a gross distortion of a US president's constitutional powers. And disparaging democratic values in the United States can have repercussions in other countries. Historian Ruth Ben-Ghiat warns that the American president's descent into authoritarianism gives other leaders around the world permission to ignore democratic norms. "The moves of Trump in this same direction embolden foreign leaders who know the US is now an autocratic ally and there will be no consequences for repressive behavior."[1227]

Imperialism

In addition to mimicking other authoritarians, Trump also fantasizes about international conquest. "America First" isolationism was the focus of his first term, but in his second term, Trump promoted imperialism. Trump expressed admiration for William McKinley, issuing an executive order on his first day back in office to restore the name Mount McKinley to North America's highest peak, which had been known by its Indigenous name, Denali, since 2015.[1228] While Trump admired McKinley for his favorable views on tariffs, McKinley was also our most imperialist president, annexing Hawaii and taking Puerto Rico, Guam, and the Philippines in the Spanish-American War.[1229] Trump's order lauded McKinley for his "expansion of territorial gains for the Nation." Attempting to rename the "Gulf of Mexico" the "Gulf of America" was likewise a move that showed Trump's desire to dominate others.

Trump has spoken of buying Greenland, seizing the Panama Canal, and making Canada the "fifty-first state."[1230] Such statements are insulting to the sovereignty of other countries. Greenland is a territory of Denmark, a founding member of NATO and a longtime ally of the United States. The Panama Canal was turned over to the country that surrounds it in 1999, under terms negotiated by Jimmy Carter in 1977.[1231] And based on the volume of the booing of the crowds at NHL hockey games played north of the border when the US national anthem was played in the early months of 2025, it seems Canada is quite content to be independent of the United States.

Trump's strongman instincts were on full display when he authorized a military operation to arrest Venezuelan president Nicolás

Maduro. In a news conference to discuss the operation, Trump and his cabinet made it clear that intimidation and brute force had replaced the soft power of the twentieth century. Noting that Maduro could have left on his own terms rather than be forcibly removed, Secretary of Defense Pete Hegseth said, "He effed around and he found out."[1232] Trump mused aloud about expansionist policies toward Cuba, Colombia, Mexico, and Greenland, and called his strategy a corollary to the Monroe Doctrine.[1233] Of course, America's fifth president, James Monroe, sought to keep European powers out of the Western Hemisphere.[1234] Trump seems instead determined to control half of the planet. His take on the plan would be called, fittingly, the "Donroe Doctrine."[1235]

Trump has even expressed a desire to colonize outer space, stating during his inaugural address, "We will pursue our manifest destiny into the stars, launching American astronauts to plant the Stars and Stripes on the planet Mars."[1236] While space exploration and the scientific research it yields can bring numerous benefits to humanity, Trump's rhetoric sounded more interested in conquest than human progress.

One of Trumps most bizarre nods to colonialism came when he said he wanted to take ownership of the Gaza Strip— which would necessitate displacing approximately 1.8 million Palestinians—and turn it into "the Riviera of the Middle East."[1237] He then shared on social media an AI-generated video of what Gaza might look like under his control: The video contained scenes of a glitzy tower labeled "Trump Gaza," dollar bills raining down from the sky on a strolling Elon Musk, golden statues in Trump's likeness, and Trump lounging shirtless with Benjamin Netanyahu by a swimming pool, the two of them sipping fruity drinks.[1238] The video was a disgusting display of self-indulgence while tens of thousands of Palestinians were being slaughtered in Gaza.

It was often difficult to determine whether Trump was genuinely serious about his musings or was merely floating ideas to divert the public's attention away from unfavorable headlines. But at least one political activist thought imperialism appealed to Trump's young, male supporters: According to the late Charlie Kirk, the assassinated founder of the political group Turning Point USA and a MAGA ally, the idea of taking over territory "makes America dream again, that we're not just this sad, low-testosterone, beta male slouching in our chair, allowing the world to run over us. It is the resurrection of masculine American energy. It is the return of Manifest Destiny."[1239] While the idea of foreign conquest might excite some "alpha males," it was likely to wreak havoc on international relations. John Bolton, Trump's former national security adviser, said the president had no coherent foreign policy strategy. According to Bolton, Trump makes decisions that are "transactional, ad hoc, episodic, and really viewed from the prism of how it helps Donald Trump."[1240]

Tariffs

In addition to shaking up the world order with military force, Trump also imposed tariffs to obtain leverage against foreign trade partners. Trade deficits with other countries seemed to offend Trump's sense of entitlement to US dominance: "We have been ripped off for decades by nearly every country on Earth, and we will not let that happen any longer," Trump said during an address to Congress in March.[1241] "Other countries have used tariffs against us for decades, and now it's our turn to start using them against those other countries." According to Trump, tariffs—taxes imposed on imported goods—would protect US manufacturing, attract businesses to American shores, and generate revenue.[1242]

Some economists, however, warned that tariffs would only increase the costs of supplies, parts, and products for American businesses that would then be passed on to consumers in the form of higher prices.[1243] Scott Lincicome, a trade expert at the libertarian think tank the Cato Institute, said Trump's view on tariffs "reflects a fundamental misunderstanding of how the global economy works."[1244] In fact, Lincicome noted, the tariffs were essentially "taxes for American consumers and manufacturers."[1245] *The Wall Street Journal* called Trump's tariffs "The Dumbest Trade War in History."[1246] Also in the

Journal, former senator Phil Gramm and professor Donald J. Boudreaux, both economists, wrote that Trump's tariffs were based on "a series of verifiably false grievances." They predicted "a worldwide recession," in which "the US economy will be less efficient, economic growth will be stunted, and most Americans will be worse off."[1247] They noted that even McKinley, who championed tariffs in 1890, ultimately backed down when he realized that "commercial wars are unprofitable."[1248] Trump himself acknowledged that his plan would cause "a disturbance."[1249] In August 2025, an appeals court struck down some, but not all, of Trump's tariffs; the case would go on to the Supreme Court, which found the tariffs illegal in 2026.[1250]

For American businesses, the uncertainty surrounding tariffs made it difficult to plan for building plants, manufacturing products, or hiring workers, as they were unsure how much their production costs might rise. When Walmart warned that tariffs would require it to raise prices, Trump blasted the retail giant on social media, writing, "Walmart should STOP trying to blame Tariffs as the reason for raising prices throughout the chain. Walmart made BILLIONS OF DOLLARS last year, far more than expected. Between Walmart and China, they should, as is said, 'EAT THE TARIFFS,' and not charge valued customers ANYTHING. I'll be watching, and so will your customers!!!"[1251]

If tariffs were so unpopular—61 percent of Americans disapproved of them, with only 38 percent in favor[1252]—why was Trump willing to risk tanking the stock market and throwing the economy into turmoil? One reason may have been that he could use them to create leverage against trade partners to get them to agree to his demands.[1253] For example, he said he would impose 25 percent tariffs on Mexico and Canada to force them to stem the flow of immigrants and illegal drugs over their borders with the United States, even though the levies seemed unlikely to solve those problems. Tariffs were a weapon Trump threatened to use against foreign leaders to pressure them into giving him what he wanted: He threatened 50 percent tariffs on India if that country continued to buy Russian oil, not to punish India but to pressure Russia to negotiate a ceasefire with Ukraine.[1254]

Regardless of the domestic impact, Trump was willing to use tariffs to bend foreign governments to his will. He seemed to believe that any negative results to the stock market or the economy were mere short-term consequences—the cost of getting what he wanted.

In addition, tariffs provided a way for Trump to curry favor with MAGA supporters by stoking grievance. When announcing the tariffs, Trump stated, "For decades, our country has been looted, pillaged, raped and plundered by nations near and far, both friend and foe alike," he said. "American workers, auto workers, farmers, and skilled craftsmen—we have a lot of them here with us today—they really suffered gravely."[1255] *The New York Times* referred to America's trade partners as Trump's "trade hostages," noting that tariff deals gave Trump "the opportunity to flex his negotiating prowess in relatable terms and show off the splashy sums he is pulling into America, adding to the reality show intrigue of his trade agenda."[1256]

After several fits and starts for tariffs caused chaos in the stock market, Trump declared that April 2, 2025, would be known as "Liberation Day," when Americans would be freed from reliance on foreign goods. That day, Trump announced that, in addition to 10 percent tariffs on all trade partners, certain countries would also be required to pay "reciprocal" tariffs that punished them for their own trade barriers.[1257] The actual imposition of tariffs, however, would be delayed several more times as people reacted negatively to the news.[1258] In the meantime, the Trump administration negotiated tariff rates with various countries and the European Union. By "Liberation Day 3," August 1, 2025, Trump gave foreign trade partners six more days to negotiate deals or face severe rate increases, using an arbitrary deadline to raise the stakes. To secure better rates, Trump extracted additional promises from various nations: South Korea agreed to buy $100 billion dollars' worth of natural gas from the United States and invest another $350 billion in the country, Japan said it would establish a $550 billion fund for US investment, and the EU promised to pony up $600 billion dollars, though it was unclear how those funds would be used or whether the terms were enforceable.[1259] According to Steven Rattner, former counselor to the

US Treasury, fears of adverse economic consequences from Trump's tariffs likely played a role in a negative jobs report coinciding with the August 1 deadline.[1260] Trump's response was to fire the head of the Bureau of Labor Statistics, Erika McEntarfer, claiming without evidence that she had "rigged" the numbers.[1261] "Shooting the messenger"—a tactic once unimaginable in American politics—signaled that federal employees could now be axed simply for displeasing the boss. Trump's mob-style approach to governance meant that, under his rule, the first job of every federal employee was not to follow the old rules but to obey the new boss.

Columbia Business School professor Daniel Ames, who teaches negotiation strategy, said that foreign governments may simply have been exploiting Trump's vanity by offering eye-popping investment numbers that were, in fact, hollow promises. "Donald Trump is a gifted storyteller, and I think when his counterparts recognize this, they can play to it," Ames said. "If you're negotiating with a narcissist, you look for ways to make them feel like they've won."[1262] All the collateral damage Trump caused with tariffs seemed like merely an exercise in proving to the world that he was in charge.

Capturing Congress

Tariffs were most certainly not part of the conservative agenda leading up to Trump's presidencies. President Ronald Reagan, a supporter of open markets, warned of the harms caused by restrictions on free trade, which he said would "raise the costs of the goods and services that American consumers across the land would have to pay. They would invite retaliation by our trading partners abroad; would in turn lose jobs for those American workers in industries that would be the victims of such retaliation; would rekindle inflation; would strain international relations; and would impair the stability of the international financial and trading systems. The net result of these counterproductive proposals would not be to protect consumers or workers or farmers or businesses. In fact, just the reverse would happen. We would lose markets, we would lose jobs, and we would lose our prosperity."[1263] Yet, in 2025, the party of Reagan offered no objection when Trump imposed tariffs without authorization from Congress, an apparent violation of the Constitution's separation of powers. In fact, when an ad funded by the Province of Ontario accurately quoted Reagan's words, Trump called the message "fake" and halted trade talks with Canada.[1264]

Article I of the Constitution gives Congress the power "to lay and collect Taxes, Duties, Imposts and Excises."[1265] Trump justified his tariffs by invoking the International Emergency Economic Powers Act of 1977, arguing that Congress had delegated to the president the authority to impose tariffs when it enacted the statute.[1266] IEEPA, as it is known, authorizes the president (1) to regulate certain economic transactions (2) during a national emergency. Trump's tariffs were a stretch on both grounds.

First, IEEPA says nothing about tariffs. Most presidents have used IEEPA to impose sanctions against foreign governments, international terrorist organizations, or drug cartels by implementing trade embargoes or prohibiting financial transactions in the United States.[1267] Until Trump, no president had used IEEPA to levy tariffs.[1268] For example, Jimmy Carter used IEEPA to impose sanctions on the government of Iran during the 1979 hostage crisis. President George W. Bush invoked IEEPA to sanction the government of Iraq during the second Gulf War, and the Taliban after the 9/11 attacks.[1269] Nothing in the text of the statute suggests that it authorizes a president to levy tariffs.

Second, Trump's purported "emergency" was a trade deficit that had existed for decades.[1270] In response, the House Committee on Foreign Affairs reported that "emergencies are by their nature rare and brief, and are not to be equated with normal, ongoing problems."[1271] According to Ilya Somin, a libertarian law professor at George Mason University's Antonin Scalia Law School, Trump was "declaring utterly bogus emergencies for the sake of trying to expand his power, undermine the Constitution, and destroy civil liberties."[1272] While the chief executive needs to have emergency powers to take action during a genuine crisis, such powers can easily be abused.

According to Frank O. Bowman III, a University of Missouri law professor, "Declaring everything an emergency begins to move us in the direction of allowing the use of government force and violence against people you don't like."[1273]

In the 1952 landmark case of *Youngstown Sheet and Tube Company v. Sawyer*, the Supreme Court rejected President Harry S Truman's argument that he had the authority to seize steel mills during a labor strike because the Korean War created an emergency entitling him to do so as commander in chief.[1274] In a concurring opinion in that case, Justice Robert H. Jackson wrote that the Founding Fathers were suspicious of a powerful executive who might improperly exploit emergencies. The framers of the Constitution, he wrote, "knew what emergencies were, knew the pressures they engender for authoritative action, knew, too, how they afford a ready pretext for usurpation." In fact, he wrote, "emergency powers would tend to kindle emergencies."[1275] If a trade deficit could constitute an emergency sufficient to trigger IEEPA, it would give the president limitless powers to squeeze foreign governments at will.

Yet throughout months of confusion and lapsed deadline after lapsed deadline, Congress did not take action to prevent Trump from doing as he wished. In the absence of congressional pushback, private litigants went to the courts to challenge Trump's tariffs. In the spring of 2025, groups of businesses and states sued the Trump administration for abusing its authority under IEEPA. During oral argument, the US Court of International Trade expressed skepticism that IEEPA's emergency provisions were intended to create leverage for a trade deal. At the hearing, Senior Judge Jane A. Restani, a Reagan appointee, said, "It may be a very dandy plan, but it has to meet the statute."[1276] The three-judge panel found that the president lacked "unbounded authority" to impose tariffs on every country in the world.[1277] In response to the decision, a White House spokesman said, "It is not for unelected judges to decide how to properly address a national emergency."[1278] In fact, all federal judges are, of course, unelected, and blocking abuses of executive or legislative power is precisely what they are constitutionally commanded to do.

On appeal to the Federal Circuit Court of Appeals, an eleven-judge panel expressed skepticism regarding Trump's arguments, noting that IEEPA does not mention the word "tariffs."[1279] Said one judge during the hearing, "It's just hard for me to see that Congress intended to give the president in IEEPA the wholesale authority to throw out the tariff schedule that Congress has adopted after years of careful work, and revise every one of these tariff rates."[1280] The Supreme Court would later agree.

Soft Power

Full of bluster and swagger, Trump seems to enjoy wielding America's hard power—military strength and economic pressure. He has showed little regard for the value of soft power, the ability to influence world affairs through mutual respect and shared values.[1281] A term popularized by Harvard political science professor Joseph S. Nye Jr., "soft power" is achieved not through coercive tactics but through more subtle forms of influence, such as foreign aid and shared political values.[1282]

Hard power comes with potential negative consequences, such as fiscal costs, injuries and deaths of soldiers and civilians, and resentment that can deepen divisions or strengthen the power of authoritarian leaders by giving them a convenient enemy to blame for domestic problems.[1283] While hard power is a necessary option for the United States, it should not be the only option. Soft power has enabled the United States to "win hearts and minds" in other countries by providing a model of freedom, democracy, human rights, and the rule of law that citizens abroad seek to emulate.[1284]

Nye argued that voluntary cooperation achieved through soft power is more enduring than coercion achieved with hard power.[1285] For example, the United States accumulated soft power by helping to rebuild Europe after World War II. We gain soft power whenever we take in refugees or provide humanitarian aid, such as the assistance once administered by USAID.[1286] Food, medical assistance, and disaster relief all help build bonds of affection with the

United States, but USAID was one of the first agencies to be axed by DOGE. International broadcasting through the Voice of America, Radio Free Europe, and Radio Free Asia once helped spread the message of democracy and rebut propaganda and disinformation in foreign countries.[1287] Shortly after taking office, Trump defunded these outlets, on the grounds that their reporting was "biased."[1288] Kari Lake, Trump's adviser to the US Agency for Global Media, said her agency, which manages America's international outlets, was "not salvageable." "From top to bottom," Lake said, "this agency is a giant rot and burden to the American taxpayer."[1289] Such comments seem to miss the point of soft power.

One significant source of soft power is the education of international students in the United States.[1290] In 2023, more than 1.5 million international students studied in the United States. These students—future leaders in their respective countries—frequently return home with positive views of Americans and our values, which influence their thinking as they take the reins of power in business and government in their native countries. By attacking international students at US universities, Trump dismantled decades of accumulated soft power. Soft power also took a hit every time Trump took sides against an ally or disparaged one of our neighbors. While supporters of the MAGA movement may have enjoyed Trump's tough talk, the "masculine American energy" was damaging our hard-won alliances around the world—partnerships we may need in the future.

New World Order

As Trump ignored soft power and employed hard power ham-handedly to impose tariffs on other countries, we saw allies turning away from America and toward one another. Can you blame Mexico and Canada for losing faith in the United States after Trump breached his own first-term trade agreement with them? And why would any other country want to enter into a deal with Trump after he had made it clear he was willing to ignore his commitment to America's treaty obligations?[1291] Predictably, instead of relying on the United States, our traditional allies began negotiating trade and defense agreements without us. Jacob Funk Kirkegaard, a Brussels-based senior fellow at the Peterson Institute for International Economics, said that these countries shared the values of "predictable, rules-based international affairs—obviously a goal that the Trump administration no longer shares."[1292] In this situation," he said, "where the traditional, core western political and military institutions are being subject to neglect, or contempt, by the Trump administration, the European Union, but also the UK, Canada, Japan, are going to be looking to strengthen other channels."[1293]

When Trump stonewalled Zelensky, for instance, the Ukrainian president began seeking assistance from Canada and several European countries.[1294] By spring and summer of 2025, countries such as Japan, Canada, Great Britain, and the European Union were holding meetings without the United States. Britain and the EU reached agreements regarding access to markets as well as security and defense.[1295] Canada and Britain began working on military collaboration. Britain, Canada, Australia, New Zealand, and Norway collaborated to address Israeli misconduct in its war in Gaza by banning the travel and freezing the assets of two far-right Israeli government officials. In May 2025, Britain, France, and Canada banded together to issue a stern rebuke to Israel over the humanitarian crisis in Gaza.[1296] The EU worked to put together trade deals with India and countries in South America.[1297] All of this activity was being accomplished without the United States. In a pointed post on social media, EU trade commissioner Maros Sefcovic wrote, "We negotiate. We do not isolate."[1298]

By playing the role of a self-serving opportunist, Donald Trump succeeded mostly in alienating America from our allies. Even though it seemed unlikely that other countries would eliminate the United States as a global partner altogether, pursuing other agreements would reduce their reliance on an unreliable administration. According to Kirkegaard, "America first means America first, even if it means America more alone."[1299]

It's a Small World

Umar Farouk Abdulmutallab was sentenced to life in prison. He now spends his days at the supermax prison in Florence, Colorado, the nation's most secure federal penitentiary. I sometimes wonder whether he regrets his mission and his complete disregard for the consequences of his actions.

Likewise, on the world stage, the Trump regime sometimes seems to cut off its nose to spite its face. All of the "deals" Trump rolled up seemed to cause more damage to the United States than benefit; vague, undocumented billion-dollar deals with foreign governments were Pyrrhic victories at best. Trump's chest-thumping style may appeal to MAGA followers, but it's hard to imagine that abandoning allies, imposing tariffs, deposing leaders, seizing oil, and dismantling decades of goodwill built with soft power were worth whatever advantage they gained. When the world is viewed through the transactional lens of personal gain, the only question becomes, "What's in it for me?" By contrast, diplomacy achieves goals both for the nation and its allies. It requires patience, partnerships, and collaboration—skills Trump has never demonstrated and for which he seems to have no respect. In the end, he might get what he wants on foreign policy, but the collateral damage will far exceed whatever benefits his policies could achieve.

PART III

How We Take It Back

ELEVEN

LESSONS FROM HISTORY

In 1980, 50 percent of deaths from car accidents involved alcohol.[1300] As a high school student at the time, I can remember the way people would shrug at drunk drivers: What could you do about people who liked to stop at the bar on their way home from work and tip a few? Judges would frequently let drunk drivers off with a slap on the wrist. But that all changed after one mother decided she had seen enough.

One evening, as Candace Lightner's thirteen-year-old daughter, Cari, walked down the street with a friend, a three-time offender for driving under the influence came barreling down the road. His car hit Cari so hard that she was knocked out of her shoes and thrown 125 feet through the air to her death. Determined to prevent other children from suffering a similar fate, Candace would lobby her state legislature to increase penalties for endangering the lives of others. Cari would become the face of the thousands of innocent victims killed by drunk drivers every year. Soon, others would join Candace Lightner's effort in the organization that became known as MADD—Mothers Against Drunk Driving. Its mission was to help victims and their families and also to "increase public awareness of the problem of drunk and drugged driving."[1301] With press conferences, candlelight vigils, public demonstrations, victim impact panels, youth summits, court monitoring, and billboards, MADD successfully lobbied for federal legislation that provided $125 million in incentive grants requiring states to pass laws to curtail drunk driving, such as license revocation and legal limits on blood alcohol levels for drivers.[1302] Subsequent legislation would raise the drinking age to twenty-one and implement "zero-tolerance" laws for drinking by drivers under that age.[1303] MADD popularized the term "designated driver" and changed the terminology from car "accident" to "crash" to emphasize the preventable nature of drunk driving; the organization would later partner with professional sports leagues and Waymo, the autonomous vehicle rideshare company. Over time, MADD helped normalize the idea that drunk driving was not only criminal but also socially unacceptable. Today, about 30 percent of car crashes involve alcohol[1304]—still far too many, but a significant reduction thanks to the work of MADD, which has saved thousands of victims whose lives were not taken by a drunk driver.

I find the MADD story inspiring. It shows what a determined group of citizens at the grassroots level can accomplish with hard work and strong motivation, and it reminds me that we have the power in our democracy to shape policy and change outcomes, even regarding matters of life and death.

When it comes to the corruption of our democracy, we have similar power to effect change. Since our nation's founding, ordinary Americans have successfully fought to end slavery, for the right to vote, for access to public education, to legally marry the person they love, and for other measures toward fulfilling the promise of America. Similarly, we each have the power to move our country forward in a way that serves all Americans, not toward a restoration of what was but toward a vision of what can be: a more perfect union. Lessons from history provide a starting point for new ideas and a source of hope for success.

History also shows that criminals, even mob families, can be brought down. No one solution works for all crimes, but exposure of wrongdoing, legislative changes, prevention efforts, collective action, accountability, and courage all have a role to play.

The Progressive Era

One era of history that parallels our own, of course, is the Gilded Age, when robber barons became fabulously wealthy through rapacious capitalism. As described earlier, high tariffs in this era protected American corporations from foreign competition.[1305] Collusion within industries, among companies sometimes governed by the same boards of directors, drove out domestic competition and allowed corporations to achieve monopoly power. Not only does such power drive out other companies, in the absence of competition, monopolistic control of an industry often leads to products of lower quality and higher prices that gouge customers.

During the Gilded Age, corporate leaders paid bribes to politicians to secure favorable treatment, often at the expense of workers and consumers.[1306] Forty percent of industrial laborers earned wages below the poverty level of five hundred dollars per year, while tariffs raised consumer prices by as much as 50 percent.[1307] Meanwhile, wealthy families like the Vanderbilts engaged in conspicuous consumption, throwing lavish balls at their Fifth Avenue mansions with the aim to outdo each other for coverage in the society pages of newspapers—a profound change of tone for a country founded on the idea of equality.[1308] There would be no more life of dignified restraint for these captains of industry. Consequently, according to Holy Cross history professor Edward T. O'Donnell, farmers and workers felt the system was exploiting them by allowing the wealthy to extract all of the profit from their labor.[1309] This was the America of President William McKinley, the subject of Donald Trump's admiration. Today, of course, we see echoes of those wealth disparities, in Meta's Mark Zuckerberg donning a sequined jumpsuit to serenade his wife at a no-holds-barred birthday party and Amazon's Jeff Bezos taking over Venice for a destination wedding attended by celebrities and wealthy elites.[1310] It is not enough for them to be fabulously wealthy; they want to also make sure the rest of us can see their riches and envy them.

McKinley's successor, Theodore Roosevelt, had different ideas. He championed reform and ushered in the Progressive Era, a time that offers important lessons for our own.[1311] According to historian Richard Hofstadter, the Progressive Era sought to "restore a type of economic individualism and political democracy that was widely believed to have existed earlier in America and to have been destroyed by the great corporation and the corrupt political machine."[1312] Roosevelt, who assumed office upon McKinley's assassination, won reelection in 1904 by campaigning for a "square deal" for ordinary Americans, a platform that would rein in corporate greed, protect consumers, and even conserve natural resources—outcomes we could use today.[1313] Known as a "trust buster," Roosevelt vigorously enforced antitrust laws to break up monopoly power that harmed consumers. The term "trust" came to be used for large corporate entities when Standard Oil used the trust as a corporate structure to avoid various state tax laws.[1314] During his political career, Roosevelt advocated for workers' compensation, child labor laws, the eight-hour workday, and pure food and drug laws.[1315] Roosevelt was also known as "the conservation president," doubling the number of national parks and signing legislation that allowed presidents to designate national monuments.[1316] When laying the cornerstone for Yellowstone National Park in Wyoming in 1903, Roosevelt said, "I cannot too often repeat that the essential feature in the present management of the Yellowstone Park, as in all similar places, is its essential democracy—it is the preservation of the scenery, of the forests, of the wilderness life and the wilderness game for the people as a whole, instead of leaving the enjoyment thereof to be confined to the very rich who can control private reserves."[1317] Making government work for all Americans—not just the wealthy—was a hallmark of the Progressive Era.

Roosevelt's successors continued reforms. William Howard Taft pushed for reduced tariffs and the implementation of a progressive income tax. Woodrow Wilson pursued a similar agenda, resulting in the creation of the Federal Trade Commission to protect consumers and the passing of the Clayton Act, which further restricted monopolies. The Progressive Era also increased the democratic power of the people with the 1913 passage of the Seventeenth Amendment, which empowered voters to elect US senators directly, and the 1920 ratification of the Nineteenth Amendment, which granted women the right to vote.[1318] These changes were the result of leadership and political will. We can surely achieve similar reforms today. As detailed in the following chapter, economic and policy changes can help us restore the balance of wealth and power.

One catalyst for change was public awareness. Muckraking journalists and other writers in the Progressive Era helped expose the corruption and inequities in society.[1319] One of these investigative reporters was Ida Tarbell, who wrote a nineteen-part series for *McClure's* magazine exposing the strong-arm tactics of Standard Oil. In 1911, the Supreme Court found Standard Oil in violation of the Sherman Act, which prohibits harmful monopolies, and ordered it to be broken up into thirty-four smaller companies.[1320] Tarbell also wrote a book called *The Tariff in Our Times*, which demonstrated how tariffs benefited trusts and harmed consumers.[1321]Also in this era, Upton Sinclair's *The Jungle* exposed hazardous working conditions and food contamination in the meatpacking industry. The book led to the enactment of the Meat Inspection Act and the Pure Food and Drug Act in 1906.[1322] Even before the Progressivist heyday, Jacob Riis's 1890 book *How the Other Half Lives* revealed the living conditions of immigrants and working-class Americans in the slums of New York. The book contained shocking photos of families living in squalor in crowded tenements, highlighting the wealth disparity between the haves and have-nots in American society.[1323] All of these writers influenced Theodore Roosevelt, who even toured the tenements of New York with Riis.[1324]

Today's journalists play an essential role in reporting on misconduct and informing the public about the consequences of MAGA policies and tactics. There is a reason the president has targeted media outlets for vengeance and abuse: They have the platform to expose the ways in which his government is harming the public. Unmuzzling these witnesses to history is an integral part of the fix.

The lessons of the Progressive Era offer inspiration for this moment. The political reforms of that era were successful because of an alliance between populists and progressives. As writer David Brooks has noted, such a union of political interests "has the benefit of scrambling outdated twentieth-century categories of left and right, and could help promote the notion that we are one nation, culturally cohesive but economically and demographically diverse. It rejects the Trumpian idea that we are sentenced to an endless class or culture war."[1325]

Two World Wars

One of the most important lessons of the twentieth century was the need for alliances to promote peace. The United Nations was formed in the aftermath of World War II, which took an astonishing sixty million lives—fifteen million service members and forty-five million civilians worldwide.[1326] That death toll was nearly triple the number from World War I, when a then-shocking twenty-one million people died.[1327] Its moniker as "the war to end all wars" was short-lived.[1328] Following World War II, leaders sought to avoid such bloodshed in the future by forming the United Nations. The UN Charter recognizes the sovereignty of member nations, prohibits unprovoked aggression, and promotes peaceful resolutions to disputes.[1329]

Trump's attack on Venezuela was a blatant violation of these principles. By ignoring the lessons of the twentieth century, Trump's muscular approach to international diplomacy risks catastrophic results. As political commentator David French wrote, Trump's 2026 military operation to capture Venezuelan president Nicolás Maduro was the kind of "gunboat diplomacy" that was used before we learned the hazards of imperialism. "The Venezuela attack," he wrote, "harks back to a different time, before the nineteenth-century world order unraveled, before two catastrophic world wars and before the creation of international legal and diplomatic structures designed to stop nations from doing exactly what the United States just did."[1330] Trump's flex of US military power seemed to be another part of his worldview: using power to get what he wants. As French warned, "When a strong state operates under the principle that war is just another extension of policy, it is tempted to operate a bit like a mob boss. Every interaction with a weaker nation is tinged in some way with the threat of force: Nice little country you have there — shame if something happened to it."[1331] Indeed, when the Trump administration anointed Maduro's vice president Delcy Rodríguez to lead Venezuela, Trump said, "If she doesn't do what's right, she is going to pay a very big price, probably bigger than Maduro."[1332] Secretary of State Marco Rubio echoed the intimidation theme, explaining that ongoing US naval presence in the region would provide "leverage" over Rodriguez.[1333] Threats, intimidation, and brute force have replaced the diplomacy and alliances of the past eighty years.

But those who forget history, as the saying goes, are doomed to repeat it. We must remember the lessons—and the profound loss of life—from those two massive wars. Alliance and diplomacy, not military aggression, are the path to peace and security. In addition to the United Nations, the North Atlantic Treaty Organization also assures safety in numbers. By providing a commitment to collective defense, NATO serves as a deterrent for an attack on any of its members. As tempting as it may be to seize natural resources from other countries and assert our control over them, surrendering to short-term gains risks long-term harms as the world becomes a more dangerous place. By violating international law and norms, the United States loses its moral authority as a model democracy and gives license to other countries to do the same. As we learned after World War II, the path to enduring peace is through respect for the self-determination of sovereign nations, fidelity to alliances, and collective defense to deter military aggression. We must elect leaders who share that vision.

World War II Accountability

The defeat of fascism in the mid-twentieth century, likewise still offers valuable lessons today. A critical component of restoring world order after World War II was holding accountable the individuals responsible for committing atrocities. The Trial of the Major War Criminals before the International Military Tribunal (also known as the Nuremberg Trials), held over almost a year from 1945 to 1946, laid bare to the world the crimes against humanity that were committed by twenty-two German military and political leaders.[1334] Robert H. Jackson, on a highly unusual leave of absence from his position as a Supreme Court justice, served as the lead prosecutor.[1335] In his opening statement, Jackson explained the importance of holding the Nazis accountable: "We are able to do away with domestic tyranny and violence and aggression by those in power against the rights of their own people only when we make all men answerable to the law."[1336]

While the misconduct of the Trump administration is certainly not comparable to the persecution, torture, and genocide of more than ten million people, accountability for wrongdoing is still essential. As in other criminal cases, punishment serves to protect the public from future misconduct by deterring others from engaging in similar behavior and provides some measure of justice to victims. While prosecution cannot undo the harms of the crimes themselves, judgment announces to the world that what the perpetrator did was wrong. Importantly, accountability also provides a historical record from which society can learn and respond by implementing reforms. That history records—and condemns—the horrors of the Nazi regime is due in no small part to the Nuremberg trials.

Efforts to hold Trump accountable for his efforts to subvert the 2020 election were cut short when Trump was reelected president in 2024; special counsel Jack Smith dismissed the cases against Trump because of the Justice Department's view that a sitting president cannot be prosecuted. But both the election interference case and the government documents case charged serious criminal conduct, and both can and should be resuscitated when Trump leaves office in 2029. One could imagine that the incoming administration in 2029—whether Republican or Democratic—may be inclined to turn the page rather than dwell on the past. Recall Gerald Ford's desire to end Watergate's "long national nightmare."[1337] Perhaps that makes sense for political reasons. But allowing the Trump regime to escape accountability would be a mistake, in my view, because it would send a message that Americans will tolerate politicians who abuse us and our democratic system. It would reward Oliver Wendell Holmes's "bad man" who seeks to exploit the system rather than act in good faith to comply with it. Letting Donald Trump off the hook would also allow him to rewrite history by claiming that he was exonerated of any crime when he most certainly was not. While the Supreme Court has ruled that a former president is immune from criminal prosecution, its decision was limited to conduct committed in the scope of his official duties. Smith had presented a compelling case that his superseding indictment, which removed allegations relating to Trump's official conduct, was viable despite the Court's opinion.[1338] Only by pursuing the case after Trump leaves office can the people hold Trump accountable for his alleged corruption, which was profound—a conspiracy to subvert democracy itself.

Reconstruction and the Civil Rights Movement

Contrary to Trump's 2025 criticism that America's Smithsonian museums devoted too much focus to "how bad slavery was," in my view, the enslavement of our fellow Americans was such a distortion of the principles we claim to cherish that I believe the topic cannot be featured enough. The denial of freedom and equality to an entire segment of society based on race was a defining feature of American history; the fact that it was so reprehensible makes it all the more important that we do not forget that shameful chapter of our nation's past, so that we can continue to learn from it. We can always benefit from the stories of society's oppression, resistance, and reform.

One of the lessons of the Reconstruction Era is that winning a war does not necessarily lead to immediate change. Following the Civil War, the South still harbored great resistance to recognizing the full citizenship of African Americans. Emancipation in the 1860s gave hope to formerly enslaved Americans and their allies, but equality did not come quickly or easily. Amendments to the Constitution eliminated slavery, gave citizenship to formerly enslaved people, and purported to give all citizens equal protection of the law—but that was not the end of the story. Following the Civil War, Reconstruction quickly gave way to the era of Jim Crow, during which domestic terrorism against Blacks—rape, arson, mob attacks, and lynching—was common and widespread.[1339] Authorities in the South maintained white supremacy by suppressing voting rights for Black men and overlooking crimes committed against Black citizens. Ku Klux Klan members attacked fellow Americans who exercised their newly won rights by doing things such as running for public office.[1340] Jim Crow laws segregated and discriminated against Black Americans, forcing them to attend separate—and inferior—schools, and to use separate parks, hotels, restrooms, restaurants, and drinking fountains.[1341] Trains and buses had separate sections: "Whites Only" and "Colored."[1342] It would be almost another hundred years before the Civil Rights Act and Voting Rights Act of the 1960s brought about significant change for Black Americans.

Some of the strategies that succeeded in bringing about change during the civil rights movement of the mid-twentieth century were nonviolent resistance and public awareness. Martin Luther King Jr. wrote that "the Christian doctrine of love operating through the Gandhian method of nonviolence was one of the most potent weapons available to oppressed people in their struggle for freedom."[1343] A key to King's strategy was gaining the "friendship and understanding" of those with opposing viewpoints rather than humiliating them.[1344] He preached understanding, not hate, and "a deep faith in the future."[1345] In our highly polarized times, when candidates and public officials seem to deliberately stoke division in society for political gain, finding friendship and understanding with our rivals seems almost out of reach. However, if we, the people, are to reclaim our power, we must resist the efforts of political leaders to divide and conquer us. Only by banding together across racial, religious, gender, geographic, and economic divides can we reclaim our power.

As with the Progressive Era, another essential element of the civil rights movement's success was raising public awareness. But by the middle of the twentieth century, the media were not confined to newspaper articles and books. Television provided a powerful medium for showing people across the country the grim reality of life in the South. Seeing images of well-dressed young Black men, women, and even children, being doused with fire hoses or attacked by police dogs while protesting for their rights shocked viewers, showing that respect for human dignity was more important than any racial divide. In today's splintered media environment, it is more difficult to break through with messages or stories than it was in the early 1900s or even the 1960s. Still, a media campaign focused on the plight of working-class families, immigrants, rural Americans, or people living in poverty can cross political divides. We can reach people where they are by using today's preferred modes of communication, such as podcasts and social media. Hate-laced rants about immigrants, minorities, and members of the transgender community are a tactic designed to pit Americans against each other. To reclaim our collective power, we need to overcome the political rhetoric that divides us.

Post-Watergate Reforms

Another era of American history that can be instructive is the post-Watergate years. Richard Nixon was forced to resign as president over the scandal, in which, in an effort to obtain intelligence against Nixon's political opponents, campaign-funded burglars broke into the Democratic National Committee headquarters in the Watergate office complex to install listening devices and were caught by a night watchman. Nixon's complicity in the cover-up was revealed in a conversation that occurred in the Oval Office and was captured on a tape recorder, which was equipped to capture conversations automatically.[1346] In one recording, Nixon could be heard agreeing with a plan to have the CIA instruct the FBI to stand down in its investigation of the financing of the break-in.[1347] Battles over the release of the Nixon tapes to the congressional committee investigating the scandal led to "the Saturday Night Massacre," in which Nixon directed Attorney General Elliott Richardson to fire Special Counsel Archibald Cox. Richardson refused and resigned, as did his deputy, William Ruckelshaus. The next leader in line at the Justice Department, Robert Bork, finally lowered the axe on Cox but refused to eliminate the special counsel's office. Soon, Leon Jaworski replaced Cox, and public outrage made it clear that Nixon's days in office were numbered.[1348] Urged to leave office by members of his own Republican party, he resigned to avoid impeachment.[1349]

Like the business scandals of the Progressive Era and the brutal repression of the civil rights movement, the Watergate saga also came to the public's attention through the work of the media. Investigative reporters Bob Woodward and Carl Bernstein of *The Washington Post* helped connect the Watergate burglary with Nixon's reelection campaign.[1350] Their reporting in the *Post* gave the story visibility as congressional hearings were getting underway.[1351] Exposing wrongdoing in any form has a significant impact on public opinion.

Sparked by public outcry over the scandal, Congress enacted several reforms to improve transparency and promote integrity. The Presidential Records Act of 1978 made it clear that government records belong to the people, not the president, and set standards for creating, accessing, and maintaining public records.[1352] The act provided that memos or recordings documenting official presidential meetings and other government activities belonged to the people and were to be safeguarded by the National Archives. The Ethics in Government Act, also passed in 1978, introduced financial disclosure requirements and conflict-of-interest rules for federal officials.[1353] In addition, the White House and the Justice Department implemented policies to enhance DOJ's independence from political influence.

Also in the 1970s, the Senate's Church Committee uncovered abuses perpetrated by the FBI. Named for Senator Frank Church, the committee found that the FBI had engaged in invasive activities as part of an operation dubbed COINTELPRO (Counterintelligence Program).[1354] Formed to investigate national security threats during the Cold War, COINTELPRO eventually began targeting American civil rights leaders such as Martin Luther King, Vietnam War protesters, and individuals suspected of being "subversives."[1355] The Church Committee found that the FBI worked to "divide, confuse," and "weaken" domestic groups, in part by gathering and disclosing disparaging information about their leaders.[1356] The abuses of COINTELPRO led to reforms such as the Foreign Intelligence Surveillance Act, which created rules governing wiretapping for national security purposes. Later, DOJ issued the *Attorney General's Guidelines for Domestic FBI Operations* (the "AG Guidelines")[1357] and the FBI's *Domestic Investigations Operations Guide*,[1358] or the "DIOG," as it is known within the federal law enforcement community. The DIOG requires FBI personnel "to ensure that all investigations and intelligence collection activities are conducted within constitutional and statutory parameters and that civil liberties and privacy are protected."[1359] For example, the DIOG prohibits any "investigation based solely on the exercise of First Amendment rights."[1360]

These examples illustrate that while reforms to the Justice Department are challenging, they are not impossible. According to Jack Goldsmith, a former DOJ official in the administration of George W. Bush, "This is the hardest of issues because the Constitution charges the president with enforcing the law. So, the DOJ can never be fully legally independent, and indeed, we wouldn't want it to be, since the president's law enforcement priorities are an important element of democratic governance. What one wants to avoid is corruption and politicization in law enforcement." Learning from the reforms of the post-Watergate era, Goldsmith says, "The reform solution going forward is to make crystal clear where the lines of independence lie; to back up those lines where possible with criminal prohibitions, which is tricky but doable; and to ensure that the lines of independence are articulated clearly throughout the executive branch." As described in the next chapter, we can follow this guidance by codifying the rules regarding communication and the Principles of Federal Prosecution.[1361]

Lessons from Around the World

Besides examining our own past, we can also learn lessons from the experiences of other countries, where democracies have emerged after periods of backsliding and even dictatorships. The history of authoritarians is instructive. Political scientist Marcel Dirsus, author of *How Tyrants Fall: And How Nations Survive*, defines tyrants as leaders who "govern with brutality in one form or another."[1362] Based on his ruthless and often lawless treatment of immigrants and perceived enemies, Donald Trump meets that definition. Informed by the fates of authoritarian governments throughout history, Dirsus concludes that dictators do not last forever. "Tyrants are much more vulnerable than they seem," Dirsus says. "And in recent years we have wasted far too much time talking about the fragility of democracies, and not enough about the fragility and weaknesses of dictatorships."[1363]

According to Dirsus, the most effective way to overthrow a tyrant is through nonviolent protest movements. Dirsus cites the work of Harvard government professor Erica Chenoweth, who has studied resistance campaigns in 389 countries between 1945 and 2014 and has developed a "3.5 Percent Rule."[1364] The rule notes that when just 3.5 percent of a country's population mobilizes in nonviolent protest against authoritarian regimes, their movements have largely succeeded in ousting those regimes in favor of democratic forms of government. That is an astonishingly low threshold, one that should give hope to nonviolent protest movements in the United States.

In their book, *Why Civil Resistance Works: The Strategic Logic of Nonviolent Conflict*, Chenoweth and political scientist Maria J. Stephan dissect case studies from several countries to understand the reasons for the success of nonviolent movements.[1365] First, nonviolent protest movements can attract large numbers of participants.[1366] Many people are reluctant to oppose their government in ways that might draw attention to themselves, fearing arrest, physical harm, or retribution. Political violence is a dangerous nonstarter that would betray American democracy, and, according to Chenoweth and Stephan, fails to reliably achieve an effective, durable, and peaceful democracy. However, speaking out has become increasingly risky in the United States, where we have seen politicians, members of the media, law firms, intellectuals, and Congress bow to pressure. Some scholars have left the country due to the political climate: Professors Timothy Snyder, Marci Shore, and Jason Stanley, all experts in authoritarianism, resigned from their posts at Yale University to take positions in Toronto.[1367] Rutgers history professor Mark Bray, who studies fascism and resistance movements that form against it, moved his family from New Jersey to Spain because of death threats.[1368] Ordinary people may feel even less empowered to sign their name to a letter to the editor or an opinion piece that criticizes the government. Peaceful protest, on the other hand, while not risk-free, has a relatively low barrier to entry and minimal risk. Peaceful protestors derive a sense of safety in numbers and in the relative anonymity that comes with holding a sign or marching with like-minded citizens. Importantly, the power of numbers also helps bolster the resolve of those who are in the fight.

Second, nonviolent mobilization works because a diverse protest movement can raise challenges to an authoritarian regime across multiple issues, making it difficult to ignore or defeat.[1369] When resistance movements encompass multiple demographic groups, characterized by various factors such as age, gender, race, and class, they amplify their collective power. Some people may mobilize in support of immigration policy, while others may be more inclined to address issues such as academic freedom or voting rights. Nonviolent protest has room at the table for everyone to push back on multiple fronts. It would be delicious irony to see Donald Trump's MAGA movement defeated by diversity itself.[1370]

Third, large and diverse opposition groups can employ a variety of tactics that can frustrate the government's efforts. Marches, social media campaigns, boycotts, sit-ins, leafleting, town hall meetings, and other activities can frustrate a government that must constantly choose how and whether to respond.[1371] While not every message will break through to the public consciousness, some of them will.

Fourth, when Americans observe their friends, neighbors, or others with whom they identify participating in a protest, they become inclined to sympathize with the cause. When someone we know and respect expresses an opinion, we are more likely to consider the merits of their view. Even those who do not march in the streets may become unified in spirit with the protesters. This can have a persuasive effect at election time.

As an example, we can look to the not-so-distant past in Chile. The South American country successfully ousted its authoritarian leader, Augusto Pinochet, in 1990 through protests and the mobilization of civil society. Pinochet, who was declared president by a military junta in 1974, confined dissidents to concentration camps and "disappeared" his political enemies, capturing the press and business elites to silence his critics. A new constitution in 1980 allowed him to remain in office after his term ended. By 1988, believing he was impervious to electoral defeat, El Generalissimo called for a presidential election. He had no opponent, mind you; he simply wanted a referendum to reaffirm his own presidency. The public took the opening and organized mass protests. A key to the success of the movement in Chile was the participation of wide swaths of society—not just idealistic and risk-taking university students but also faith leaders, union heads, businesspeople, and professionals, such as doctors and dentists. The archbishop of the Catholic Church in Santiago spoke out, giving the cause moral authority. Crowds at soccer matches began to chant for the leader's ouster. Political factions set aside their differences to unite in ousting Pinochet from office. The following year, fair elections restored democracy to Chile. The people, through mass protest and coalition building, had regained power.[1372]

In the United States, it will take dedicated organizing to build alliances with a sufficient number of people to oust MAGA extremists. To get there, we can learn the lesson of Chile: If we can set aside differences and form coalitions, we can focus on the aspects of democratic society that matter most—the democratic process and the rule of law. Regardless of where we stand on policy matters, we must work to build unity in supporting the free press, independent courts, a robust Congress, business autonomy, scientific research, and free expression in the arts.

Marcel Dirsus cites another reason that nonviolent demonstrations succeed: They give an administration no good options. "Mass protests can be very effective, even in deeply entrenched authoritarian regimes. If enough people take to the streets, the regime is forced to make a decision: either allow the protests to continue, which shows they are not in control, or use violence to suppress them. However, using violence risks causing a backlash and could weaken their coalition because of the cost of repression."[1373] As one world leader has observed, "History proves all dictatorships, all authoritarian forms of government, are transitory. Only democratic systems are not transitory." That leader? Someone who understands the threat of public protests: Vladimir Putin.[1374]

A peaceful protest movement also contributed to the downfall of Ferdinand Marcos, the dictator who dismantled democracy in the Philippines. During his two decades as president, Marcos established martial law, punished his critics, and crushed institutions that could check his power. His abuses of power enabled him to corruptly appropriate public funds for himself and his allies but led to economic ruin for his country.[1375] When Filipinos decided they had had enough, they rose up through a movement called "People Power."[1376] For three days in February 1986, hundreds of thousands of citizens took to the streets to protest Marcos and his false claim that he had defeated Corazon Aquino in the recent presidential election.[1377] Activists in the People Power movement had been working for years to publicize Marcos's unjust enrichment at the expense of the populace.[1378] When Marcos ordered the military to clear protesters, some soldiers refused. The nation's Catholic radio station helped to spread the news of the protest movement.[1379] The protests caused the United States to withdraw its support of Marcos, and he was forced into exile.[1380] The People Power Revolution was a vivid reminder that in a democracy, authority derives from the people.

Another important lesson from other countries is about the "cult of personality," wherein a government is centered around its leader. One way dictatorships end is with the demise of the dictator: When a charismatic leader leaves office or dies of natural causes, it is often impossible to replace him. For example, when the fascist leader Francisco Franco died in 1975, Spain transitioned quickly to a democracy.[1381] Trump will not remain in office forever, and, as University of Florida law professor Neil Buchanan put it, his "life expectancy is certainly not measured in decades."[1382]

Of course, we cannot simply hope that Trump's exit from the political stage will immediately collapse the MAGA movement and restore democracy. We can learn lessons from other democracies about how to actively rebound from far-right regimes. From Poland, we can see the importance of appealing to rural and working-class voters, currently strong supporters of the MAGA movement. In 2023, Polish voters ousted their right-wing populist leader, Jarosław Kaczyński, who had spent the prior ten years dismantling democratic institutions. Kaczyński and his Law and Justice Party appealed to voters who had felt left behind in Poland's new economy and by its membership in the European Union. (Sound familiar?) He built a coalition of rural residents, the working class, older voters, and devoutly religious people to create an "illiberal democracy." Kaczyński and his party appealed to traditional values by stoking culture wars and claiming an identity that was "Polish," "Catholic," and "anti-Western." His opponent, Donald Tusk, did not give up on these voters, though. Instead, he embraced them, campaigning in rural areas and working-class communities. Though Tusk came from the more affluent and industrialized part of Poland, he campaigned outside his base and won on the issues that mattered to rural and working-class voters.[1383] Of course, Turk lost office in 2025 to a conservative opponent—a reminder of the fragility of political popularity.[1384]

Michigan senator Elissa Slotkin, a Democrat who previously served as a member of Congress in a red district, has used a strategy similar to that of Tusk; she has said that the key to her success was to campaign in rural areas and "lose less badly" there. By gaining voters in the reddest parts of her district, she was able to cobble together sufficient votes to win her district three times.[1385] That strategy should be adopted by moderate Republicans and Democrats seeking to defeat MAGA politicians. One of the lessons of recent years is that even in urban areas, working-class voters have felt left behind. Candidates must find ways to address *their* needs, rather than just the social and cultural issues favored by the college-educated and professional classes. Office seekers must show up in rural and working-class communities and answer their residents' hard questions to earn their support. For voters who are barely eking out a living, "democracy" and "rule of law" seem like abstract terms that won't put food on the table. Kitchen-table issues—the cost of food, gas, health care, child-rearing, retiring, etc.—are what matter most to many Americans. Successful campaigns need not dwell in the past, but they can't ignore the concerns of farmers and factory workers. Candidates must find a way to appeal to the hopes of their voters by promising a vision for a better future.[1386]

One other lesson from Poland is the importance of young voters. In addition to campaigning in rural parts of his country, Tusk also worked to earn the support of young people, winning large victories among voters aged eighteen to twenty-nine as well as a moderate majority of voters aged thirty to forty-nine.[1387] In the United States, young voters represent a huge base of potential support, with only 16 percent of eligible voters casting ballots in all three presidential and midterm elections between 2020 and 2024.[1388] In 2024, Trump worked hard to earn their votes, appearing on numerous podcasts to speak to younger voters.[1389] This largely untapped demographic could be harnessed by other candidates for huge gains. Their votes count as much as anyone else's, and, if a party can attract them now, it may be able to count on their support for decades to come.

An Aboveboard Influence Campaign

Sometimes the odds against making meaningful change seem daunting, if not impossible, to overcome, especially when the powerful and the wealthy use the political system to advance their own interests. However, the success of Mothers Against Drunk Driving demonstrates that ordinary people can make a significant difference in public life. MADD's story shows that a multifaceted approach—one that includes raising public awareness—can be effective in creating social change. As President Barack Obama said during his speech to commemorate the fiftieth anniversary of the march across the Edmund Pettus Bridge in Selma, Alabama, what makes America exceptional is our ability to change: "What greater form of patriotism is there than the belief that America is not yet finished, that we are strong enough to be self-critical, that each successive generation can look upon our imperfections and decide that it is in our power to remake this nation to more closely align with our highest ideals?"[1390] Honoring the ordinary men and women who marched across the bridge, Obama said, "What enormous faith these men and women had. Faith in God, but also faith in America."[1391]

TWELVE

BUILDING GUARDRAILS

Seven-year-old Aiyana Stanley-Jones was sleeping on the couch with her grandmother on the night the Detroit police came to their door. They lived with the rest of their family in the lower floor of a duplex on Detroit's east side. The Detroit Police Department's elite Special Response Team, armed with assault weapons, raid shields, and a warrant for a murder suspect, approached the home shortly after midnight on that night in May 2010.

This was no ordinary raid: As the officers burst through the door, the Arts & Entertainment network's reality television show *The First 48* was filming the event from outside.[1392] Perhaps to enhance the drama for the cameras, one officer fired a flash-bang grenade through a window; these explosive devices, with their ear-shattering noise and blast of light, are sometimes used in law enforcement operations to disorient subjects, giving police a momentary advantage.[1393] Ron Scott, spokesman for the Detroit Coalition Against Police Brutality, would later call the raid "a military assault on a private dwelling."[1394] Officers would eventually find their suspect in the upstairs unit of the duplex—but not before Aiyana's grandmother was startled from her sleep by the flash-bang to find strange men entering their home in the dark. Witness descriptions differed as to what happened next: The lead officer asserted that the grandmother approached him and swiped at his weapon, an MP5 machine gun, a claim she denied.[1395] Either way, the gun went off, and a bullet struck Aiyana in the neck. She would soon be pronounced dead at a nearby hospital.[1396]

Maybe Aiyana's death was an unavoidable accident. But several factors increased the danger to her innocent life. Approaching the home after dark, using the flash-bang grenade, and especially inviting a reality TV crew along to record the incident for its entertainment value all seemed to me unnecessary steps that were more performative than practical.

The case offers an essential lesson in governance: Doing things the safe way—the boring way—may not be glamorous, but it is often most effective. The second Trump administration has been anything but dull. It is filled with splashy announcements seemingly designed more to score quick political points than to achieve long-lasting improvements: Sending in the National Guard to suppress immigration protests, taking over policing in Washington, DC, and demanding law firms and universities bend to the president's will all seemed like tactics more focused on amassing power than solving real problems. As Elon Musk once said about a SpaceX rocket launch, "I am not saying it will get to orbit, but I am guaranteeing excitement. It won't be boring."[1397] That statement could be a metaphor for Donald Trump's presidency, which has been compared to a reality TV show.[1398] In his first term, he announced Supreme Court picks in prime time, before cameras.[1399] On the day that he publicly humiliated Ukrainian president Volodymyr Zelensky at the White House in February 2025, Trump gloated, "This is going to be great television."[1400] Of course, in reality television, it's all a game—who knows what is true and what is fiction? But, as journalist Megan Garber wrote in *The Atlantic*, "the ambiguities that make reality so engrossing as a mode of entertainment make it hazardous as a mode of politics."[1401]

One downside of Trump's focus on entertainment value has been his tendency to announce one new thing after another, creating a sense of chaos. According to Ben Rhodes, the deputy national security for President Obama, "Trump's approach is more of a pyramid scheme than a plan," binging on "short-term 'wins' at the expense of the future."[1402] Whenever Trump makes an outrageous announcement, such as the possibility of pursuing a third term in office,[1403] his critics react, as he no doubt knew they would. Of course, the devious power of Trump's communications strategy is that he makes it difficult to discern when he is creating a distraction and when he is floating an idea he wants to normalize. But many of Trump's most over-the-top acts have seemed designed more to rouse the MAGA movement and score political victories than to improve the quality of American life. By going after violent crime or immigrants, he has effectively baited Democrats into coming to their defense so that he could then label them soft on crime or border security. His attacks on Harvard and other universities were met with cheers from those whom he had convinced were looked down upon by "the elite." But while Trump's bare-knuckled tactics may have gained power for himself, they do nothing to advance national interests.

How, then, are ordinary Americans of either party, or independents, to right the ship? In a democracy, of course, we do not need to wait for someone else to articulate a plan for the future. Rather than hoping that a politician or a party will come to our rescue, we have the power to shape our own future. We can start by building guardrails to prevent power-hungry despots from stealing our democracy.

Prevent Abuses of Power

One thing you can say about Donald Trump and the authors of Project 2025 is that they knew how to find the weaknesses in our system of government and exploit them. Even Oliver Wendell Holmes would have to give grudging credit to Trump's talents as the quintessential "bad man" who finds loopholes in the law. Our Constitution provides a framework for governance, but in many ways, it presumes that public officials will act in good faith to advance the interests of the nation. While Congress and the courts may check a president's power, the Constitution also recognizes that his powers as commander in chief of the armed forces and as chief executive require him to make quick decisions and act nimbly, especially in an emergency. As a result, the Constitution serves as a rough framework rather than a detailed manual for running the country. Over the past 250 years, through statutes and case law, we have worked to flesh out the concepts outlined in the Constitution, but new rules and norms are occasionally needed to address new problems. Maintaining our constitutional separation of powers means the presidency can never be abuse-proof; nevertheless, several steps can be taken to protect the country from a corrupt team running the White House.

Raise Standards for Government Officials

If we cannot prevent a demagogue from winning the White House, we can at least set up some guardrails to keep out their cronies. Trump appointed his personal lawyers, Fox News hosts, and others to top government positions, often based on their fealty to him rather than their qualifications. They, in turn, carried out his orders. Congress has the power to set criteria for presidential appointees through legislation, not only for cabinet nominees but also for other high-level government officials in various agencies. For example, the Judiciary Act of 1789 requires that the attorney general of the United States be someone who is "learned in the law."[1404] The head of the Defense Department must be a civilian who has been out of the military for at least seven years.[1405] For posts that require specific expertise, Congress could mandate professional training and experience. For example, Congress could require the head of Health and Human Services to hold a degree in medicine or public health, keeping out hacks like Robert F. Kennedy Jr. It also could impose experience requirements that would disqualify someone like election denier Paul Ingrassia, whom Trump nominated to run the Office of Special Counsel in 2025, just three years after he had graduated from law school.[1406]

In addition, to avoid any appearance of a conflict of interest, Congress could bar individuals who have served on a president's campaign or as his personal lawyers from holding top DOJ posts. During the second Trump administration, his Justice Department was led by Attorney General Pam Bondi, one of Trump's impeachment lawyers, as well as Todd Blanche and D. John Sauer, who had helped defend Trump in his criminal cases. When Blanche interviewed convicted sex offender Ghislaine Maxwell during the political firestorm relating to the release of the files of her coconspirator Jeffrey Epstein, it was unclear whether his loyalties were to the Department of Justice or Trump, who had an interest in clearing his name.[1407] A rule barring personal lawyers from serving in a presidential administration would give those who do serve arm's-length objectivity. No one has a right to a government appointment. Barring political allies from key positions would insulate officials from political influence, protect their integrity, and avoid any appearance of partiality.

Another way to curtail unchecked presidential control of executive agencies is to amend the laws governing "acting" officials, those who serve in high-level government positions on a temporary basis without Senate confirmation. As Trump once said, "I like acting. It gives me more flexibility."[1408] Appointing acting officials also gives him more control: As Trump played musical chairs with interim and acting US attorneys, or used one individual to occupy multiple high-level positions, he evaded the constitutional confirmation process that ensures Senate advice and consent before nominees may lead government agencies. Trump was exploiting another loophole in the law.

To shore up this gap, we should amend the Federal Vacancies Reform Act. Former government officials Bob Bauer and Jack Goldsmith, who served in the administrations of different parties, make several recommendations to improve this process in their book, *After Trump: Reconstructing the Presidency*. They suggest limiting acting officials to either an appointee already confirmed by the Senate for some other position or the first assistant of the official who has vacated the office.[1409] The statute should further clarify that the first assistant must already be in office.[1410] Such a reform would ensure that the acting official is either a Senate-vetted appointee or someone with extensive career experience. This change would prevent a president from appointing someone who fulfills neither of those criteria, such as Matthew Whitaker, whom Trump appointed to serve as acting attorney general during his first term. Bauer and

Goldsmith also suggest shortening the duration of an acting official's term from its current 210 days to 120 days, to give the president a sense of urgency to fill the vacancy.[1411]

Restore Department of Justice Independence

As a former Justice Department employee, I am pained by Trump's transformation of an independent law enforcement agency into a potent political tool. Trump's accusations that his predecessors "weaponized" the department provided a guise for Trump to do just that himself. The firing of agents and prosecutors who worked on the January 6 prosecutions and the cases against Trump, the transactional dismissal of bribery charges against New York mayor Eric Adams in exchange for assistance in immigration enforcement, and the initiation of investigations against Trump's perceived enemies all violated DOJ norms. The problem with norms is that they set expectations but are not enforceable. Policies can be changed from one administration to the next. But if a president does not care enough about the country's long-term future to obey norms, then we must consider structural changes to safeguard against the abuse of DOJ's immense power.

Of course, if a president wants to target political rivals for criminal prosecution, he needs the help of others at the Justice Department. One of the most important post-Watergate norms was the implementation of DOJ's Principles of Federal Prosecution.[1412] While these principles are merely policies and lack the power of law, parts of them could be codified into law. For example, one provision prohibits prosecutors from taking any action against a person based on the person's political association, affiliation, or beliefs.[1413] Another important post-Watergate norm is the limit on communications between the White House and the Justice Department. Only officials at the highest levels are permitted to communicate, so as to avoid even the appearance that the president or White House is controlling prosecutorial decisions that should be based on fact and law and not on politics. Again, though, this practice is only a norm, not a law.

Throughout both his presidencies, Trump demanded that the Justice Department ignore these standards, publicly calling for the prosecution of rivals like Barack Obama, Hillary Clinton, James Comey, Letitia James, and more. During Trump's first administration, norms mostly held within the department, as Attorney General William Barr publicly refuted claims of a stolen presidential election and other DOJ officials refused to go along with Trump's baseless claims of fraud. During his second administration, the Justice Department was brought under Trump's thumb. Attorney General Pam Bondi's statements and actions, along with Ed Martin's "name and shame" philosophy at the Weaponization Working Group, obediently channeled the boss's views and orders.[1414]

Although under the Constitution's separation of powers federal prosecutors have broad discretion in choosing which defendants and offenses to charge, baseless, politically motivated lawsuits and prosecutions serve no valid government interest and undermine the rule of law. The Constitution's Due Process Clause already prohibits prosecutors from engaging in selective prosecution, which occurs when a person is targeted based on an arbitrary factor, such as race or political affiliation. But to demonstrate selective prosecution, a defendant must show that other individuals were treated differently under similar circumstances—an almost impossible standard to meet, given that it requires proof of something that didn't happen. As long as we want to hold public officials accountable for their criminal misconduct, we cannot completely eliminate politics from prosecution, but we can reduce its influence.

One meaningful reform would be to clarify the rules about communications between the White House and the Justice Department. A 2020 report by the Center for American Progress (CAP) recommended codifying the communication policy.[1415] CAP's recommendation had four components. First, the rules regarding communications should include "detailed guidance" on which communications are permitted and which are not. While it is essential to prohibit political meddling in DOJ's work, a president must also be able to fulfill his duties as chief executive and commander in chief.

According to the CAP report, the rule should provide examples of the kinds of communications that are and are not permissible. For instance, an attorney general should be prohibited from sharing information with the president about investigations involving his political allies or rivals. On the other hand, high-level DOJ officials should be permitted to share information about charges that might affect foreign policy, such as the unsealing of an indictment against a foreign diplomat. Clarity in the rules regarding permissible and prohibited communications would protect the integrity of prosecutions and public confidence in the criminal justice system.

Second, the communications policy should be expanded to cover communications between the Justice Department and other public officials. This reform would help to avoid improper influence on cabinet officials or other presidential appointees outside the Justice Department.

Third, Congress could also require that any communications between the White House and the Justice Department be reported to DOJ's inspector general. The IG could issue regular reports to congressional oversight committees disclosing communications between the White House and DOJ, appropriately redacted or summarized to protect ongoing investigations. Awareness of these disclosures would have a healthy chilling effect on officials, reminding them to avoid improper influence.

Finally, to make it more difficult for future administrations to change the communication policy, DOJ should codify it in the *Federal Register*. Using the rulemaking process would accomplish several goals: With its notice-and-comment requirements, the policy would become subject to public scrutiny. In addition, it would benefit from the input of outside critics. Perhaps most importantly, the policy would become more difficult to change, because it would need to go through a similar notice-and-comment process rather than potentially being eliminated with the stroke of a pen.

Another place to look for guidance on mitigating the president's ability to use criminal prosecution as a political weapon is the military justice system. In courts-martial, the law prohibits what is known as "undue command influence." As set forth in a federal statute, superior officers may not direct a subordinate "to make a particular disposition in a specific case or otherwise substitute the discretion of . . . such officer for that of the subordinate."[1416] Such a statute would deter the president from making public statements about targets of criminal prosecution, as his statements could be used by a defendant as evidence of a violation of the prohibition on unlawful command influence, potentially resulting in dismissal of the case. Additionally, this measure would reinforce the current policy on communication between the White House and the Justice Department. Such a law would discourage the use of DOJ as a tool for harassment and reputational harm. One likely outcome of this reform would be to deter a president from making public comments about locking up his rivals or calling them "crooked," for fear that his statements would be used as evidence of undue command influence. Eliminating such rhetoric by the president would, in turn, reduce the threats and harassment hurled at a president's political opponents and turn down the temperature on political violence.

An even more radical idea that would solve the problem of DOJ independence once and for all is to separate it entirely from the executive branch. If the president lacked control over the Justice Department, it would operate free from political pressure and bias. In fact, in the 1970s, Senator Sam Ervin introduced a bill to do just that. After presiding over the Watergate hearings, the Democrat from North Carolina said, "I have become convinced of the utter necessity of removing the department, insofar as that it is possible, from the play of partisan politics."[1417] Indeed, many states have attorneys general who are elected separately from the governors of their states and operate independently. Bauer and Goldsmith reject this idea as a bridge too far, and I tend to agree with them, but in the spirit of brainstorming, it is worthy of consideration.[1418] Because the Constitution contemplates only three branches of government, a constitutional amendment likely would be required to create an agency that exists outside of that structure.[1419] An independent DOJ could still be subject to appropriate checks and balances from the other branches: The attorney general could be appointed by the president, with the advice and consent of the Senate, to serve for a term that would exceed any presidential administration, such as ten years. An attorney general who abused their position could be removed by impeachment.

The downside of this structure is that an independent DOJ would be less responsive to the will of the people because its leader could not be removed except for high crimes or misdemeanors. So if, for example, prosecutors prioritized marijuana enforcement when the people preferred to see resources dedicated to combating the harms of fentanyl, they would lack the ability to vote out of office the presidential administration responsible for that decision. However, other methods could be used to pressure the Justice Department to focus on matters with public support. Congress could hold oversight hearings to expose how DOJ was using its appropriated funds; Congress could also withhold funding for programs it found inappropriate or unimportant. While an independent DOJ might not be a perfect solution, it is the kind of bold idea we might need to restore integrity to the Justice Department after Trump's demolition of norms. It would insulate criminal prosecution from politics—an essential requirement for the rule of law.

Codify the DIOG

One of the most important post-Watergate reforms was the creation of the FBI's *Domestic Investigations Operations Guide*. As discussed earlier, the DIOG is a policy manual that safeguards against the kinds of rogue operations that led to abuses in the 1960s and 1970s against social movements—their organizers, leaders, and supporters—as well as against President Richard Nixon's perceived enemies. Enacting a charter for the FBI was one of the reforms considered by the Church Committee. Instead, committee members were satisfied that the new internal policy rules were sufficient. With its requirement for predication, protection for constitutional rights, and respect for privacy, the DIOG has provided strong guardrails against FBI abuse. Now that we have seen an administration abuse its investigative powers, it is time to revisit this idea. One way to give these provisions teeth would be to codify them in the *Federal Register*. As discussed above regarding White House communications policies, using the rulemaking process would raise awareness of these rules, subject them to public input, and make it difficult for an internal leader to change them.

Ban Law Enforcement Masks

The use of masks by ICE agents and other law enforcement officers has lent a sinister aura to officers, a counterproductive perception when public trust is essential to effective policing. As I learned in my work in law enforcement, officers are most effective when they have the respect of the people they serve. Proposed federal legislation, the "No Anonymity in Immigration Enforcement Act," would prohibit ICE agents from wearing masks or face coverings.[1420] Enacting that bill would be a good start, but we should go further and ban them for all federal agents, with only limited exceptions, such as health concerns or undercover work. In addition, Congress could make grant funding to state and local law enforcement agencies conditional on imposing similar bans. Such measures have already been introduced in several states.[1421] While federal officials have defended the use of masks to protect agents from threats, harassment, and doxxing, the loss of accountability and the fear masks instill outweigh this interest. Public officials should be subject to public scrutiny and accountability.

Clarify the Definition of "Emergency"

One legal provision that Trump has regularly exploited is the ability to declare emergencies and then wield the extra power granted in them to address the crisis. As discussed earlier, his tariffs were based on his claims of an economic emergency. He declared simultaneous emergencies at the southern border and in Chicago; Portland, Oregon; and other cities. Of course, a president must be able to respond to genuine emergencies, which can be difficult to define in advance. A president also must be permitted to use economic sanctions as a tool in diplomatic negotiations with other countries. But Trump has demonstrated how a chief executive can take emergency powers and run wild with them.

To ensure that a president uses his economic powers responsibly, the International Emergency Economic Powers Act[1422] should be amended to clarify that it does not authorize the president to impose tariffs, retaining that power for Congress, as set forth in the Constitution. Such an amendment would leave the president free to use other economic levers, such as sanctions, including the prohibition on financial transactions and the freezing of assets in the United States, and import and export bans—but not tariffs, which ultimately harm the American people. If, on the other hand, Congress wanted to give the president some emergency tariff power, it could require the president to report back to Congress within a set period, such as thirty days after imposition, to justify the action, which Congress would then have to ratify. Such a system would give the president the power to act quickly to impose tariffs when necessary, while subjecting them to congressional oversight to avoid abuse.

In addition to addressing the emergency provisions of IEEPA, Congress should also clarify when the president may deploy the National Guard in American cities. Of course, under some circumstances, it may be necessary for the president to use the National Guard to execute federal law when the local government refuses, such as during the civil rights movement, when several governors blocked Black students from entering schools reserved for white students. Preserving emergency power is necessary, but it requires guardrails to avoid abuse. In June 2025, when the president called up the California National Guard for deployment to Los Angeles over the objection of the state's governor and the city's mayor, he relied on a statute that permits him to deploy federal troops during "a rebellion or danger of a rebellion" against the US government or when ordinary law enforcement is unable to execute the law.[1423]

Due to the statute's lack of clarity, Trump's assertion of power was legally murky, and litigation ensued after California sought to remove the troops in response to his order. A federal district judge initially found that the protests against immigration raids "fell far short of 'rebellion'" and entered a temporary restraining order.[1424] In addition, the court found that Immigration and Customs Enforcement agents were, in fact, able to execute the law.[1425] An appeals court disagreed, ruling that the statute gives the president wide latitude to decide for himself what constitutes a rebellion. After the trial, the same district court renewed its order striking down the use of the National Guard in Los Angeles, finding that the situation did not amount to a rebellion.[1426] Therefore, the court reasoned, the president's use of troops violated the Posse Comitatus Act, which prohibits the military from performing ordinary law enforcement activities, such as searches, seizures, and arrests.[1427] Courts in other cases reached mixed results, reflecting the vague language of the statutes that give the president authority to use military troops in US cities. In December 2025, the US Supreme Court declined to lift a lower court's temporary order banning national guard troops from the streets of Chicago.[1428]

To reduce the risk of a president's abuse of power while preserving his ability to respond to genuine emergencies, Congress should amend the statute to clarify what does and does not constitute a rebellion. For example, it could require a declaration by the mayor or governor that they have lost the ability to protect the peace with state and local law enforcement officers, a situation that was not present in Los Angeles. Such a requirement would honor the sovereignty of state government. The statute could also provide that if a governor or mayor is part of the lawlessness, then a president may activate troops so long as his decision is ratified by Congress within a short period, such as ten days, to maintain the activation of troops. Such a provision would provide a check on the president's ability to abuse emergency power in that context.

In addition, Congress should amend the even more potent Insurrection Act, which allows the president to use regular armed forces, not just the National Guard, and overrides the Posse Comitatus Act.[1429] Bauer and Goldsmith have warned that the vague language of the Insurrection Act is particularly dangerous because it offers the president almost unbridled discretion that would limit judicial review. For example, one provision allows the president to invoke the act's powers "as he considers necessary" when it is "impracticable to enforce" the law against "obstructions," "combinations," or "assemblages."[1430] Providing that kind of power to a president focused on retribution is like putting a grenade in the hand of a toddler. Congress should specify the circumstances under which any president should be allowed to invoke this potentially dangerous weapon.

Another statute in need of revision is the Home Rule Act, which governs Washington, DC. Trump invoked the statute in August 2025 when he declared an emergency in the nation's capital based on its rate of violent crime, even though the rate was then at a thirty-year low. While most would agree with the goal of reducing violent crime, local residents balked at a federal takeover to achieve it. Under the Home Rule Act of 1973, a president may take over the district's Municipal Police Department during a federal emergency for "federal purposes."[1431] Enforcement against street crime is typically a matter reserved for the states, though federal statutes permit federal law enforcement agents to enforce crimes of carjacking, armed robberies of commercial establishments, drug trafficking, and firearms offenses. Trump used agents from the FBI, ICE, and the Drug Enforcement Administration, as well as members of the National Guard, to patrol the nation's capital. Tellingly, most agents were visibly posted in tourist areas like the National Mall instead of neighborhoods with high crime rates, indicating that Trump's move was more to establish a show of force than to reduce violent crime.[1432]

To curtail this type of overreach in the future, Congress could amend the Home Rule Act. Because the Constitution delegates power to Congress to govern Washington, DC, Congress could enact legislation to clarify that ordinary law enforcement activities are excluded from the type of emergencies contemplated by the statute that allows Trump to take over the municipal police department.

Extend Ethics Laws to the President and Vice President

One corrupting influence in Trump's second administration is the use of his office for financial gain. Organizing dinners for the highest investors in his crypto meme coins, and selling branded merchandise created the impression that the presidency is for sale. Accepting the "palace in the sky" jet from Qatar suggested a patronage relationship that left Trump beholden to that nation's leaders. Soliciting donations from US business leaders gave the appearance of favoritism in government regulation and enforcement.

Whenever individuals, business owners, or investors provide something of value to a public official, it creates a conflict of interest. The risk is that the official will use their position to reward the generosity of their benefactor instead of working for the public good. Like Benjamin Franklin's snuff box, a gift to a public official creates at least an impression of a patronage relationship, and tends to undermine public confidence in the official's ability to make decisions solely based on the best interest of the United States. The Constitution prohibits government officials from accepting foreign emoluments—that is, gifts or other things of value from a foreign national—without the permission of Congress.[1433] In addition, the president is prohibited from accepting emoluments from the United States or any state.[1434] His only compensation is his four-hundred-thousand-dollar annual salary and fifty-thousand-dollar expense account. The Constitution is silent as to whether the president may accept a gift from a private citizen.

To promote good government, free from conflicts of interest, Congress should expand the Ethics in Government Act, passed in the wake of Watergate, to prohibit the president from accepting gifts or using his office to generate income outside his salary. Similar prohibitions exist in other parts of government: For example, following the indictment of Detroit mayor Kwame Kilpatrick in a massive corruption scheme, the City of Detroit revised its charter to ban gifts to public officials from anyone who might have business before the city.[1435] One of Kilpatrick's defenses at trial was that the lavish benefits he had received—in the form of cash, travel, and even custom-tailored suits—were all just gifts. By banning all gifts, Detroit undercut any such defense in the future and made it clear that city officials should work for the people and not for those who shower them with handouts.

In fact, the Ethics in Government Act already prohibits all other executive-branch employees from accepting gifts valued at more than twenty dollars from a source that might have matters pending before their agency.[1436] When I served in government, my colleagues and I all received annual ethics training, and we took it as a given that we could not accept gifts in our official capacities. There are modest exceptions for gifts from family members or personal friends, or for life events, such as weddings and the births of babies. Ethics officers provide guidance for gifts that come close to the line. But the act currently applies only to "employees" and not the president. Congress could amend this statute to include the president, who has no constitutional entitlement to emoluments. Forgoing any gifts during a four-year presidential term seems like a small price to pay for the privilege of serving as president of the United States. The definition of "gifts" should also include donations to inaugural funds and galas, which should be funded publicly, and modestly. Any private donations for presidential libraries should be offered and accepted only after a president has left office.

In addition, a president who has financial holdings—including investments or business interests—should be required to completely divest from those holdings or put them in a blind trust administered by an independent entity. Handing control of the Trump Organization to Trump's son has done little to dispel the notion that Donald Trump is profiting from his presidency through hotel deals in foreign countries, cryptocurrency, and self-promoting merchandise. A third party is needed to avoid actual or apparent conflicts of interest.

Empower the Courts

One concern about abuse of executive power is the lack of recourse against a president who refuses to obey court orders. The only real constitutional check on a president who violates a court order is impeachment, and when Congress is under the president's thumb, that guardrail becomes meaningless. One way to overcome this threat is by giving the Supreme Court the power to enforce its orders. Currently, all federal law enforcement agencies fall under the executive branch, including the US Marshals Service, which provides security at federal courthouses. What if, instead, Congress enacted legislation to move the Marshals Service to the judicial branch? If a member of the executive branch were found in contempt of a court order, the court could direct the marshals to jail them until they complied for up to a certain period, perhaps eighteen months. Separation-of-powers concerns would likely protect the president from custody, but a president can act only through his subordinates. Government employees would be far more reluctant to violate a court order if they knew that jail time was a potential consequence.

In addition to providing the courts with enforcement capabilities, Congress should also create an inspector general for the Supreme Court. The inspector general could investigate cases of fraud, waste, and abuse in the courts. Additionally, it could investigate judges and justices for ethics violations, such as accepting gifts that create the appearance of impropriety or bias. By placing this inspector general within the Supreme Court and under the supervision of the chief justice, such a statute would mitigate separation-of-powers concerns.

State and Local Power

In addition to federal institutions, state and local officials can also push back against abuse of presidential power. States' rights were long the domain of social conservatives who resisted efforts to recognize abortion rights, voting rights, and other individual rights guaranteed by the US Constitution. With MAGA Republicans in control of the White House and Congress, they now seem to have forgotten about their allegiance to states' rights. However, in our republic, state sovereignty is guaranteed by the Tenth Amendment to the Constitution, which reserves to the states all powers not specifically delegated to the federal government. As a result, state attorneys general have succeeded in lawsuits challenging some of Trump's most extreme executive orders when they impacted the states they served. For example, because Trump's plan to redefine birthright citizenship would adversely affect people living in his state, Washington attorney general Nick Brown was able to bring suit on behalf of those residents.[1437] Attorneys general must take a vigorous role in safeguarding the citizens of their states from presidential overreach.

Besides attorneys general, governors also have the power to contest a president's orders to activate their states' National Guard troops, who may be diverted from their normal work to respond to a crisis manufactured by the president. For example, some National Guard troops called up by Trump to respond to protests in Los Angeles in 2025 would otherwise have been responding to California wildfires.[1438] State and local officials should highlight the plight of individuals victimized by wildfires, whose homes might have been saved if the California National Guard had not been deployed to patrol the streets of Los Angeles.

In Massachusetts, Governor Maura Healey proposed state funding for medical research in 2025 to offset losses of federal funds.[1439] Later, after the Centers for Disease Control and Prevention (CDC) changed its recommendations to limit vaccine use, Healey directed insurance companies in her state to provide coverage for vaccines based on guidance from the state's department of public health rather than following the CDC's recommendations.[1440] Similarly, California, Oregon, and Washington joined together in 2025 to form a "Health Alliance" to review scientific data together and make recommendations on vaccines to their residents.[1441] Political stunts come at a cost, and strong governors can fight back on behalf of the people of their states. Of course, some states will vary in their views: Florida, led by Republican Governor Ron DeSantis, decided to end all vaccine mandates.[1442]

In addition to state officials, local leaders play a role in stopping presidential abuses as well. Even if Trump's Justice Department will not hold his cronies accountable, state prosecutors can. Most states prohibit crimes such as bribery, extortion, and fraud. County prosecutors and district attorneys can bring them to justice through criminal prosecution for violating state laws. For example, during the first Trump administration, the Manhattan district attorney prosecuted former Trump adviser Steve Bannon for defrauding investors by soliciting donations to fund the construction of a wall between the United States and Mexico.[1443] The state court prosecution came after Trump had pardoned Bannon to evade federal charges that ensnared his alleged coconspirators.

As the Trump regime drives America deeper into authoritarianism, lawyers and other professionals can fight back by working in state and local governments, where they can protect state sovereignty and the people they serve.

Build Resilience to Disinformation

Trump's use of disinformation has been an unprecedented effort to rewrite history. His extortion of research universities based on false or misleading accusations threatened to harm one of America's greatest strengths. While we cannot MAGA-proof all of our institutions of democracy, we can take some steps to protect them.

A variety of proposals to combat disinformation are set forth in my book *Attack from Within*, and I won't repeat them here; however, one essential step is to promote independent journalism. As large media corporations are captured by patronage, smaller publications and investigative reporters are more important than ever to provide independent voices unbought by a president who can control their corporate mergers. However, it has become increasingly challenging for small publications to survive. We have frequently seen local newspapers close down in the face of changing economic models. As news has shifted from print to online, advertising revenue can no longer support local newspapers, leaving many small communities as "news deserts." The loss of funding for public radio also leaves smaller communities without resources to sustain them.

One way to support small local publications is through grants from nonprofit organizations committed to supporting journalism, such as community foundations funded by private donors, with governance structures to ensure editorial independence. In addition, new outlets such as Substack newsletters have provided fresh voices and perspectives on such issues as law, history, and politics, with most publishers offering a free option as well as bonus content for paid subscribers. To ensure an informed electorate, we should encourage the exploration of new formats as technology evolves. A vigorous free press can help correct inaccuracies and expose government abuses, enabling the people to hold wrongdoers politically accountable. So deeply did the founders value the right to the free press that Thomas Jefferson once said, "Were it left to me to decide whether we should have a government without newspapers or newspapers without a government, I should not hesitate a moment to prefer the latter."[1444]

And while we can't always stop bad actors from trafficking in disinformation, we can build resilience against disinformation through education on topics such as media literacy and civics. Media-literacy training for children in schools and for adults in public libraries, faith communities, civic groups, or community colleges can help people identify tactics of disinformation and think critically about what they see, hear, and read. These services can be provided by states or by community organizations. In addition to media literacy, civics education should be restored. As our educational priorities have shifted toward STEM fields (science, technology, engineering, and math), civics education has paid the price. For every fifty dollars the government spends on STEM education, it spends five cents on civics.[1445] However, Americans who lack a basic understanding of civics are more vulnerable to disinformation about how our government works. When Trump and MAGA influencers claim judges are restricting his use of executive power, someone with a basic understanding of civics can recognize the false claim for what it is—checking a president's abuse of power is exactly what courts are supposed to do. A person who understands civics also understands the constitutional respect for states as separate, sovereign entities, shedding light on the impropriety of Trump's use of the National Guard in US cities. Restoring civics education would help safeguard Americans from the harms of disinformation.

Protect Knowledge

One of the most profound ways Trump abused his power during his second term was to demand that recipients of federal funds bend to his will. He used the leverage of grant money to attack academic freedom, DEI programs, scientific research, and campus speech. He defied the will of Congress by impounding funds that had been appropriated for specific purposes, such as humanitarian aid, research, and education. One solution to this problem would be for Congress to retain its constitutional power of the purse by eliminating the executive branch as the administrator for federal grants. The Government Accountability Office, a nonpartisan, independent agency that works for Congress,[1446] could oversee the disbursement of funds to universities and other grant recipients to prevent a president from interfering with the will of the people, as reflected in the decisions of their elected representatives. A president might challenge such a change as a violation of the Constitution's Vesting Clause, which confers power to the president to execute the law, but a counterargument can be made that if Congress is funding the grants, then Congress can simply allocate the money to the recipients without using the president as the middleman.

In addition, states can offset cuts to academic research by appropriating their own funds to universities, as Governor Healey has proposed in Massachusetts. Protecting medical research is essential, but we should also recognize the value of the arts and humanities. It was through popular movies, documentaries, and other arts that citizens in South Korea kept alive the memory of the military state and all of its horrors, prompting strong resistance and a quick reversal when the president declared martial law in 2024.[1447]

Preserving collective memory and historical knowledge is essential to maintaining our resilience against oppression. Trump's executive order to remove materials from government cultural institutions that "inappropriately disparage Americans" whitewash history.[1448] Among the items taken down from Fort Pulaski National Monument, in Georgia, was a photograph known as *The Scourged Back*, a famous image from the Civil War era. The horrific photo depicts a formerly enslaved man with severe scars across his back from whippings. Alan Spears, the senior director for cultural resources at the National Parks Conservation Association, said the image "shocked the nation and the world with its honest depiction of the vicious nature of slavery."[1449] To remove such a powerful image from public display is to lose the opportunity to reflect on its lessons. We must keep alive our memories not only of America's greatest achievements but also of the times when we failed to live up to our values. Only by grappling with the darker moments of the nation's history can we rise above them.

Election Laws

Another area where guardrails can protect democracy is election laws. All other rights and policy choices flow from free and fair elections. But in recent decades, election laws have evolved to shift leverage toward the rich and powerful. The Supreme Court has all but gutted the Voting Rights Act of 1965, which prevented state legislatures from discriminating against voters based on race.

Trump's second term was marked by a Congress that was unwilling to fulfill its duties as a separate and coequal branch of government. Our constitutional system is designed so that each branch provides checks and balances on the others. But with rare exception, the GOP-controlled Congress acted as a rubber stamp for Trump's nominees. Republicans uttered nary a peep when Trump refused to spend appropriated funds. They looked the other way when Trump imposed tariffs on other countries, even though the power to tax belongs to Congress. The legislature allowed the president to fire board members and heads of independent agencies in violation of its own statutes. And the concept of impeachment became a relic of a bygone era.

Several electoral reforms would help to make Congress less beholden to the president and more responsive to voters. While it is impossible to cure every abuse of executive power we saw in Trump's second term, a vigorous Congress that safeguards its own power would be an essential check on a strongman president. We can restore power to the people by reforming campaign finance laws, clarifying term limits, and making elected representatives more responsive to the voters they serve.

Improve campaign finance laws

When it comes to disparities in political power, one of the greatest harms to American politics in recent decades was the Supreme Court's 2010 decision in *Citizens United v. Federal Election Commission.*[1450] The case was built on *Buckley v. Valeo*, a 1976 case in which the court struck down part of the Federal Election Campaign Act. The goal of that law, the court wrote in 1971, was "the prevention of corruption and the appearance of corruption spawned by the real or imagined coercive influence of large financial contributions on candidates' positions and on their actions if elected to office."[1451] The statute reflected the obvious perception that politicians who accept money to gain office are beholden to the donors who put them there. The law was an effort to remove the stench of money from politics. Although the court upheld the statute's limits on contributions to candidates' campaign funds, it struck down restrictions on expenditures as violating the First Amendment's free speech and free assembly protections.[1452]

The Court's distinction seems illogical, at least in hindsight. First, it is not at all evident that money equals speech. Money may *fund* speech, in the form of political advertising, but the two are not quite the same thing. I suppose jurists who spend time in the company of the wealthy are apt to see things differently from the ordinary citizen. A different makeup of the court could just as easily have reached a different conclusion.

Second, even if money is speech, our Constitution does not require permitting unlimited expenditures on election campaigns. Like all rights, the right to free speech under the Constitution may be restricted by the government if the limits are narrowly tailored to achieve a compelling governmental interest. For example, Congress has passed laws criminalizing speech when it amounts to perjury, a threat, or a conspiracy because those laws meet that standard. Eliminating bribery from politics certainly fulfills a compelling governmental interest. But the court in *Buckley* found that the limits on campaign expenditures were insufficiently narrow. The unsigned opinion stated that while large donations directly to a candidate might amount to bribery, there was less risk that campaign expenditures would be "given as a *quid pro quo* for improper commitments from a candidate."[1453] That reasoning seems laughable now.

In today's world of campaign fundraising, expenditures are where all the action is. Spending millions of dollars on political ads creates an opportunity for influence peddling. Moreover, the court in *Buckley* focused on the risk of corruption rather than on the imbalance of power. As Professor Zephyr Teachout has suggested, what if the court had instead interpreted the statute as promoting the compelling governmental interest of equality among voters?[1454] When billionaires can stack the deck in their favor by spending millions on their preferred candidate, voters with fewer assets are unable to match their level of influence in the election's outcome. Through that lens, the court might have upheld the statute at issue in *Buckley*, on the grounds that preventing inequality among voters was a compelling government interest and that the solution—limiting campaign expenditures to a nominal amount that was affordable to a large number of Americans—was narrowly tailored to achieve that objective.[1455]

Four decades later, in *Citizens United*, the court compounded the problem. After witnessing the impact of money on American politics since *Buckley*, the court had an opportunity to rectify its mistake and overturn that decision in *Citizens United*. Instead, the court did something worse, extending *Buckley's* First Amendment protections to corporations, labor unions, and other organizations.[1456] These entities were now able to pool their assets, allowing them to make even larger expenditures than individuals. As a result, *Citizens United* opened the door to so-called "dark money," allowing independent political committees to fund political advertising without disclosing their donors.[1457] Again, the court ignored the importance of equality for ordinary voters and focused on the importance of "speech" in the form of "donations" by the wealthy.[1458] Moreover, the court now seemed to think that even patronage was not a real threat. Justice Anthony Kennedy, writing for the majority, said, "independent expenditures, including those made by corporations, do not give rise to corruption or the appearance of corruption."[1459] As in *Buckley*, the court in *Citizens United* again failed to foresee how the future would unfold. The less-than-prescient Justice Kennedy wrote, "With the advent of the Internet, prompt disclosure of expenditures can provide shareholders and citizens with the information needed to hold corporations and elected officials accountable for their positions and supporters." Nope. Because super PACs are not required to disclose their members, the identities of the individuals contributing to them are largely unknown, leading to the term "dark money."

Today, super PACs are behemoths of dark money that wield outsized influence over elections. In the 2024 elections, super PACs spent $2.6 billion, with conservative committees outspending their progressive counterparts by a ratio of nearly two to one.[1460] This spending can influence elections by misleading voters into believing that certain causes have more popular support than they actually do. Without transparency in donor lists, super PACs often take on grassroots- or patriotic-sounding names, such as "Fairshake" or "America," when, in fact, they are funded by billionaires and special interest groups. The influence of super PACs only continues to grow: According to the Brennan Center for Justice, in 2024, super PACs supporting Donald Trump or Kamala Harris reaped a total of $865 million from donors who contributed $5 million or more each. These high-end donors accounted for 75 percent of the funding to super PACs in 2024.

What's more alarming is that this number more than doubled from 2020, when super PACs collected $406 million. Elon Musk alone contributed more than $239 million to the America PAC to fund door-to-door canvassing and ads for Trump.[1461] Musk also spent more than nineteen million dollars to support Republican candidates for the House of Representatives.[1462] Musk, of course, stood to benefit enormously from the Trump administration through government contracts with his companies and his role as the head of the Department of Government Efficiency.

In recent years, the cryptocurrency industry has emerged as a significant player in election funding, leveraging vast sums to influence election outcomes in its favor. Fairshake, for example, is a super PAC reportedly funded primarily by three large crypto firms, though nondisclosure rules hide its complete donor list.[1463] During the 2024 primary election for a US Senate seat in California, Fairshake spent millions targeting Representative Katie Porter, one of the Democrats in the race. Porter was a populist who had become well-known for using a whiteboard during congressional hearings to highlight financial harms to consumers. Without even mentioning crypto, Fairshake attacked Porter in ads that called her a "bully" and "liar," and falsely suggested that she had taken campaign donations from large oil companies and pharmaceutical firms. Porter's popular support tanked, and she was defeated soundly in the primary, earning only 15 percent of the vote. According to a *New Yorker* exposé, Fairshake's goal was more about crypto than it was about Porter, seeking "to warn anyone running for office that, if you are anti-crypto, the industry will come after you."[1464] That's hardly a fair shake for candidates or the rest of us.

Without intervention, we can expect the influence of billionaires and special interest groups in elections to keep increasing, given the leverage they can wield through super PACs. Is it any wonder that tax cuts for the wealthy were extended during the second Trump administration? One way to address the harms of *Buckley* and *Citizens United* is for Congress to pass the DISCLOSE Act, proposed federal legislation that would enhance transparency in campaign expenditures.[1465] First introduced in 2010, the bill would require super PACs to reveal the names of their donors, identify the super PACs in the ads they fund, and prohibit the use of shell corporations to mask the sources of contributions.[1466] While the DISCLOSE Act would not eliminate big donors from politics, it would at least allow us to see *which* billionaires and industries are making expenditures to *which* committees, allowing us to identify potential conflicts of interest. The DISCLOSE Act has failed to pass in the years since the *Citizens United* decision, mainly along party lines, with Republicans opposing it.[1467] Changing the makeup of Congress may be a necessary first step to passing the bill, which would help engender nonpartisan good government.

A more drastic measure to rein in campaign expenditures altogether would be to pass a constitutional amendment to overturn *Buckley* and *Citizens United.* Senator Jeanne Shaheen, a Democrat from New Hampshire, has proposed the Democracy for All Amendment, which would authorize Congress and state legislatures to put reasonable limits on campaign expenditures. According to Shaheen, the amendment would "curb the concentration of political influence held by the wealthiest Americans."[1468] While candidates who benefit from the status quo may oppose such an amendment, it should appeal to many members of Congress, who often lament the time they spend on fundraising rather than lawmaking. The amendment should also appeal to working-class Democrats, Republicans, and independents, whose interests are underrepresented by groups that make massive campaign expenditures. According to the Center for Public Integrity, a non-partisan news organization, 75 percent of Americans support an amendment that would reverse the results of *Citizens United.*[1469] We have amended our Constitution twenty-seven times. Surely, we can find support for an amendment that would reduce the influence of special interests in favor of equal voting rights.

One idea short of a constitutional amendment to prevent corporations from making campaign expenditures would be to change state laws governing corporate power.[1470] Because a corporation is an organization created by law, the law can be changed to limit its powers. State legislation or ballot initiatives could be used to define corporations as lacking the power to make political expenditures. Organizers in Montana have drafted a ballot proposal called the Transparent Election Initiative that would do just that. The initiative would not overturn *Citizens United*, but it would neutralize its consequences.

Shore up presidential term limits

While we are amending the Constitution, another improvement would be to clarify the language of the Twenty-Second Amendment, passed in 1951 following Franklin D. Roosevelt's four terms in office.[1471] Term limits had been debated since the Constitutional Convention, but George Washington's tradition-setting retirement from office after two terms made an amendment unnecessary until Roosevelt. The goal of setting term limits was to prevent a president from amassing power and using their position to reward supporters who would keep them in office.[1472]

The common understanding of the amendment is that it limits presidents from serving more than two terms. But the text is murky. It provides, "No person shall be *elected* to the office of the President more than twice."[1473] That language could be slippery enough to give the "bad man" an opening to exploit. Trump could ascend to a third term by routes other than election. As *Politico* imagined, J. D. Vance could run for president with Trump as VP, telling voters he would step aside immediately to allow Trump to serve a third term: "Vote Vance to Make Trump President Again."[1474] While the Twelfth Amendment says that no one who is "constitutionally ineligible to the office of President shall be eligible to that of Vice President," that language, too, builds on the same loophole—a person is not barred from *serving* a third or subsequent term, they just can't be *elected* more than twice.[1475]

Trump has repeatedly floated the idea of serving beyond his second term. After winning the 2024 election, Trump said, "I suspect I won't be running again unless you say, 'He's so good we've got to figure something else out.'"[1476] Is it all a joke? Is it something to take seriously? Literally? With Trump, one never knows. He spent much of his second term pushing the limits of presidential power. Why should we expect him to stop at term limits?

If Trump were to attempt to remain in power, he would not be the first leader to overstay their term. Mila Versteeg, a law professor at the University of Virginia, studied 234 heads of state in the twenty-first century and found that one-third of them tried to evade legal term limits.[1477] Many succeeded, including Recep Tayyip Erdoğan in Turkey and Vladimir Putin in Russia—both leaders Trump admires.[1478] Versteeg concluded that those who managed to stay in power did so not by violating the law but by exploiting gray areas or persuading courts to adopt their interpretation of the law.[1479]

A constitutional amendment could revise the language of the Twenty-Second Amendment to clarify that no person may *serve* as president more than twice. Such an amendment would reflect the current understanding of the limits and goals of the 1951 effort to prevent corruption of the presidency by allowing one person to use patronage to retain power and become entrenched in office.

End gerrymandering

Ending gerrymandering is also essential to preserving our democracy. Gerrymandering—the drawing of political districts to benefit one group over another—is a deliberate way to distort the results of elections. The drawers of district lines may engage in what's known as "cracking" or "packing," in which they use unorthodox line-drawing to enhance their own power. Cracking is dividing members of a particular voting bloc into smaller districts to dilute their power; packing occurs when members of a particular group are assigned to a single district to limit their influence. Either of these strategies can give an unfair advantage to the group that is drawing the lines.

When one party controls a legislature, gerrymandering can be nearly impossible to combat. That's because of a 2019 Supreme Court decision, *Rucho v. Common Cause*.[1480] In that case, the court reaffirmed that race-based gerrymandering is illegal, but held that courts lack the power to strike down *political* gerrymandering. That is, when legislatures crack or pack districts to help Republicans or Democrats, the issue is a political question that courts cannot address. As a result, parties in power often engage in gerrymandering when they have the chance. In dissenting from the court's decision, Justice Elena Kagan wrote that gerrymandered districts are "anti-democratic in the most profound sense" and "imperil our system of government."[1481]

In 2025, the GOP-controlled legislature in Texas not only proposed a gerrymandered map that would add five more Republican seats in Congress but did so outside of the ordinary ten-year cycle, after the decennial census.[1482] Trump publicly advocated for the passage of the new maps on social media, claiming, incredibly, that because he had won Texas in the 2024 presidential election, he was "entitled to five more seats."[1483] Giving him five more seats in Texas for the 2026 midterms would provide him with a greater likelihood of retaining Republican control of the House. In protest, Democratic lawmakers fled the state to prevent a quorum and block the legislation.[1484] They ultimately returned, and the bill became law.[1485] At Trump's urging, Republican legislatures in Missouri and North Carolina followed suit, redrawing their states' congressional maps in hopes of winning another seat for their party.[1486] In response, California voters in November 2025 approved a plan to gerrymander their own state that would redraw district lines to offset the five seats Democrats expected to lose to Republicans in Texas.[1487] It was an antidemocracy nuclear arms race that assured mutual destruction.

As discussed earlier, thriving democracies practice the kinds of mutual tolerance and forbearance that Steven Levitsky and Daniel Ziblatt highlight in *How Democracies Die*.[1488] In the context of gerrymandering, mutual tolerance and forbearance require drawing district lines that respect city and county lines, compactness, contiguity, communities of interest, and other usual standards, rather than ways that maximize a party's power or accede to a president's commands.

One way to achieve fair and representative legislative districts is to use independent districting commissions. For example, in

Michigan, the Independent Citizens Redistricting Commission consists of thirteen commissioners, of whom four "affiliate" with the Democratic Party, four with Republicans, and five identify as independents.[1489] Other states with independent commissions include California, New York, and Colorado.[1490] Not only do independent commissions draw district maps in ways that do not tilt power in favor of any one party, they also preserve confidence in the political system. Creating independent districting commissions in other states would help to achieve fairness. When people perceive that the system is fair, they are more likely to engage in politics, and participation is an essential component of a healthy democracy. In December 2025, Indiana's GOP-controlled state senate rejected gerrymandered maps that would have favored Republicans, offering hope that some lawmakers care more about drawing lines fairly than about winning at all costs.[1491]

Proportional representation

Other developed democracies around the world provide examples the United States could look to for guidance in eliminating the harms of gerrymandering through a system called proportional representation. In a 2022 open letter to Congress, more than two hundred American political scientists described proportional representation as a system in which each congressional district has multiple representatives, rather than just one.[1492] In such a system, candidates—and their parties—would win seats in proportion to the number of votes they earn; the size of Congress would expand as voters elect multiple members to represent their district..[1493] For instance, consider a congressional race today in which 60 percent of the voters choose the Democratic candidate and 40 percent select the Republican. In our current system, the Democrat would win the seat. The 40 percent of the electorate who voted for the winner's opponent would have a representative in Washington who does not reflect their values. Today, with so many reliably red and blue districts on the map, these party preferences are entrenched. In a proportional representation system, this same district might get five representatives. Under the scenario described above, with 60 percent of voters favoring Democrats and 40 percent favoring Republicans, the outcome of the election would be three Democrats and two Republicans in Congress. As a result, all voters would have their views represented, and the tendency to appeal to the party's most extreme elements would dissipate.[1494] Such a system would also open the possibility of more than two political parties, representing the interests of the moderate voters currently underrepresented in our two-party system.

Proportional representation would cure some of the problems with our current winner-take-all approach to congressional elections. Today, because the same party consistently wins 90 percent of districts, congressional elections have become meaningless for most voters. House members are selected in primary elections with low voter turnout, thereby favoring candidates with extreme left or right views.[1495] Consequently, according to scholars advocating for the new system, Congress is "polarized and held hostage by obstructionist politics," making it difficult or impossible to pass meaningful legislation.[1496] Instead of addressing national issues, members of Congress often spend their time investigating opponents or blocking efforts to make meaningful change so as to score political points. A larger, more diverse group of representatives in Congress would be more amenable to the kinds of compromise that brought us the Immigration and Nationality Act, the Social Security Act, and the Voting Rights Act, legislative achievements of prior decades that would seem unimaginable today. Proportional representation would bring us closer to the framers' original vision of Congress, described by John Adams as "in miniature, an exact portrait of the people at large. It should think, feel, reason, and act like them."[1497] In fact, similar systems are used in most established democracies.[1498] Representative Donald S. Beyer Jr., a Virginia Democrat, has proposed the Fair Representation Act, which would use proportional representation in congressional elections.[1499] This solution could end the gridlock in Congress that prevents the American government from accomplishing significant reforms.

Ranked-choice voting

Beyer's proposal for proportional representation also comes with a twist—ranked-choice voting. Ranked-choice voting allows voters to list multiple candidates on their ballot in the order of their preference, rather than being limited to a single winner-take-all choice.[1500] In ranked-choice voting, if any candidate wins a majority of all votes cast, that candidate is named the winner. If no candidate achieves a majority, then the candidate who came in last place is eliminated from the race, and the voters whose first-choice candidate was eliminated have their second-choice votes counted. This process continues until one candidate wins a majority of votes.[1501] Ranked-choice voting helps reduce extremism by preventing two candidates from splitting the moderate vote and allowing a more extreme candidate to win an election by a plurality. By introducing compromise, ranked-choice voting tends to eliminate candidates not favored by any significant segment of the electorate. While some voters do not get their first choice in office, they often get a candidate they can live with.

Variations on ranked-choice voting have been implemented in federal elections in Alaska and Maine, as well as local elections in many other states.[1502] Florida is the only state that has banned ranked-choice voting.[1503] Some critics suggested the 2025 Democratic primary for mayor of New York showed that ranked-choice voting doesn't work because it failed to produce the consensus it promises, with voters splitting their support between party stalwart and former New York governor Andrew Cuomo and the upstart Zohran Mamdani and largely ignoring the other candidates.[1504] These critics may have a point, or they may under-estimate the appeal of a candidate focused on affordability during times of wide wealth disparity. Regardless, the method has worked in other parts of the country. Senator Lisa Murkowski, the moderate Republican from Alaska, was elected through ranked-choice voting. Mary Peltola, a Democrat, won an open House seat in Alaska in 2022, defeating the state's former governor, Sarah Palin, who had been endorsed by Trump.[1505] In Maine, another state with ranked-choice voting, Democrat Jared Golden won reelection to the House in 2024 by building bipartisan support in a rural district that was won by Trump in the last three elections; the Associated Press called the contest "one of the few truly competitive races nationwide."[1506] If ranked-choice voting can reduce polarization in politics and bolster participation by giving voters a real choice, it seems like an experiment worth trying.

Popular vote compact

Another way voters can take charge of their decisions is by enacting the National Popular Vote Interstate Compact. The agreement would ensure that the candidate in a presidential election who wins the popular vote would be declared the winner in a given state.[1507] Currently, our electoral college system delivers a winner-take-all approach: State legislatures decide how to allocate their electoral votes, with only Maine and Nebraska apportioning their votes to more than one candidate. In all other states, the winning candidate is awarded all of the state's electoral votes. The electoral college was one of the significant compromises of the Constitutional Convention, but that plan had plenty of flaws even at its outset, including the apportionment of each enslaved person as three-fifths of a citizen. As the nation's population has grown and migrated from rural to urban areas, the system has become undemocratic because it gives disproportionate power to states with smaller populations. For example, voters in Wyoming now have four times the influence of voters in California. That's because Wyoming has one electoral vote for every 195,000 people, while California has one electoral vote for every 712,000 people, giving residents of the Cowboy State more say in the outcome of a presidential election.[1508]

With many states decidedly red or blue, today's presidential campaigns are waged in a handful of swing states, so that casting a vote elsewhere is all but futile. The current system allows a candidate to win the presidency with only 23 percent of the popular vote. Indeed, in recent years, the winner of the popular vote, such as Al Gore and Hillary Clinton, has often lost the electoral vote. In 2016, Clinton won *two million* more votes than Trump, who still won the electoral vote. These factors lead to low turnout because voters are aware of the relative value of their ballots. Disengagement from electoral politics erodes our democracy and can leave people feeling powerless and discontent.

Of course, a constitutional amendment could change the system to a popular vote. However, in light of the political challenges associated with such a change—for example, the fact that a constitutional amendment requires ratification by three fourths of the state legislatures in the nation—a different route might be more effective. The answer may lie in the National Popular Vote Interstate Compact.[1509] That agreement would authorize participating states to award all of their electoral votes to the candidate who wins the popular vote. If states controlling 270 or more of the 538 electoral votes signed on, they could throw the election to the winner of the popular vote. To date, fifteen states, controlling 196 electoral votes, have already entered into the compact; the plan would become operational when states that control seventy-four more electoral votes sign on. That would end one of the ways in which a minority of voters can control the outcome of a presidential election, a phenomenon Steven Levitsky and Daniel Ziblatt call our country's "tyranny of the minority."[1510] In this way, the National Popular Vote Compact could restore true democracy to the American people.

The Long View

Of course, not every abuse of power can be cured. The "bad man" will always exist. Trump's team of lawyers, looking for loopholes, have found a number of ways to exploit the gray areas of the law. For example, Trump's use of executive orders to target law firms and the media is difficult to counter in ways other than through lawsuits. His gamble on the Supreme Court's growing acceptance of the once-fringe unitary executive theory allowed him to ignore laws that had restricted his ability to fire inspectors general and members of bipartisan oversight boards. These and other abuses likely cannot be eliminated under our constitutional structure that emphasizes separation of powers. But removing dark money from politics can help restore power to the people. Clarifying language to prevent a president from serving more than two terms would mitigate a chief executive's ability to amass power and reward patrons. In addition, a strong and independent Congress could use its authority to check a president's abuses. If we can use some of the methods discussed above to elect responsible and independent members of Congress, then we can avoid many of these downstream consequences. Likewise, a Congress that checks a president who abuses his power to silence critics in the press or academia leads to a healthier society. A nation with a strong and vigorous free press can expose corrupt uses of power and raise public awareness, enabling voters to make informed choices. A country with academic freedom can teach history and engage in scientific research that protects and advances the best interests of its citizens.

Sound Decisions, Not Splashy Announcements

As for seven-year-old Aiyana Stanley-Jones, the City of Detroit would ultimately pay $8.25 million to settle the wrongful death case brought by her family.[1511] However, no one could be truly happy with that result, because it could not bring her back. Playing for the cameras turned out to be a tragedy for everyone involved. I don't fault the Detroit Police Department for pursuing a murder suspect, but I often wonder what would have happened if the officers had attempted to locate their suspect during daylight hours. Or if they had refrained from using the flash-bang grenade. Or if they had declined to allow *The First 48* to come along to capture the drama for the entertainment pleasure of its viewers. A careful, thoughtful approach would have been less exciting but may have been more effective. Likewise, in governing, instead of focusing on short-term, splashy acts that score political points, we need to approach public policy with maturity to make the hard decisions necessary for meaningful, long-term improvements in American society.

THIRTEEN

VISION FOR THE FUTURE

The blaze began in the early morning hours at a tidy brick home in the suburban community of Novi, Michigan. Five young men—all undocumented immigrants from Mexico—had been living in the basement of the otherwise vacant home, which was owned by Roger Tam, operator of a nearby restaurant where the five were employed. The young men stayed in the house as a benefit and condition of their employment; each day, Tam would pick them up and drive them to work for their twelve-hour shifts at the restaurant. But on this morning, when Tam arrived, he found the house in flames. Trapped in the basement, where they were locked away at night, all five young men died of smoke inhalation. Miguel and Pablo were twenty-three. Leonel and Simeon were five years younger. Brayan was sixteen.[1512]

In contrast to the disdain with which immigrants are regarded by many Americans today, the public reaction to that case was nothing but compassion for the young men. Although they had entered the country without lawful authorization, they had journeyed to the United States and were working six days a week in hopes of a better life. Learning their stories made them more than statistics. More than "illegal aliens." More than "other."

One important lesson from that case is how our perceptions differ when we put a human face on a news story. When we see the humanity in others, we feel compassion for their plight. While president, Donald Trump has stoked resentment, in part, by pushing the narrative that immigrants from Latin American countries are "animals" and unworthy of the same kind of lives as the rest of us. It is easy to provoke rage when discussing faceless statistics. But when we learn the story of an individual, all but the most heartless among us feel compassion for them.

Telling the stories of those who are harmed by abuses of authority can be an important way to combat tyranny and reclaim the power of the people. When the public learns about the realities of political violence, the hardship endured by immigrants, the harm to refugees who are denied humanitarian aid, or the loss of grant funds to medical researchers, we are inclined to appreciate the real harms of ruthless policies. We, the people, have the power to tell those stories. Through journalism, lawsuits, social media, and public protest, we can persuade others to act with empathy. As we propose policy changes, we can use those stories to help us advance toward a more perfect union.

Stories can help lead our country to a better place. But leadership requires more than just resistance to the status quo. In addition to safeguarding our government against corruption and abuse, we need to propose a future where everyone can thrive. Regardless of party, people yearn for a vision of the future that promises peace, health, and a better life for their children. As Ben Rhodes, the former deputy national security advisor, writes, by reacting to every move Trump makes, Democrats have dug themselves into a deeper hole, constantly promoting "resistance" rather than articulating a vision for the future.[1513] According to Rhodes, "Every day brings a new battle, generating outrage that overwhelms their capacity to present a coherent alternative. The party spends more time defending what is being lost than imagining what will take its place."[1514]

To deflate the MAGA movement, Democrats, moderate Republicans, independents, or third parties will need to share a blueprint for improvements. Key parts of that plan must include economic prosperity for all Americans, solutions for our broken immigration system, evidence-based plans to reduce violent crime, and meaningful ways to promote new technologies while protecting humanity and our planet. Voters want to know not just what you are against but what you are *for*. The outline for our future should be one that is inclusive, not one that deliberately pits some segments of society against others. We must avoid the temptations of short-term desires at the expense of long-term necessities. For example, reducing wealth disparity in America will require electing a Congress that works for the people. Fixing our immigration system will take time and compromise. We must acknowledge the risks associated with climate change and technology while embracing the possibilities of human achievement. We can surely incentivize innovation without abandoning protection for communities and our planet.

But even the best plan requires buy-in. Evidence-based solutions make good sense, but persuasion comes not just from facts and figures but also from "feels." To help people understand the stakes, we need not only policy wonks but communicators. While Trump has governed by evoking fear and longing for the past, America has always been about upward mobility and hope for a better future. Putting faces on issues and telling the stories of real people can inspire ordinary Americans to get out and work toward change.

Income Equality

First, increasing economic justice must be seen as a priority. Despite its great wealth, ranking number one in the world in gross domestic product (GDP), the United States ranks only twenty-fourth among all countries in happiness.[1515] Studies have shown that many factors can influence happiness, such as income, peace, and strong social connections; however, one essential component is economic equality.[1516] As detailed earlier, corporate tax cuts, the elimination of taxes on capital gains, automation, the growing role of technology in business, and offshore manufacturing have all contributed to the enormous wealth gap in our country that has only grown since the 1980s. That disparity breeds resentment, as more and more Americans feel left behind and worse off than their parents' generation. That's because they are. In New York City, previously little-known state assemblyman Zohran Mamdani was elected mayor in 2025 by campaigning on the importance of affordability in essential needs, such as housing and childcare, after asking Trump voters why they had voted for the president.[1517] It is no surprise that every presidential election since 2012 has been a change election, with voters casting out the incumbent party in hopes of something better.

And it is not just that many Americans are economically disadvantaged—it's that at the same time, many others enjoy fabulous wealth. Social media and television lay bare for all to see the extravagant riches of the billionaires who are enjoying the spoils of disparity. The same instincts that drive voters to resent "elite" Democrats fueled the Occupy Wall Street movement a decade earlier. According to former labor secretary Robert Reich, income inequality leads to educational, racial, and class inequality.[1518] That leaves people susceptible to the manipulations of a tyrant, who exploits those disparities and blames these so-called elites, immigrants, and DEI programs for their loss. The demagogue talks about the good old days, and many voters find such messages appealing, because they remember the time when the middle class prospered. But that prosperity was fueled by long-gone economic policies that reined in corporate greed. By stoking grievance and resentment against people of color, immigrants, and members of the LBGT community minorities, MAGA politicians dissuade people from banding together across demographic groups in a populist alliance. As a result, they convince people to vote against their own economic self-interest, all while enabling the rich to get richer. Reich blames both Republicans and Democrats who "don't want to bite the hand that feeds them."

Undoubtedly, capitalism is a core American value that has significantly contributed to our nation's rise as a superpower. But corporate greed is creating a caste system that is very un-American. Some executives enjoy seven- and eight-figure salaries while more than thirty-five million people live in poverty.[1519] Just as they did in the Gilded Age, millionaires, and now billionaires, live in ostentatious mansions, while other Americans have no home at all. It doesn't have to be this way. We can restore quality of life for lower- and middle-income Americans through several strategies. As described below, targeted regulation and other legal authorities can help advance the dual interests of progress and prosperity for all Americans. In fact, by making America more affordable, candidates can build coalitions that include urban and rural voters.

A more progressive income tax

One way to offset wealth disparities in our country is to look to the period before the Reagan administration, when middle-class America thrived. One hallmark of that era was a progressive income tax, in which the wealthy paid a higher rate than their lower-income counterparts. Today, the highest earners are taxed at only 37 percent of their earnings, in contrast to the 70 percent rate that existed in the 1970s. While the wealthiest Americans might oppose such a change, there are more of us than there are of them. If we can persuade members of Congress to vote in their constituents' best economic interests, a progressive income tax would benefit all of American society by reducing wealth inequality and poverty.

In addition to adjusting income tax rates, we should also reduce tariffs on most imported goods because the higher import costs are typically passed on to consumers as a hidden tax.[1520] We can use the stories of individuals suffering from economic hardship to bring these messages home. Candidates for office, advocacy groups, and journalists should highlight the stories of working parents struggling to make ends meet to put a human face on the growing wealth gap in American society and spark public demand for change.

Manufacturing and unions

Another method for restoring income equality would be to subsidize manufacturing wages in essential industries. As the economy becomes more dependent on the technology sector, Americans without training in writing computer code or developing AI are finding their skills devalued. Yet manufacturing skills are essential for maintaining national security by reducing dependence on foreign countries for the production of items such as weapons, vehicles, medicine, and food. In addition, maintaining a strong economy and a competitive advantage requires us to produce computer chips and other components essential to modern economic activity. An obstacle to American manufacturing is the availability of less expensive labor in other countries. Oppressively low wages in China, for example, allow corporations to produce goods there more cheaply and thereby offer lower prices to consumers. In the United States, wages and benefits far exceed those paid to workers overseas, reflecting our values that workers should be fairly compensated and not exploited. As a result, many American companies have moved their factories offshore.

We can address this problem by using government subsidies to improve the wages and benefits of American manufacturing workers. We need not support every manufacturing sector, only those that are essential to maintaining autonomy in national security and emerging technologies. We may be content to import toys and clothing from foreign factories, but the goods that make us self-sufficient should be made in America. Corporations, whose priority is the bottom line, have shown themselves incapable of keeping jobs in the United States. As a result, we should use the additional tax revenue collected from corporations and the wealthiest Americans to subsidize manufacturing wages in key industries.

In addition, we must support the labor unions that built America's middle class. Unions enable collective bargaining that gives them the ability to match the power of a large corporation, whose instincts would otherwise be to minimize costs by reducing wages and benefits. Union negotiators achieve higher wages and better working conditions for unionized workers, which government subsidies can offset. Stories of blue-collar workers making cars and trucks on the assembly line have inspired pride in Detroit for decades. Unions help drive the American dream by providing opportunities for upward mobility.

During Trump's second term, he issued an executive order removing collective bargaining protections for large segments of federal workers in the name of "national security."[1521] The order, covering twenty-two agencies, used a broad definition to include employees at agencies with little apparent connection to national security, such as the Social Security Administration, the Department of Veterans Affairs, and the Department of the Interior.[1522] In a lawsuit, unions representing federal employees argued that the president's real goal was retaliation and control; they cited White House statements that "certain federal unions have declared war on President Trump's agenda" and that Trump would "not tolerate mass obstruction that jeopardizes his ability to manage agencies with vital national security missions."[1523] An appeals court decided in favor of Trump, ruling that courts cannot second-guess a president's decisions regarding national security.[1524] Trump's aggressive move to strip union protections from almost five hundred thousand federal workers was met with little public outcry.[1525] It was part of his larger effort to assert more control over the federal workforce, but what did it mean for unions outside of government work? The lack of resistance could empower a president or Congress to likewise chip away at union protections in the private sector under the guise of national security.

Future leaders must recognize the importance of union rights for employees to match the bargaining power of ever-larger corporations. If we are to preserve America's middle class, labor unions must be part of the equation. We need to lift up the workers who use their hands to provide Americans with the durable goods we depend on to thrive.

Home ownership

Besides wages and union protections, we must also address challenges in housing. One of the essential parts of the American dream is to own one's own home. Yet today in the United States, the average age of a first-time home buyer is thirty-eight years old.[1526] In 1980, the typical first-time home buyer was a person in their late twenties.[1527] Buying a home not only provides someone with housing security and the pride of ownership but also makes for a valuable investment asset, due to appreciation in value and tax deductions on interest payments. Buying a starter home often leads the homeowner down a path toward a larger home.

Homeownership benefits not only individual owners but also the communities in which they reside. People who own their own homes contribute to stable neighborhoods because of their investment in the community. They are more likely to spend time caring for and improving their home. Residents who know their neighbors are more likely to look out for one another. Families who are secure in their home avoid the disruptions that arise when children are required to change schools or parents need to find new doctors or even new ways to travel to their jobs. For all of these reasons, helping people to buy their first home would help middle-class Americans and the nation as a whole.

One way to help Americans buy their first home would be to provide down-payment vouchers and larger tax credits for mortgage payments. In the same way that some Americans qualify for food stamps, home buyers with incomes below a certain middle-class threshold could receive vouchers for purchasing a home; tax breaks could help them to make the mortgage payments over time. With greater economic justice, Americans would enjoy a higher quality of life, greater happiness and, consequently, more resilience against a tyrant seeking to amass power. To reduce wealth disparity, we should foster greater solidarity across our differences and focus on initiatives that improve our quality of life, rather than constantly spinning our government's wheels investigating the sins of the opposing party. Again, by using stories of families struggling to buy their first home, we can help inspire the policy changes needed to make these goals a reality.

Consumer protections

Another way to help protect ordinary Americans from the growing power of corporate greed would be to strengthen consumer protection laws and antitrust enforcement. In early 2025, the Trump administration began hollowing out the Consumer Financial Protection Bureau (CFPB).[1528] Formed in the wake of the 2008 financial crisis, the agency protects customers from abusive practices by banks and financial services companies. Trump said it was "very important to get rid of" CFPB, calling its employees "a vicious group of people."[1529] Elon Musk posted online, "RIP CFPB."[1530] Union members challenged the president's ability to destroy an agency created by Congress, but Trump voters voiced little objection.[1531] By strategically pandering to the wishes of his supporters on cultural issues, Trump deftly gained the political power to take action that harmed their financial interests. In dismantling CFPB, he removed a government institution that prevented large banks and big business from exploiting consumers of all political persuasions. A new vision must reverse the administration's efforts to tear down structures that protect ordinary Americans.

Additionally, we should revitalize our antitrust laws to rein in corporate greed. Mergers and acquisitions have consolidated markets in banking, health care, the media, and countless other sectors, leading to monopoly power that enables companies to gouge customers. And yet, antitrust enforcers and courts have seemed to yawn. For example, in 2024, Google was found to have engaged in illegal activities to freeze out competitors.[1532] The company entered into sales contracts for its products that required computer hardware makers, browser developers, and internet service providers to make Google their default search engine. The result of Google's predatory practices was unparalleled profits for itself and higher costs for people buying computers, cell phones, and wireless service plans. The consequence for the company's predatory behavior? A slap on the wrist. The minimal penalties that ended the case against Google sent its stock soaring. The upshot was a clear message to corporations that violating antitrust laws was a price worth paying.[1533] According to Bloomberg markets analyst John Authers, concentration of corporate power is at an unprecedented high in the tech industry. In this time of "greedflation," he writes, "dominant companies find it easier to set prices and hold down payrolls while rewarding shareholders—and this pumps up the inequality that has polarized the nation."[1534]

The solution lies in antitrust enforcement. As Authers advises, "The political stars are aligned for a new antitrust crusade."[1535] Antitrust laws protect competition in the marketplace, leading to product innovation and lower prices for consumers. Today's concentration of power in various sectors would have had Theodore Roosevelt up in arms. We need a new trustbuster. A new vision for leadership should include vigorous enforcement of the antitrust laws passed during the Gilded Age. In fact, antitrust enforcement enjoys bipartisan support from Democrats and Republicans who champion the middle class.[1536] Mitigating monopolistic greed would improve products and services, reduce consumer costs, and narrow the wealth gap that has fueled anger and division in our country.

Immigration

Another area of our politics that requires attention is immigration. We need to recognize that our immigration system is a mess. For too long, it has seemed that most members of both parties do not really want to fix the system because politics makes it too difficult. Allowing entry into the United States without knowing who we are admitting is a threat to our national security. Democrats seek the big tent of inclusion but take political hits from critics who rightly point out that porous borders threaten our safety. Republicans balk at the expenditure of public funds for undocumented immigrants but don't want to lose the cheap labor immigrants provide to certain industries. The result is gridlock.

While the second Trump administration focused on removing undocumented immigrants from the country, it did little to improve the immigration system; its conduct seemed more about flexing power and stoking anti-immigrant sentiment than real solutions. While there is no quick fix, several compromise steps could move us toward long-term improvement. The Center for American Progress, a public policy research organization, has proposed ideas to improve the US immigration system, including prohibiting asylum claims by immigrants who cross the border illegally.[1537] In addition, it proposes that immigrants who file asylum claims at the border would no longer be paroled into the country but would instead be held in custody for up to thirty days. If their claim is rejected, they would be released but prohibited from entering the United States. Of course, such a solution requires sufficient resources to decide cases within thirty days. CAP's proposed reform would also raise the standard of proof in asylum cases, to make it more difficult to game the system with bogus claims.

Jennifer Gorland, a former immigration judge who served in the Obama, Biden, and Trump administrations, shared with me her insights and ideas for improving the immigration system. First, rather than focusing all of our efforts on removing people who have entered or remained in violation of the law, we should find ways to promote *legal* immigration. Finding ways for immigrants to enter the United States lawfully, to serve our own needs, would be a win-win for our nation as well as source countries. For example, providing more work visas for people in South and Central America would improve our relations with these countries and help us fill worker shortages in various industries such as farming, hospitality, and construction. We currently face a severe shortage of workers in the building trades, leaving government-funded infrastructure projects idle.[1538] Work visas that permit immigrants to train as welders, carpenters, and electricians could help fill jobs where retirements are outnumbering new recruits.[1539] Immigrants could provide the labor needed to make badly needed improvements to America's crumbling bridges, tunnels, roads, pipes, and power lines. In addition, we should also encourage colleges and universities to offer scholarships to international students on the condition that they return to their home countries to perform work that will improve the quality of life there. For example, such conditions could include requiring them to work on reducing domestic and gang violence, thereby leading to fewer immigrants seeking to flee their homes for the safety of the United States.

Second, many immigrants who arrive at the US border seek asylum on grounds for which there is no statutory relief, such as escaping domestic or gang violence. The asylum statute addresses claims based only on "race, religion, nationality, membership in a particular social group, or political opinion."[1540] Because asylum seekers are entitled to a hearing, they are permitted entry if they can demonstrate that they would be persecuted if they returned to their home country. But a clogged immigration system that is substantially over capacity means they may not get a hearing for years. Some simply disappear into the country and live in the shadows without documentation, a risky existence that makes them susceptible to arrest and deportation. When they ultimately receive their hearing, most of those who show up are ordered removed because they are unable to demonstrate any statutory basis to remain.[1541] Uneven application of the law, permitting some to stay anyway, gives false hope to others seeking relief.

Instead of going through this meaningless exercise, we should invest resources in source countries to address the conditions that cause people to flee their homes. Severe problems prompt people to make dangerous journeys to the United States. By addressing the root causes they seek to escape, we may be able to reduce the flood of people arriving at our borders. It is in our national interest to address this issue. Restoring USAID would be an important first step. The agency not only provides humanitarian relief, but it also promotes economic development, health, and education.[1542] In countries with high rates of domestic violence, trained USAID workers could help develop organizations devoted to reducing assaults and providing shelters for survivors. Similarly, we could provide aid to foreign countries to help them combat gang violence in their own countries so that their residents see less need to escape their surroundings to avoid becoming victims or recruits. As climate change increases the number of refugees, we should increase—not decrease—the humanitarian aid we provide, using funds not just to feed, clothe, shelter, and heal people but to help them build infrastructure systems to help them sustain themselves. We should see such expenditures as investments in our own security.

In addition, we should amend the asylum statute to clarify who qualifies. For example, admission criteria based on membership in a "particular social group" is currently applied inconsistently because of uncertainty about its meaning. As a result, the language incentivizes immigrants who are ineligible for asylum to try anyway. This provision is often used to permit asylum for people who have been persecuted because of their sexual orientation. For example, in Uganda and Senegal, it is illegal to be gay. We should rephrase the statute's language to specify that asylum is available for individuals who have been persecuted for their sexual orientation, and eliminate the vague "social group" language. This revision would give clear notice to immigrants as to whether they are eligible for asylum, deterring people from coming to our border when they have no chance to stay. In addition, we should amend the asylum statute to provide fair notice that gang threats and domestic violence do not amount to the kind of persecution for which asylum was designed. This would help to reduce the backlog in our immigration courts and prevent immigrants from suffering the indignities of detention and deportation.

Third, we should replicate with Mexico the agreement we have with Canada. Under that arrangement, when an immigrant enters Canada from a third country before coming to the United States, they must return to Canada to litigate their asylum claim. A similar agreement with Mexico would eliminate the entry of immigrants from other countries and would substantially diminish the volume of immigrants seeking asylum in the United States. This move would alleviate the burden on our immigration courts and reduce the number of immigrants living in the country without legal status, many of whom never return to court and live in the shadows of American society. To incentivize Mexico to agree to such a deal, we could offer them something of value in exchange, such as a substantial number of work visas for Mexican citizens. The availability of work visas for Mexican citizens would also reduce the number of people entering illegally.

Fourth, we should negotiate with other countries to take back their own citizens. Men from Venezuela were sent to the terrorist prison in El Salvador in part because Venezuela would not accept them. If we are going to negotiate "deals," then we should look for ways to return immigrants to their home countries rather than ways to send them to third countries like El Salvador or South Sudan. For some countries, a deal may be a nonstarter, but one bargaining chip could be to offer US work visas for a set number of immigrants from each country, with a pathway to citizenship, to incentivize them to cooperate.

Fifth, instead of just arresting and deporting people already living in America one at a time, regardless of any danger they pose, we should use proactive investigations to disrupt immigration fraud schemes. Smugglers worldwide prey on immigrants seeking to come to America; migrants sometimes pay tens of thousands of dollars to their so-called "travel agents" for passage through various countries and into the United States, usually using false documents. We must use global alliances to disrupt these rings in source countries. In immigration court, litigants often present documents from their home country, such as birth certificates and marriage certificates, that cannot be authenticated. As AI enables the creation of more sophisticated counterfeit documents, we must develop methods to detect them. We should also explore systems that utilize AI to assist investigators in distinguishing genuine from counterfeit immigration documents. In addition, we should focus not only on immigrants who are working in the United States without legal status but also on the employers who hire them. Although the Trump administration arrested undocumented immigrants in the parking lots of Home Depot stores, it did little to bring criminal prosecutions against the contractors that hired them. To deter this practice, we should prioritize the prosecution of employers who knowingly hire people without legal authorization to work.

Finally, we should provide citizenship to the immigrants in this country covered by Deferred Action for Childhood Arrivals (DACA).[1543] This policy prevents removal from the United States of people who were brought to the United States as children; many of them are now adults with no connections to or even recollections of their home countries. They have been left in legal limbo for too long and should be granted citizenship. This would be part of a compromise package that would need to be accepted by immigration hawks who balk at any amnesty program like this, in exchange for comprehensive reforms to shore up the border.

By putting human faces and names on the plights of families, we can counter the cruelty cultivated by the Trump administration, and elicit the compassion needed to address one of our most intractable issues. Just as Laken Riley and Kilmar Abrego Garcia became household names, we need to recognize the individual humanity of the people in our immigration system to build the kind of empathy that can motivate change.

Violent Crime

When Trump took over policing in Washington, DC, he said he was cracking down on violent crime. However, research and experience show that his heavy-handed tactics are the exact opposite of the strategy that has led to a decline in crime rates in American cities over the past few years. When I served as US attorney in Detroit, our office partnered with federal, state, and local stakeholders as well as researchers to study and implement best practices. At that time, I recall that one of the stories we heard from experts was a variation on the parable of the starfish thrower. As the parable goes, a boy finds thousands of starfish washed up on the beach, where they will certainly die. He starts throwing them back into the water, one by one, but for each starfish he throws in, more wash ashore. A man comes along and tells him that his efforts are futile because he cannot possibly throw them all back. The boy replies that he may be unable to save all of them, but he can save this one. As he continues to throw the starfish back, the man begins to help. The variation on the story was that the man turns around and walks away. When the boy asks where he is going, the man says he is going to find out how the starfish are ending up on the beach in the first place and prevent them from landing there at all. It is a metaphor, of course, for crime prevention.

Some politicians promote the idea that law enforcement officers can arrest individuals who commit crimes without limit. And to protect public safety from immediate harm, you must arrest, prosecute, and punish offenders. But if *all* you do is arrest and imprison, you will never stop the flow of offenders, and members of the public will continue to be victimized. To achieve long-term public safety, government programs must address the root causes of crime. According to Thomas Abt, a former Justice Department official who now leads the Center for the Study and Practice of Violence Reduction at the University of Maryland, a large law enforcement presence reduces crime only in the short term. "The reason that surges are not particularly effective, and are generally disfavored by crime researchers and others who look at this stuff for a living, is because it's a resource-intensive way of temporarily reducing crime. If it does in fact reduce crime, that doesn't address any of the underlying conditions."[1544]

In Detroit, we coordinated efforts among law enforcement agencies and community partners from the business and nonprofit sectors. Federal, state, and local law enforcement agencies collaborated to do what each does best: Federal agencies traced guns, provided intelligence about international drug cartels and violent gangs, and offered investigative techniques not available to state officials, like wiretaps and grand jury subpoenas. State police lent troopers for traffic stops and crime lab support. And local police officers, who knew their communities best, patrolled the streets. Federal and state prosecutors worked cooperatively to charge cases in the forum where the laws were most effective, based either on the strength of the penalty or the efficiency of the process. We saw tremendous results, including the lowest homicide total since the mid-1960s.

Part of the strategy was community interruption of violence, which takes various forms but is a proven method for reducing violent crime.[1545] Arrest data and criminal history were used to identify individuals at high risk for engaging in violent crime. In Detroit, as part of an initiative known as Ceasefire, offenders were required to participate in a violence-reduction program as a condition of parole or probation. In Chicago's Peacekeepers Program, "violence interrupters," who are trusted community members, recruit these individuals. Once enrolled in a program, these high-risk individuals are offered a range of services, including education, job training, and assistance in finding employers willing to hire people with a felony record. In addition, participants are offered cognitive behavioral therapy to help them make better choices during conflicts on the streets. As a result, people learn to make better decisions, put down their guns, and live safely without resorting to violence. In Detroit, we saw significant reductions in gang violence in areas where the program operated. The program has evolved and grown in Detroit through the use of violence interrupters, known locally as ShotStoppers.[1546] The programs were funded through federal grants and support from the business and nonprofit communities. In Chicago, a similar program led to a 73 percent drop in recidivism over a two-year period.[1547]

The Trump administration's cuts to grant funding was detrimental to these strategies that were making a significant impact on violent crime.[1548] Police patrols have value in deterring crime and serving the public. But a show of military force merely creates the *appearance* of an administration that is tough on crime. Real results require nuance and the support of communities through the collaboration of law enforcement, business, philanthropy, and local residents. Telling stories about not only victims of crime but also people who have turned their lives around can help persuade the public that investments in prevention are crucial to long-term success in reducing crime.

Other Urgent Issues

A vision for America's future must include plans to address issues around technology and climate change. Human advancement requires scientific research and open inquiry, free from political pandering. As artificial intelligence advances rapidly, we must establish guardrails to protect data privacy, prevent bias, and mitigate the harms of "hallucinations" and other hazards. At the very least, we can require labeling of deepfake photos and videos generated with AI, demand transparency into when AI is used in government and private services, and require large AI companies to submit to audits and oversight to ensure their practices are in the public interest. With a Congress that reflects the will of the people rather than the desires of billionaires, we can achieve these things.

An additional concern for the twenty-first century is the reality that our planet is heating up every day. Extreme weather events such as hurricanes, floods, and wildfires are becoming more frequent. The loss of habitable locations will lead to more refugee crises as more people compete for scarcer resources. We cannot reverse the damage we have already caused to our environment, but we can prevent new harm. Industries that spew pollution want to ignore climate change or pretend it doesn't exist, so that they can maximize profits without costly abatement programs. Donald Trump has pandered to this viewpoint: During a 2025 address to the United Nations General Assembly, Trump said, "This 'climate change,' it's the greatest con job ever perpetrated on the world, in my opinion." Trump continued, "All of these predictions made by the United Nations and many others, often for bad reasons, were wrong. They were made by stupid people that have cost their countries fortunes and given those same countries no chance for success. If you don't get away from this green scam, your country is going to fail."[1549]

We can't allow leaders to continue perpetuating this lie, or we and our planet will pay the price. Not only should we be concerned for the Earth, we must also be mindful of the competitive advantage we are losing to China, which has invested heavily in developing clean energy. China is leading the world in supplying equipment for alternative energy, such as solar panels and wind turbines.[1550] As the United States clings to fossil fuels to appease big oil and coal companies, we are losing economic power to a hostile foreign adversary. Again, stories may be the way to cut through the debate. Stories about the victims of wildfires and hurricanes can make a compelling case for addressing the realities of global warming and climate change. A vision for the future must include solutions to address technology and climate change.

Unity

Any vision for the future needs to include unity. The divide-and-conquer mentality may be an effective way to campaign, but it is a terrible way to govern. Politics is the art of compromise. Future leaders must be able to build coalitions among disparate groups of voters to break the partisan poison that infects our politics. To build political alliances among a diverse range of groups, we must reject the pursuit of political purity and focus on shared priorities. I know plenty of middle-aged moderates who say they are fiscally conservative and socially progressive. Many voters today are just the opposite. In a democracy, we must respect the will of the people, even if we don't share the majority view on every issue. Sometimes, society moves more slowly to adapt to change than we would like. Most voters don't think of themselves as being "far right" or "far left" but as individuals with genuine concerns in search of pragmatic answers.

Just as Donald Trump was able to build coalitions among business leaders, the religious right, and voters who felt economically left behind, America's next generation of leaders can also find common ground among various groups. Progressives and populists share many goals, such as providing the working class with good-paying jobs, affordable housing, and access to health care. By focusing on kitchen-table issues rather than culture wars, candidates can bring more supporters into the tent. We don't have to sacrifice our values to support candidates willing to make compromises, but we may need to be more patient as we seek to convince our fellow citizens of our views. Likewise, libertarian Republicans likely share with progressives a deep commitment to free speech and other civil liberties that Trump and the MAGA movement have demolished in the interest of promoting their own views. These groups share a disdain for executive orders targeting law firms, universities, and the media for engaging in activity that is protected by the First Amendment. Freedom is a value around which many Americans can rally.

Trump has united voters only through their hatred of common enemies, such as immigrants, the transgender community, or "the left," portraying any political opponent as part of a monolithic force of evil. But eventually, voters will grow tired of the rhetoric as they see their wallets shrink. A candidate who can find ways to unify various groups of voters can build a winning coalition. Deliberately stoking division is antithetical to our Constitution, which talks about "we, the people," not "us versus them."

We can overcome the appeal of the culture wars ourselves, right now, by choosing to see ourselves and each other as individuals, and resist efforts to cast us as "the right" versus "the left." The "either/or fallacy," the debater's trick, baits us into choosing between only two choices. In fact, the world is far more nuanced, and we have infinite choices about how to shape our future. We must think for ourselves and see others not as our enemies, but as our fellow Americans seeking to achieve common goals.

Call Me By My Name

One of the most effective ways to capture public attention is by highlighting the people harmed by current policies and neglect. Roger Tam would be sentenced to only nine months in prison for harboring undocumented immigrants after the judge found that their deaths were accidental. Still, Miguel, Pablo, Leonel, Simeon, and Brayan left an indelible impression on me and everyone who touched the case. The young men had come to America to work long days for low wages, meals, and a roof over their heads in hopes of a better life. Instead, their lives were tragically cut short. We all can inspire others by embracing our shared humanity. We all have more in common than we have differences. To advance as a nation, we must find a unity of purpose while preserving our individual humanity. If we can overcome the deliberate political tactics that divide us, we can restore our national purpose of life, liberty, and the pursuit of happiness.

FOURTEEN

CIVIC AWAKENING

In 2005, Donald Trump launched Trump University, touting the program as a way for people to learn his secrets to success in real estate and moneymaking.[1551] Thousands enrolled in seminars and paid tuition; one "Gold Elite" course cost as much as thirty-five thousand dollars. Trump promoted his university as a way for ordinary Americans to achieve financial power. In one web video, Trump said his courses would "teach you better than the best business school." Instead, some who bought in found instructors with no qualifications in real estate. In 2011, the Better Business Bureau gave Trump University a grade of D-minus after receiving twenty-three complaints.[1552] In 2010, former students filed a class action lawsuit in California, alleging that the university provided nothing more than extended "infomercials."[1553] In court documents, one former employee called the university a "fraudulent scheme" that "preyed upon the elderly and uneducated to separate them from their money."[1554] Others described psychological tactics used by sales staff to exploit the emotions of prospective students, some of whom were even encouraged to max out their credit cards to pay tuition.[1555] Those who followed Trump, even paid to be like him, at some point realized they were being defrauded. They woke up. They organized. They fought back and they won, leading to a settlement in their favor that brought the collapse of Trump University.

In my work as a prosecutor, I have learned that con artists can get away with their crimes for only so long. One of the truly useful insights Donald Trump shares in *The Art of the Deal* is that sooner or later, you must deliver what you promise, or else people will catch on to the scam. "You can't con people, at least not for long," he wrote. "You can create excitement, you can do wonderful promotion and get all kinds of press, and you can throw in a little hyperbole. But if you don't deliver the goods, people will eventually catch on."[1556] The same is true of leaders who use intimidation and traffic in lies.

At some point, Americans who took Trump's bait and voted against their own financial self-interest will realize that they are no wealthier than they were before. In fact, they will find that they are comparatively poorer than the highest earners as the income gap grows, fueled by Trump's MAGA policies. If his tariffs persist, they will cause consumer prices to rise, leaving working-class voters with less money for other expenses. At some point, people will notice that crime rates are not lower in cities where Trump took over police departments with a show of military force. Long-term crime rates will increase or remain unchanged because the root causes of poverty have gone unaddressed and grant funds devoted to the effort have been cut. Even after the deportation of immigrants, we will see people continue to seek a better life in America if we don't invest in improvements that reduce the likelihood they will flee their homes in the first place. Taking away grant funding for scientific research and ignoring or lying about scientific fact will prevent progress in public health and lead to the return of diseases once thought eradicated, like measles and polio. Eventually, the people will catch on that Trump's daily reality show of signing ceremonies, executive orders, pageantry, and online posts has not solved any real problems and, in fact, has achieved only bigger problems and deeper division.

But when? And by the time people catch on, will it be too late to recover essentials such as the independence of the Justice Department, the vigor of Congress, or the rule of law? Will our voting districts be so gerrymandered that we are unable to elect the leaders of our choice? Will the wealthiest Americans be able to make such large campaign contributions that electoral office will simply go to the highest bidders, transforming America into an oligarchy?

I know from my work in crisis response that most of us harbor a "normalcy" bias—that is, we tend to ignore signs of danger because we assume that ordinary conditions will prevail. This normalcy bias can be dangerous in a crisis because people tend to remain in harm's way even after it is time to evacuate. Some of the people who died in the September 11 attacks continued working at their desks in the South Tower of the World Trade Center even after the North Tower had been hit by a plane.[1557] As we see unprecedented attacks on our democracy, it is tempting to believe that everything is still fine. For many of us, life goes on as usual. But things are not normal in the United States. When protest is criminalized and troops occupy city streets, when the president extorts law firms and universities, when masked agents make arrests, and when people are "erroneously" deported without due process, it is time to take action.

We, the people, have the power to expose the con now, before it is too late to recover our institutions of democracy. In today's world, many Americans seem content to amuse themselves with celebrity gossip, spectator sports, online gambling, TikTok videos, and other passive forms of entertainment. This is a freedom we have in our country. But citizenship comes with the responsibility to educate ourselves about issues and participate in our democracy. Numerous strategies are available to help us, as individuals, show the rest of the country that the emperor has no clothes. But we must act with urgency, before we miss the opportunity to correct the course of American history.

Lawsuits

One of the most successful forms of resistance against the Trump regime's assertions of power has been litigation. During a time when Trump faced few checks from other pillars of democracy, such as Congress, lawsuits were remarkably successful. As reported in *The Atlantic*, "a legal resistance led by a patchwork coalition of lawyers, public-interest groups, Democratic state attorneys general, and unions has frustrated Trump's ambitions. Hundreds of attorneys and plaintiffs have stood up to him, feeding a steady assembly line of setbacks and judicial reprimands for a president who has systematically sought to break down limits on his own power."[1558] *Just Security*, a digital law journal based at the New York University School of Law, posted a legal tracker with continuous updates.[1559] According to the tracker, five hundred legal challenges were filed against the Trump administration in the first ten months of 2025. Courts blocked at least part of the president's actions in 144 of those cases, with 246 other cases awaiting a court ruling. In dozens of those cases, plaintiffs obtained favorable final rulings against Trump with no government appeal.[1560] Lawsuits blocked or slowed the closure of federal agencies, the firing of government employees, the extortion of law firms, the imposition of tariffs, and many other Trump initiatives.[1561]

In addition to stopping executive overreach, lawsuits also exposed some of the administration's most troubling conduct: the ruthlessness of DOGE, the predawn deportations, the disdain for due process and the rule of law. Media reports publicizing court opinions finding against the Trump Administration—sometimes in scathing terms—helped raise awareness of the administration's efforts to expand executive power.[1562] Opinions like the one written by Judge Harvie Wilkinson of the Fourth Circuit Court of Appeals alerted the public to the breathtaking lawlessness of Trump's erroneous removal of Kilmar Abrego Garcia without due process and refusal to return him: "This should be shocking not only to judges," the Reagan appointee wrote, "but to the intuitive sense of liberty that Americans far removed from courthouses still hold dear."[1563] While Trump was dashing off executive orders with ever more bold assertions of power, lawyers were beating them back in court.

When Judge William Young found that the Trump administration had violated the First Amendment rights of students when it took immigration enforcement action against them in retaliation for speaking out in favor of Palestinians, he began his written opinion with a note he had received from an anonymous sender. The note stated, "Trump has pardons and tanks. What do you have?" Beneath the note, Judge Young responded, "Dear Mr. or Ms. Anonymous, Alone, I have nothing but my sense of duty. Together, we the people of the United States—you and me—have our magnificent Constitution. Here's how that works out in a specific case."[1564] He then proceeded to recount the government's actions in the case, analyze them under the law, and declare them unconstitutional. His response to the anonymous note was a powerful reminder of our founding document's separation of powers among the three coequal branches of government.

All Americans opposed to the tyranny of Trump should draw inspiration from the success of these lawsuits. We need more lawyers to champion these causes by representing labor unions, wrongfully terminated federal workers, immigrants, protesters, university students, and other ordinary people who often lack the resources to hire expensive attorneys. In apparent fear of retaliation, some law firms have turned their backs on people who seek to challenge the president in court. Lawyers ready to advocate for the people can take jobs with offices of state attorneys general or advocacy organizations, such as the American Civil Liberties Union, which are still performing the vital work of defending democratic norms.

Of course, lawsuits depend not only on the lawyers who advocate for these causes but also on plaintiffs who are eligible to sue. Because only those who have suffered actual harm have legal standing to bring a case in court, individuals need to volunteer to challenge unlawful government action—no small sacrifice in light of the threats and harassment it might invite. Plaintiffs, too, should be emboldened by the early successes of many suits in the courts. In the words of one school official who overcame initial reluctance and ultimately decided to step up as a plaintiff to challenge cuts by the Department of Education, "You are in 1938 Berlin. Which kind of person are you?"[1565]

Besides lawyers and plaintiffs, others can help these causes by funding their efforts through donations to organizations like the State Democracy Defenders Fund and Democracy Forward, which filed a hundred cases against the Trump administration in its first nine months.[1566] While some courts ruled in favor of Trump's initiatives, many court orders provide a playbook for checking his most egregious abuses of power. Our constitutional protections for free expression, due process, equal protection, and separation of powers, as well as our statutory rights to fair notice, just cause, and freedom from arbitrary decisions are all worth fighting for in court. If we lose these rights, we lose our democracy.

Collective Action

One of the great strengths of democratic movements is the power of collective action. Any of us who looks at the state of our country on our own may feel despair and helplessness. In fact, one of the goals of authoritarian leaders is to make opponents feel hopeless, so that they will fall in line and obey. However, when we come together in groups, we can gain strength and confidence. Jim Clark, president of the Boys and Girls Clubs of America, has written that collective action can achieve accelerated results and increase impact; he describes the image of a rowing crew, able to use their oars collectively to move a boat faster and more efficiently than a single rower ever could.[1567] When it comes to mobilizing political change, collective action can have the same effect.

Collective action can topple tyrants. That's why authoritarians stoke division in society, to prevent oppositional organizing and resistance. As historian Ruth Ben-Ghiat has written, "Authoritarianism depends on breaking the horizontal bonds of solidarity and empathy that lead people to risk their safety to protest injustices against others. . . . Weak authoritarians fear empathy, a sense of justice and morality, love for others, and collective action."[1568] Protesters who speak out against the Trump administration's abuses of power, she writes, "are on the right side of history. A reckoning will come for the aggressors as more Americans open their eyes to the criminal nature of this administration."[1569]

In October 2025, charitable organizations banded together to form "NATO for Non-Profits," modeled after the post–World War II alliance that provides collective defense for its members.[1570] Their stated goal was to protect each other if they were targeted by Trump in retaliation for their work. In a crisis, members would issue statements of support, lend resources, and otherwise rally around the target. As with NATO, an attack on one would be seen as an attack on all. Led by Vanita Gupta, who served in top Justice Department positions during the Obama and Biden administrations, the group was formed in response to Trump's memorandum on "countering domestic terrorism."[1571] Trump's memo directed federal agencies to dismantle "networks" organizing "under the umbrella of self-described anti-fascism."[1572] Some nonprofit leaders feared the directive could be interpreted broadly to bring the power of the federal government down on any organization that did not share Trump's views.

A lesson from other countries facing authoritarian crackdowns on civil society is that organizations end up expending resources on defending themselves rather than performing their work serving vulnerable communities.[1573] By banding together, members of NATO for Nonprofits could share that load. That same week, 3,700 groups signed on to a letter opposing Trump's memo as an effort to "intimidate and silence charitable groups through executive action." The signatories included a diverse array of nonprofit organizations, such as the American Association of University Women, the Immigrant Legal Resource Center, chapters of the ACLU, fair housing centers, reproductive health care networks, environmental groups, children's defense funds, and churches.[1574] They wrote, "Efforts by the president of the United States to defund, discredit, and dismantle nonprofit groups he simply disagrees with are reprehensible and dangerous—a violation of a fundamental freedom in America."[1575] Noting the importance of solidarity, the letter added, "We stand with those wrongly targeted and with each other. No exceptions."[1576] As Gupta explained, "The only way through this moment is with collective action. When you have an administration that tries to silence people through the cudgel of the federal government, the only way through is to work together."[1577]

For individuals who want to get involved, many existing organizations are ready-made for political activism. Local Republican and Democratic Party clubs have the ear of their members of Congress, US senators, and state officials. Joining a county or district party organization can give any one of us a direct line to elected leaders to urge them to challenge MAGA politicians and policies. Nonpartisan organizations such as the League of Women Voters, which works to educate voters and protect and expand voting rights, have chapters throughout the country.[1578] In addition, grassroots groups like Indivisible, with local chapters in many communities, recognize that defending democracy is not a matter of party politics but of preserving America as we know it. Indivisible provides its member groups with informational materials to help train volunteers and organize action, such as calling members of Congress, talking to voters, and participating in protests.

Even if we are unable to find a local group to join, we can participate in demonstrations, such as the nationwide "Hands-Off" and "No Kings" protests. Protests can provide ordinary people with an opportunity to amplify their voices and send a message to elected officials. Even if the president is indifferent, members of Congress or local elected officials might take note, causing them to reconsider their support for an unpopular leader. Political demonstrations can also inspire onlookers. For people who are not paying attention to politics, a massive protest can prompt them to stop and consider what is happening to their country. For people who are concerned but don't know what they can do, seeing people from all walks of life participating in demonstrations may inspire them to join the cause. Rallies provide an opportunity to invite friends to come along, including those who may never have participated in a protest in their lives. Among the signs seen at some of the demonstrations was one that read, "This is my first protest." For critics who say protesters are simply preaching to the choir, the demonstrations still hold value by galvanizing participants through the positive energy of others in the crowd. Sometimes it can feel empowering to know that we are not alone in our views. And large protests signal to the world that a leader is losing political support.

In October 2025, an estimated four to seven million people participated in No Kings protests in big cities and small towns, including in counties won by Trump in 2024.[1579] Trump's GOP supporters sought to undermine the event by accusing participants of being paid protesters or agitators.[1580] House Speaker Mike Johnson, a staunch Trump ally, called the day's events "hate America" rallies that attracted "all the pro-Hamas wing and, you know, the antifa people."[1581] But in fact, the protests were attended by a diverse assembly of patriotic Americans—high school students, teachers, veterans, and grandparents. I even saw a priest at a joyful gathering in Gettysburg, Pennsylvania, where hundreds of participants cheered each time a car passed by and honked its horn in approval. Many protesters carried whimsical signs with messages such as "The only monarchs should be butterflies" and "Too many issues, not enough sign." The No Kings rallies were a celebration of America. They showed that a large segment of the population cared enough about preserving democracy to show up on a Saturday afternoon and take to the streets. No wonder far-right politicians sought to diminish the value of the protests. The turnout was a beacon of hope against a regime that was trampling on the rule of law, and a good reminder that America's decline into authoritarianism is not inevitable, because the people still hold the power.

Boycotts are another way that individuals can band together to amplify their voices. Just as the Montgomery bus boycott in response to the arrest of Rosa Parks for refusing to move to the back of the bus in 1955 helped to spark the civil rights movement in the American South, boycotts of news outlets and television networks can pressure them to resist Trump's efforts to muzzle speech he dislikes. Canceled subscriptions and low ratings can provide a powerful incentive for media companies to avoid self-censorship simply to appease the president. For example, when ABC suspended Jimmy Kimmel from his late-night comedy show, subscribers canceled their streaming subscriptions to Disney+, an arm of the network's parent company.[1582] While viewers terminate their subscriptions for various reasons, the three million customers who canceled their subscriptions in September 2025 greatly exceeded the usual total of 1.2 million every three months.[1583] ABC returned Kimmel to the air after a six-day hiatus, perhaps motivated by a desire to retain viewers. If for-profit media companies won't permit free speech or cover important news the administration finds uncomfortable, audiences can switch to other outlets that will, including a growing number of nonpartisan, nonprofit news sites such as the Marshall Project, ProPublica, *MinnPost*, *CalMatters*, and *The Texas Tribune*. Consumers have power, and we should use it.

Education

Another vital way to expose a con artist is through education. We can learn and we can teach. We need not become overwhelmed by the litany of issues about which we might hope to learn. Instead, we can identify one issue that matters to us—whether it is medical research, health care, public education, or some other concern—and educate ourselves about it. We don't need an advanced degree to learn about the topics we are passionate about; we can inform ourselves by reading the work of experts. Credible journalism and peer-reviewed journals contain findings supported by evidence. With access to online resources, we can read source material, such as statutes and case law. We can attend candidate debates and town hall meetings, where we can ask questions and determine whether potential leaders are genuinely committed to solving problems or simply seeking to avoid confrontation. Lectures at local universities, community colleges, places of worship, civic organization meetings, and local libraries all provide opportunities to learn more about issues that matter to us.

During Trump's first year back in office, some universities held teach-ins, gatherings where professors provided information about various aspects of history, political science, and law. Teach-ins began at the University of Michigan in 1965 as an alternative to sit-ins or walk-outs in opposition to the Vietnam War. Instead, professors used their collective knowledge to host an all-night educational event open to students and community members, during which they lectured, debated, and answered questions. Teach-ins have become popular in the ensuing decades because they offer an opportunity for deeper engagement by helping people contextualize current events. I participated in teach-ins at the University of Michigan in early 2025. Organized by faculty members outside regular business hours and open to students on a voluntary basis, the teach-ins drew large crowds and encouraged active audience engagement. Those who attended seemed eager to understand the sudden and profound changes to the way our government was being run. Professors at other universities did the same.

In October 2025, academics, journalists, citizens, and even podcasters gathered at the Smithsonian National Museum of American History for a teach-in in support of history and museums.[1584] Alarmed by Trump's efforts to whitewash some of American history's stains, organizers of the event explained that America's past does not "belong to" any political party or leader.[1585] Instead, history is "rooted in archives and evidence" that includes an "understanding of the country's contentious past—its joys and its sorrows, its benefits and its harms, its brilliant promise and its unrealized dreams."[1586] Importantly, planners of the teach-in intended to model civil discourse as "an alternative to the 'debate-me-bro' culture that defines so much of political life in the US today, showing that activism works best when it is not about scoring rhetorical points but rather deepening our understanding of the issues and nation we seek to shape."[1587] Teachers, journalists, and storytellers can help to preserve our history, all of it. Thinking deeply about our past, including the unpleasant parts—especially the unpleasant parts—is essential to moving forward.[1588]

Communication

Another critical tactic for resistance is communication. During the Arab Spring, large groups of protesters were able to organize across the Middle East by using social media, a relatively new technology in 2011.[1589] By setting dates, times, and locations for demonstrations, individuals were able to bring about extensive public showings of opposition to oppression. Their ability to organize led to the resignation of Egypt's Hosni Mubarak and sparked hope for a better future.[1590] Their success was short-lived, as leaders responded with arrests and violence, but their use of social media to get their message out was inspiring.[1591] Of course, social media can also be a vector for disinformation and government propaganda. However, more than at any other time in history, we have the ability to communicate widely through social media, allowing us to share our message with a large community of people. We need not wait for someone else to organize a protest or a teach-in. We can do it ourselves, communicating the logistics to the world in a single online post.

Communicating can also take the form of speaking out on behalf of others. Too often during Trump's second term, leaders have kept their heads down and their mouths shut. In the famous quote often attributed to eighteenth-century philosopher Edmund Burke, "The only thing necessary for evil to triumph is that good men do nothing,"[1592] People who care about preserving democracy must speak up. We all have voices and can express our views on injustice. During 2025, Republicans were complicit with Trump and, with few exceptions, Democrats seemed cowed or confused. But voices outside of politics, such as business and faith leaders, can perhaps be even more persuasive than elected officials. For instance, in February 2025, Catholic bishops in Michigan issued a joint statement calling on lawmakers to seek legislation that not only would protect our borders but also create "a humane immigration system that welcomes refugees and immigrants by providing a fair pathway to citizenship." Their statement denounced "harmful rhetoric that broadly demeans our immigrant brothers and sisters" and called for the "unyielding support and respect for the human dignity of all migrant people in our midst."[1593] Business leaders, university presidents, professional associations, and others with a platform have an obligation to speak up for American values, even when it is risky to do so.

Ordinary people, too, can speak out, through social media, letters to the editor, and letters to their members of Congress to stand up for democracy. We can also discuss our views with friends and neighbors. People tend to trust those they know best. As a result, we can wield a great deal of influence within our social circle and raise awareness about the harms that flow from the corruption, cruelty, and mob-style tactics of Donald Trump and MAGA politics.

Even when we disagree with our neighbors, we can be most persuasive when we use empathic listening.[1594] Rather than browbeating our neighbors, we must listen more than we speak. We can respond by asking questions, showing curiosity, and respecting their views. We may not "win" the argument then and there, but if we can plant a seed that causes others to reconsider their positions, we will have made progress.

Resistance

An important response to a power-hungry tyrant is resistance. Just as the mob boss relies on acquiescence, so, too, does the authoritarian leader. During Trump's second term as president, too many law firms, media outlets, universities, and political leaders capitulated to his coercive demands. Others put their heads down in hopes of avoiding attention. *The New York Times* reported that it was becoming more difficult for reporters to find experts who would go on the record to criticize Trump out of apparent fear of retribution, a development the paper referred to as "a chill spreading over political debate in Washington and beyond."[1595] But the brave souls who fought back deserve our praise. The law firms that filed suit challenging punitive executive orders against them and won made our democracy just a little bit stronger. So did the media outlets that surrendered their press credentials rather than agree to a Pentagon press policy that prohibited reporting on information not approved by the Defense Department.[1596] When seven major universities rejected a "compact" that would provide preferred funding if they agreed to adhere to Trump's views, they struck a blow in favor of academic freedom and merit-based grants, refusing to succumb to the fear of the consequences of refusing Trump's "deal."[1597] As Maurene Comey, daughter of the former FBI director, wrote in an email message to her colleagues after she was fired from her position as a federal prosecutor, "Fear is the tool of the tyrant."[1598] Authoritarians seek to silence their opponents through threats and intimidation. That's because public criticism is a danger to them. John Gotti was convicted at trial through the testimony of Sammy "The Bull" Gravano, an underboss in the Gambino crime family who broke the gangster code of silence.[1599] Speaking out against an authoritarian leader can sometimes reveal the information needed to deflate their influence and control.

Nullification

Another power the people have is jury nullification. Jurors who refuse to indict or convict a defendant even when the evidence is sufficient are said to "nullify" the law, finding in favor of a defendant in the broader interests of justice. A famous case of jury nullification occurred in 1733 when John Peter Zenger was charged with seditious libel in New York for publishing newspaper articles critical of the British colonial governor.[1600] Even though the judge instructed the jury that they needed to find only that Zenger had published the articles, which Zenger had unquestionably done, the jury returned a not-guilty verdict after only ten minutes of deliberation.[1601] The people were rebelling against oppressive laws in a case that is now seen as a courageous stand in defense of the free press.

Nullification can occur not only at trial but also at the grand jury stage of a case. The Fifth Amendment to the Constitution provides that no person may be brought to trial on a federal felony charge unless they have first been indicted by a grand jury; the protection is based on the belief that a body of citizens should serve as a check on the government's power to take away someone's liberty. As of early September 2025, *The New York Times* reported seven instances in which a Washington, DC, grand jury had refused to return an indictment, including three times in the same case.[1602] I know from my own experience as a federal prosecutor that a grand jury's refusal to return an indictment is extremely rare. That's because prosecutors typically exercise appropriate discretion to avoid overcharging cases, and supervisors carefully review proposed indictments before they are presented to a grand jury. In such cases, where the evidence amounts to probable cause, grand jurors should respect the rule of law and return an indictment. Similarly, trial jurors should find defendants guilty at trial when the evidence amounts to proof beyond a reasonable doubt. Nonetheless, grand jury and trial jurors retain the ability to decide against the government when they believe a case is not in the best interests of justice.

To the extent that Trump's Department of Justice and its successors abuse their power to prosecute people who engaged in fabricated "lawfare," nullification is a tool ordinary people can use against unjust prosecutions. Even a single holdout juror can create a hung jury, requiring the government to try the case again or, if it believes the likelihood of conviction would be no higher with a different jury, to dismiss the case. The Founding Fathers gave jurors the power to prevent the government from oppressing the people through unjust prosecutions and convictions. Jurors have a duty to exercise that power.

Satire

One underappreciated way to expose the corruption and hypocrisy of an authoritarian leader is humor. When a tyrant makes obviously false claims, we can use satire to demonstrate their absurdity. Mockery brings attention to lies in ways that combative argument sometimes cannot.

As historian Ruth Ben-Ghiat has written, authoritarians may love a good fight, but they hate to be humiliated:

> Authoritarians do have their own twisted sense of humor. Most of them are sadists, so they enjoy humiliating people, including their sycophantic enablers. Benito Mussolini loved to make fun of anti-fascists who had "repented" to reduce their prison sen-

> tences; he would read their confession/conversion statements out loud in Parliament, mocking them for having capitulated to him.
>
> Trump behaves similarly, whether he is humiliating his GOP lackeys on television or mocking a disabled reporter. The point is to cultivate cruelty in his followers. Getting them to laugh *with him* means, at least in that moment, that they are not laughing *at him*—being ridiculed is the thing strongmen most fear.[1603]

Laughing at a tyrant, of course, undermines his authority. Humor reveals his weaknesses and attacks his vulnerabilities. When Trump raged that "radical leftists" were taking over the streets of Portland and Chicago, images of protesters wearing inflatable frog and unicorn suits created a visual rebuttal.[1604] As one protester said, silly costumes helped to "combat that specific narrative that we are violent and we are agitating."[1605] Another protester said that the costumes kept the atmosphere "light-hearted" and showed Trump and government agents "that we are not scared of them."[1606] Satire should avoid being mean-spirited, as in the manner of Rush Limbaugh, who stoked discontent and bred cynicism.[1607] If the goal is lifting up democracy, then the message should be uplifting.

History has shown that laughter can be a powerful force in politics. In 1940, one of the greatest threats to Nazi leaders was the popularity of Charlie Chaplin's comedy film, *The Great Dictator*, which poked fun at Hitler.[1608] Political cartoonists like Thomas Nast, Patrick Oliphant, and Herbert Block lampooned the leaders of their times. As far back as the 1870s, Nast shaped public opinion regarding the corruption of Boss Tweed and the Tammany Hall political machine with his cartoons in *Harper's Weekly*.[1609] In 2025, Ann Telnaes submitted a cartoon to her editors at *The Washington Post* depicting tech and media titans kneeling before a golden statue of Trump and offering bags of money; among the depicted gift bearers was Amazon executive chairman Jeff Bezos, owner of the *Post*.[1610] When an editor refused to publish the work, apparently fearing repercussions from the president or their boss, Telnaes resigned. The episode spoke to the power of a cartoon.

Humor is most effective when it reflects reality. For example, in November 2025, a jury acquitted Sean Dunn, a thirty-seven-year-old Air Force veteran, of assault for throwing a Subway sandwich at a Customs and Border Protection agent after the Trump regime took over police functions on the streets of Washington, DC.[1611] After failing to obtain an indictment before a grand jury, prosecutors proceeded to trial on a misdemeanor assault charge against Dunn, who admitted to throwing the sandwich as an act of protest.[1612] The case seemed to be more about failure of proof than nullification; prosecutors were unable to prove, beyond a reasonable doubt, that the agent had the requisite reasonable fear of physical harm from the sandwich when he was wearing *a bulletproof vest.*[1613] After the jury found Dunn not guilty, social media platforms were filled with puns referring to the incident as an assault "with a deli weapon" or the "Reuben Missile Crisis."[1614] The jokes mocked the decision by DC US attorney Jeanine Pirro to bring criminal charges in a case where the facts fell far short of satisfying the legal definition of "forcible assault," highlighting the heavy-handed tactics of the Trump Justice Department.[1615] The charges were particularly jarring in contrast to the pardons that were given to January 6 defendants who attacked police with flagpoles, baseball bats, and other makeshift weapons that injured police officers.[1616] While law enforcement agents deserve to be protected, prosecutors are ethically obliged to seek criminal charges only where the evidence is sufficient to obtain and sustain a conviction. This was a ridiculous charging decision that deserved to be ridiculed.

Viral online posts and comedy sketches can reach a broader audience than ordinary political commentary; the viewers of comedy shows are likely a different audience than those of *Meet the Press*. The animated television series *South Park* saw a surge in ratings after it began skewering Trump during his second term.[1617] I saw reason for hope through satire in the fall of 2025, when *Saturday Night Live* parodied Attorney General Pam Bondi and Homeland Security Secretary Kristi Noem.[1618] In a sketch mocking Bondi's appearance before a Senate committee, comedienne Amy Poehler mirrored the attorney general's combative testimony, saying she spells her name with an "i" because "I ain't going to answer any of your questions." The joke landed because the real Pam Bondi had shown great disdain for congressional oversight during the hearing. Tina Fey then joined the sketch as Noem, complete with baseball cap and machine gun. When asked why she would laugh at the last scene of the film *Old Yeller*, in which a beloved dog gets shot, Fey responded, "Dogs don't just get shot. Heroes shoot them." The joke was a reference to Noem's admission in her autobiography of having killed her own dog, a fourteen-month-old pointer named Cricket.[1619] The bit rang true because of the ruthlessness with which Noem enforces immigration laws.

The sketch reminded me of Fey's 2008 portrayal of Sarah Palin, the running mate of John McCain in that year's presidential campaign. In a series of skits, Fey exposed Palin as inexperienced and unprepared to govern. Satire that mocks Trump and his fawning cronies can have a similar awakening effect on public opinion.

Campaigning

If we want to replace a regime that is destroying our democracy, we have the power to work together toward that goal. Any of us can volunteer to work on a political campaign in our own communities. Larger campaigns will have paid staffers, but all campaigns need volunteers. If there is a candidate or an issue we care about, we can volunteer to knock on doors, make calls at phone banks, distribute literature, or drive the candidate to events. State and local races matter. Our lives are more directly affected by state and local government than by the federal government. Supporting strong candidates at the lower levels of government is the way we build the bench of future leaders in Congress and the White House. Finding local campaigns in need of volunteers is as simple as an online search. Better yet, we can run for public office ourselves. We need people of integrity to lead. While some may think they lack the necessary ambition to hold office, leaders worth electing are those who are in it not for themselves but for the people they serve. If you have never thought of running for public office because you believe it is not for you, please think again. We need honorable people who lead for the right reasons—to serve the public, not to fulfill their personal ambition. Groups like Run For Something and Emily's List offer resources for political candidates, including those running for the first time.[1620] Campaigning for and serving in public office are enormous sacrifices. But if we want to see change in our politics—and improve our communities—we need good people to say yes to running.

Voting

Lastly, of course, all eligible voters must register and vote. MAGA personalities like Donald Trump and Kash Patel, who portray progressive public officials as corrupt and stoke doubts about the fairness of our elections, create cynicism that can cause many Americans to disengage from politics altogether. Replacing democratic participation with blind obedience is one of the goals of a tyrant. But every vote matters, as I learned through a vivid example in the early 2000s. One August evening during primary campaign season, my husband and I were assembling a trampoline for our children in our side yard. As we were struggling to tug the woven mat taut enough to connect it to the perimeter supports, Yousef Rabhi came by on his campaign rounds. He was a first-time candidate and a political unknown running for county commissioner.

My husband and I had already discussed his race and had decided to vote for his opponent in the upcoming election. When Rabhi asked if he could talk with us about his campaign, we politely declined, given our focus on assembling the trampoline. But rather than move on, Rabhi offered to help. We welcomed the assistance, and with an extra set of hands, we were able to complete the assembly—but not for another twenty minutes or so, a significant time sacrifice for a candidate seeking to maximize the number of doors he could knock on. As we worked, we asked Rabhi to share his policy views, and we were impressed. Once he left, my husband and I agreed that we would vote for him. We did, and he won—by *one* vote.[1621] He would go on to win higher office in Michigan, sparked, at least in part, by that first victory. Our votes changed the outcome of the election. Of course, everyone who voted for Rabhi says the same thing. And all of us are right. We must commit to voting and to encouraging and assisting others to do the same. If elected leaders are to serve all of the people, then all of the people must participate in choosing them.

Not only must all eligible voters cast a ballot, we also need to make wise choices when we do. We need to elect leaders who will not merely advance our preferred side in the culture wars but will restore integrity to government by being honest with voters and treating all people with dignity and respect. Seating such leaders may require us to reject the kinds of political purity that some voters demand. But compromise and long-term solutions to controversial policy issues, such as immigration, are the only way we can move forward as a nation.

Leadership Over Power

No book about American power would be complete without discussing Robert A. Caro's seminal treatment of the topic in his Pulitzer Prize–winning book *The Power Broker*.[1622] Caro's biography of Robert Moses explores in detail how the New York City Public Works and Parks Department commissioner wielded power without ever holding elective office. According to Caro, Moses's early idealism eroded during his decades in power. He gradually came to rule by fear—amassing dossiers of officials' secrets and using them to coerce subservience.[1623] Even if he had no derogatory information about a person, he would use "innuendo or outright falsehood" to disparage them in the press.[1624] As Caro writes, "He practiced McCarthyism long before there was a McCarthy."[1625] In addition to punishing those who crossed him, Moses also used lucrative public works contracts to reward the banks, labor unions, contractors, insurers, and real estate companies that went along with his demands: carrots and sticks.[1626] In essence, he was creating his own mob-style leverage.

Of course, Moses built significant public infrastructure projects in New York. He is responsible for many of the bridges, tunnels, and highways that connect the city's five boroughs. But rather than seeking ideas to benefit the public, Moses answered to no one; as Caro writes, "he shaped New York and its suburbs into the image he personally conceived."[1627] Without the input of the people, or even of the engineers who disagreed with his opinions, he built a city with no regard to democratic accountability. In configuring the New York City we know today, Moses ruthlessly dispossessed 250,000 people from their homes, tearing apart neighborhoods and communities.[1628] His highways "flooded the city with cars" as Moses was "systematically starving" the subways and commuter railways, leading to the traffic jams that New York still battles today, now with congestion pricing.[1629] His vast suburbs of "sprawling, low-density" housing doomed New York City to eternal transportation challenges.[1630] By bullying his way past public oversight, Moses ended up overpaying by forty million dollars on a single project.[1631] According to Caro, "he had used the power of money to undermine the democratic processes of the largest city in the world, to plan and build its parks, bridges, highways, and housing projects on this basis of his whim alone."[1632] New York served as a model for other cities—many of which replicated Moses's mistakes.

The Power Broker demonstrates the dangers of allowing one person to accumulate too much power. Caro writes of its corrupting force:

> Power is not an instrument that its possessor can use with impunity. It is a drug that creates a need for larger and larger dosages. And Moses was a user. . . . Slowly but inexorably, he began to seek power for its own sake. . . . Increasingly, the projects became not ends but means—the means of obtaining more and more power.[1633]

By examining Trump's executive orders raising unfounded allegations against law firms and universities, his misleading and deceptive public statements, his use of emergency declarations to activate military troops, his aggressive use of executive authority to impound funds appropriated by Congress or to impose tariffs, and his willingness to blow up NATO, one could reasonably conclude that, like Robert Moses, the forty-seventh president was taking these steps not as ends unto themselves but as means of accumulating more power.

The framers of our Constitution, fresh from a revolution for independence from a monarchy, understood the risks of excessive power. Rather than reward the "bad man" who looks for loopholes in the founders' separation-of-powers design, we should look for leaders who seek to execute the law according to the will of the people. Regardless of our politics, we cannot tolerate public servants who will deliver our preferred policies while violating the law to do it. We can use the second Trump administration as an opportunity to recognize that the legal process matters more than any substantive policy choice of the moment. If we lose control of the rule of law, a president can become a dictator. And even if MAGA supporters like what they see from the forty-seventh president, the next dictator to come along may have different ideas about how to rule over our country and its nuclear-armed military forces. Our system of government includes checks and balances to prevent any one branch from amassing too much power, but no system is airtight. It presumes that we will elect good people who will do their best to advance the interests of the country. In choosing a leader, character matters.

Our nation's most lauded leaders were flawed, to be sure, but they possessed virtues worthy of our great country. While carving the images of American presidents into the face of a mountain defaces natural resources and lands revered by Native American tribes, the presidents chosen to be immortalized on Mount Rushmore reveal something about our national character. They were glorified because of their perceived embodiment of certain qualities: George Washington is remembered for his honor and humility, leading the Continental Army to victory in the American Revolution against Britain and then, after serving as our first president, voluntarily relinquishing power following his second term. Thomas Jefferson is noted for his reason and skills of persuasion in support of individual liberty. Abraham Lincoln is honored for his integrity as "Honest Abe" and his skills as a unifier during the Civil War. Theodore Roosevelt is recognized for his optimism and his efforts to promote economic fairness for America's workers and consumers. We can find candidates who possess similar traits to these leaders, rather than short-term dealmakers who seek to divide us in order to amass their own power. Much about our system of government presumes good faith from our leaders. We can't make every grant of authority foolproof against abuse. We, the people, have an obligation to choose better people to lead our country.

The Fix

Donald Trump would eventually pay twenty-five million dollars to settle the lawsuit over Trump University.[1634] He never admitted liability, claiming that he was agreeing to settle only to avoid a protracted trial. But the hefty sum can hardly be seen as mere nuisance value. If the plaintiffs are to be believed, then the flimsy foundation on which his scheme was built was destined to fail. As Trump himself said, if you fail to deliver, at some point, people catch on.

The same is likely true of his deeply warped manner of governing. Trump is masterful at diverting people's attention away from their own best interests. One would hope that at some point, even Trump voters will realize that his mob-style governing, which has benefited himself and the ultrarich, has been a bad deal for most Americans. As writer David Brooks has observed, Trumpism can be seen "as a multipronged effort to amputate the higher elements of the human spirit—learning, compassion, science, the pursuit of justice—and supplant those virtues with greed, retribution, ego, appetite. Trumpism is an attempt to make the world a playground for the rich and ruthless, so it seeks to dissolve the sinews of moral and legal restraint that make civilization decent."[1635] I am betting that most Americans would miss that decency when it is gone. I also believe we can awaken enough of our citizenry before it comes to that.

One reason authoritarian regimes eventually fail is the tendency of their leaders to corrupt government institutions and surround themselves with sycophants. According to University of Chicago professors Georgy Egorov and Konstantin Sonin, the tendency of authoritarians to purge competent government officials and replace them with unqualified loyalists leads to the loss of the expertise and candid advice needed to run a government competently.[1636] For example, Vladimir Putin invaded Ukraine in 2022, expecting a quick victory. More than four years later, the war continued to rage on, a miscalculation that Egorov and Sonin attribute to the failures of Putin's yes-men advisers. Putin's "colossal mistake," they write, was inevitable because "a descent into ineptitude is a natural outcome of autocracies."[1637] Trump and his MAGA movement, built on a similarly flawed structure, seem destined to a similar fate. If they are not stopped, they may take the rest of the country down with them.

We are already seeing some cracks in Trump's coalition. Former Georgia congresswoman Marjorie Taylor Greene, once one of Trump's most loyal surrogates, split with him over his refusal to disclose the Epstein files and the 2025 government shutdown over health care costs, among other issues. As Trump amassed power, rewarded loyalists, and punished his enemies, Greene remained a MAGA purist. As described in *Politico*, she stayed true to the movement's "populist, anti-establishment and anti-elite roots,"[1638] even as it became clear that Trump's policies favored the billionaire class. Greene said, "I'm not some sort of blind slave to the President, and I don't think anyone should be. I serve in Congress. We're a separate branch of the government, and I'm not elected by the President. I'm not elected by anyone that works in the White House. I'm elected by my district."[1639] The first stirring of awakening sometimes comes from the most unlikely place. As Trump's populist supporters increasingly continue to recognize that his policies favor the rich, their disillusionment seems inevitable.

But we need not wait for Trump's government to fail on its own. We have the ability to fix it ourselves, and to do it right now, before it is too late. The key is to use our powers of litigation, organizing, education, campaigning, voting, and other tactics to help our fellow Americans understand that our country is better than the corruption, cruelty, and chaos that Trump has fueled. As citizens, we have not just the ability but a responsibility to preserve our democracy. Of course, it is tempting to take the easy path and simply look away. Most of us can occupy ourselves by focusing solely on our families and our jobs and leave the heavy lifting to someone else. Or, we may be inclined to believe that America will endure it because it always has. Some people are no doubt afraid to stick their necks out lest they become a target of Trump's retribution. Fear is contagious—but so is courage. When people see others resisting tyranny or organizing to promote democracy, they become more inclined to join in. Just as organized crime families go underground when investigators are brave enough to take them on, divisive politicians will change their stripes if public opinion turns on them.

We can be a country that is united in lifting people up rather than casting them out, a nation that is collectively moving toward more equality and opportunity, with less economic and racial injustice. Grievance and resentment look backward. Hope looks forward. With the will of the people, we can send the Donald Trumps of the world to the scrap heap of history and achieve our best version of America. Of course, our nation will not fix itself. It will take work and participation by its citizens. We can draw inspiration from Shirley Chisholm, America's first Black congresswoman, who said, "You don't make progress by standing on the sidelines, whimpering and complaining. You make progress by implementing ideas."[1640] Together, we can create our own leverage to restore American greatness. We can provide something society can't live without—freedom and democracy.

With unity of purpose, we can fix our country and make its promises a reality for all Americans.

ACKNOWLEDGMENTS

This book is based in part on my work and observations as a federal prosecutor at the US Attorney's Office for the Eastern District of Michigan, where I was honored to serve for almost twenty years. My colleagues in that office were dedicated public servants who prosecuted crimes and defended the federal government in court without fear or favor. The American people would be proud to see the work they did every day with integrity and diligence. In return, they received only modest pay, but also the deep satisfaction of representing the interests of the United States. The abuse of the Department of Justice during the Trump administration causes me great pain, but the people I know who remain at DOJ give me hope that its integrity can be restored.

I was able to write this book because of the constant support of my husband, whose partnership allows me to take on projects that would otherwise be unimaginable. He is a nonstop source of encouragement and comfort who often reminds me to laugh at the absurdity of it all. He prefers to stay out of the spotlight and, true to his wishes, remains nameless here.

I draw inspiration from our children, who will inherit the country we leave them. They deserve the same freedom and opportunity my husband I have enjoyed. They are kind, bright, and good people, and they bring us joy no matter where they are. My mother, Beverly McQuade, helps me to be the best version of myself. My father, Robert McQuade, of blessed memory, was an important ally during a time when girls and women struggled for equality. He convinced me that I could do anything. My sister, Kim McQuade, keeps me humble. My father-in-law, a selfless pillar of kindness who also prefers to be unnamed, is a model of the value of hard work and determination.

I am grateful to my editor, Greg Ruggiero, who helped to sharpen the ideas for this book and make their expression sing. He made the writing and editing process an absolute delight. Michael Vandergriff, my research assistant, provided tremendous help, bringing enthusiasm to his work and mine. Thanks to Kate Hurley for her assistance in researching and summarizing source material. I am grateful to everyone at Seven Stories Press, including Dan Simon and Ruth Weiner, for their tremendous work and their confidence in me. I appreciate their commitment to finding authors and publishing books about human rights and social justice. Thanks to Molly Pisani and all of the other copy editors and fact checkers for their meticulous and outstanding work. I am grateful to Rodrigo Corral for designing another magnificent cover for this book. The image of White House china, broken and repaired, perfectly captures not only the fragility of democracy but also our ability to restore it. Kintsugi, a Japanese art, uses gold to highlight an object's cracks as part of its history and beauty rather than hiding them. In the same way, we must remember our nation's history, including its darker chapters, to understand and appreciate who we are and who we can be.

Thank you to House Minority Leader Hakeem Jeffries for inspiring this book's focus with his description of President Trump's first one hundred days in office as "chaos, cruelty, and corruption."[1641]

Thank you to my colleagues and students at the University of Michigan Law School, where I am privileged to work with people who are smart, curious, and ethical. Julian Mortenson, Don Herzog, Len Niehoff, and Evan Caminker, in particular, helped me think about the limits of executive power and free speech. During a time when so much of the news of the day is depressing, these brilliant minds are continually finding new ways to use the law to solve problems. They make me optimistic for our future.

Many thanks to the hardworking people at NBC News and MS NOW for giving me a platform to explain the news to their viewers. I am grateful for the opportunity to help people understand how the legal system works, so that they can form their own opinions based on law and facts. I am fortunate to have friends who supported me during this project, including my podcast #SistersInLaw, Kimberly Atkins Stohr, Joyce Vance, and Jill Wine-Banks, along with our producers at Politicon. I am grateful for the opportunity to analyze legal news each week with these astute observers of our legal system. And thank you to the viewers and listeners who share words of support; I appreciate every one.

Thank you to Jennifer Gorland for generously sharing her observations and insights from her work as an immigration judge. My conversations with Elie Honig, Marissa Pollick, Maureen Murrett, and Sarah Clark also helped shape my ideas. I am grateful for my former boss Judge Bernard A. Friedman, an eternal mentor and wonderful friend. With every punctuation mark and word choice in this book, I thought of the lessons from my former editors at *The Michigan Daily* and the *Rochester Democrat and Chronicle*, my first real job. Mary and Jim Holleran were only a few years older than me, but they were my second parents when I was living in western New York, on my own for the first time. Thank you to my friends Kathy Nicholl, Tammy Machowicz Olsztyn, and Pam Williams for your constant love and support, even from far away. And thanks to the Grenada girls, the Bursley gang, the Pi Phis, the N-Mates, the USAO Queens, the Durkans, and my tennis friends for always picking me up with kindness and laughs when I need them most.

And thanks to you, the reader, for choosing to learn more about how we can take our country back from the corrupt con artists who are dismantling our democracy to amass power for themselves. The founders warned us they would come. We can see them systematically destroying our country and the freedom it stands for, but I remain hopeful that together, we can fix it.

—Barbara McQuade
Ann Arbor, Michigan

NOTES

Introduction: The Fix Was In

1. Tresa Baldas and Jim Schaefer, "Contractor: I Denied Ferguson, Lost Projects," *Detroit Free Press*, October 27, 2012.
2. United States v. Kilpatrick, 798 F.3d 365 (6th Cir. 2015).
3. Alexandra Harland, "Weekly Wrap-Up of Kilpatrick Federal Trial," *ClickOnDetroit*, October 26, 2012, https://www.clickondetroit.com/news/2012/10/26/weekly-wrap-up-of-kilpatrick-federal-trial/.
4. Mary M. Chapman, "Former Mayor of Detroit Guilty in Corruption Case," *New York Times*, March 11, 2013.
5. "Bobby Ferguson, Friend of Kwame Kilpatrick, Granted Early Release from Prison," Fox 2 Detroit, April 29, 2021, https://www.fox2detroit.com/news/bobby-ferguson-friend-of-kwame-kilpatrick-granted-early-release-from-prison.
6. "Bobby Ferguson, Friend of Kwame Kilpatrick."
7. Yoni Appelbaum, "I Alone Can Fix It," *The Atlantic*, July 2016.
8. Zephyr Teachout, *Corruption in America: From Benjamin Franklin's Snuff Box to Citizens United* (Harvard University Press, 2014), 2.
9. Teachout, *Corruption in America*, 283.
10. "Adlai Stevenson Quotes," Adlai Today, McLean County Museum of History, accessed September 6, 2025, https://mchistory.org/adlai-today/quotes.
11. Teachout, *Corruption in America*, 3.
12. Trump v. J.G.G., 604 US ___, 3 (2025).
13. Nina Totenberg, "Trump Calls for the Impeachment of a Judge, as Lawsuits Pile Up," NPR, March 18, 2025, https://www.npr.org/2025/03/18/nx-s1-5332086/trump-lawsuits.
14. George Washington, "Farewell Address," 1796, https://www.georgewashington.org/farewell-address.jsp#google_vignette.
15. Nicholas von Hoffman, *Citizen Cohn: The Life and Times of Roy Cohn* (Doubleday, 1988).
16. Michael Kruse, "Trump's Long War with Justice," *Politico*, August 23, 2018, https://www.politico.com/magazine/story/2018/08/23/donald-trump-jeff-sessions-justice-department-war-219592/.
17. Michael Kruse, "The Final Lesson Donald Trump Never Learned from Roy Cohn," *Politico*, September 19, 2019, https://www.politico.com/magazine/story/2019/09/19/roy-cohn-donald-trump-documentary-228144/.
18. Kruse, "The Final Lesson Donald Trump Never Learned from Roy Cohn."
19. Kruse, "The Final Lesson."
20. Kruse, "The Final Lesson."
21. Ron Elving, "President Trump Called for Roy Cohn, But Roy Cohn Was Gone," NPR, January 7, 2018, https://www.npr.org/2018/01/07/576209428/president-trump-called-for-roy-cohn-but-roy-cohn-was-gone.
22. Kathryn Krawczyk, "Trump Apparently Told Don McGahn He 'Never Had a Lawyer Who Took Notes,'" *The Week*, April 23, 2019, https://theweek.com/speedreads/836099/trump-apparently-told-don-mcgahn-never-lawyer-who-took-notes.

23. Kruse, "The Final Lesson."
24. Niccolò Machiavelli, *The Prince*, trans. George Bull (Penguin Books, 2003).
25. Machiavelli, *The Prince*, 54.
26. R. J. Roger, *The Don: 36 Rules of the Bosses*, Joost Effers (Citadel Press, 2024), 36.
27. Elving, "President Trump Called for Roy Cohn."
28. Donald Trump with Tony Schwartz, *Trump: The Art of the Deal*, reissue (Ballantine Books, 2015), 53.
29. Trump with Schwartz, *The Art of the Deal*, 53.
30. Ximena Bustillo and Hilary Fung, "Trump Is Found Guilty on 34 Felony Counts. Read the Counts Here," NPR, May 30, 2024, https://www.npr.org/2024/05/30/g-s1-1848/trump-hush-money-trial-34-counts.
31. Bustillo and Fung, "Trump Is Found."
32. Peter Charalambous, "Sentencing Finalizes Trump's Conviction, Ends Embarrassing Chapter in His Return to the White House," ABC News, January 10, 2025, https://abcnews.go.com/US/sentencing-finalizes-trumps-conviction-ends-embarrassing-chapter-return/story?id=117566581.
33. Eugene Kiely, "Timeline of FBI Investigation of Trump's Handling of Highly Classified Documents," FactCheck.org, August 30, 2022, https://www.factcheck.org/2022/08/timeline-of-fbi-investigation-of-trumps-handling-of-highly-classified-documents/.
34. Elise Hammond, Maureen Chowdhury, Tori B. Powell, and Mike Hayes, "Trump Indicted in Special Counsel's 2020 Election Interference Probe," CNN Politics, August 1, 2023, https://www.cnn.com/politics/live-news/trump-2020-election-probe-08-01-23.
35. Kate Brumback and Eric Tucker, "Trump and 18 Allies Charged in Georgia Election Meddling as Former President Faces 4th Criminal Case," *Associated Press News*, August 15, 2023, https://apnews.com/article/trump-georgia-election-investigation-grand-jury-willis-d39562cedfc60d64948708de1b011ed3.
36. Katelyn Polantz, Hannah Rabinowitz, and Sara Murray, "Georgia Appeals Court Disqualifies Fulton County DA Fani Willis from Prosecuting Trump," CNN, December 19, 2024, https://www.cnn.com/2024/12/19/politics/fani-willis-donald-trump-georgia/index.html; Greg Allen and Steve Inskeep, "Judge Cannon Dismisses Trump Documents Case over Special Counsel Appointment," NPR, July 15, 2024, https://www.npr.org/2024/07/15/nx-s1-5040311/judge-cannon-dismisses-trump-documents-case-over-special-counsel-appointment; Louis Jacobson and Amy Sherman, "Key Facts from the Supreme Court's Immunity Ruling and How It Affects Presidential Power," PBS News, July 1, 2024, https://www.pbs.org/newshour/politics/key-facts-from-the-supreme-courts-immunity-ruling-and-how-it-affects-presidential-power.
37. Rebecca Beitsch, "Smith Moves to Drop Jan. 6, Classified Documents Cases Against Trump," *The Hill*, November 25, 2024, https://thehill.com/regulation/court-battles/5008336-justice-department-dismisses-trump-case/.
38. James A. Morone, "Why the Legend of Al Capone Still Fascinates," *New York Times*, December 2, 2016.
39. Morone, "Why the Legend of Al Capone."
40. Morone, "Why the Legend of Al Capone."
41. Steve Benen, "Two Years Later, Trump Won't Let Go of Al Capone Comparison," *MaddowBlog*, MSNBC, May 14, 2024, https://www.msnbc.com/rachel-maddow-show/maddowblog/two-years-later-trump-wont-let-go-al-capone-comparison-rcna152130.
42. Morone, "Why the Legend of Al Capone."
43. Samuel Earle, "Trump's Third Act? American Gangster," op ed, *New York Times*, March 25, 2024.
44. Maureen Dowd, "Donald Trump, Our Foundering Father," op ed, *New York Times*, July 5, 2025.
45. Jonathan Lambert, "Study: 14 Million Lives Could Be Lost Due to Trump Aid Cuts," NPR, July 1, 2025, https://www.npr.org/sections/goats-and-soda/2025/07/01/nx-s1-5452513/trump-usaid-foreign-aid-deaths.

46. Kelly McCarthy and Melanie Schmitz, "How Trump's Tax Cut and Spending Megabill Would Impact SNAP Recipients," ABC News, July 2, 2025, https://abcnews.go.com/GMA/News/trump-big-beautiful-bill-cuts-SNAP-affordable-food-benefits/story?id=123415329.
47. Robert Tracy McKenzie, "America Is Great Because America Is Good, Part One," *Faith and American History*, July 27, 2016, https://faithandamericanhistory.wordpress.com/2016/07/27/america-is-great-because-america-is-good-part-one/.
48. Ali Watkins, "Trump Says He Has No Plans to Call Walz After Shootings in Minnesota," *New York Times,* June 17, 2025.
49. Caroline Wazer, "Yes, Musk Said 'The Fundamental Weakness Of Western Civilization Is Empathy.' Here's Context," *Snopes*, March 10, 2025, https://www.snopes.com/fact-check/elon-musk-empathy-quote/.
50. Amanda Terkel and Megan Lebowitz, "From 'Rapists' to 'Eating the Pets': Trump Has Long Used Degrading Language Toward Immigrants," NBC News, September 19, 2024, https://www.nbcnews.com/politics/donald-trump/trump-degrading-language-immigrants-rc-na171120.
51. Zolan Kanno-Youngs, Shawn McCreesh, "Trump Calls Somalis 'Garbage' He Doesn't Want in the Country," *New York Times*, December 2, 2025.
52. Eric Tucker, Alanna Durkin Richer, Ben Finley, and Lindsay Whitehurst, "Kilmar Abrego Garcia Returned to the US, Charged with Transporting People in the Country Illegally," *Associated Press News*, June 7, 2025, https://apnews.com/article/abrego-garcia-justice-department-el-salvador-a547f3a228c92d4e69be799354037c7f.
53. Tucker, Richer, Finley, and Whitehurst, "Kilmar Abrego Garcia Returned to the US."
54. "The Abrego-Garcia Indictment," *New York Times*, June 6, 2025.
55. Tucker, Richer, Finley, and Whitehurst, "Kilmar Abrego Garcia Returned to the US."
56. Todd Blanche (@DAGToddBlanche), "Welcome back." X, June 6, 2025, https://x.com/DAGToddBlanche/status/1931088509168689269.
57. Ana Faguy, "US Government Wants to Deport Kilmar Ábrego García to Uganda," BBC News, August 23, 2025, https://www.bbc.com/news/articles/cewyppwwo9jo.
58. Adam Liptak and Mattathias Schwartz, "Supreme Court Lets Trump Deport Eight Migrants to South Sudan," *New York Times*, July 3, 2025.
59. Angélica Franganillo Díaz and John Fritze, "Supreme Court Allows Trump to Remove Migrants to South Sudan and Other Turmoil-Filled Countries," CNN Politics, June 23, 2025, https://www.cnn.com/2025/06/23/politics/supreme-court-migrants-south-sudan-turmoil-filled-countries.
60. Díaz and Fritze, "Supreme Court Allows Trump to Remove Migrants."
61. Jason Zengerle, "The Ruthless Ambition of Stephen Miller," op ed, *New York Times*, July 13, 2025.
62. Nathan Taylor Pemberton, "Trolling Democracy," op ed, *New York Times*, July 13, 2025.
63. Pemberton, "Trolling Democracy."
64. The White House (@whitehouse), Instagram, reel, February 18, 2025, https://www.instagram.com/reel/DGOclSlxOev/?hl=en.
65. Megan Loe, "Trump Posted Meme About Chicago That Said, 'I Love the Smell of Deportations in the Morning,'" *Snopes*, September 8, 2025, https://www.snopes.com/fact-check/trump-chicago-meme-post/.
66. Stuart A. Thompson, "How Trump Is Using Fake Imagery to Attack Enemies and Rouse Supporters," *New York Times*, October 21, 2025.
67. Pemberton, "Trolling Democracy."
68. Mike Collins (@repmikecollins), "Or we could buy him a ticket on Pinochet Air for a free helicopter ride back," X, February 1, 2024, https://x.com/RepMikeCollins/status/1753131697799868658.
69. Jonathan Franklin, "Chilean Army Admits 120 Thrown into Sea," *The Guardian*, January 8, 2001.
70. Savannah Kuchar, "People Know 'They're Going to Die': Democrat Hits GOP Senator over Viral Town Hall Exchange," *USA Today*, June 1, 2025.
71. Kuchar, "People Know 'They're Going to Die.'"
72. Kuchar, "People Know 'They're Going to Die.'"

73. Pemberton, "Trolling Democracy."
74. Hanna Rosin, "Jeffrey Goldberg on the Group Chat That Broke the Internet," *The Atlantic*, March 24, 2025.
75. Rosin, "Jeffrey Goldberg on the Group Chat."
76. Rosin, "Jeffrey Goldberg on the Group Chat."
77. Tim Balk and Ashley Cai, "A Half Dozen Trump Officials Hold More Than One Big Job," *New York Times*, July 11, 2025.
78. Balk and Cai, "A Half Dozen Trump Officials."
79. Loreben Tuquero, "How Fake Citations Appeared in RFK Jr.'s MAHA Report: Here Are Generative AI's Red Flags in Studies," *PolitiFact*, May 30, 2025, https://www.politifact.com/article/2025/may/30/MAHA-report-AI-fake-citations/.
80. Emily Kennard and Margaret Manto, "The MAHA Report Cites Studies That Don't Exist," *NOTUS*, May 29, 2025, https://www.notus.org/health-science/make-america-healthy-again-report-citation-errors.
81. Tuquero, "How Fake Citations Appeared."
82. Tuquero, "How Fake Citations Appeared."
83. Centers for Disease Control and Prevention, "Measles Data and Research," accessed August 30, 2025, https://www.cdc.gov/measles/data-research/index.html; Perri Klass, MD, "What to Know About Measles When Traveling," *New York Times*, July 1, 2025.
84. Lena H. Sun, "US Measles Cases Reach 33-Year High as Outbreaks Spread," *Washington Post*, July 7, 2025.
85. Mary Kekatos, Cheyenne Haslett, and Youri Benadjaoud, "Mass Layoffs, Major Vaccine Policy Changes: Timeline of Turmoil at CDC," ABC News, August 28, 2025, https://www.msn.com/en-us/health/other/mass-layoffs-major-vaccine-policy-changes-timeline-of-turmoil-at-cdc/ar-AA1Lrsfa?ocid=BingNewsSerp.
86. Kekatos, Haslett, and Benadjaoud, "Mass Layoffs, Major Vaccine Policy Changes."
87. Chiara Eisner, "Government Papers Found in an Alaskan Hotel Reveal New Details of Trump-Putin Summit," NPR, August 16, 2025, https://www.npr.org/2025/08/16/nx-s1-5504196/trump-putin-summit-documents-left-behind.
88. Maureen Dowd, "Trump's Cabinet of Incompetents," op ed, *New York Times*, July 12, 2025.
89. Josh Campbell and Kit Maher, "Homeland Security Secretary Kristi Noem's Purse Stolen," CNN Politics, April 21, 2025, https://www.cnn.com/2025/04/21/politics/homeland-security-kristi-noem-purse-stolen/.
90. Gabe Cohen and Michael Williams, "FEMA's Response to Texas Flood Slowed by Noem's Cost Controls," CNN Politics, July 10, 2025, https://www.cnn.com/2025/07/09/politics/fema-texas-flood-noem.
91. Cohen and Williams, "FEMA's Response to Texas Flood."
92. Maxine Joselow, "FEMA Didn't Answer Thousands of Calls From Flood Survivors, Documents Show," *New York Times*, July 11, 2025.
93. Christopher Flavelle and Lisa Friedman, "Acting FEMA Chief Told Staff He Didn't Know About US Hurricane Season," *New York Times*, June 2, 2025.
94. Ari Daniel, "Farewell to USAID: Reflections on the Agency That President Trump Dismantled," NPR, July 1, 2025, https://www.npr.org/sections/goats-and-soda/2025/07/01/g-s1-75222/usaid-trump-humanitarian-rubio-musk.
95. Adriana Gomez Licon, "Musk Waves a Chainsaw and Charms Conservatives Talking Up Trump's Cost-Cutting Efforts," *Associated Press News*, February 21, 2025, https://apnews.com/article/musk-chainsaw-trump-doge-6568e9e0cfc42ad6cdcfd58a409eb312.
96. Tara Copp and Anthony Izaguirre, "Trump Administration Tries to Bring Back Fired Nuclear Weapons Workers in DOGE Reversal," *Associated Press News*, February 16, 2025, https://apnews.com/article/nuclear-doge-firings-trump-federal-916e6819104f04f44c345b7dde4904d5.
97. Copp and Izaguirre, "Trump Administration Tries."
98. "How We'll Personally Feel the Loss of Federal Workers," *Slate*, July 4, 2025, https://slate.com/news-and-politics/2025/07/doge-workers-emergency.html.
99. "How the Stock Market Made Back All Its Losses After Trump Escalated the Trade War," *Associated Press News*, May 4, 2025, https://apnews.com/article/trump-tariffs-stock-market-bonds-dollar-pause5409392268729ba0ada7077d0eea9e4e.

100. "How the Stock Market Made Back All Its Losses"; Ana Swanson, "What Is a Trade Deal? Trump Takes an Expansive View," *New York Times*, July 8, 2025.
101. Jeanna Smialek and Ana Swanson, "As Trump Sows Tariff Confusion, Rules of Global Commerce Give Way to Chaos," *New York Times*, July 11, 2025.
102. Jack Nicas and Ana Ionova, "Behind Trump's Decision to Tax Brazil to Save Bolsonaro," *New York Times*, July 11, 2025.
103. Smialek and Swanson, "As Trump Sows Tariff Confusion."

1. Carrots and Sticks

104. Francis Ford Coppola, *The Godfather*, Paramount Pictures, 1972.
105. *Merriam-Webster Dictionary*, "don," accessed August 17, 2025, https://www.merriam-webster.com/dictionary/don.
106. Coppola, *The Godfather*.
107. Open hearing before the US Senate Select Committee on Intelligence, 115th Cong. (2017) (statement for the record of James B. Comey), 2–3, available at https://www.intelligence.senate.gov/2017/06/01/hearings-open-hearing-former-fbi-director-james-comey/.
108. Statement for the record of James B. Comey, 3.
109. Statement for the record of James B. Comey, 3.
110. Eric Tucker and Julie Pace, "Comey to Congress: President Trump Told Him 'I Need Loyalty,'" PBS News, June 7, 2017, https://www.pbs.org/newshour/politics/comey-congress-president-trump-told-need-loyalty.
111. Statement for the record of James B. Comey, 7.
112. David Post, "Trump Fires FBI Director James Comey," op ed, *Washington Post*, May 9, 2017.
113. Christal Hayes, "'A Blind Loyalty to Donald Trump': Read Michael Cohen's Statement Before Learning His Prison Sentence," *USA Today*, December 12, 2018.
114. Hayes, "'A Blind Loyalty to Donald Trump.'"
115. Colleen Long, "Cohen Says Trump Behaved 'Much Like a Mobster Would Do,'" *Associated Press News*, February 28, 2019, https://apnews.com/article/88e83c32a9d54d82abe3ac52bfad22e4.
116. Isaac Stanley-Becker, "Calling Michael Cohen a 'Rat,' Trump Brings 'American Underworld' Lingo to the White House," *Washington Post*, December 17, 2018.
117. Anushka Patil, "Trump Blasts Lawmaker for Remaining Democrat After Receiving Pardon," *New York Times*, December 2025.
118. Patil, "Trump Blasts Lawmaker."
119. Patil, " Trump Blasts Lawmaker."
120. Lexie Schapitl and Barbara Sprunt, "Ethics Committee Releases Gaetz Report, Lists Sex, Drug Allegations," NPR, December 23, 2024, https://www.npr.org/2024/12/23/nx-s1-5233060/matt-gaetz-ethics-report-released.
121. Lexie Schapitl, Deirdre Walsh, and Elena Moore, "Former Rep. Matt Gaetz Withdraws as Trump's Attorney General Pick," NPR, November 21, 2024, https://www.npr.org/2024/11/21/g-s1-35211/gaetz-out-attorney-general-trump.
122. Kelsey Ables and Maegan Vazquez, "Trump Names Self-Styled 'Alpha Male' Influencer Ambassador to Malaysia," *Washington Post*, July 11, 2025; Nick Adams, "Thank You, Mr. President. This Nomination Is the Honor of a Lifetime," *Nick's Picks* (blog), Substack, July 10, 2025, https://nickadamsmaga.substack.com/p/thank-you-mr-president-this-nomination.
123. Vanessa Friedman, "Trump Lapel Pins and Gold Cards," *New York Times*, April 22, 2025.
124. Ruth Ben-Ghiat, "Pete Hegseth and the Autocratic Strategy of Engineered Incompetence," *Lucid* (blog), Substack, January 15, 2025, https://lucid.substack.com/p/pete-hegseth-and-the-autocratic-strategy.
125. Ben-Ghiat, "Pete Hegseth and the Autocratic Strategy."
126. Hannah Arendt, *The Origins of Totalitarianism* (Penguin Classics, 2017), p 339.
127. Mark Hertling, "Does Pete Hegseth Have What It Takes to Be Secretary of Defense?" *The Bulwark*, January 7, 2025, https://www.thebulwark.com/p/does-pete-hegseth-have-what-it-takes.
128. Hertling, "Does Pete Hegseth Have?"

129. Hertling, "Does Pete Hegseth Have?"
130. Hertling, "Does Pete Hegseth Have?"
131. Hertling, "Does Pete Hegseth Have?"
132. Jane Mayer, "Pete Hegseth's Secret History," *New Yorker*, December 1, 2024.
133. Mayer, "Pete Hegseth's Secret History."
134. Mayer, "Pete Hegseth's Secret History."
135. Hertling, "Does Pete Hegseth Have?"
136. Mayer, "Pete Hegseth's Secret History."
137. Mayer, "Pete Hegseth's Secret History."
138. Mayer, "Pete Hegseth's Secret History."
139. "Text of the Email That Pete Hegseth's Mother Sent Him," *New York Times*, November 29, 2024.
140. Juliann Ventura, "Hegseth's Mother Complained About His Treatment of Women: NYT," *The Hill*, November 29, 2024, https://thehill.com/policy/defense/5015482-hegseth-nomination-mother-women/.
141. Zachary B. Wolf, "Trump Administration Signal Chat Leak Reveals Chaotic Security Lapses," CNN, March 25, 2025, https://www.cnn.com/2025/03/25/politics/europe-emoji-signal-chat-trump-what-matters.
142. Greg Jaffe and Helene Cooper, "Under Hegseth, Chaos Prevails at the Pentagon," *New York Times*, April 22, 2025.
143. Mayer, "Pete Hegseth's Secret History."
144. Robin Givhan, "What We Learned About Pete Hegseth in Nearly Five Hours of Questions," *Washington Post*, January 14, 2025.
145. "Dr. Mark T. Esper," US Department of War, accessed December 2, 2025, https://www.defense.gov/About/Biographies/Biography/Article/1378166/dr-mark-t-esper/.
146. Maggie Haberman, "Trump Proposed Launching Missiles into Mexico to 'Destroy the Drug Labs,' Esper Says," *New York Times*, May 5, 2022.
147. Kelsey Carolan, "Esper: Trump Asked About Shooting Protesters 'In the Legs or Something' After George Floyd Death," *The Hill*, May 2, 2022, https://thehill.com/policy/defense/3473642-esper-trump-asked-about-shooting-protesters-in-the-legs-or-something-after-george-floyd-death/.
148. Michel Martin and Tinbete Ermyas, "Former Pentagon Chief Esper Says Trump Asked About Shooting Protesters," NPR, May 9, 2022, https://www.npr.org/2022/05/09/1097517470/trump-esper-book-defense-secretary.
149. Barbara Starr, Ryan Browne, and Nicole Gaouette, "Trump Fires Defense Secretary Mark Esper," CNN, November 9, 2020, https://www.cnn.com/2020/11/09/politics/trump-fires-esper/index.html.
150. Carolan, "Esper: Trump Asked About Shooting Protesters."
151. Elizabeth Crisp, "Slotkin to Hegseth: Esper Had 'More Guts and Balls Than You,'" *The Hill*, June 18, 2025, https://thehill.com/homenews/senate/5357477-hegseth-slammed-by-slotkin-over-protester-orders/.
152. Eric Schmitt, "Hegseth Defends Deployment of Troops to Los Angeles at Testy Hearing," *New York Times*, June 10, 2025.
153. Zachary Cohen, "Hegseth Orders National Guard Troops in DC to Carry Weapons," CNN, August 22, 2025, https://www.cnn.com/2025/08/22/politics/hegseth-orders-national-guard-troops-dc-carry-weapons.
154. Annie Karni, "Tillis Says Hegseth 'Unfit' for Pentagon Post," *New York Times*, July 9, 2025.
155. Karni, "Tillis Says Hegseth 'Unfit.'"
156. Brian Klaas, "How Tyrants Fall," review of *How Tyrants Fall: And How Nations Survive*, by Marcel Dirsus, *The Garden of Forking Paths*, July 18, 2024, https://www.forkingpaths.co/p/how-tyrants-fall.
157. Brian Klaas, "Putin and the Dictator Trap," *The Atlantic*, March 16, 2022.
158. Devlin Barrett and Maggie Haberman, "Trump Says He Will Nominate Kash Patel to Run FBI," *New York Times*, November 30, 2024.
159. Barrett and Haberman, "Trump Says He Will Nominate."

160. Zeke Miller, Eric Tucker, and Will Weissert, "Trump Uses Mass Firing to Remove Independent Inspectors General at a Series of Agencies," *Associated Press News*, January 25, 2025, https://apnews.com/article/trump-inspectors-general-fired-congress-unlawful-4e8bc57e132c-3f9a7f1c2a3754359993.
161. Miller, Tucker, and Weissert, "Trump Uses Mass Firing."
162. Andrea Hsu, "Trump Fires EEOC and Labor Board Officials, Setting Up Legal Fight," NPR, January 28, 2025, https://www.npr.org/2025/01/28/nx-s1-5277103/nlrb-trump-wilcox-abruzzo-democrats-labor.
163. Nina Totenberg, "Supreme Court Allows Trump to Fire Members of Independent Agency Boards—for Now," NPR, May 22, 2025, https://www.npr.org/2025/05/22/nx-s1-5366714/supreme-court-nlrb-mspb.
164. Totenberg, "Supreme Court Allows Trump."
165. Erin Doherty and Dan Mangan, "Trump Tells Fed's Lisa Cook She's Fired; She Says He Has No Authority to Do So," CNBC, August 25, 2025, https://www.cnbc.com/2025/08/25/trump-fires-lisa-cook-fed-powell.html?msockid=3fca96abf6c0612e28d08350f7446078.
166. Doherty, "Trump Tells Fed's Lisa Cook."
167. Doherty, "Trump Tells Fed's Lisa Cook."
168. Doherty, "Trump Tells Fed's Lisa Cook."
169. Doherty, "Trump Tells Fed's Lisa Cook."
170. Glenn Thrush, Devlin Barrett, and Adam Goldman, "Justice Dept. Fires Prosecutors Who Worked on Trump Investigations," *New York Times*, January 27, 2025.
171. Ryan Lucas, "DOJ Says Will Not Fire FBI Agents Who Acted in 'Ethical' Way Over Jan. 6 Cases," NPR, February 5, 2025, https://www.npr.org/2025/02/05/g-s1-46641/fbi-january-6-fired-justice.
172. Kyle Cheney and Josh Gerstein, "DOJ Fires Dozens of Prosecutors Who Handled Jan. 6 Cases," *Politico*, January 31, 2025, https://www.politico.com/news/2025/01/31/doj-purges-prosecutors-january-6-cases-00201904.
173. Spencer S. Hsu, "Seven Top DC Prosecutors Demoted in Purge by Trump's US Attorney," *Washington Post*, February 28, 2025.
174. Hsu, "Seven Top DC Prosecutors."
175. Ximena Bustillo and Anusha Mathur, "The DOJ Has Been Firing Judges with Immigrant Defense Backgrounds," NPR, November 6, 2025, https://www.npr.org/2025/11/06/g-s1-96437/trump-immigration-judges-fired.
176. Stephen Fowler, "Judge Grants Top Whistleblower Advocate Reprieve After He Sued Trump Over Firing," NPR, February 10, 2025, https://www.npr.org/2025/02/10/nx-s1-5292259/hampton-dellinger-trump-special-counsel.
177. "About OSC," US Office of Special Counsel, accessed December 2, 2025; Barbara McQuade, "Trump Taps Extreme Jan. 6 Apologist for Key Watchdog Role. That Won't End Well." *MSNBC Opinion*, June 2, 2025, https://www.msnbc.com/opinion/msnbc-opinion/trump-jan-6-podcast-paul-ingrassia-job-senate-rcna210246.
178. Vaughn Hillyard, Michael Kosnar, Lindsey Pipia, and Dareh Gregorian, "Trump Nominates Former Podcast Host with History of Inflammatory Comments for Top Ethics Job," NBC News, May 30, 2025, https://www.nbcnews.com/politics/trump-administration/trump-nominates-former-podcast-host-history-inflammatory-comments-top-rcna210041.
179. "John C. Eastman," Claremont Institute, accessed December 2, 2025, https://www.claremont.org/bio/john-c-eastman/; Hayes Brown, "John Eastman's Georgia Surrender and the January 6 Fallout," MSNBC Opinion, August 22, 2023, https://www.msnbc.com/opinion/msnbc-opinion/john-eastman-georgia-surrender-january-6-rcna101187.
180. Paul Ingrassia (@PaulIngrassia), "Interesting read with a lot of good information. I believe a combination of releases (and potentially even shutting down the DC Jail permanently) and pardons are in order. In addition, President Trump should ask Congress to offer reparations to the tune of $1 million per family (at least) as restitution to remunerate the defendants and their families for their losses," X, December 16, 2024, https://x.com/PaulIngrassia/status/1868739699734360563.
181. Paul Ingrassia (@PaulIngrassia), "In addition, Congress should make J6 a national holiday—and memorialize the occasion as tribute to the victims and their families, particu-

larly those who lost their lives." X, December 16, 2024, https://x.com/PaulIngrassia/status/1868739699734360563.

182. Daniel Lippman, "Ingrassia Withdraws Nomination After Racist Texts," *Politico,* October 22, 2025, https://www.politico.com/news/2025/10/21/trump-pulls-ingrassia-nomination-racist-texts-00617041.
183. Doug Bock Clark, "She Pushed to Overturn Trump's Loss in the 2020 Election. Now She'll Help Oversee US Election Security," *ProPublica,* August 26, 2025, https://www.propublica.org/article/heather-honey-dhs-election-security.184. Clark, "She Pushed to Overturn Trump's Loss."
185. Clark, "She Pushed to Overturn Trump's Loss."
186. David A. Graham, "Bill Barr's Departure Reveals the Hollowness of Trumpism," *The Atlantic,* December 14, 2020.
187. Graham, "Bill Barr's Departure Reveals."
188. Robert Farley, "What Trump Asked of Pence," FactCheck.org, August 3, 2023, https://www.factcheck.org/2023/08/what-trump-asked-of-pence/.
189. Andrew Restuccia and Siobhan Hughes, "Trump's Tweet About Pence Seen as Critical Moment During Riot," *Wall Street Journal,* July 21, 2022.
190. Restuccia and Hughes, "Trump's Tweet About Pence."
191. Marc Fisher, "Trump Follows Tested 'Counterpuncher' Playbook in Face of Indictments," *Washington Post,* August 17, 2023.
192. Ron Elving, "President Trump Called for Roy Cohn, But Roy Cohn Was Gone," NPR, January 7, 2018, https://www.npr.org/2018/01/07/576209428/president-trump-called-for-roy-cohn-but-roy-cohn-was-gone.
193. Donald Trump with Tony Schwartz, *Trump: The Art of the Deal,* reissue (Ballantine Books, 2015), 58–59.
194. Elving, "President Trump Called for Roy Cohn."
195. Fisher, "Trump Follows Tested 'Counterpuncher' Playbook."
196. Donald J. Trump (@realDonaldTrump), "IF YOU GO AFTER ME, I'M COMING AFTER YOU!" Truth Social, August 4, 2023, https://truthsocial.com/@realDonaldTrump/posts/110833185720203438.
197. Gregory Svirnovskiy and Josh Gerstein, "Trump Goes After Leonard Leo and the Federalist Society in Fury over Court Ruling," *Politico,* May 29, 2025, https://www.politico.com/news/2025/05/29/trump-goes-after-leonard-leo-and-the-federalist-society-in-fury-over-court-ruling-00375813.
198. Svirnovskiy and Gerstein, "Trump Goes After Leonard Leo."
199. Svirnovskiy and Gerstein, "Trump Goes After Leonard Leo."
200. Katie Rogers, "What, Exactly, Was That Cabinet Meeting?" *New York Times,* August 26, 2025.
201. Frank Bruni, "The Chilling Displays of Devotion That Trump Demands of His Enablers," *New York Times,* April 17, 2025.
202. Bruni, "The Chilling Displays of Devotion."
203. Michelle Stoddart, "'Homegrowns Are Next': Trump Doubles Down on Sending American 'Criminals' to Foreign Prisons," ABC News, April 14, 2025, https://abcnews.go.com/Politics/homegrowns-trump-doubles-sending-convicted-us-citizens-foreign/story?id=120802863
204. Bruni, "The Chilling Displays of Devotion."
205. Bruni, "The Chilling Displays of Devotion."
206. Minho Kim, "Rubio Attacks Zelensky, Firmly Defending Trump and Vance," *New York Times,* March 2, 2025.
207. Kim, "Rubio Attacks Zelensky"; Caroline Vakil, "Rubio Praises Trump After Explosive Zelensky Meeting," *The Hill,* February 28, 2025, https://thehill.com/homenews/administration/5169943-trump-rubio-endorsement-ukraine/.
208. Bruni, "The Chilling Displays of Devotion."

2. Invincibility Theater

209. Frank Witsil, "SEC: Fraudster Hatched New Scheme While Serving Time at Ferndale Home," *Detroit Free Press*, August 13, 2019, https://www.freep.com/story/news/local/michigan/2019/08/13/antonio-bravata-sec-billionaire-boys/1997649001/.
210. "Former Brighton Resident and Son Convicted in Real Estate Investment Fraud," press release, US Attorney's Office, Eastern District of Michigan, FBI Archives, March 27, 2013, https://archives.fbi.gov/archives/detroit/press-releases/2013/former-brighton-resident-and-son-convicted-in-real-estate-investment-fraud.
211. Donald Trump with Tony Schwartz, *Trump: The Art of the Deal*, reissue (Ballantine Books, 2015), 80.
212. Trump with Schwartz, *The Art of the Deal*, 80.
213. Trump with Schwartz, *The Art of the Deal*, 77.
214. Trump with Schwartz, *The Art of the Deal*, 58.
215. Trump with Schwartz, *The Art of the Deal*, 58.
216. Trump with Schwartz, *The Art of the Deal*, 105.
217. Trump with Schwartz, *The Art of the Deal*, 177.
218. Michael Kruse, "The Escalator Ride That Changed America," *Politico*, June 14, 2019, https://www.politico.com/magazine/story/2019/06/14/donald-trump-campaign-announcement-tower-escalator-oral-history-227148/.
219. "The Apprentice," IMDb, accessed December 3, 2025, https://www.imdb.com/title/tt0364782/.
220. Russ Buettner and Susanne Craig, "The Star-Making Machine That Created 'Donald Trump,'" *New York Times*, September 14, 2024.
221. Michelle Ye Hee Lee, "Fact Check: Has Trump Declared Bankruptcy Four or Six Times?" *Washington Post*, September 26, 2016.
222. Tessa Stuart, "Donald Trump's 13 Biggest Business Failures," *Rolling Stone*, March 14, 2016, https://www.rollingstone.com/politics/politics-news/donald-trumps-13-biggest-business-failures-59556/.
223. Buettner and Craig, "The Star-Making Machine."
224. Jill Colvin, "Trump Displays Steak, Water, Wine to Defend Business Record," *Associated Press News*, March 9, 2016, https://apnews.com/domestic-news-domestic-news-events-general-news-united-states-presidential-election-23a5260fcffc47408cc67458e3844775; Stuart, "Donald Trump's 13 Biggest Business Failures."
225. Elliot Spagat, "Trump Paying $25M After Judge Approves Trump University Deal," *Associated Press News*, March 31, 2017, https://apnews.com/article/17e975d3ccba4a92a9b023dff8437b21.
226. David Harrison, "Put Some Gold on It: Trump Is Obsessed with Rebuilding Versailles. But He's No Sun King," *Slate*, May 30, 2025, https://slate.com/news-and-politics/2025/05/trump-oval-office-gold-decor-rococo-versailles.html.
227. Emily Keegin, "Trump's Oval Office Is a Gilded Rococo Nightmare. Help," *New York Times*, May 27, 2025.
228. Talia Lakritz, "Before-and-After Photos Show Changes Trump Has Made to the White House Decor, So Far," *Business Insider*, August 4, 2025, https://www.businessinsider.com/donald-trump-white-house-decor-oval-office-photos-2025-4.
229. Matt Viser, "In Cabinet Meeting, Trump Takes a Golden Opportunity to Talk Interior Decor," *Washington Post*, July 8, 2025.
230. Alex Gangitano and Dominick Mastrangelo, "Trump's Plan for White House Ballroom Sparks Outrage from His Critics," *The Hill*, July 8, 2025, https://thehill.com/homenews/administration/5432723-200m-ballroom-trump-legacy/.
231. Lee Moran, "Donald Trump's Ballroom Price Tag Suddenly Massively Jumps Again," *HuffPost*, December 17, 2025, https://www.huffpost.com/entry/donald-trump-ballroom-update_n_69425a2ae4b04337be6b68f6.
232. Timothy L. O'Brien, "Trump Is Turning the White House into a Golden Goose," *Bloomberg Opinion*, October 24, 2025, https://www.bloomberg.com/opinion/articles/2025-10-24/east-wing-demolition-trump-and-the-white-house-golden-grift; Rebecca Schneid and Connor Greene, "Who Is Paying for Trump's $250 Million Ballroom—and What They Might Get in

Return," *Time,* October 23, 2025, https://time.com/7327752/trump-white-house-ballroom-funding-donors/.

233. Monica Alba and Raquel Coronell Uribe, "White House Fires Board That Reviews Presidential Construction Projects in Washington," NBC News, October 2025, https://www.nbcnews.com/politics/donald-trump/white-house-fires-commission-fine-arts-board-trump-ballroom-projects-rcna240405.
234. Peter York, "Trump's Dictator Chic," *Politico Magazine*, March/April 2017, https://www.politico.com/magazine/story/2017/03/trump-style-dictator-autocrats-design-214877/.
235. York, "Trump's Dictator Chic."
236. Matt Viser, "In Cabinet Meeting, Trump Takes a Golden Opportunity."
237. Domenico Montanaro, "4 Takeaways from Trump's Second Inaugural Address," NPR, January 20, 2025, https://www.npr.org/2025/01/20/g-s1-43759/trump-inaugural-address-key-moments.
238. Aimee Picchi, "Trump Proposes Offering $5 Million 'Gold Card' to Wealthy Immigrants. Here's How It Would Work," CBS News MoneyWatch, March 5, 2025, https://www.cbsnews.com/news/trump-gold-card-eb5-visa-5-million-immigration-oligarch-cbs-news-explains/.
239. Zolan Kanno-Youngs, Eric Schmitt, and John Ismay, "Trump Announces New 'Trump Class' of Warships," *New York Times*, December 22, 2025.
240. Mallory Shelbourne and Sam Lagrone, "Trump Unveils New Battleship Class; Proposed USS Defiant Will Be Largest U.S. Surface Combatant Since WWII," *US Naval Institute News*, December 22, 2025, https://news.usni.org/2025/12/22/trump-unveils-new-battleship-class-proposed-uss-defiant-will-be-largest-u-s-surface-combatant-since-wwii.
241. Kanno-Youngs, Schmitt, and Ismay, "Trump Announces New 'Trump Class.'"
242. Ellen Mitchell, "5 Things to Know as Trump Rolls Out Golden Dome Missile Defense Shield," *The Hill*, May 20, 2025, https://thehill.com/policy/defense/5280612-trump-golden-dome-missile-defense/.
243. Cat Zakrzewski, "Donald Trump Has Wrapped His Political Career in the American Flag," *Washington Post,* July 4, 2025.
244. Zakrzewski, "Donald Trump Has Wrapped."
245. "Prosecuting Burning of the American Flag," executive order, White House, August 25, 2025, https://www.whitehouse.gov/presidential-actions/2025/08/prosecuting-burning-of-the-american-flag/; Texas v. Johnson, 491 US 397 (1989).
246. Zakrzewski, "Donald Trump Has Wrapped."
247. Miriam Waldvogel, "5 Things to Know about Trump's $45 Million Military Parade," *The Hill,* June 14, 2025, https://thehill.com/policy/defense/5347224-trump-military-parade-criticism-cost/; Carolina A. Miranda, "The Tepid Theatrics of Trump's Parade," op ed, *Washington Post,* June 17, 2025.
248. Keith McMillan, "Trump Received 'Bone Spurs' Diagnosis as a 'Favor,' Doctor's Daughters Allege," *Washington Post,* December 26, 2018.
249. Miranda, "The Tepid Theatrics of Trump's Parade."
250. Miranda, "The Tepid Theatrics of Trump's Parade."
251. Nardine Saad and Kwasi Gyamfi Asiedu, "What We Know About White House Plans for 'Arc de Trump,'" BBC, October 16, 2025, https://www.bbc.com/news/articles/cy7e8lv176go.
252. Saad and Asiedu, "What We Know About White House Plans."
253. Jill Cowan and Mimi Dwyer, "Federal Agents March Through L.A. Park, Spurring Local Outrage," *New York Times*, July 7, 2025.
254. Shawn Hubler, "Judge Says Trump's Use of Troops in L.A. Is Illegal," *New York Times*, September 2, 2025.
255. Cowan and Dwyer, "Federal Agents March Through L.A. Park."
256. Ken Klippenstein, "Exclusive: Operation Excalibur in Los Angeles Was Show of Force," KenKlippenstein.com, July 7, 2025, https://www.kenklippenstein.com/p/exclusive-operation-excalibur-in.
257. Cowan and Dwyer, "Federal Agents March Through L.A. Park."
258. Cowan and Dwyer, "Federal Agents March Through L.A. Park."

259. Kaanita Iyer, "Following LA and DC, Trump Wants to Send the National Guard to Other US Cities. Here's How He Can Do It," CNN, August 26, 2025, https://www.cnn.com/2025/08/26/politics/trump-national-guard-us-cities.
260. Lucy Gilder and Jake Horton, "Is Crime in Washington DC 'Out of Control,' as Trump Claims?" BBC, August 11, 2025, https://www.bbc.com/news/articles/c8600x7dnn40.
261. Donald Judd, "Trump Says He's Withdrawing National Guard from Chicago, Los Angeles and Portland," CNN, December 31, 2025, https://www.cnn.com/2025/12/31/politics/trump-national-gaurd-withdrawl-chicago-los-angeles-portland.
262. Irie Sentner and Paul McLeary, "Trump, Justifying Domestic Military Action, Tells Leaders to 'Handle' the 'Enemy from Within,'" *Politico*, September 30, 2025,https://www.politico.com/news/2025/09/30/trump-military-cities-training-ground-00587977.
263. Julie Bosman, Jazmine Ulloa, and Hamed Aleaziz, "Chicago Braces for Trump's Immigration Crackdown," *New York Times*, September 5, 2025.
264. Michelle Goldberg, "This Is What Autocracy Looks Like," op ed, *New York Times*, June 9, 2025.
265. Goldberg, "This Is What Autocracy Looks Like."
266. Adam Cancryn, "Trump's Crime Crackdown Is Also His Midterm Sales Pitch," CNN, August 28, 2025, https://www.cnn.com/2025/08/28/politics/midterm-election-trump-crime-crackdown.
267. Gilder and Horton, "Is Crime in Washington DC."
268. Daniel Dale, "Fact Check: "Trump Falsely Claims Washington, DC, Now Has No Crime At All," CNN, September 3, 2025, https://www.cnn.com/2025/09/03/politics/fact-check-trump-washington-dc-crime.
269. Dale, "Fact Check: Trump Falsely Claims."
270. Luke Broadwater, "Trump Says Having 'a Little Fight With the Wife' Should Not Count as a Crime," *New York Times*, September 8, 2025.
271. Dale, "Fact Check: Trump Falsely Claims."
272. Zeeshan Aleem, "Trump's 'Department of War' Launch Is More Than Just a Shallow Rebrand," MSNBC Daily, September 5, 2025, https://www.msnbc.com/opinion/msnbc-opinion/trump-department-of-war-defense-name-executive-order-rcna229314.
273. "Fact Sheet: President Donald J. Trump Restores the Department of War," White House, September 5, 2025, https://www.whitehouse.gov/fact-sheets/2025/09/fact-sheet-president-donald-j-trump-restores-the-united-states-department-of-war/.
274. "Fact Sheet: President Donald J. Trump Restores the Department of War."
275. David E. Sanger, "The Return of the 'War Department' Is More Than Nostalgia. It's a Message," *New York Times*, September 5, 2025.
276. "Secretary of War Pete Hegseth Addresses General and Flag Officers at Quantico, Virginia," transcript, Department of War, September 30, 2025, https://www.war.gov/News/Transcripts/Transcript/Article/4318689/secretary-of-war-pete-hegseth-addresses-general-and-flag-officers-at-quantico-v/.
277. Megan Loe, "Trump Posted Meme About Chicago That Said, 'I Love the Smell of Deportations in the Morning,'" Snopes, September 8, 2025, https://www.snopes.com/fact-check/trump-chicago-meme-post/.
278. Sanger, "The Return of the 'War Department.'"
279. Kinsey Crowley, "Did Trump End 7 Wars? Here Is What He Says," *USA Today*, September 5, 2025, https://www.usatoday.com/story/news/politics/2025/09/04/trump-7-wars/85969451007/; Laya Neelakandan, "Trump and India's Modi Split over US Role in Pakistan Ceasefire," CNBC, June 18, 2025, https://www.msn.com/en-us/politics/government/modi-denies-trump-s-claim-that-he-stopped-the-war-between-india-and-pakistan/ar-AA1H03Rq.
280. Terrence McCoy, Ana Vanessa Herrero, and Samantha Schmidt, "Officials, Locals Undercut Trump Claims About Venezuela Drug Boats," *Washington Post*, October 20, 2025.
281. McCoy, Herrero, and Schmidt, "Officials, Locals Undercut Trump Claims."
282. Franco Ordoñez and Ryan Lucas, "As Strikes on Alleged Drug Boats Grow, So Do Questions About Their Legality and Goal," NPR, October 24, 2025, https://www.npr.org/2025/10/24/nx-s1-5584173/trump-drug-boats-venezuela-maduro.

283. Ordoñez and Lucas, "As Strikes on Alleged Drug Boats Grow."
284. Michael Schmitt, "Attacking Drug Cartels in the Territory of Another State," *Just Security*, October 17, 2025, https://www.justsecurity.org/122756/drug-cartels-venezuela-territory/.
285. McCoy, Herrero, and Schmidt, "Officials, Locals Undercut Trump Claims."
286. Ordoñez and Lucas, "As Strikes on Alleged Drug Boats Grow."
287. Ashleigh Fields, "Torture Memos Author: Admiral, Soldiers 'Should Not Have Obeyed' Orders to 'Kill Everybody,'" December 2, 2025, *The Hill*, https://thehill.com/policy/defense/5629370-john-yoo-condemns-second-boat-strike/.
288. Charlie Savage, "The Peril of a White House That Flaunts Its Indifference to the Law," *New York Times*, October 24, 2025.
289. NPR Staff, "Trump Says US Will 'Run' Venezuela and Sell Seized Oil in Remarks on the Strikes," NPR, January 3, 2026, https://www.npr.org/2026/01/03/g-s1-104346/trump-venezuela-maduro-press-conference.
290. Tess Bridgeman, Michael Schmitt, and Ryan Goodman, "Expert Q&A on U.S. Military Actions on Venezuela and Boat Strikes," *Just Security*, January 6, 2026, https://www.justsecurity.org/126156/faq-venezuela-boat-strikes/.
291. US Const. art VI.
292. Stephen Collinson, "Trump's New US Mission Statement: Strength, Force, Power," CNN, January 6, 2026, https://www.cnn.com/2026/01/06/politics/trump-greenland-venezuela-colombia-miller-analysis.
293. NPR Staff, "Trump Says US Will 'Run' Venezuela."
294. Michelle Goldberg, "Don't Call It Regime Change. This Is Something Else Entirely," *New York Times*, January 2026.
295. Taylor Penley, "DHS Secretary Noem Gives Helicopter, Horseback Tour of Agents' Enhanced Border Measures," Fox News, February 4, 2025, https://www.foxnews.com/media/dhs-secretary-noem-gives-helicopter-horseback-tour-agents-enhanced-border-measures.
296. Mike Brest, "Hegseth Shows Support for Military Rank and File with Germany Workout," *Washington Examiner*, February 11, 2025, https://www.washingtonexaminer.com/policy/defense/3316935/hegseth-rank-and-file-military-workout-troops-germany/.
297. Kevin Sheehan and Chris Nesi, "Teen Bloods Gang Member Nabbed in NJ by US Marshals, with Former Trump Attorney Alina Habba in Tow," *New York Post*, April 2, 2025, https://nypost.com/2025/04/02/us-news/teen-bloods-gang-member-nabbed-by-feds-nj-cops-with-alina-habba-in-tow/.
298. Aaron Zitner, Nancy A. Youssef, and Sadie Gurman, "Constantly in Motion, Trump's Cabinet Portrays a White House That's Always Winning," *Wall Street Journal*, April 26, 2025.
299. Scott Wong, "Trump Signs Big Tax-Cut and Spending Bill into Law in July Fourth Ceremony," NBC News, July 4, 2025, https://www.nbcnews.com/politics/white-house/trump-signs-big-tax-cut-spending-bill-law-july-fourth-ceremony-rcna216753.
300. Sara Chernikoff and Ramon Padilla, "Comparing Trump's Day 1 Executive Orders to Past Presidents: See Graphics," *USA Today*, January 23, 2025, https://www.usatoday.com/story/graphics/2025/01/23/how-many-executive-orders-did-trump-sign/77881247007/.
301. Chris Megerian, Zeke Miller, and Lisa Mascaro, "Trump White House Rescinds Memo Freezing Federal Money after Widespread Confusion," *Associated Press News*, January 29, 2025, https://apnews.com/article/donald-trump-pause-federal-grants-aid-6d41961940585544fa43a3f66550e7be.
302. Megerian, Miller, and Mascaro, "Trump White House Rescinds Memo."
303. Emma Colton, "Trump Unloads on Judge Boasberg, 'Radical Left Judges' for Halting Deportations of Violent Illegal Aliens," Fox News, March 30, 2025, https://www.foxnews.com/politics/trump-unloads-judge-boasberg-radical-left-judges-halting-deportations-violent-illegal-aliens?msockid=3fca96abf6c0612e28d08350f7446078.
304. "Fact Sheet: President Donald J. Trump Directs Administration to Make Federal Architecture Beautiful Again," White House, August 28, 2025, https://www.whitehouse.gov/fact-sheets/2025/08/fact-sheet-president-donald-j-trump-directs-administration-to-make-federal-architecture-beautiful-again/.
305. "Fact Sheet: President Donald J. Trump Directs Administration."

306. Marco Margaritoff, "Kellyanne Conway Praises Trump for Taking over Cultural Institutions: 'It's Super Exciting,'" *HuffPost*, August 31, 2025, https://www.huffpost.com/entry/kellyanne-conway-praises-trump-taking-control-cultural-institutions_n_68b31ee1e4b072bf-6d64c05e; Giselle Ruhiyyih Ewing, "Trump Says He's Fired National Portrait Gallery Director amid Washington Arts Scene Takeover," *Politico*, May 30, 2025, https://www.politico.com/news/2025/05/30/trump-portrait-gallery-smithsonian-00377156.
307. Shawn McCreesh, "A Memorial to Kennedy? It's Trump's Now, Too," *New York Times*, December 23, 2025.
308. Brett Samuels, "Trump Teases Marble Armrests for Kennedy Center: 'Unlike Anything Ever Done Or Seen Before!,'" *The Hill*, December 26, 2025, https://thehill.com/blogs/in-the-know/5663851-trump-kennedy-center-marble-armrests/.
309. Samara Angel and Jonathan Katz, "Defending American Arts, Culture, and Democracy," Brookings Institution, February 28, 2025, https://www.brookings.edu/articles/defending-american-arts-culture-and-democracy/.
310. Sarah Mervosh, "ACLU Sues Defense Department Schools Over Book Bans," *New York Times*, April 15, 2025.
311. Ewing, "Trump Says He's Fired National Portrait Gallery Director."
312. "Restoring Truth and Sanity to American History," executive order, White House, March 27, 2025, https://www.whitehouse.gov/presidential-actions/2025/03/restoring-truth-and-sanity-to-american-history/.
313. "Restoring Truth and Sanity to American History."
314. Frank Langfitt and A. Martínez, "National Parks Removing Historical Items Trump Administration Found 'Disparaged' US," NPR, September 17, 2025, https://www.npr.org/2025/09/17/nx-s1-5543315/national-parks-removing-historical-items-trump-administration-found-disparaged-u-s.
315. Maxine Joseloe, "Park Service Is Ordered to Take Down Some Materials on Slavery and Tribes," *New York Times*, September 16, 2025.
316. Ed Shanahan, Katherine Rosman, and Liam Stack, "US Park Service Strikes Transgender References from Stonewall Website," *New York Times*, February 13, 2025.
317. Deena Zaru, "Trump Admin Removes Memorial Honoring People Enslaved by George Washington in Philadelphia," ABC News, January 23, 2026, https://abcnews.go.com/US/trump-admin-removes-memorial-honoring-people-enslaved-george/story?id=129472615.
318. Zolan Kanno-Youngs, "Trump Says Smithsonian Focuses Too Much on 'How Bad Slavery Was,'" *New York Times*, August 19, 2025.
319. Kanno-Youngs, "Trump Says Smithsonian Focuses"; Chris Hayes, "Defense Dept. Backtracks After GOP's 'War on Woke' Tries to Cancel Jackie Robinson," MSNBC Daily, March 21, 2025, https://www.msnbc.com/top-stories/latest/trump-erase-history-jackie-robinson-rcna197514.
320. Margaritoff, "Kellyanne Conway Praises Trump."
321. Margaritoff, "Kellyanne Conway Praises Trump."
322. Peter Chawaga, "Rob Manfred Admits Donald Trump's Role in MLB Decision on Rose Reinstatement," *Newsweek*, June 5, 2025, https://www.newsweek.com/sports/mlb/rob-manfred-admits-donald-trumps-role-mlb-decision-pete-rose-reinstatement-2081393.
323. Chawaga, "Rob Manfred Admits Donald Trump's Role."
324. Joe Pierre, MD, "Why Do People Choose Authoritarianism over Democracy?" *Psychology Today*, March 22, 2025, https://www.psychologytoday.com/us/blog/psych-unseen/202404/why-do-people-choose-authoritarianism-over-democracy.
325. Pierre, "Why Do People Choose Authoritarianism."
326. Angel and Katz, "Defending American Arts, Culture, and Democracy."
327. Angel and Katz, "Defending American Arts, Culture, and Democracy."
328. Angel and Katz, "Defending American Arts, Culture, and Democracy."

3. Disinformation Warfare

329. Allan Lengel, "Criminals Who Alter Face and Fingerprints Don't Always Have Luck," Ticklethewire.com, accessed September 1, 2025, https://ticklethewire.com/criminals-who-alter-face-and-fingerprints-dont-always-have-luck/.
330. Lengel, "Criminals Who Alter Face."
331. Lengel, "Criminals Who Alter Face."
332. Niccolò Machiavelli, *The Prince*, trans. George Bull (Penguin Books, 2003).
333. Daniel Dale, "Fact Check: Trump Made More Than 20 False Claims in His Inauguration Day Remarks," CNN Politics, January 20, 2025, https://www.cnn.com/politics/fact-check-trump-inauguration/index.html.
334. Joey Garrison, "'Did I Say That?' President Trump Backs Off After Calling Zelenskyy a Dictator," *USA Today*, February 27, 2025, https://www.yahoo.com/news/did-president-trump-backs-off-205816121.html.
335. "Federal Letter to Harvard on Governance, Admissions, and DEI Reform," Harvard University Office of Research Funding," April 11, 2025, https://www.harvard.edu/research-funding/wp-content/uploads/sites/16/2025/04/Letter-Sent-to-Harvard-2025-04-11.pdf.
336. Donald Trump with Tony Schwartz, *Trump: The Art of the Deal*, reissue (Ballantine Books, 2015), 56.
337. Sal Gilbertie, "Egg Prices Will Remain High for Quite a While, USDA Data Shows," *Forbes*, February 18, 2025, https://www.forbes.com/sites/salgilbertie/2025/02/18/usda-data-indicates-egg-prices-will-remain-high-for-quite-a-while/; Brakkton Booker, "Trump Talks of a Third Term amid Growing Concerns About a Constitutional Crisis," *Politico*, February 21, 2025, https://www.politico.com/news/2025/02/21/trump-third-term-white-house-022002.
338. Greg Sargent, "Trump's Own Pollster Just Hit Him with Very Bad News—and a Warning," *New Republic*, February 25, 2025, https://newrepublic.com/article/191841/trump-approval-rating-pollster-bad-news-warning.
339. Will Weissert, "Trump's Remarks on Canada Becoming the 51st State Raise a Lot of Questions," *Associated Press News*, February 13, 2025, https://apnews.com/article/how-canada-could-become-us-state-42360e10ded96c0046fd11eaaf55ab88; Ido Vock, "Why Does Trump Want Greenland and What Do Its People Think?" BBC News, March 24, 2025, https://www.bbc.com/news/articles/c74x4m71pmjo.
340. Kaanita Iyer, "Following LA and DC, Trump Wants to Send the National Guard to Other US Cities: Here's How," CNN, August 26, 2025, https://www.cnn.com/2025/08/26/politics/trump-national-guard-us-cities.
341. Rachel Scott, Isabella Murray, and Michelle Stoddart, "Trump Hangs Plaques Mocking Biden, Obama along White House Colonnade," ABC News, December 17, 2025, https://abcnews.go.com/Politics/trump-hangs-plaques-mocking-biden-obama-white-house/story?id=128492648.
342. Naftali Bendavid, "In Trump's First Month, a Relentless Effort to Remake the Presidency," *Washington Post*, February 20, 2025.
343. Jonathan Turley, "Donald Trump Just Won the Greatest Jury Verdict in American History," op ed, *The Hill*, November 6, 2024, https://thehill.com/opinion/campaign/4976533-trump-prosecutions-lawfare-end/.
344. "Section 9-27.000: Principles of Federal Prosecution," *Justice Manual*, US Department of Justice, 2018, accessed December 3, 2025, https://www.justice.gov/jm/jm-9-27000-principles-federal-prosecution.
345. United States v. Trump, No. 23-cr-80101, ECF No. 85 (S.D. Fla. Mar. 7, 2025).
346. United States v. Trump, ECF No. 85, 2.
347. United States v. Trump, No. 23-cr-257, ECF No. 281 (D.DC Nov. 2024).
348. United States v. Trump, ECF No. 281 (D.DC Nov. 2024).
349. United States v. Trump, No. 23-80101-CR-CANNON, slip op. (S.D. Fla. July 15, 2024).
350. United States v. Trump, No. 23-87822, ECF No. 79 (11th Cir. Feb. 2025).
351. "Ending the Weaponization of the Federal Government," executive order, White House, January 20, 2025, https://www.whitehouse.gov/presidential-actions/2025/01/ending-the-weaponization-of-the-federal-government/.

352. Valerie Pavilonis, "Fact Check: Thousands of Black Lives Matter Protesters Were Arrested in 2020," *USA Today*, February 22, 2022, https://www.usatoday.com/story/news/factcheck/2022/02/22/fact-check-thousands-black-lives-matter-protesters-arrested-2020/6816074001/.
353. Alanna Durkin Richer, Michael Kunzelman, and Jacques Billeaud, "Records Rebut Claims of Unequal Treatment of Jan. 6 Rioters," *Associated Press News*, August 30, 2021, https://apnews.com/article/records-rebut-claims-jan-6-rioters-55adf4d46aff57b91af2fdd3345dace8.
354. "Restoring the Integrity and Credibility of the Department of Justice," memorandum, Office of the Attorney General, US Department of Justice, February 5, 2025, https://www.justice.gov/ag/media/1388506/dl?inline.
355. Ben Protess, Jonah E. Bromwich, Maggie Haberman, Kate Christobek, Jesse McKinley, and William K. Rashbaum, "Trump Convicted on All Counts to Become America's First Felon President," *New York Times*, May 30, 2024.
356. "Attorney General James Wins Landmark Victory in Case Against Donald Trump," press release, Office of the New York State Attorney General, February 16, 2024, https://ag.ny.gov/press-release/2024/attorney-general-james-wins-landmark-victory-case-against-donald-trump.
357. Iyer, "Following LA and DC."
358. Alan Feuer, "Trump Grants Sweeping Clemency to All Jan. 6 Rioters," *New York Times*, January 20, 2025.
359. Alan Feuer and Glenn Thrush, "Trump Pardons Giuliani and Others Involved in Effort to Overturn 2020 Election," *New York Times*, November 10, 2025.
360. Tom Dreisbach, "How Trump's 'Will Be Wild!' Tweet Drew Rioters to the Capitol on Jan. 6," NPR, July 13, 2022, https://www.npr.org/2022/07/13/1111341161/how-trumps-will-be-wild-tweet-drew-rioters-to-the-capitol-on-jan-6.
361. Brian Naylor, "Read Trump's Jan. 6 Speech, a Key Part of Impeachment Trial," NPR, February 10, 2021, https://www.npr.org/2021/02/10/966396848/read-trumps-jan-6-speech-a-key-part-of-impeachment-trial.
362. Naylor, "Read Trump's Jan. 6 Speech."
363. Naylor, "Read Trump's Jan. 6 Speech."
364. Mychael Schnell, "Cheney: Trump 'Summoned the Mob, Assembled the Mob and Lit the Flame of This Attack,'" *The Hill*, June 9, 2022, https://thehill.com/policy/national-security/3518354-cheney-trump-summoned-the-mob-assembled-the-mob-and-lit-the-flame-of-this-attack/.
365. Dan Barry and Alan Feuer, "'A Day of Love': How Trump Inverted the Violent History of Jan. 6," *New York Times*, January 5, 2025.
366. Barry and Feuer, "'A Day of Love.'"
367. Jake Traylor, "Trump Calls People Charged and Convicted for Jan. 6 Riots 'Hostages,'" *Meet the Press Blog*, NBC News, November 3, 2023, https://www.nbcnews.com/meet-the-press/meetthepressblog/trump-calls-people-charged-convicted-jan-6-riots-hostages-rcna123617.
368. Sarah Fortinsky, "Trump Calls Jan. 6 Defendants 'Warriors,'" *The Hill*, June 9, 2024, https://thehill.com/homenews/campaign/4713140-trump-calls-j6-defendants-warriors/.
369. Fortinsky, "Trump Calls Jan. 6 Defendants."
370. Fortinsky, "Trump Calls Jan. 6 Defendants."
371. Donald J. Trump and J6 Prison Choir, "Justice for All," posted March 3, 2023, by Donald J. Trump – Topic, YouTube, 2:20, https://www.youtube.com/watch?v=DvDd6H5t-sM; Barry and Feuer, "'A Day of Love.'"
372. "Former President Trump Holds Rally in Waco, Texas," C-SPAN, March 25, 2023, video, 2:42, https://www.c-span.org/program/campaign-2024/former-president-trump-holds-rally-in-waco-texas/625539.
373. Spenser S. Hsu, "US to Pay Nearly $5 Million to Family of Jan. 6 Rioter Ashli Babbitt," *Washington Post*, May 19, 2025.
374. Hsu, "US to Pay Nearly $5 Million."
375. Justin Jouvenal, "Internal Probe Clears Capitol Police Officer in Shooting of Ashli Babbitt," *Washington Post*, August 23, 2021.

376. Haley Britzky and Holmes Lybrand, "US Air Force to Provide Military Funeral Honors for Rioter Killed on January 6," CNN, August 28, 2025, https://www.cnn.com/2025/08/28/politics/us-air-force-funeral-ashli-babbitt.
377. The White House, "01.06.21," accessed January 7, 2026, https://www.whitehouse.gov/j6/.
378. The White House, "01.06.21."
379. Ed Martin (@EagleEdMartin), "No MAGA left behind," X, May 28, 2025, https://x.com/EagleEdMartin/status/1927092000848855360; Aaron Blake, "'No MAGA Left Behind': Trump's Pardons Get Even More Political," CNN, May 28, 2025, https://www.cnn.com/2025/05/28/politics/analysis-trump-pardons-politics.
380. Shaila Dewan, "Political Violence Is Part of the American Story. It Is Also Changing," *New York Times*, June 28, 2025.
381. Steve Karnowski, "Minnesota Lawmaker Shot to Death at Home Will Lie in State at Capitol Ahead of Funeral," *Associated Press News*, June 29, 2025, https://apnews.com/article/minnesota-lawmakers-shot-funeral-119d4589c28205b4faec41f5c59a823c.
382. Karnowski, "Minnesota Lawmaker Shot to Death."
383. Sabrina Souza, Amanda Musa, Dakin Andone, and Lex Harvey, "Man Accused of Setting Fire to Pennsylvania Governor's Home Denied Bail," CNN, April 14, 2025, https://edition.cnn.com/2025/04/14/us/pennsylvania-governor-arson-what-we-know-hnk/index.html.
384. Calvin Woodward, "Trump Was on the Links Taking a Breather from the Campaign. Then the Secret Service Saw a Rifle," *Associated Press News*, September 16, 2024, https://apnews.com/article/trump-assassination-attempt-2024-election-f0ace849dda2b99cb281aed5b9a7ea95.
385. Rachel Treisman, "Who Is Brian Thompson, the UnitedHealthcare CEO Gunned Down in New York?" NPR, December 4, 2024, https://www.npr.org/2024/12/04/nx-s1-5215881/brian-thompson-unitedhealthcare-ceo-shot-new-york; Joe Hernandez, "What We Know About the Palm Springs Fertility Clinic Bombing," NPR, May 19, 2025, https://www.npr.org/2025/05/19/nx-s1-5403669/what-we-know-palm-springs-ivf-clinic-bombing; Andrew Goudsward and Jasper Ward, "Three Charged in Arson Attacks at Tesla Dealerships, Charging Stations," *Reuters*, March 20, 2025, https://www.reuters.com/world/us/us-attorney-general-says-alleged-arsonists-targeting-tesla-face-charges-2025-03-20/.
386. Isabella Helms, "Round-the-Clock Watch: UM Regents Get 24/7 Security amid Threats," *Michigan News Source*, July 3, 2025, https://www.michigannewssource.com/2025/07/round-the-clock-watch-um-regents-get-24-7-security-amid-threats/.
387. Alexandra Hutlzer and Michelle Stoddart, "Trump Doubles Down on Blaming 'Radical Left' After Vow to Go After Political Violence," ABC News, September 12, 2025, https://abcnews.go.com/Politics/trump-doubles-blaming-radical-left-after-vow-after/story?id=125509965.
388. Dewan, "Political Violence Is Part."
389. Dewan, "Political Violence Is Part."
390. Amy Qin, "Xenophobia and Hate Speech Are Spiking Heading into the Election," *New York Times*, November 1, 2024.
391. Qin, "Xenophobia and Hate Speech."
392. "Transcript: Read Trump's Full Second Inaugural Address," PBS NewsHour, January 20, 2025, https://www.pbs.org/newshour/politics/transcript-read-trumps-full-second-inaugural-address.
393. Donald J. Trump (@realDonaldTrump), "I am going to lead a movement to get rid of MAIL-IN BALLOTS, and also, while we're at it, Highly "Inaccurate," Very Expensive, and Seriously Controversial VOTING MACHINES, which cost Ten Times more than accurate and sophisticated Watermark Paper, which is faster, and leaves NO DOUBT, at the end of the evening, as to who WON, and who LOST, the Election. We are now the only Country in the World that uses Mail-In Voting. . . . Remember, the States are merely an "agent" for the Federal Government in counting and tabulating the votes. They must do what the Federal Government, as represented by the President of the United States, tells them, FOR THE GOOD OF OUR COUNTRY, to do," Truth Social, August 18, 2025, https://truthsocial.com/@realDonaldTrump/115049485680941254.
394. Robert Farley, Saranac Hale Spencer, and Alan Jaffe, "Fact-Checking Trump's Claims About Mail-In Ballots, Voting Machines and States' Role," FactCheck.org, August 19, 2025, https://

www.factcheck.org/2025/08/factchecking-trumps-claims-about-mail-in-ballots-voting-machines-and-states-role/.
395. Farley, Spencer, and Jaffe, "Fact-Checking Trump's Claims."
396. Jane C. Timm, "Fox News and Dominion Reach $787.5. Million Settlement in Defamation Lawsuit," April 18, 2023, NBC News, https://www.nbcnews.com/media/fox-news-settles-dominion-defamation-lawsuit-rcna80285.
397. "Dominion Voting Systems reaches settlement in its $1.3 billion defamation lawsuit against Guiliani," CBS News, September 27, 2025, https://www.cbsnews.com/news/dominion-voting-systems-rudy-guiliani-reach-settlement-defamation-lawsuit/.
398. "Fact Sheet: President Donald J. Trump Protects the Integrity of American Elections," White House, March 25, 2025, https://www.whitehouse.gov/fact-sheets/2025/03/fact-sheet-president-donald-j-trump-protects-the-integrity-of-american-elections/.
399. Nick Corasaniti, "Trump Is Trying to Gain More Power Over Elections. Is His Effort Legal?" *New York Times*, March 25, 2025.

4. Above the Law

400. "John Gotti," History.com, accessed September 2, 2025, https://www.history.com/articles/john-gotti.
401. "John Gotti."
402. Selwyn Raab, "John Gotti Dies in Prison at 61; Mafia Boss Relished the Spotlight," *New York Times*, June 11, 2002.
403. Raab, "John Gotti Dies."
404. "D.A. Bragg Announces 34-Count Trial Conviction of Donald J. Trump," press release, Manhattan District Attorney, May 30, 2024, https://manhattanda.org/d-a-bragg-announces-34-count-felony-trial-conviction-of-donald-j-trump/.
405. Steven Levitsky and Daniel Ziblatt, *How Democracies Die* (Crown, 2018), 8.
406. Levitsky and Ziblatt, *How Democracies Die*, 9.
407. Oliver Wendell Holmes Jr., "The Path of the Law," *Harvard Law Review* 10 (1897): 457.
408. Richard Primus, "Trump's Third-Term Ambitions Are Very Revealing," *The Atlantic*, May 14, 2025.
409. Liset Cruz, Ali Bianco, Megan Messerly, Abhinanda Bhattacharyya, and Anna Wiederkehr, "37 Ways Project 2025 Has Shown Up in Trump's Executive Orders," *Politico*, February 5, 2025, https://www.politico.com/interactives/2025/trump-executive-orders-project-2025/.
410. Sarah Fortinsky, "Trump Executive Orders and Actions: By the Numbers," *The Hill*, January 21, 2025, https://thehill.com/homenews/administration/5098445-trump-executive-orders-first-day/.
411. Trump v. United States, No. 23-939, 603 U.S. ___, 40 (2024).
412. "Ensuring Accountability for All Agencies," executive order, White House, February 18, 2025, https://www.whitehouse.gov/presidential-actions/2025/02/ensuring-accountability-for-all-agencies/.
413. "Ensuring Accountability for All Agencies."
414. Natalie Allison, Ann E. Marimow, and Andrew Ackerman, "Trump Order Challenges Independence of FCC, FTC and Financial Regulators," *Washington Post*, February 18, 2025.
415. Allison, Marimow, and Ackerman, "Trump Order Challenges Independence."
416. "Ensuring Accountability for All Agencies."
417. "Restoring Accountability to Policy-Influencing Positions Within the Federal Workforce," executive order, White House, January 20, 2025, https://www.whitehouse.gov/presidential-actions/2025/01/restoring-accountability-to-policy-influencing-positions-within-the-federal-workforce/.
418. Donald J. Trump (@realDonaldTrump)," Following my Day One Executive Order, the Office of Personnel Management will be issuing new Civil Service Regulations for career government employees. Moving forward, career government employees, working on policy matters, will be classified as "Schedule Policy/Career," and will be held to the highest standards of conduct and performance. If these government workers refuse to advance the policy interests of the President, or are engaging in corrupt behavior, they should no longer

have a job. This is common sense, and will allow the federal government to finally be "run like a business." We must root out corruption and implement accountability in our Federal Workforce!" Truth Social, April 18, 2025, https://truthsocial.com/@realDonaldTrump/posts/114360632714487285.

419. Charles S. Clark, "Deconstructing the Deep State," *Government Executive*, accessed August 8, 2023, https://www.govexec.com/feature/gov-exec-deconstructing-deep-state/.
420. Robert P. Beschel Jr., "DOGE Was Bad. Schedule F Will Be Worse," *The Atlantic*, April 28, 2025.
421. "Restoring Accountability to Policy-Influencing Positions."
422. Molly Redden, Andy Kroll, and Nick Surgey, "'Put Them in Trauma': Inside a Key MAGA Leader's Plans for a New Trump Agenda," *Government Executive*, October 28, 2024, https://www.govexec.com/management/2024/10/inside-key-maga-leaders-plans-new-trump-agenda/400607/.
423. Nur Ibrahim, "Unpacking Trump Admin's New Hiring Plan for Federal Workers—Including Question About Implementing Presidential Policy," Snopes, June 4, 2025, https://www.snopes.com/fact-check/trump-policy-hiring-plan/.
424. Erich Wagner, "Here's How Trump's New Vice Presidential Pick Stacks Up on Federal Workforce Issues," *Government Executive*, July 15, 2024, https://www.govexec.com/management/2024/07/heres-now-trumps-new-vice-presidential-pick-stacks-federal-workforce-issues/398056/.
425. Rebecca Hersher and Julia Simon, "Energy Dept. Tells Employees Not to Use Words Including 'Climate Change' and 'Green,'" NPR, September 30, 2025, https://www.npr.org/2025/09/30/nx-s1-5557324/trump-doe-ban-words-climate-change-science.
426. Shannon Bond, Jenna McLaughlin, and Stephen Fowler, "Trump Administration Uses Taxpayers Dollars to Blame Democrats for Government Shutdown," NPR, October 1, 2025, https://www.npr.org/2025/09/30/nx-s1-5558393/government-shutdown-trump-ethics-hatch-act.
427. Bond, McLaughlin, and Fowler, "Trump Administration Uses Taxpayer Dollars."
428. Bond, McLaughlin, and Fowler, "Trump Administration Uses Taxpayer Dollars."
429. Alexandra Skores and Hanna Park, "Multiple Airports Refuse to Play Kristi Noem Video That Blames Democrats for Government Shutdown," CNN, October 15, 2025, https://www.cnn.com/2025/10/13/us/kristi-noem-tsa-video.
430. Seung Min Kim and Kevin Freking, "Trump Pick to Lead Federal Watchdog Agency Withdraws After Offensive Text Messages Were Revealed," *Associated Press News*, October 21, 2025, https://apnews.com/article/trump-special-counsel-ingrassia-texts-d11db9dc83767040f56a16766a3c240b.
431. Naftali Bendavid, "Trump Attacks Watergate Laws in Massive Shift of Ethics System," *Washington Post*, June 21, 2025.
432. Bendavid, "Trump Attacks Watergate Laws."
433. Bendavid, "Trump Attacks Watergate Laws."
434. David Yaffe-Bellany, Matthew Goldstein, and Eric Lipton, "Trump Offers Private Dinner to Top 220 Investors in His Memecoin," *New York Times*, April 23, 2025.
435. Eric Lipton, Ben Protess, and David Yaffe-Bellany, "Trump Organization Plans an Ethics Policy Without Banning Foreign Deals," *New York Times*, December 5, 2024.
436. Lipton, Protess, and Yaffe-Bellany, "Trump Organization Plans an Ethics Policy."
437. Lipton, Protess, and Yaffe-Bellany, "Trump Organization Plans an Ethics Policy."
438. Lipton, Protess, and Yaffe-Bellany, "Trump Organization Plans an Ethics Policy."
439. Will Weissert, "Trump's Middle East Visit Comes as His Family Deepens Its Business, Crypto Ties in the Region," *Associated Press News*, May 14, 2025, https://apnews.com/article/trump-business-interests-family-middle-east-cryptocurrency-cbb7d2354304ce0308800819944cf3f8.
440. Nick Schifrin and Sonia Kopelev, "Trump Arrives in Saudi Arabia as He Sets New Course for American Policy in Middle East," PBS News, May 14, 2025, https://www.pbs.org/newshour/show/trump-arrives-in-saudi-arabia-as-he-sets-new-course-for-american-policy-in-middle-east.

441. Vivian Nereim, "Trump's Pledge to the Middle East: No More 'Lectures on How to Live,'" *New York Times*, May 14, 2025.
442. Nereim, "Trump's Pledge to the Middle East."
443. Nereim, "Trump's Pledge to the Middle East."; Domenico Montanaro, "Here Are 5 Takeaways from Trump's First Major Foreign Trip to the Middle East," NPR, May 16, 2025, https://www.npr.org/2025/05/16/nx-s1-5400447/trump-middle-east-trip-qatar-air-force-one.
444. Shawn McCreesh, "'Things Happen': Trump Brushes Off the Murder of Khashoggi," *New York Times*, November 18, 2025.
445. Jonathan Karl and Katherine Faulders, "Trump Administration Poised to Accept 'Palace in the Sky' as a Gift for Trump from Qatar: Sources," ABC News, May 11, 2025, https://abcnews.go.com/Politics/trump-administration-poised-accept-palace-sky-gift-trump/story?id=121680511.
446. Franco Ordoñez and Deirdre Walsh, "Trump Says He'd Be 'Stupid' to Turn Down Qatar's Offer of a New Plane," NPR, May 12, 2025, https://www.npr.org/2025/05/11/g-s1-65838/qatar-plane-trump.
447. Ordoñez and Walsh, "Trump Says He'd Be 'Stupid.'"
448. Ordoñez and Walsh, "Trump Says He'd Be 'Stupid.'"
449. US Const. art. I, § 9, cl. 8.
450. *The Federalist* No. 68 (Alexander Hamilton), New York, March 14, 1788, available at the Avalon Project, Lillian Goldman Law Library, Yale Law School, https://avalon.law.yale.edu/18th_century/fed68.asp.
451. Ordoñez and Walsh, "Trump Says He'd Be 'Stupid.'"
452. 31 USC § 1341.
453. Tyler Pager, "Donor Who Gave $130 Million to Pay Troops Is Reclusive Heir to Mellon Fortune," *New York Times*, October 25, 2025.
454. Pager, "Donor Who Gave $130 Million."
455. 5 USC § 7353.
456. David Gura, "A Crypto Winter or a Meltdown? Recession Fears and Layoffs Hit Cryptocurrencies," NPR, June 14, 2022, https://www.npr.org/2022/06/14/1105025475/a-crypto-winter-or-a-meltdown-recession-fears-and-layoffs-hit-crypto-currencies.
457. Natalie Sherman, Kayla Epstein, and Michelle Fleur, "Fallen 'Crypto King' Sam Bankman-Fried Gets 25 Years for Fraud," BBC News, March 28, 2024, https://www.bbc.com/news/business-68677487.
458. Talia Kaplan, "Trump Warns Crypto 'Potentially a Disaster Waiting to Happen,'" Fox Business, August 31, 2021, https://www.foxbusiness.com/politics/crypto-potentially-a-disaster-waiting-to-happen-trump.amp.
459. Chris Cameron, "Trump, Appealing to Bitcoin Fans, Vows US Will Be 'Crypto Capital of the Planet,'" *New York Times*, July 27, 2024.
460. Robert Weissman, interview by Amy Goodman and Juan González, "Mt. Everest of Corruption": Crypto Investors Buy Access to President; Trump Expands Bitcoin Holdings," *Democracy Now!*, May 28, 2025, https://www.democracynow.org/2025/5/28/trump_crypto.
461. Eric Lipton, David Yaffe-Bellany, and Ben Protess, "Secret Deals, Foreign Investments, Presidential Policy Changes: The Rise of Trump's Crypto Firm," *New York Times*, April 29, 2025.
462. David Yaffe-Bellany and Kenneth P. Vogel, "The 'Trump Pump': How Crypto Lobbying Won Over a President," *New York Times*, July 9, 2025.
463. Yaffe-Bellany and Vogel, "The 'Trump Pump.'"
464. Maria Aspan, "Trump Has a Pro-Cryptocurrency Platform—While Harris Chases the Crypto Vote," NPR, September 25, 2024, https://www.npr.org/2024/09/25/nx-s1-5056183/trump-has-a-pro-cryptocurrency-platform-while-harris-chases-the-crypto-vote.
465. Aspan, "Trump Has a Pro-Cryptocurrency Platform."
466. Will Weissert and Alan Suderman, "Trump Hosts Top Crypto Investors as Some Industry Leaders Fear He's Putting Personal Profits First," *Associated Press News*, May 22, 2025, https://apnews.com/article/trump-crypto-projects-industry-scam-memecoin-0e2d7ca5170bf594d44a391884ec52b3.

467. Yaffe-Bellany and Vogel, "The 'Trump Pump'"; David Yaffe-Bellany, Matthew Goldstein, and Eric Lipton, "Trump Offers Private Dinner to Top 220 Investors in His Memecoin," *New York Times*, April 23, 2025.
468. Devlin Barrett, "Justice Dept. Disbands Cryptocurrency Enforcement Unit," *Washington Post*, April 8, 2025; "Ending Regulation by Prosecution," memorandum, Office of the Deputy Attorney General, US Department of Justice, April 7, 2025, https://www.justice.gov/dag/media/1395781/dl?inline.
469. Weissert and Suderman, "Trump Hosts Top Crypto Investors."
470. "SEC Charges Crypto Entrepreneur Justin Sun and His Companies for Fraud and Other Securities Law Violations," press release, US Securities and Exchange Commission, March 22, 2023, https://www.sec.gov/newsroom/press-releases/2023-59.
471. "Weissman interview by Goodman and González ("'Mt. Everest of Corruption'"), May 28, 2025.
472. Stephen Fowler, "Trump Opened a New Golf Course in Scotland. It's Not His Only New Venture as President," NPR, July 29, 2025, https://www.npr.org/2025/06/26/nx-s1-5446114/trump-wealth-business-crypto-brand; *Financial Disclosure Report: President Donald J. Trump*, US Office of Government Ethics, July 2025 (PDF on file with author).
473. Home page, World Liberty Financial, accessed September 2, 2025, https://www.worldliberty-financial.com/.
474. Lipton, Yaffe-Bellany, and Protess, "Secret Deals, Foreign Investments"; Alan Suderman, "Trump Signs Executive Order to Establish Government Bitcoin Reserve," *Associated Press News*, March 6, 2025, https://apnews.com/article/bitcoin-reserve-trump-crypto-sacks-5c91a1ab3dab9a8c86d4bc42b8db3f8f.
475. Weissert and Suderman, "Trump Hosts Top Crypto Investors."
476. Yaffe-Bellany, Goldstein, and Lipton, "Trump Offers Private Dinner."
477. Lipton, Yaffe-Bellany, and Protess, "Secret Deals, Foreign Investments."
478. Yaffe-Bellany and Vogel, "The 'Trump Pump.'"
479. Eric Lipton, David Yaffe-Bellany, Bradley Hope, Tripp Mickle, and Paul Mozur, "Anatomy of Two Giant Deals: The U.A.E. Got Chips. The Trump Team Got Crypto Riches," *New York Times*, September 15, 2025.
480. Lipton, Yaffe-Bellany, Hope, Mickle, and Mozur, "Anatomy of Two Giant Deals."
481. Lipton, Yaffe-Bellany, Hope, Mickle, and Mozur, "Anatomy of Two Giant Deals."
482. Lipton, Yaffe-Bellany, Hope, Mickle, and Mozur, "Anatomy of Two Giant Deals."
483. David Yaffe-Bellany and Kenneth P. Vogel, "Trump Pardons the Founder of the Cryptocurrency Exchange Binance," *New York Times*, October 23, 2025.
484. Yaffe-Bellany and Vogel, "Trump Pardons the Founder."
485. Yaffe-Bellany and Vogel, "Trump Pardons the Founder."
486. Julia Mueller, "Trump Pardoned Man 1 Month After Mother Attended $1M per Person Fundraiser: Report," *The Hill*, May 27, 2025, https://thehill.com/homenews/administration/5319932-trump-pardon-paul-walczak/; "Owner of Florida Health Care Companies Sentenced for Employment Tax Crimes," press release, US Department of Justice, April 11, 2025, https://www.justice.gov/opa/pr/owner-florida-health-care-companies-sentenced-employment-tax-crimes.
487. Mueller, "Trump Pardoned Man."
488. "Owner of Florida Health Care Companies Sentenced."
489. Michael Gold, "Social Media, Pleas from Allies and Prison Essays: How Santos Won His Freedom," *New York Times*, October 18, 2025.
490. Gold, "Social Media, Pleas from Allies."
491. Grace Ashford, Michael Gold, Nicholas Fandos, and Nate Schweber, "George Santos Pleads Guilty to Wire Fraud and Identity Theft," *New York Times*, August 19, 2024.
492. Gold, "Social Media, Pleas from Allies."
493. Gold, "Social Media, Pleas from Allies."
494. Gold, "Social Media, Pleas from Allies."
495. Gold, "Social Media, Pleas from Allies."

496. Robert Frank, "Donald Trump Jr. Co-Founds New Private Members Club, Executive Branch, with a $500,000 Fee," CNBC, April 28, 2025, https://www.cnbc.com/2025/04/28/donald-trump-jr-private-members-club-executive-branch.html.
497. Frank, "Donald Trump Jr. Co-Founds New Private Members Club."
498. Alisha Haridasani Gupta, "What Does President Trump's New Perfume Smell Like?" *New York Times*, July 1, 2025.
499. Gupta, "What Does President Trump's New Perfume Smell Like?"
500. Trump Store, accessed October 29, 2025, https://www.trumpstore.com/.
501. Monica Torres, "Expert Says 1 Big Claim About 'Trump Mobile' Is Simply 'Not Plausible,'" *HuffPost*, June 24, 2025, https://www.huffpost.com/entry/trump-mobile_l_685984f5e4b0b13879323798.
502. Fowler, "Trump Opened a New Golf Course in Scotland."
503. Michael Adams and Paul Katzeff, "What Are Meme Coins? Are They Worth Investing In?" *Investor's Business Daily*, May 13, 2024, https://www.forbes.com/advisor/investing/cryptocurrency/what-are-meme-coins-are-they-worth-investing-in/.
504. Donald J. Trump (@realDonaldTrump), "My NEW Official Trump Meme Is HERE! It's Time to Celebrate Everything We Stand For: WINNING! Join My Very Special Trump Community. GET YOUR $TRUMP NOW. Go to http://gettrumpmemes.com — Have Fun!" X, January 17, 2025, https://x.com/realdonaldtrump/status/1880446012168249386.
505. Chandelis Duster, "What to Know About Trump Cryptocurrency Meme Coins," NPR, January 20, 2025, https://www.npr.org/2025/01/20/nx-s1-5268759/donald-trump-melania-cryptocurrency-meme-coins.
506. Yaffe-Bellany, Goldstein, and Lipton, "Trump Offers Private Dinner."
507. Yaffe-Bellany, Goldstein, and Lipton, "Trump Offers Private Dinner."
508. Yaffe-Bellany, Goldstein, and Lipton, "Trump Offers Private Dinner."
509. Yaffe-Bellany, Goldstein, and Lipton, "Trump Offers Private Dinner."
510. Yaffe-Bellany, Goldstein, and Lipton, "Trump Offers Private Dinner."
511. Weissert and Suderman, "Trump Hosts Top Crypto Investors."

5. Silencing Critics

512. Tresa Baldas, "Ontario Man Admits 'Sextorting' Two Detroit Area Teens," *Detroit Free Press*, January 15, 2016, https://www.freep.com/story/news/2016/01/15/sextortion-canada/78710888/.
513. Daisuke Wakabayashi and Michael N. Grynbaum, "Trump Sues the *New York Times* for Articles Questioning His Success," *New York Times*, September 16, 2025.
514. Stephen Collinson, "Why Trump Is Relishing His Duel with Harvard and Other Elite Schools," CNN, March 6, 2025, https://edition.cnn.com/2025/04/16/politics/harvard-trump-columbia-elite-universities-funding/index.html.
515. "Addressing Risks from Perkins Coie LLP," executive order, White House, March 6, 2025, https://www.whitehouse.gov/presidential-actions/2025/03/addressing-risks-from-perkins-coie-llp/.
516. Aaron Pellish and Jeremy Herb, "Ex-Intel Official Who Created Controversial Trump-Russia Dossier Speaks Out," CNN, October 18, 2021, https://www.cnn.com/2021/10/17/politics/christopher-steele-dossier-trump.
517. Robert S. Mueller III, *Report on the Investigation into Russian Interference in the 2016 Presidential Election*, vol. 1 (US Department of Justice, 2019), 1–2, available at https://www.documentcloud.org/documents/5955240-Full-Mueller-Report/.
518. Donald J. Trump interview with George Stephanopoulos, "ABC News' Oval Office Interview with President Trump," transcript, ABC News, June 13, 2019, https://abcnews.go.com/Politics/abc-news-oval-office-interview-president-donald-trump/story?id=63688943.
519. Caroline Sullivan, "Five Court Wins That Impacted Voters This Election," *Democracy Docket*, November 22, 2022, https://www.democracydocket.com/analysis/five-court-wins-that-impacted-voters-this-election/.
520. Paul Dans and Steven Groves, eds., *Mandate for Leadership: The Conservative Promise* (Heritage Foundation, 2025), 561, https://static.heritage.org/project2025/2025_MandateForLeadership_FULL.pdf.

521. United States v. Trump, No. 1:23-cr-278290 (D.DC 2025), ECF No. 185.
522. United States v. Trump, No. 1:23-cr-278290 (D.DC 2025), ECF No. 185.
523. United States v. Trump, No. 1:23-cr-278290 (D.DC 2025), ECF No. 184.
524. Zach Montague, "Trump Appeals Ruling Blocking Executive Order Against Perkins Coie," *New York Times*, June 30, 2025.
525. Melissa Quinn, "Judge Finds Trump Executive Order Punishing Susman Godfrey Law Firm Unconstitutional," CBS News, June 27, 2025, https://www.cbsnews.com/news/judge-strikes-down-trump-executive-order-punishing-susman-godfrey-law-firm/.
526. Perkins Coie LLP v. US Department of Justice, et al., Civil Action No. 25-716 (BAH), memorandum opinion, US District Court for the District of Columbia (filed May 2, 2025) (Howell, J.).
527. "Addressing Risks from Paul Weiss," executive order, White House, March 14, 2025, https://www.whitehouse.gov/presidential-actions/2025/03/addressing-risks-from-paul-weiss/.
528. "Addressing Risks from Paul Weiss."
529. Daniel Barnes, "Inside the Fallout at Paul Weiss After the Firm's Deal with Trump," *Politico*, June 29, 2025, https://www.politico.com/news/2025/06/29/paul-weiss-brad-karp-trump-fall-out-00420354.
530. James Booth, "Paul Weiss Partner Pay Hits $7.5M Following London Expansion Drive," *Financial News London*, February 27, 2025, https://www.fnlondon.com/articles/paul-weiss-partner-pay-hits-7-5m-following-london-expansion-drive-60febc71; Debra Cassens Weiss, "BigLaw Firm Will Pay Up to $20M to Top Partners, an Amount Needed 'To Be at the Big Table,'" *ABA Journal*, May 20, 2024, https://www.abajournal.com/news/article/biglaw-firm-to-pay-up-to-20m-to-top-partners-an-amount-needed-to-be-at-the-big-table.
531. Matt Shuham, "Trump and a Powerhouse Law Firm Are Telling Different Stories About Their Shocking Agreement," *HuffPost*, March 21, 2025, https://www.huffpost.com/entry/paul-weiss-agreement-white-house-differences_n_67dda2cae4b00872325325f5.
532. Shuham, "Trump and a Powerhouse Law Firm."
533. Shuham, "Trump and a Powerhouse Law Firm."
534. Shuham, "Trump and a Powerhouse Law Firm."
535. Shuham, "Trump and a Powerhouse Law Firm."
536. Ankush Khardori, "Trump's Law Firm Deals Are Already a Mess," *Politico*, July 10, 2025, https://www.politico.com/news/magazine/2025/07/10/trump-law-firms-deals-mess-column-00445259.
537. Khardori, "Trump's Law Firm Deals Are Already a Mess."
538. Timothy Snyder, *On Tyranny: Twenty Lessons from the Twentieth Century* (Crown: 2017), 17.
539. Justin Henry, "Paul Weiss Loses Ex-US Attorney Williams after Trump Deal," *Bloomberg Law*, June 6, 2025, https://news.bloomberglaw.com/business-and-practice/former-us-attorney-damian-williams-leaves-paul-weiss-for-jenner.
540. Roy Strom, "Trump Says He'll Enlist Big Law Dealmakers for Coal, Tariffs," *Bloomberg Law*, April 8, 2025, https://news.bloomberglaw.com/business-and-practice/trump-says-hell-enlist-big-law-dealmakers-for-coal-tariffs.
541. Henry, "Paul Weiss Loses Ex-US Attorney."
542. Daniel Barnes, "Inside the Fallout at Paul Weiss."
543. Neera Tanden (@neeratanden), "Paul Weiss' actions will live in infamy," X, May 3, 2025, https://x.com/neeratanden/status/1918703276482085373.
544. Michael S. Schmidt, "When Silence Speaks Volumes," *New York Times*, July 11, 2025.
545. Katelyn Polantz, "Trump's Crackdown on Law Firms Is Chilling the Future of Pro Bono Legal Work," CNN, May 7, 2025, https://www.cnn.com/2025/05/07/politics/trump-law-firm-crackdown-pro-bono-work.
546. Shayna Jacobs, Clara Ence Morse, and Mark Berman, "Nation's Biggest Law Firms Back Off from Challenging Trump Policies," *Washington Post*, October 26, 2025.
547. Jacobs, Morse, and Berman, "Nation's Big Law Firms Back Off."
548. Brad S. Karp and Gary M. Wingens, "The Law Did Not Create This Crisis, But Lawyers Will Help End It," *New York Times*, June 25, 2018.

549. Ian Bassin and Maximillian Potter, "On Anticipatory Obedience and the Media," *Columbia Journalism Review*, October 8, 2024, https://www.cjr.org/analysis/anticipatory-obedience-bassin-potter-scheppele-orban-trump-hungary-media-punish.php.
550. Michael M. Grynbaum, "Trump Calls the News Media the 'Enemy of the American People,'" *New York Times*, February 17, 2017.
551. Dana Milbank, "Trump Attacked the Free Press, and He Got Exactly What He Deserved," op ed, *Washington Post*, May 19, 2017.
552. Russ Buettner, Susanne Craig, and Mike McIntire, "The President's Taxes: Long-Concealed Records Show Trump's Chronic Losses and Years of Tax Avoidance," *New York Times*, September 27, 2020.
553. Robert Parry, "US Journalism's New 'Golden Age'?" *Consortium News*, May 22, 2017, https://consortiumnews.com/2017/05/22/us-journalisms-new-golden-age/.
554. Milbank, "Trump Attacked the Free Press."
555. Dan Mangan, "Jeff Bezos Killed Washington Post Endorsement of Kamala Harris, Paper Reports," CNBC, October 25, 2024, https://www.cnbc.com/2024/10/25/jeff-bezos-killed-washington-post-endorsement-of-kamala-harris-.html.
556. Mangan, "Jeff Bezos Killed Washington Post Endorsement."
557. Dominick Mastrangelo, "Washington Post Restructuring Newsroom; Columnist Resigns," *The Hill*, March 10, 2025, https://thehill.com/homenews/media/5186150-washington-post-overhaul-bezos/.
558. Liam Riley, "Jeff Bezos Congratulates Trump for 'Extraordinary Political Comeback and Decisive Victory,'" CNN, November 6, 2025, https://www.cnn.com/2024/11/06/media/jeff-bezos-congratulates-trump-victory-amazon-post/.
559. Clare Malone, "Is Jeff Bezos Selling Out *The Washington Post*?" *New Yorker*, May 12, 2025.
560. Malone, "Is Jeff Bezos Selling Out."
561. "Pentagon Cancels $10bn 'Jedi' Contract," BBC News, July 6, 2021, https://www.bbc.com/news/business-57739636; Don Reisinger, "Why Amazon Is Challenging the Trump Administration over a Defense Department Cloud Contract," *Inc.*, February 10, 2020, https://www.inc.com/don-reisinger/jeff-bezos-has-officially-launched-an-all-out-offensive-on-donald-trump-but-who-will-win.html.
562. Malone, "Is Jeff Bezos Selling Out."
563. Huo Jingnan, Shannon Bond, and Bobby Allyn, "Meta Says It Will End Fact-Checking as Silicon Valley Prepares for Trump," NPR, January 7, 2025, https://www.npr.org/2025/01/07/nx-s1-5251151/meta-fact-checking-mark-zuckerberg-trump.
564. Malone, "Is Jeff Bezos Selling Out"; Chris Morris, "Amazon Prime Says It Will Stream All Seven Seasons of 'The Apprentice,' and Trump Is Likely to Reap Royalties from the Deal," *Fortune*, March 11, 2025, https://fortune.com/2025/03/11/amazon-prime-stream-the-apprentice-trump/.
565. Giselle Ruhiyyih Ewing, "ABC and Stephanopoulos to Pay Trump $15M, Apologize in Defamation Suit Settlement," *Politico*, December 14, 2024, https://www.politico.com/news/2024/12/14/trump-abc-stephanopoulos-settlement-00194391.
566. Ewing, "ABC and Stephanopoulos to Pay Trump $15M"; E. Jean Carroll v. Donald J. Trump, Case 1:20-cv-07311-LAK, memorandum opinion granting plaintiff's motion to dismiss defendant's counterclaim (S.D.N.Y. Aug. 7, 2023).
567. Brian Stelter, "Why ABC News Settled with Donald Trump for $15 Million," CNN, December 16, 2024, https://www.cnn.com/2024/12/16/media/george-stephanopoulos-trump-settlement-abc.
568. Donald J. Trump (@realDonaldTrump), "CBS and 60 Minutes defrauded the public by doing something which has never, to this extent, been seen before. They 100% removed Kamala's horrible election changing answers to questions, and replaced them with completely different, and far better, answers, taken from another part of the interview. This was Election changing "stuff," Election Interference and, quite simply, Election Fraud at a level never seen before. CBS should lose its license, and the cheaters at 60 Minutes should all be thrown out, and this disreputable "NEWS" show should be immediately terminated. With the new Democrat scandal that just arose with respect to USAID illegally paying large sums of money to *Politico* and other media outlets, the question must be asked, was CBS paid for committing

this FRAUD??? Many other questions to come! This will go down as the biggest Broadcasting SCANDAL in History!!!" Truth Social, February 6, 2025, https://truthsocial.com/@realDonaldTrump/posts/113956631326391344.

569. David Folkenflik, "Paramount Agrees to Pay $16 Million to Settle Trump's CBS Lawsuit," NPR, July 2, 2025, https://www.npr.org/2025/07/02/nx-s1-5290171/trump-lawsuit-paramount-cbs-60-minutes-kamala-harris.
570. Folkenflik, "Paramount Agrees to Pay $16 Million."
571. Folkenflik, "Paramount Agrees to Pay $16 Million."
572. Yurii Stasiuk and Nicole Markus, "CBS Cancels Stephen Colbert's Show Days After Trump Settlement Criticism," *Politico*, July 18, 2025, https://www.politico.com/news/2025/07/18/cbs-cancels-stephen-colbert-00462089.
573. Stasiuk and Markus, "CBS Cancels Stephen Colbert's Show."
574. Miriam Waldvogel, "Trump Refiles Lawsuit against Iowa Pollster in State Court," *The Hill*, July 1, 2025, https://thehill.com/regulation/court-battles/5378784-trump-lawsuit-des-moes-register-poll/.
575. Waldvogel, "Trump Refiles Lawsuit."
576. Brian Stelter, Katelyn Polantz, Hadas Gold, and Paula Reid, "Trump Sues *Des Moines Register* and Top Pollster over Final Iowa Survey," CNN, December 17, 2024, https://edition.cnn.com/2024/12/17/media/trump-lawsuit-des-moines-register-ann-selzer-poll/index.html.
577. Liam Reilly, "Trump Has Long Threatened the Media. Press Freedom Groups Fear He Might Make Good on It," CNN, November 7, 2024, https://www.cnn.com/2024/11/07/media/trump-news-media-press-freedom-threats.
578. David Folkenflik, "Judge Orders White House to Allow AP Access to News Events," NPR, April 9, 2025, https://www.npr.org/2025/04/08/nx-s1-5342369/ap-white-house-court-ruling-oval-office-gulf-of-mexico-america.
579. Julie Pace, "The AP's Freedom of Speech—And Yours," *Wall Street Journal*, March 26, 2025.
580. David Bauder, "Associated Press Seeks Full Appeals Court Hearing on Access to Trump Administration Events," *Associated Press News*, June 10, 2025, https://apnews.com/article/trump-white-house-ap-access-press-freedom-23aefe14ee2e85dafe499c2a07a1e2f8.
581. Bauder, "Associated Press Seeks Full Appeals Court Hearing."
582. Brian Stelter, "Pentagon Boots CNN and *The Washington Post* from Workspace in Favor of Smaller Conservative Outlets," CNN, February 7, 2025, https://www.cnn.com/2025/02/07/media/pentagon-press-rotation-defense-department.
583. Ashleigh Fields, "Conservative Commentator Questions Zelensky over Attire: 'Why Don't You Wear a Suit?'" *The Hill*, February 28, 2025, https://thehill.com/policy/international/5170029-conservative-commentator-questions-zelensky-over-attire-why-dont-you-wear-a-suit/.
584. Fields, "Conservative Commentator Questions Zelensky."
585. Connor Stringer, "The MAGA Reporter Whose Humiliation of Zelensky Sparked a Geopolitical Crisis," *The Telegraph* (London), March 1, 2025, https://www.telegraph.co.uk/world-news/2025/03/01/maga-brian-glenn-humiliation-zelensky-trump-vance/.
586. "Trump Signs Executive Order Directing Federal Funding Cuts to PBS and NPR," PBS News, May 2, 2025, https://www.pbs.org/newshour/politics/trump-signs-executive-order-directing-federal-funding-cuts-to-pbs-and-npr.
587. David Folkenflik, "Trump's FCC Chief Opens Investigation into NPR and PBS," NPR, January 30, 2025, https://www.npr.org/2025/01/30/nx-s1-5281162/fcc-npr-pbs-investigation.
588. Folkenflik, "Trump's FCC Chief Opens Investigation."
589. Dominick Mastrangelo, "Trump's FCC Probing Comcast, NBC over DEI Policies," *The Hill*, February 12, 2025, https://thehill.com/homenews/media/5141303-comcast-fcc-diversity-equity-inclusion/.
590. Mastrangelo, "Trump's FCC Probing Comcast."
591. Wyatte Grantham-Philips, "What to Know About Jimmy Kimmel's Return to His Late-Night TV Show," *Associated Press News*, September 26, 2025, https://apnews.com/article/jimmy-kimmel-show-suspended-charlie-kirk-ae43c600bd0f2a4c7d3c12077e91b211.

592. Kevin Breuninger, "Ted Cruz Compares FCC Chair Carr to Mafia Boss in Jimmy Kimmel Warnings," CBNC, September 19, 2025, https://www.cnbc.com/2025/09/19/ted-cruz-jimmy-kimmel-fcc-carr-mafia.html?msockid=3fca96abf6c0612e28d08350f7446078.
593. Breuninger, "Ted Cruz Compares FCC Chair Carr to Mafia Boss."
594. Breuninger, "Ted Cruz Compares FCC Chair Carr to Mafia Boss."
595. Grantham-Philips, "What to Know About Jimmy Kimmel's Return."
596. Breuninger, "Ted Cruz Compares FCC Chair Carr to Mafia Boss."
597. Breuninger, "Ted Cruz Compares FCC Chair Carr to Mafia Boss."
598. Grantham-Philips, "What to Know About Jimmy Kimmel's Return."
599. Grantham-Philips, "What to Know About Jimmy Kimmel's Return."
600. Minho Kim and Megan Mineiro, "Trump Urges Congress to 'Kill' Voice of America as Its Leader Defends Gutting It," *New York Times*, June 25, 2025; Minho Kim, "Trump Administration Rescinds Voice of America Layoffs After Errors in Notices," *New York Times*, June 27, 2025.
601. Nick Schifrin, Dan Sagalyn, and Zeba Warsi, "What Is Voice of America and Why Trump Is Dismantling the Broadcaster," PBS News, March 17, 2025, https://www.pbs.org/newshour/show/what-is-voice-of-america-and-why-trump-is-dismantling-the-broadcaster.
602. Schifrin, Sagalyn, and Warsi, "What Is Voice of America."
603. John Haltiwanger, "Why Authoritarians Attack Universities First," *Foreign Policy*, April 16, 2025, https://foreignpolicy.com/2025/04/16/trump-authoritarians-universities-fascism-jason-stanley/.
604. Haltiwanger, "Why Authoritarians Attack Universities First."
605. Haltiwanger, "Why Authoritarians Attack Universities First."
606. Anna Dumont, "What Autocrats Want from Academics: Servility," *Chronicle of Higher Education*, March 20, 2025, https://www.chronicle.com/article/what-autocrats-want-from-academics-servility?sra=true.
607. Dumont, "What Autocrats Want from Academics."
608. Dumont, "What Autocrats Want from Academics."
609. Stephen Collinson, "Why Trump Is Relishing His Duel with Harvard and Other Elite Schools," CNN, April 16, 2025, https://edition.cnn.com/2025/04/16/politics/harvard-trump-columbia-elite-universities-funding/index.html.
610. Bianca Quilantan, "College Presidents Testifying on Campus Antisemitism," *Politico*, December 5, 2023, https://www.politico.com/news/2023/12/05/college-presidents-testifying-campus-antisemitism-00130277.
611. Collinson, "Why Trump Is Relishing His Duel with Harvard"; Zoe Sottile and Eva Rothenberg, "Here's What Led Up to Harvard President Claudine Gay's Resignation," CNN, January 2, 2024, https://www.cnn.com/2024/01/02/business/timeline-harvard-president-claudine-gay-resignation.
612. Collinson, "Why Trump Is Relishing His Duel with Harvard."
613. "Columbia University Caves to Demands to Restore $400M from Trump Administration," *The Guardian*, March 21, 2025, https://www.theguardian.com/us-news/2025/mar/21/columbia-university-funding-trump-demands.
614. Giselle Ruhiyyih Ewing, "Anti-Defamation League Decries Trump's Use of 'Centuries-Old Antisemitic Trope' at Rally," *Politico*, July 4, 2025, https://www.politico.com/news/2025/07/04/trump-antisemitic-trope-response-00440000.
615. Ewing, "Anti-Defamation League Decries Trump's Use."
616. Emma Green, "Why the Charlottesville Marchers Were Obsessed with Jews," *The Atlantic*, August 15, 2017.
617. Jonathan Weisman, "Jewish Allies Call Trump's Dinner with Antisemites a Breaking Point," *New York Times*, November 28, 2022.
618. Weisman, "Jewish Allies Call Trump's Dinner."
619. Laura Meckler, Dan Rosenzweig-Ziff, Susan Svrluga, Perry Stein, and Emily Davies, "Inside the Powerful Task Force Spearheading Trump's Assault on Colleges, DEI," *Washington Post*, July 24, 2025.
620. Meckler, Rosenzweig-Ziff, Svrluga, Stein, and Davies, "Inside the Powerful Task Force."
621. Collinson, "Why Trump Is Relishing His Duel with Harvard."

622. "Columbia University Caves to Demands to Restore $400M."
623. Haltiwanger, "Why Authoritarians Attack Universities First."
624. Betsy Klein and Dalta Faheid, "University of Virginia President Resigns amid Pressure from the Trump Administration," CNN, June 27, 2025, https://www.cnn.com/2025/06/27/us/university-of-virginia-president-resigns.
625. Klein and Faheid, "University of Virginia President Resigns."
626. Klein and Faheid, "University of Virginia President Resigns."
627. Klein and Faheid, "University of Virginia President Resigns."
628. Anemona Hartocollis, Michael S. Schmidt, and Tyler Pager, "President of Northwestern, a School Attacked by the G.O.P., Will Resign," *New York Times*, September 4, 2025.
629. Sam Stevenson, "Donald Trump Secures $75 Million Northwestern Deal: 'Huge Win,'" *Newsweek*, November 29, 2025, https://www.newsweek.com/donald-trump-northwestern-deal-11128551.
630. Stevenson, "Donald Trump Secures $75 Million Northwestern Deal."
631. Matt Moret, "Penn Revokes Lia Thomas' Records, Bans Trans Athletes under Trump Administration Deal," *The Athletic* (blog), *New York Times*, July 1, 2025, https://www.nytimes.com/athletic/6467404/2025/07/01/trump-lia-thomas-transgender-athletes-penn/.
632. Moret, "Penn Revokes Lia Thomas' Records."
633. "Joint Letter Regarding Compliance with Federal Anti-Discrimination and Funding Requirements," US Department of Education and US Department of Justice letter to Harvard University, April 11, 2025, https://www.harvard.edu/research-funding/wp-content/uploads/sites/16/2025/04/Letter-Sent-to-Harvard-2025-04-11.pdf.
634. "Joint Letter Regarding Compliance," Apr. 11, 2025.
635. Collinson, "Why Trump Is Relishing His Duel with Harvard"; Danielle Douglas-Gabriel, "Trump Wields His 'Secret Weapon': College Accreditation," *Washington Post*, July 12, 2025.
636. Douglas-Gabriel, "Trump Wields His 'Secret Weapon.'"
637. "How Trump Has Targeted Harvard's International Students—and What the Latest Court Ruling Means," *Associated Press News*, June 20, 2025, https://apnews.com/article/harvard-trump-judge-international-students-8267f58489cfb1f4013330b78fa02c1b; Alan Blinder, "Judge Rules Trump Administration Illegally Canceled Harvard Funding," New York Times, September 3, 2025.
638. "Chairmen Jordan and Fitzgerald Subpoena Harvard University," press release, House Judiciary Committee, June 26, 2025, https://judiciary.house.gov/media/press-releases/chairmen-jordan-and-fitzgerald-subpoena-harvard-university.
639. Dakin Andone, "Websites Serving Harvard Undergrad Women, Minority and LGBTQ Students Taken Down, *Crimson* Reports," CNN, July 10, 2025, https://www.cnn.com/2025/07/10/us/harvard-student-diversity-websites-removed.
640. Andone, "Websites Serving Harvard Undergrad Women."
641. M. Gessen, "Welcome to Trump's Mafia State," transcript, *The Opinions* (podcast), *New York Times*, April 21, 2025, https://www.nytimes.com/2025/04/21/opinion/trump-universities-mafia-state.html.
642. Gessen, "Welcome to Trump's Mafia State."
643. Evan Goldstein and Len Gutkin, "'We're in the Midst of an Authoritarian Takeover,'" *Chronicle of Higher Education*, March 11, 2025, https://www.chronicle.com/article/were-in-the-midst-of-an-authoritarian-takeover.
644. Gessen, "Welcome to Trump's Mafia State."
645. "Canadian Resident Sentenced in Sextortion Case," press release, US Department of Justice, August 10, 2016, https://www.justice.gov/usao-edmi/pr/canadian-resident-sentenced-sextortion-case.
646. David Pressman, "I Watched It Happen in Hungary. Now It's Happening Here," *New York Times*, July 23, 2025.

6. Doing Injustice

647. United States v. Eric Adams, indictment, No. 24 Cr. 556 (S.D.N.Y. Sept. 2024).

648. Danielle R. Sassoon, US Attorney, SDNY, letter to Attorney General Pamela Jo Bondi, re: United States v. Eric Adams, No. 24 Cr. 556 (DEH), February 12, 2025; available at https://static01.nyt.com/newsgraphics/documenttools/24535586a908999e/3801d435-full.pdf.
649. Sassoon letter to Bondi, February 12, 2025.
650. Sassoon letter to Bondi, February 12, 2025.
651. "Danielle Sassoon," Federalist Society, accessed December 7, 2025, https://fedsoc.org/bio/danielle-sassoon.
652. Luc Cohen, "Who Is Danielle Sassoon, the Prosecutor Who Stood Up to Trump's DOJ over Eric Adams' Case?" *Reuters*, February 14, 2025, https://www.reuters.com/world/us/who-is-danielle-sassoon-prosecutor-who-stood-up-trumps-doj-over-eric-adams-case-2025-02-14/.
653. April Rubin and Sareen Habeshian, "DOJ Moves to Drop Eric Adams Charges After 7 Prosecutors Resign," *Axios*, February 14, 2025, https://www.axios.com/2025/02/15/eric-adams-charges-dropped-justice-department.
654. Jonah E. Bromwich and William K. Rashbaum, "3 Adams Case Prosecutors Resign Rather Than Express Regret to Justice Dept.," *New York Times*, April 22, 2025.
655. Bromwich and Rashbaum, "3 Adams Case Prosecutors Resign."
656. Rich Schapiro and Tom Winter, "Trump's Border Czar Tells NYC Mayor He'll Be 'Up His Butt' If He Breaks Vow to Help ICE," NBC News, February 14, 2025, https://www.nbcnews.com/politics/justice-department/trumps-border-czar-tells-eric-adams-butt-nyc-mayor-breaks-vow-help-ice-rcna192201.
657. United States v. Adams, No. 24 Cr. 556, memorandum opinion, (S.D.N.Y. Apr. 2025).
658. United States v. Adams, memorandum opinion.
659. Peter Stone, "Pam Bondi Turning DOJ into Trump's 'Personal Law Firm,' Top Experts Warn," *Guardian*, May 2, 2025, https://www.theguardian.com/us-news/2025/may/02/trump-doj-pam-bondi.
660. "Communications with the White House and Congress," memorandum, US Department of Justice, May 11, 2009, https://www.justice.gov/oip/foia-library/communications_with_the_white_house_and_congress_2009.pdf/dl; "Section 9-27.000: Principles of Federal Prosecution," *Justice Manual*, US Department of Justice, 2018, https://www.justice.gov/jm/jm-9-27000-principles-federal-prosecution.
661. Robert H. Jackson, "The Federal Prosecutor" (speech, Conference of United States Attorneys, Washington, DC, April 1, 1940), Robert H. Jackson center, https://www.roberthjackson.org/speech-and-writing/the-federal-prosecutor/.
662. Berger v. United States, 295 US 78, 88 (1935).
663. Quinta Jurecic, "Trump's Attacks on Justice Department Independence, Then and Now," *Lawfare*, March 27, 2025, https://www.lawfaremedia.org/article/trump-s-attacks-on-justice-department-independence--then-and-now.
664. Trump v. United States, No. 23-393, 603 US ___ (2024).
665. Jurecic, "Trump's Attacks on Justice Department Independence."
666. Perry Stein, Jeremy Roebuck, and Derek Hawkins, "Trump Visits Justice Department for Speech That Breaks All Norms," *Washington Post*, March 14, 2025.
667. "Speech: Donald Trump Addresses the Staff at the Department of Justice," transcript, *Roll Call*, March 14, 2025, https://rollcall.com/factbase/trump/transcript/donald-trump-speech-department-of-justice-march-14-2025/.
668. Michelle L. Price and Colleen Long, "What to Know About Pam Bondi, Trump's New Pick for Attorney General," *Associated Press News*, November 25, 2024, https://apnews.com/article/things-to-know-pam-bondi-eec1d16075c7debda62223b475e3977d.
669. Josh Gerstein, "Trump Promised to Get Revenge. Here Are His Targets," *Politico*, November 6, 2024, https://www.politico.com/news/2024/11/06/trump-retribution-enemy-list-00187725.
670. Ken Dilanian, "Firings, Pardons and Policy Changes Have Gutted DOJ Anti-Corruption Efforts, Experts Say," NBC News, June 3, 2025, https://www.nbcnews.com/politics/justice-department/firings-pardons-policy-changes-gutted-doj-anti-corruption-efforts-expe-rcna200571.
671. "Pausing Foreign Corrupt Practices Act Enforcement to Further American Economic and National Security," executive order, White House, February 10, 2025, https://www.whitehouse.gov/presidential-actions/2025/02/pausing-foreign-corrupt-practices-act-enforcement-to-further-american-economic-and-national-security/.

672. "Ending the Weaponization of the Federal Government," executive order, White House, January 20, 2025, https://www.whitehouse.gov/presidential-actions/2025/01/ending-the-weaponization-of-the-federal-government/.
673. Memorandum from the Attorney General to All Department Employees, "Total Elimination of Cartels and Transnational Criminal Organizations," memorandum, Office of the Attorney General, Department of Justice, February 5, 2025, https://www.documentcloud.org/documents/25514910-doj-eliminating-cartels/.
674. "General Policy Regarding Charging, Plea Negotiations, and Sentencing," memorandum, Office of the Attorney General, Department of Justice, February 5, 2025, https://www.justice.gov/ag/media/1388541/dl?inline.
675. "General Policy Regarding Charging, Plea Negotiations, and Sentencing."
676. Ryan J. Reilly, Sarah Fitzpatrick, and David Rohde, "Justice Department Office That Prosecutes Public Corruption Slashed in Size, Sources Say," NBC News, March 11, 2025, https://www.nbcnews.com/politics/justice-department/justice-department-office-prosecutes-public-corruption-slashed-size-so-rcna195928.
677. Jeremy Roebuck, Perry Stein, Cat Zakrzewski, and Carol D. Leonnig, "Justice Dept. Scales Back Crypto Cases in Line with Trump Directives," *Washington Post*, April 8, 2025.
678. Dilanian, "Firings, Pardons, and Policy Changes Have Gutted."
679. "Frequently Asked Questions," FBI, accessed September 5, 2025, https://www.fbi.gov/about/faqs.
680. Katelyn Polantz, Zachary Cohen, and Casey Gannon, "Exclusive: Trump Adviser Kash Patel Has Appeared Before Grand Jury in Mar-a-Lago Document Probe," CNN, October 20, 2022, https://www.cnn.com/2022/10/20/politics/kash-patel-mar-a-lago-grand-jury-testimony/index.html.
681. David Klepper, "Music to Trump's Ears: Whitewashing Jan. 6 Riot With Song," *Associated Press News*, April 21, 2023, https://apnews.com/article/j6-choir-trump-national-anthem-capitol-riot-79618f1f2a689c308dfdc34d54d327ea.
682. Natalia Drozdiak and Chris Strohm, "Trump Picks Loyalist 'Deep State' Critic Patel to Head FBI," *Bloomberg News*, November 30, 2024, https://www.bloomberg.com/news/articles/2024-11-30/trump-picks-loyalist-deep-state-critic-patel-to-head-the-fbi.
683. Timothy Noah, "The Who's Who on Kash Patel's Crazy Enemies List," *New Republic*, December 3, 2024.
684. Noah, "The Who's Who."
685. Noah, "The Who's Who."
686. Drozdiak and Strohm, "Trump Picks Loyalist 'Deep State' Critic."
687. Drozdiak and Strohm, Trump Picks Loyalist 'Deep State' Critic."
688. Adam Goldman, "F.B.I. Reassigns Agents Who Knelt During Racial Justice Protests in 2020," *New York Times*, April 30, 2025.
689. John Shiffman, Sarah N. Lynch, Joseph Tanfani, and Aram Roston, "'Slap in the Face': Bongino Appointment Sends Shockwaves Through FBI," *Reuters*, February 27, 2025, https://www.reuters.com/world/us/slap-face-bongino-appointment-sends-shockwaves-through-fbi-2025-02-27/.
690. Shiffman, Lynch, Tanfani, and Roston, "Slap in the Face."
691. Luke Barr, "Missouri Attorney General Appointed Co-Deputy Director of FBI," ABC News, August 18, 2025, https://abcnews.go.com/Politics/missouri-attorney-general-appointed-deputy-director-fbi/story?id=124764098.
692. Adam Goldman, "F.B.I. Suspends Employee on Patel's So-Called Enemies List," *New York Times*, April 11, 2025.
693. Robert S. Mueller, *Report on the Investigation into Russian Interference in the 2016 Presidential Election*, vol. 1 (Department of Justice, 2019), available at https://www.justice.gov/archives/sco/file/1373816/dl?inline=.
694. Charlie Savage, Adam Goldman, and Alan Feuer, "F.B.I. Pick Pushed False and Misleading Claims About Trump Investigations," *New York Times*," January 23, 2025.
695. Jeremy Roebuck, "FBI Fires Agents Photographed Kneeling During 2020 George Floyd Protests," *Washington Post*, September 27, 2025.

696. Adam Goldman, "The F.B.I. Is Using Polygraphs to Test Officials' Loyalty," *New York Times*, July 10, 2025.
697. Ryan J. Reilly, "DOJ 'Weaponization' Group Will Shame Individuals It Can't Charge, New Head Says," NBC News, May 13, 2025, https://www.nbcnews.com/politics/justice-department/doj-weaponization-group-will-shame-individuals-cant-charge-crimes-new-rcna206553.
698. "US Charges Five Chinese Military Hackers for Cyber Espionage Against US Corporations and a Labor Organization for Commercial Advantage," press release, US Attorney's Office for the Western District of Pennsylvania, May 19, 2014, https://www.justice.gov/usao-wdpa/pr/us-charges-five-chinese-military-hackers-cyber-espionage-against-us-corporations-and.
699. United States v. Internet Research Agency LLC, et al., No. 1:18-cr-00032-DLF (D.DC filed Feb. 16, 2018) (Indictment).
700. Reilly, "DOJ 'Weaponization' Group Will Shame Individuals."
701. Reilly, "DOJ 'Weaponization' Group Will Shame Individuals."
702. Eagle Ed Martin, @EagleEdMartin, biography section, X, accessed December 7, 2025, https://x.com/EagleEdMartin.
703. Kyle Cheney, "Ed Martin Jr., a Crusader for Jan. 6 Defendants, Now Oversees Their Absolution," *Politico*, January 29, 2025, https://www.politico.com/news/2025/01/29/ed-martin-jr-jan-6-defendants-00201269.
704. Caitlin Yilek, "Trump Replaces Controversial US Attorney Pick Ed Martin: 'Disappointing,'" CBS News, May 8, 2025, https://www.cbsnews.com/news/trump-ed-martin-us-attorney-nomination-withdrawn/; Alanna Durkin Richer and Michael Kunzelman, "New Top Prosecutor for DC Advocated for Jan. 6 Rioters and Echoed Trump's False 2020 Election Claims," *Associated Press News*, January 28, 2025, https://apnews.com/article/justice-department-jan-6-dc-us-attorney-9418cccb045d64c65b7ce85a220c45ac.
705. Yilek, "Trump Replaces Controversial US Attorney Pick Ed Martin"; Jordan Rubin, "Trump's DC Prosecutor Dismissed Jan. 6 Case Against Client He Represented," *Deadline: Legal Blog*, MSNBC, February 6, 2025, https://www.msnbc.com/deadline-white-house/deadline-legal-blog/ed-martin-jan-6-lawyer-padilla-us-attorney-rcna191041.
706. Adele M. Stan, "Trump's Pick for Federal Prosecutor in DC Gives Hacks a Bad Name," *New Republic*, February 3, 2025.
707. Eagle Ed Martin, @EagleEdMartin, home page, X, accessed December 7, 2025, https://x.com/EagleEdMartin.
708. Ed Martin (@EagleEdMartin), "Dear @elon, Please see this important letter. We will not tolerate threats against DOGE workers or law-breaking by the disgruntled. All the best. Ed Martin," February 3, 2025, https://x.com/EagleEdMartin/status/1886456136032817488.
709. Ed Martin (@EagleEdMartin), "Dear @elon, Please see this important letter."
710. Alan Feuer, "In Fiery Words, the Federal Prosecutor in Washington Promises an Inquiry into Allegations Raised by Musk," *New York Times*, February 7, 2025.
711. "Read Interim US Attorney Ed Martin's Letters to Democratic Lawmakers," *Washington Post*, February 19, 2025.
712. J. Edward Moreno, "Schumer Warns Kavanaugh and Gorsuch They Will 'Pay the Price,'" *The Hill*, March 4, 2020, https://thehill.com/homenews/senate/486007-schumer-warns-kavanaugh-and-gorsuch-they-will-pay-the-price/.
713. "Read Interim US Attorney Ed Martin's Letters to Democratic Lawmakers."
714. Rebecca Beitsch, "US Attorney Launches Probe into Whether Schumer, Garcia Made Threats to Justices, Musk," *The Hill*, February 20, 2025, https://thehill.com/homenews/administration/5156193-us-attorney-accuses-congressmen-of-threatening-public-officials/.
715. Counterman v. Colorado, 600 US 66, 74 (2023).
716. Spencer S. Hsu and Dan Rosenzweig-Ziff, "DC US Attorney Tells Georgetown He Won't Hire from Any School With 'DEI,'" *Washington Post*, March 5, 2025.
717. Hsu and Rosenzweig-Ziff, "DC US Attorney Tells Georgetown."
718. Rob Stein, "Medical Journals Hit with Threatening Letters from Justice Department," NPR, May 2, 2025, https://www.npr.org/sections/shots-health-news/2025/05/02/nx-s1-5374993/medical-journals-hit-with-threatening-letters-from-justice-department.
719. Michael S. Schmidt and Glenn Thrush, "For Those Deemed Trump's Enemies, a Time of Anxiety and Fear," *New York Times*, January 18, 2025.

720. Alexander Bolton, "GOP Senator Torpedoes Trump's Pick to Serve as US Attorney for DC," *The Hill*, May 6, 2025, https://thehill.com/homenews/senate/5285035-tom-tillis-ed-martin-us-attorney-dc/.
721. Alan Feuer and Adam Goldman, "Pardoned Jan. 6 Rioter Who Threatened Police Joins Justice Dept.," *New York Times*, July 1, 2025.
722. Donald Trump (@realDonaldTrump), "Pam: I have reviewed over 30 statements and posts saying that, essentially, "same old story as last time, all talk, no action. Nothing is being done. What about Comey, Adam "Shifty" Schiff, Leticia??? They're all guilty as hell, but nothing is going to be done." Then we almost put in a Democrat supported U.S. Attorney, in Virginia, with a really bad Republican past. A Woke RINO, who was never going to do his job. That's why two of the worst Dem Senators PUSHED him so hard. He even lied to the media and said he quit, and that we had no case. No, I fired him, and there is a GREAT CASE, and many lawyers, and legal pundits, say so. Lindsey Halligan is a really good lawyer, and likes you, a lot. We can't delay any longer, it's killing our reputation and credibility. They impeached me twice, and indicted me (5 times!), OVER NOTHING. JUSTICE MUST BE SERVED, NOW!!! President DJT," Truth Social, September 20, 2025, https://truthsocial.com/@realDonaldTrump/posts/115239044548033727.
723. Trump, "Pam: I have reviewed."
724. Trump, "Pam: I have reviewed."
725. Trump, "Pam: I have reviewed."
726. Glenn Thrush, Maggie Haberman, Alan Feuer, and Tyler Pager, "Inside the Trump Administration's Push to Prosecute James Comey," *New York Times*, September 27, 2025.
727. Thrush, Haberman, Feuer, and Pager, "Inside the Trump Administration's Push."
728. Thrush, Haberman, Feuer, and Pager, "Inside the Trump Administration's Push."
729. Devlin Barrett, Glenn Thrush, and Jonah E. Bromwich, "New York Attorney General Letitia James Is Indicted After Trump's Pressure Campaign," *New York Times*, October 9, 2025.
730. Alan Feuer and Devlin Barrett, "Judge Dismisses Cases Against Comey and James, Finding Trump Prosecutor Was Unlawfully Appointed," *New York Times*, November 24, 2025.
731. "Section 9-27.260 - Initiating and Declining Charges—Impermissible Considerations," *Justice Manual*, US Department of Justice, 2018, accessed December 3, 2025, https://www.justice.gov/jm/jm-9-27000-principles-federal-prosecution#9-27.260.
732. Bart Jansen and Karissa Waddick, "After Comey Indictment, Trump Says Other Opponents Are Next," *USA Today*, Sept. 29, 2025, https://www.usatoday.com/story/news/politics/2025/09/29/james-comey-indictment-reaction/86418110007/.
733. Charlie Savage, "Ex-C.I.A. Chief Asks to Keep Justice Dept. From Steering Case to Favored Judge," *New York Times*, December 22, 2025.
734. Savage, "Ex CIA Chief Asks to Keep Justice Dept. from Steering Case."
735. Sean James, "Chris Christie Accuses Trump of Using Justice Department Like a Mob Boss: 'Executes Hits' on Political Enemies," *Mediaite*, MSN, October 13, 2025, https://www.msn.com/en-us/news/politics/chris-christie-accuses-trump-of-using-justice-department-like-a-mob-boss-executes-hits-on-political-enemies/ar-AA1Oopt2.
736. James, "Chris Christie Accuses Trump."
737. Paul Schwartzman, Spencer Hsu, and Jeremy Barr, "TV-Ready, Loyal: Pirro, Trump's Pick for Top D.C. Prosecutor, Fits His Mold," *Washington Post*, May 9, 2025.
738. Samantha Waldenberg, "Trump Nominates Jeanine Pirro for Full Term as DC's Top Federal Prosecutor," CNN, June 17, 2025, https://edition.cnn.com/2025/06/17/politics/jeanine-pirro-us-attorney-nomination.
739. Sophia Barnes, "Pirro Says She'd Recommend Federal Officers Leave DC 'When They Make No Arrests,'" NBC Washington, August 22, 2025, https://www.nbcwashington.com/news/local/pirro-says-shed-recommend-federal-officers-leave-dc-when-they-make-no-arrests/3978676/.
740. Kevin Sheehan and Chris Nesi, "Teen Bloods Gang Member Nabbed by Feds, NJ Cops with Former Trump Attorney Alina Habba in Tow," *New York Post*, April 2, 2025, https://nypost.com/2025/04/02/us-news/teen-bloods-gang-member-nabbed-by-feds-nj-cops-with-alina-habba-in-tow/.

741. Matt Friedman, "The Risks of Habba," *Politico*, March 31, 2025, https://www.politico.com/newsletters/new-jersey-playbook/2025/03/31/the-risks-of-habba-00259965.
742. Tracey Tully, "Top US Prosecutor in New Jersey, a Trump Loyalist, Targets Governor," *New York Times*, April 11, 2025.
743. Zach Schonfeld and Rebecca Beitsch, "Habba Announces Criminal Charge Against Rep. McIver over ICE Facility Scuffle," *The Hill*, May 19, 2025, https://thehill.com/homenews/house/5308603-habba-announces-criminal-charge-against-rep-mciver-over-ice-facility-scuffle/.
744. Jonah E. Bromwich, Tracey Tully, and Devlin Barrett, "Alina Habba, a Trump Loyalist, Resigns as New Jersey's Top Prosecutor,"*New York Times*, December 8, 2025.
745. Bromwich, Tully, and Devlin, "Alina Habba, a Trump Loyalist, Resigns."
746. "Terminations," memorandum, Office of the Deputy Attorney General, January 31, 2025, https://www.warner.senate.gov/public/_cache/files/8/5/8590fa4b-e135-4ea5-b76f-0f13c097a489/57173F5183F4632CC51D21798D2BEB945EE70C717140FA62CABC283B83D628A9.memorandum-from-the-acting-deputy-attorney-general-01.31.25.pdf.
747. "Terminations."
748. Kyle Cheney and Josh Gerstein, "DOJ Fires Dozens of Prosecutors Who Handled Jan. 6 Cases," *Politico*, January 31, 2025, https://www.politico.com/news/2025/01/31/doj-purges-prosecutors-january-6-cases-00201904.
749. "Terminations."
750. "Merit System Principles (5 USC § 2301)," US Merit Systems Protection Board, accessed December 7, 2025, https://www.mspb.gov/msp/meritsystemsprinciples.htm.
751. Josh Gerstein, "Justice Department Official Defends Demand for FBI Agent Names, Cites 'Insubordination,'" *Politico*, February 5, 2025, https://www.politico.com/news/2025/02/05/justice-department-memo-fbi-insubordination-00202655.
752. Rebecca Beitsch, "Senate Confirms Bove to Appeals Court Despite Whistleblower Complaints, Controversy," *The Hill*, July 29, 2025, https://thehill.com/homenews/senate/5426437-senate-confirms-emil-bove-appeals-court/.
753. Alan Feuer and Glenn Thrush, "White House Exerts Enormous Influence Over FBI, Lawsuit Alleges," *New York Times*, September 10, 2025.
754. Feuer and Thrush. "White House Exerts Enormous Influence."
755. Feuer and Thrush, "White House Exerts Enormous Influence."
756. Feuer and Thrush, "White House Exerts Enormous Influence."
757. Feuer and Thrush, "White House Exerts Enormous Influence."
758. Cheney and Gerstein, "DOJ Fires Dozens of Prosecutors."
759. Cheney and Gerstein, "DOJ Fires Dozens of Prosecutors."
760. Katherine Faulders and Alexander Mallin, "Pam Bondi Fired At Least 20 Officials with Ties to Jack Smith Investigation: Sources," ABC News, July 12, 2025, https://www.msn.com/en-us/news/politics/pam-bondi-fired-at-least-20-officials-with-ties-to-jack-smith-investigation-sources/ar-AA1Iu651.
761. Faulders and Mallin, "Pam Bondi Fired At Least 20 Officials."
762. Perry Stein and Salvador Rizzo, "Trump's Justice Dept. Ousts National Security Officials in Latest Purge," *Washington Post*, March 8, 2025.
763. Devlin Barrett, "Justice Dept. Official Says She Was Fired After Opposing Restoring Mel Gibson's Gun Rights," *New York Times*, March 10, 2025.
764. Barrett, "Justice Dept. Official Says She Was Fired."
765. Perry Stein, "Firings Without Explanation Create Culture of Fear at Justice Dept., FBI," *Washington Post*, July 10, 2025.
766. Stein, "Firings Without Explanation Create Culture of Fear."
767. Stein, "Firings Without Explanation Create Culture of Fear."
768. Michael Feinberg, "Goodbye to All That," *Lawfare*, July 3, 2025, https://www.lawfaremedia.org/article/goodbye-to-all-that.
769. William K. Rashbaum, Jonah E. Bromwich, and Benjamin Weiser, "Fired Prosecutor Challenges Trump's Claims to Sweeping Power in Lawsuit," *New York Times*, September 15, 2025.

770. Andrew Goudsward, "Two-Thirds of the DOJ Unit Defending Trump Policies in Court Have Quit," Reuters, July 14, 2025, https://www.reuters.com/legal/litigation/two-thirds-doj-unit-defending-trump-policies-court-have-quit-2025-07-14/.
771. Goudsward, "Two-Thirds of the DOJ Unit."
772. Goudsward, "Two-Thirds of the DOJ Unit."
773. Goudsward, "Two-Thirds of the DOJ Unit."
774. Dana L. Gold, Andrea Meza, and Kevin L. Owen, counsel for Erez Reuveni, letter to to DOJ Officials, June 24, 2025, 7. Document published by *Washington Post*, June 24, 2025, https://www.washingtonpost.com/documents/ffd3273e-0656-42e8-8ed1-e2ad6c4c5bf3.pdf.
775. Gold, Meza, and Owen letter to DOJ officials.
776. Stone, "Pam Bondi Turning DOJ Into Trump's 'Personal Law Firm.'"
777. Jacey Fortin, Devlin Barrett, Ernesto Londoño, and Shaila Dewan, "Justice Dept. to End Oversight of Local Police Accused of Abuses," *New York Times*, May 21, 2025.
778. Fortin, Barrett, Londoño, and Dewan, "Justice Dept. to End Oversight."
779. Fortin, Barrett, Londoño, and Dewan, "Justice Dept. to End Oversight."
780. Chiraag Bains, "What Just Happened: The Trump Administration's Dismissal of Voting Rights Lawsuits," *Just Security*, May 27, 2025, https://www.justsecurity.org/113745/wjh-trump-dismissal-voting-rights-lawsuits/.
781. Devlin Barrett and Nick Corasaniti, "Justice Dept. Explores Using Criminal Charges Against Election Officials," *New York Times*, July 2, 2025.
782. Stone, "Pam Bondi Turning DOJ."
783. Stone, "Pam Bondi Turning DOJ"; "Investigation into Unlawful 'Straw Donor' and Foreign Contributions in American Elections," memorandum, White House, April 24, 2025, https://www.whitehouse.gov/presidential-actions/2025/04/investigation-into-unlawful-straw-donor-and-foreign-contributions-in-american-elections/; "Fact Sheet: President Donald J. Trump Addresses Risks Associated with Miles Taylor," White House, April 9, 2025, https://www.whitehouse.gov/fact-sheets/2025/04/fact-sheet-president-donald-j-trump-addresses-risks-associated-with-miles-taylor/.
784. Eileen Sullivan and Michael S. Schmidt, "Comey Tracked by Secret Service After Post Critical of Trump," *New York Times*, July 9, 2025.
785. Sullivan and Schmidt, "Comey Tracked by Secret Service."
786. Sullivan and Schmidt, "Comey Tracked by Secret Service."
787. Sullivan and Schmidt, "Comey Tracked by Secret Service."
788. Sullivan and Schmidt, "Comey Tracked by Secret Service."
789. "Pam Bondi's Hunt for Leakers Just Took a Chilling Turn," editorial, *Washington Post*, May 2, 2025.
790. American Bar Association v. US Department of Justice, No. 25-cv-1263 (CRC), slip op. (D.DC Apr. 25, 2025) (Cooper, J.).
791. ABA v. DOJ, No. 25-cv-1263 (CRC), slip op. (Cooper, J.).
792. ABA v. DOJ, No. 25-cv-1263 (CRC), slip op. (Cooper, J.).
793. ABA v. DOJ, No. 25-cv-1263 (CRC), slip op. (Cooper, J.).
794. ABA v. DOJ, No. 25-cv-1263 (CRC), slip op. (Cooper, J.).
795. Stone, "Pam Bondi Turning DOJ."

7. Enter the Broligarchs

796. Dr. Hanna was then known as Dr. Hanna-Attisha. "Pediatric Lead Exposure Presentation from Hurley Medical Center doctors concerning Flint MI," Flint Water Study Updates, September 2015, https://flintwaterstudy.org/2015/09/pediatric-lead-exposure-presentation-from-hurley-medical-center-doctors-concerning-flint-mi/.
797. Emily Kwong, Pien Huang, Rachel Carlson, and Rebecca Ramirez, "10 Years After Flint, the Fight to Replace Lead Pipes Across the US Continues," NPR, April 26, 2024, https://www.npr.org/2024/04/26/1198909905/flint-water-lead-poisoning-anniversary-chicago.
798. "Order No. 5: Elimination of the Office of Ombudsman," Emergency Manager, City of Flint, December 8, 2011, https://www.cityofflint.com/wp-content/uploads/CityPDF/005.pdf.

799. "Michigan Truth Squad: Who Approved Switch to Flint River? State's Answers Draw Fouls," *Bridge Magazine*, Center for Michigan, January 21, 2016, https://www.mlive.com/politics/2016/01/michigan_truth_squad_who_appro.html.
800. "'Missing Lead' in Flint Water Pipes Confirms Cause of Crisis," press release, University of Michigan, October 18, 2015, https://news.umich.edu/missing-lead-in-flint-water-pipes-confirms-cause-of-crisis/; Lindsey Smith, "State Admits Flint Did Not Follow Federal Rules Designed to Keep Lead Out of Water," *Michigan Public*, October 18, 2015, https://www.michiganpublic.org/news/2015-10-18/state-admits-flint-did-not-follow-federal-rules-designed-to-keep-lead-out-of-water.
801. Smith, "State Admits Flint Did Not Follow Federal Rules."
802. Kwong, Huang, Carlson, and Ramirez, "10 Years After Flint."
803. Kwong, Huang, Carlson, and Ramirez, "10 Years After Flint."
804. Anna Clark and Sarahbeth Maney, "Ten Years After the Flint Water Crisis, Distrust and Anger Linger," *ProPublica*, May 4, 2024, https://www.propublica.org/article/flint-michigan-water-crisis-ten-years-after.
805. Kelly House, "No Convictions for Flint: Attorney General Ends Water Crisis Prosecutions," *Bridge Michigan*, Center for Michigan, October 31, 2023, https://www.bridgemi.com/michigan-environment-watch/no-convictions-flint-attorney-general-ends-water-crisis-prosecutions.
806. Way Mullery, "Who Was Behind Trump During His Inaugural Address?" CNN, January 20, 2025, https://www.cnn.com/2025/01/20/us/seating-chart-trump-inaugural-address-dg/index.html.
807. Alex Isenstadt, "Trump Says in New Book Mark Zuckerberg Will 'Spend the Rest of His Life in Prison' If He Interferes in the 2024 Election," *Politico*, August 28, 2024, https://www.politico.com/news/2024/08/28/trump-zuckerberg-election-book-00176639.
808. Isenstadt, "Trump Says in New Book."
809. Joel Kaplan, "More Speech and Fewer Mistakes," Meta, January 7, 2025, https://about.fb.com/news/2025/01/meta-more-speech-fewer-mistakes/.
810. Huo Jingnan, Shannon Bond, and Bobby Allyn, "Meta Says It Will End Fact Checking as Silicon Valley Prepares for Trump," NPR, January 7, 2025, https://www.npr.org/2025/01/07/nx-s1-5251151/meta-fact-checking-mark-zuckerberg-trump.
811. *Report on Russian Active Measures Campaigns and Interference in the 2016 US Election, Volume 2: Russia's Use of Social Media*, US Senate Select Committee on Intelligence (US Government Publishing Office, 2019), 33–36.
812. Jingnan, Bond, and Allyn, "Meta Says It Will End Fact Checking."
813. Jingnan, Bond, and Allyn, "Meta Says It Will End Fact Checking."
814. Sara Dorn, "Elon Musk's Political Shift: How the Billionaire Moved from Backing Obama to Endorsing DeSantis," *Forbes*, November 27, 2022, https://www.forbes.com/sites/saradorn/2022/11/27/elon-musks-political-shift-how-the-billionaire-moved-from-backing-obama-to-endorsing-desantis/.
815. Dorn, "Elon Musk's Political Shift."
816. Kristen Grind and Megan Twohey, "In Public, Elon Musk Was Rising to Political Power as One of President Trump's Top Outside Advisers; in Private, He Was Taking Drugs and Facing Turmoil in His Family Life," *New York Times*, May 30, 2025.
817. Mike Stone and Joey Roulette, "Elon Musk's US Department of Defense Contracts," *Reuters*, February 11, 2025, https://www.reuters.com/world/us/elon-musks-us-department-defense-contracts-2025-02-11/.
818. Piper Hudspeth Blackburn, Tami Luhby, Aaron Pellish, and Matt Egan, "Elon Musk and Vivek Ramaswamy Will Lead New 'Department of Government Efficiency' in Second Trump Term," CNN, November 12, 2024, https://edition.cnn.com/2024/11/12/politics/elon-musk-vivek-ramaswamy-department-of-government-efficiency-trump/index.html.
819. Blackburn, Luhby, Pellish, and Egan, "Elon Musk and Vivek Ramaswamy Will Lead."
820. Ana Faguy and Brandon Drenon, "Vivek Ramaswamy Announces Run for Governor in Ohio," BBC News, February 25, 2025, https://www.bbc.com/news/articles/c86pwpy7vx6o.
821. Faiz Siddiqui, Hannah Natanson, Cat Zakrzewski, Alex Horton, and Elizabeth Dwoskin, "A Diminished DOGE Reels from the Departure of the 'Dogefather,' Elon Musk," *Washington Post*, June 8, 2025.

822. Ed Mazza, "'Failed Spectacularly': Critics Troll Elon Musk After 'Humiliating' Loss In Wisconsin," *HuffPost*, April 1, 2025, https://www.huffpost.com/entry/elon-musk-wisconsin-loss_n_67eca270e4b0923ef8b4847b; Hadas Gold, "'Truly a Moron': Elon Musk Escalates Spat with Trump Adviser Peter Navarro over Tariffs," CNN, April 8, 2025, https://www.cnn.com/2025/04/08/business/elon-musk-peter-navarro-comments-tariffs/index.html; Niall Stanage, "The Memo: Musk Drops Bomb on Trump's 'Big, Beautiful Bill,'" *The Hill*, June 3, 2025, https://thehill.com/homenews/5331561-elon-musk-trump-budget-bill-gop/.
823. Amy Sherman, "Is Donald Trump in the Jeffrey Epstein Files? What to Know After Social Media Fight with Elon Musk," *PolitiFact*, June 6, 2025, https://www.politifact.com/article/2025/jun/06/jeffrey-epstein-files-elon-musk-donald-trump/.
824. Donald J. Trump (@realDonaldTrump), "The easiest way to save money in our Budget, Billions and Billions of Dollars, is to terminate Elon's Governmental Subsidies and Contracts. I was always surprised that Biden didn't do it!" Truth Social, June 5, 2025, https://truthsocial.com/@realDonaldTrump/posts/114632206992330264.
825. Anna Cooban, "Elon Musk Says Some of His Social Media Posts About Trump 'Went Too Far'" CNN, June 11, 2025, https://www.cnn.com/2025/06/11/business/musk-regrets-some-posts-about-trump-intl.
826. Derek Thompson, "The Story of the Gilded Age Wasn't Wealth. It Was Corruption." *The Atlantic*, April 3, 2025.
827. "Why Did Mark Twain Call It the 'Gilded Age'"? Reference.com, accessed September 5, 2025, https://www.reference.com/history-geography/did-mark-twain-call-gilded-age-8cc9ae718f21128b-9.
828. Thompson, "The Story of the Gilded Age"; Richard White, *The Republic for Which It Stands: The United States During Reconstruction and the Gilded Age, 1865–1896*, Oxford History of the United States (Oxford University Press, 2017), 2.
829. Thompson, "The Story of the Gilded Age."
830. Jonathan Chang and Meghna Chakrabarti, "America's New Gilded Age," *On Point* (WBUR), March 14, 2025, https://www.wbur.org/onpoint/2025/03/14/america-gilded-age-trump-2024-president; Thompson, "The Story of the Gilded Age."
831. Thompson, "The Story of the Gilded Age."
832. Chang and Chakrabarti, "America's New Gilded Age."
833. Anne Branigin and Roxanne Roberts, "Trump Loves a Swanky Ballroom. So Did the Gilded Age Elite," *Washington Post*, August 13, 2025.
834. Branigin and Roberts, "Trump Loves a Swanky Ballroom."
835. Chang and Chakrabarti, "America's New Gilded Age."
836. Sam Peach, "Putin's Oligarchs: The Machinery of Wealth and Obedience," *Foreign Analysis*, July 14, 2025, https://foreignanalysis.com/putins-oligarchs/.
837. Peach, "Putin's Oligarchs."
838. Peach, "Putin's Oligarchs."
839. Peach, "Putin's Oligarchs."
840. Peach, "Putin's Oligarchs."
841. Peach, "Putin's Oligarchs."
842. Peach, "Putin's Oligarchs."
843. Peach, "Putin's Oligarchs."
844. Elaine Godfrey, "Sudden Russian Death Syndrome," *The Atlantic*, December 29, 2022.
845. Barbara Ortutay, "Trump Extends TikTok Ban Deadline for a Third Time, Without Clear Legal Basis," *Associated Press News*, June 19, 2025, https://apnews.com/article/tiktok-ban-trump-delay-executive-order-3211a98113615be44cf92b32dca69a8e.
846. Ortutay, "Trump Extends TikTok Ban Deadline."
847. Soo Rin Kim and Lalee Ibssa, "Trump's TikTok Ban Reversal Comes After Meeting Megadonor Who Has Stake in TikTok," ABC News, March 11, 2024, https://abcnews.go.com/Politics/trumps-tiktok-ban-reversal-after-meeting-megadonor-stake/story?id=108013785.
848. Hafiz Rashid, "TikTok CEO Tries Sucking Up to Trump After Supreme Court Upholds Ban," *New Republic*, January 17, 2025.

849. Tony Romm and Ana Swanson, "After US Takes Stake in Intel, Trump Pledges 'Many More' Deals," *New York Times*, August 25, 2025.
850. Ana Swanson and Lauren Hirsch, "'Golden Share' in US Steel Gives Trump Extraordinary Control," *New York Times*, June 15, 2025.
851. Swanson and Hirsch, "Golden Share in US Steel."
852. Bret Stephens, "Donald Trump's Assault on Capitalism," *New York Times*, August 26, 2025.
853. Robbie Whelan, Amrith Ramkumar, Lauren Thomas, and Josh Dawsey, "Inside Intel's Tricky Dance with Trump," *Wall Street Journal*, August 25, 2025, https://www.wsj.com/tech/inside-intels-tricky-dance-with-trump-c03f729c.
854. Whelan, Ramkumar, Thomas, and Dawsey, "Inside Intel's Tricky Dance."
855. Julia Manchester, "Trump Calls Off Plans to Deploy Federal Troops to San Francisco," *The Hill*, October 23, 2025, https://thehill.com/homenews/administration/5570089-trump-troops-san-francisco/.
856. David Nakamura, "Trump Says He Has Called Off Federal 'Surge' in San Francisco Amid Pushback," *Washington Post*, October 23, 2025.
857. Whelan, Ramkumar, Thomas, and Dawsey, "Inside Intel's Tricky Dance."
858. Stephens, "Donald Trump's Assault on Capitalism."
859. Ian Ward, "The Seven Thinkers and Groups That Have Shaped JD Vance's Unusual Worldview," *Politico*, July 18, 2024, https://www.politico.com/news/magazine/2024/07/18/jd-vance-world-view-sources-00168984.
860. Ava Kofman, "Curtis Yarvin's Plot Against America," *New Yorker*, June 9, 2025; Ward, "Seven Thinkers That Have Shaped."
861. Kofman, "Curtis Yarvin's Plot Against America."
862. Anne Applebaum, "The Most Nihilistic Conflict on Earth," *The Atlantic*, August 6, 2025.
863. Hadas Gold, "Elon Musk Wants to Privatize the Postal Service and Amtrak," CNN, March 5, 2025, https://edition.cnn.com/2025/03/05/business/musk-usps-amtrak-privatization/index.html.
864. "Trump Executive Order Ended the Prohibition on Private Federal Prisons," Southern Poverty Law Center, accessed September 7, 2025, https://www.splcenter.org/resources/guides/trump-executive-order-private-federal-prisons/.
865. Lauren-Brooke Eisen, "What Trump's Victory Means for the Private Prison Industry," Brennan Center for Justice, November 25, 2024, https://www.brennancenter.org/our-work/analysis-opinion/what-trumps-victory-means-private-prison-industry.
866. "DOJ OIG Releases Report on the Federal Bureau of Prisons' Monitoring of Contract Prisons," press release, Department of Justice Office of the Inspector General, August 11, 2016, https://oig.justice.gov/news/doj-oig-releases-report-federal-bureau-prisons-monitoring-contract-prisons.
867. Megan Mumford, Diane Whitmore Schanzenbach, and Ryan Nunn, "The Economics of Private Prisons," The Hamilton Project, Brookings Institution, October 20, 2016, https://www.hamiltonproject.org/publication/paper/the-economics-of-private-prisons/.
868. "FBI Takes Over Investigation of Idaho Prison Nicknamed 'Gladiator School,'" *New York Daily News*, March 7, 2014, https://www.nydailynews.com/2014/03/07/fbi-takes-over-investigation-of-idaho-prison-nicknamed-gladiator-school/.
869. "FBI Takes Over Investigation."
870. Susan Haigh, "The US Postal Service Has Been Struggling for Years. Now Trump's Talking About Privatizing It," *Associated Press News*, March 25, 2025, https://apnews.com/article/us-postal-service-privatization-trump-musk-dejoy-692d56e701f3853af4ce914832a33124.
871. Haigh, "The US Postal Service Has Been Struggling."
872. Haigh, "The US Postal Service Has Been Struggling."
873. Haigh, "The US Postal Service Has Been Struggling."
874. Brian Slodysko and Michael Biesecker, "Trump Appointees Have Ties to Companies That Stand to Benefit from Privatizing Weather Forecasts," *Associated Press News*, July 9, 2025, https://apnews.com/article/trump-lutnick-weather-service-privatization-conflicts-9892de853c283468e6fb970cfd898d96.

875. Paul Dans and Steve Groves, eds., *Mandate for Leadership: The Conservative Promise* (Heritage Foundation, 2023), 675, https://static.heritage.org/project2025/2025_MandateForLeadership_FULL.pdf.
876. Slodysko and Biesecker, "Trump Appointees Have Ties to Companies."
877. Slodysko and Biesecker, "Trump Appointees Have Ties to Companies."
878. Heather Somerville, Vera Bergengruen, and Joel Schectman, "How Palantir Won Over Washington—and Pushed Its Stock Up 600%, *Wall Street Journal*, August 5, 2025, https://www.wsj.com/tech/palantir-pltr-stock-success-government-contracts-f3b2d453.
879. Somerville, Bergengruen, and Schectman, "How Palantir Won Over Washington."
880. Somerville, Bergengruen, and Schectman, "How Palantir Won Over Washington."
881. Somerville, Bergengruen, and Schectman, "How Palantir Won Over Washington."
882. Somerville, Bergengruen, and Schectman, "How Palantir Won Over Washington."
883. Somerville, Bergengruen, and Schectman, "How Palantir Won Over Washington."
884. Slodysko and Biesecker, "Trump Appointees Have Ties to Companies."
885. Slodysko and Biesecker, "Trump Appointees Have Ties to Companies."
886. Slodysko and Biesecker, "Trump Appointees Have Ties to Companies."
887. Slodysko and Biesecker, "Trump Appointees Have Ties to Companies."
888. Slodysko and Biesecker, "Trump Appointees Have Ties to Companies."
889. Slodysko and Biesecker, "Trump Appointees Have Ties to Companies."
890. Ben Rhodes, *After the Fall: Being American in the World We've Made* (Random House, 2021), 8.
891. Luke Mayville, *John Adams and the Fear of American Oligarchy* (Princeton University Press, 2016), 153.
892. Shawn McCreesh, "Trump, on Tariffs, Says 'Maybe Children Will Have 2 Dolls Instead of 30,'" *New York Times*, April 30, 2025.
893. Fritz Farrow and Ivan Pereira, "Trump Hosted 'Great Gatsby' Halloween Party Hours Before SNAP Funding Lapsed," ABC News, November 1, 2025, https://abcnews.go.com/Politics/trump-hosted-great-gatsby-halloween-party-hours-snap/story?id=127091016.
894. Mayville, *John Adams and the Fear of American Oligarchy*, 152–53.
895. Kurt Andersen, *Evil Geniuses: The Unmaking of America* (Random House, 2020), 292.
896. Andersen, *Evil Geniuses*, 293.
897. Andersen, *Evil Geniuses*, 293.
898. Andersen, *Evil Geniuses*, 287; Jules Witcover, "The Dynasty That Almost Wasn't," *Politico*, September 15, 2015, https://www.politico.com/magazine/story/2015/09/the-dynasty-that-almost-wasnt-213150/.
899. Andersen, *Evil Geniuses*, 293.
900. Quoctrung Bui, "The Fall and Rise of US Inequality, in 2 Graphs," NPR, February 11, 2015, https://www.npr.org/sections/money/2015/02/11/384988128/the-fall-and-rise-of-u-s-inequality-in-2-graphs.
901. Lisa Kashinsky, Andrew Howard, and Elena Schneider, "Republicans Just Cut Medicaid. Will It Cost Them Control of Congress?" *Politico*, July 6, 2025, https://www.politico.com/news/2025/07/06/republican-medicaid-cuts-midterms-big-beautiful-bill-00440023.
902. Elena Moore, Claudia Grisales, and Deirdre Walsh, "Trump on Fourth of July Signs 'One Big Beautiful Bill' to Implement His Agenda," NPR, July 4, 2025, https://www.npr.org/2025/07/03/nx-s1-5454841/house-republicans-trump-tax-bill-medicaid; Phil Galewitz, Julie Appleby, Renuka Rayasam, and Bernard J. Wolfson, "5 Ways Trump's Megabill Will Limit Health Care Access," NPR, July 3, 2025, https://www.npr.org/sections/shots-health-news/2025/07/02/nx-s1-5453870/senate-republicans-tax-bill-medicaid-health-care.
903. Kelly McCarthy and Melanie Schmitz, "How Trump's Tax Cut and Spending Megabill Would Impact SNAP Recipients," ABC News, July 2, 2025, https://abcnews.go.com/GMA/News/trump-big-beautiful-bill-cuts-SNAP-affordable-food-benefits/story?id=123415329.
904. Saranac Hale Spencer, D'Angelo Gore, Robert Farley, Kate Yandell, Alan Jaffe, and Jessica McDonald, "Unraveling the 'Big, Beautiful Bill' Spin," FactCheck.org, July 2, 2025, updated July 3, 2025, https://www.factcheck.org/2025/07/unraveling-the-big-beautiful-bill-spin/.
905. Moore, Grisales, and Walsh, "Trump on Fourth of July Signs 'One Big Beautiful Bill.'"

906. Paul Waldman, "The GOP Megabill Fulfills JD Vance's Incredibly Depressing Vision of Patriotism," MSNBC, July 5, 2025, https://www.msnbc.com/opinion/msnbc-opinion/big-beautiful-bill-vance-immigration-ice-rcna216161.

8. Scapegoats and Pawns

907. "Castro Enterprise Leader Convicted for RICO Conspiracy and Other Violent Crimes," press release, Office of Public Affairs, US Department of Justice, June 4, 2019.
908. United States v. Chaka Castro, indictment (E.D. Mich., filed Apr. 1, 2015).
909. United States v. Castro, indictment.
910. United States v. Castro, No. 19-2300 (6th Cir. Aug. 11, 2020).
911. Russell Muirhead and Nancy L. Rosenblum, *A Lot of People Are Saying: The New Conspiracism and the Assault on Democracy* (Princeton University Press, 2019), 90.
912. Ruth Ben-Ghiat, *Strongmen: Mussolini to the Present* (W. W. Norton & Company, 2020), 74.
913. Max Fisher, "Trump Tests a Role He's Long Admired: A Strongman Imposing Order," *New York Times*, June 4, 2020.
914. Ben-Ghiat, *Strongmen*, 68.
915. Zolan Kanno-Youngs, Hamed Aleaziz, and Eileen Sullivan, "Trump Starts Immigration Crackdown, Enlisting the Military and Testing the Law," *New York Times*, January 20, 2025.
916. Kanno-Youngs, Aleaziz, and Sullivan, "Trump Starts Immigration Crackdown."
917. Aaron Pelish, "Venezuelan Little League Team Denied Entry into US Amid Trump Travel Ban," *Politico*, July 25, 2025, https://www.politico.com/news/2025/07/25/trump-travel-ban-little-league-00477894.
918. Ruth Ben-Ghiat, "What Trump and Hegseth Really Fear," *Lucid* (blog), *Substack*, June 8, 2025, https://lucid.substack.com/p/what-trump-and-hegseth-really-fear.
919. Ben-Ghiat, "What Trump and Hegseth Really Fear."
920. Ben-Ghiat, "What Trump and Hegseth Really Fear."
921. Meredith Deliso, "Laken Riley Case: Suspect Found Guilty by Judge in Campus Killing, Sentenced to Life," ABC News, November 20, 2024, https://abcnews.go.com/US/laken-riley-suspect-guilty-murder/story?id=116030068.
922. Stacey Dec, "Trump Signs Laken Riley Act, Setting Up Next Phase of Immigration Crackdown," ABC News, January 29, 2025, https://abcnews.go.com/Politics/trump-sign-laken-riley-act-setting-phase-immigration/story?id=118226963.
923. Joel Rose, "Trump Supporters Welcome the First Steps in His Immigration Crackdown," NPR, Feb. 8, 2025, https://www.npr.org/2025/02/08/nx-s1-5279370/trump-supporters-welcome-immigration-crackdown.
924. Amber Phillips, "'They're Rapists.' President Trump's Campaign Launch Speech Two Years Later, Annotated," *Washington Post*, June 16, 2017.
925. Emily Peck, "Trump Says Immigrants Are Taking 'Black Jobs,' But There's No Such Thing," *Axios*, July 31, 2024, https://www.axios.com/2024/07/31/trump-nabj-interview-black-jobs-rhetoric.
926. Ximena Bustillo, Sergio Martínez-Beltrán, "Trump Administration Strips Schools, Churches of Immigration Enforcement Protections," NPR, January 21, 2025, https://www.npr.org/2025/01/21/nx-s1-5269899/trump-immigration-enforcement-schools-churches.
927. Malcolm Ferguson, "Stephen Miller Yells at ICE Agents About New Order to Ramp Up Arrests," *New Republic*, May 28, 2025.
928. Ferguson, "Stephen Miller Yells at ICE Agents."
929. Josh Fiallo, "Stephen Miller Explicitly Ordered ICE Raid Home Depots," *Daily Beast*, June 11, 2025, https://www.thedailybeast.com/stephen-miller-explicitly-ordered-ice-raid-home-depots/.
930. Fiallo, "Stephen Miller Explicitly Ordered."
931. Bustillo, Martínez-Beltrán, "Trump Administration Strips Schools."
932. Eduardo Cuevas and Josh Meyer, "Trump Administration Floats Suspending Habeas Corpus: What's That?" *USA Today*, May 10, 2025, https://www.usatoday.com/story/news/politics/2025/05/10/trump-stephen-miller-habeas-corpus-constitution/83554334007/.

933. "Invocation of Alien Enemies Act Regarding the Invasion of the United States by Tren de Aragua," executive order, White House, March 15, 2025, https://www.whitehouse.gov/presidential-actions/2025/03/invocation-of-the-alien-enemies-act-regarding-the-invasion-of-the-united-states-by-tren-de-aragua/.
934. US Const. amend. XIV.
935. "Protecting the Meaning and Value of American Citizenship," executive order, White House, January 20, 2025, https://www.whitehouse.gov/presidential-actions/2025/01/protecting-the-meaning-and-value-of-american-citizenship/.
936. United States v. Wong Kim Ark, 169 US 649 (1898).
937. Steve Vladeck, "Bonus 112: Birthright Citizenship, 'Invasions,' and the Supreme Court," *One First*, December 21, 2024, https://www.stevevladeck.com/p/bonus-112-birthright-citizenship.
938. "Invocation of the Alien Enemies Act."
939. 50 USC § 21.
940. Katherine Yon, "The Alien Enemies Act, Explained," Brennan Center for Justice, June 17, 2020, https://www.brennancenter.org/our-work/research-reports/alien-enemies-act-explained.
941. Michael Kranish, "Jefferson's Retreat and Return to Power," *Washington Post*, November 2, 2025.
942. Yon, "The Alien Enemies Act, Explained."
943. Ryan J. Reilly, "Trump-Appointed Federal Judge Rejects Use of Alien Enemies Act to Deport Migrants," NBC News, May 1, 2025, https://www.nbcnews.com/politics/immigration/trump-appointed-federal-district-judge-rejects-use-alien-enemies-act-v-rcna204150; J.A.V. v. Trump, 2025 WL 1843651 (S.D. Tex. May 1, 2025).
944. Kyle Cheney and Josh Gerstein, "Appeals Court Rejects Trump's Bid to Deport Venezuelan Immigrants He Deems 'Alien Enemies,'" *Politico*, September 3, 2025, https://www.politico.com/news/2025/09/03/fifth-circuit-ruling-trump-alien-enemies-00541115.
945. Josh Gerstein, "The Judge Who Tried to Stop the Deportation Planes Is Not Happy with the Trump Administration" *Politico*, March 17, 2025, https://www.politico.com/news/2025/03/17/judge-boasberg-trump-deportation-hearing-00234945.
946. Gerstein, "The Judge Who Tried to Stop."
947. Gerstein, "The Judge Who Tried to Stop."
948. Mark Sherman, "Justice Department Files Misconduct Complaint Against Federal Judge Handling Deportation Case," *Associated Press News*, July 28, 2025, https://apnews.com/article/boasberg-salvador-venezuela-trump-misconduct-complaint-b5f5e982263b95f32e4229aefe312f12.
949. Gisela Salim-Peyer, "No One Was Supposed to Leave Alive," *The Atlantic*, July 23, 2025.
950. Nayib Bukele (@nayibbukele), "Today, the first 238 members of the Venezuelan criminal organization, Tren de Aragua, arrived in our country. . . . They were immediately transferred to CECOT," March 16, 2025, https://x.com/nayibbukele/status/1901245427216978290.
951. Bukele (@nayibbukele), "The United States will pay a very low fee for them, but a high one for us," X, March 16, 2025, https://x.com/nayibbukele/status/1901245427216978290.
952. Louis Casiano, "US Paid El Salvador to Take Venezuelan Tren de Aragua Members: 'Pennies on the Dollar,' White House Says," Fox News, March 17, 2025, https://www.foxnews.com/politics/us-paid-el-salvador-take-venezuelan-tren-de-aragua-members-pennies-dollar-white-house-says.
953. "Lynching Postcards, 1908," Truth in Photography, accessed October 23, 2025, https://www.truthinphotography.org/lynching-postcards.html.
954. Alex Galbraith, "'Too Late': White House Mocks Judge After Trump Admin Ignores Order Against Deportations," *Yahoo News*, March 16, 2025, https://www.yahoo.com/news/too-white-house-mocks-judge-203816948.html.
955. Joseph Bernstein, "At a Prison Appearance, a $50,000 Watch Stands Out," *New York Times*, March 28, 2025.
956. Lee Moran, "Kristi Noem's 'Utterly Reprehensible' Migrant Prisoners Video Sparks Fury," *HuffPost*, March 26, 2025, https://www.huffpost.com/entry/kristi-noem-el-salvador-prison-video_n_67e4e9ece4b0501fc770e4af; Kristi Noem (@Sec_Noem), "I toured the CECOT, El Salvador's Terrorism Confinement Center. President Trump and I have a clear message

to criminal illegal aliens: LEAVE NOW. If you do not leave, we will hunt you down, arrest you, and you could end up in this El Salvadorian prison," X, March 26, 2025, https://x.com/Sec_Noem/status/1905034256826408982.

957. Scott Neuman, "DHS Secretary Misstates Meaning of Habeas Corpus Under Senate Scrutiny," NPR, May 20, 2025, https://www.npr.org/2025/05/20/nx-s1-5405144/habeas-corpus-noem-dhs-senate.
958. Richard Fausset, "Jokey Names for Detention Centers Face Criticism for Insensitivity," *New York Times,* August 26, 2025.
959. Fausset, "Jokey Names for Detention Centers."
960. Fausset, "Jokey Names for Detention Centers."
961. Fausset, "Jokey Names for Detention Centers."
962. Ozturk v. Trump, No. 2:25-cv-00374, 2025 WL 1420540, 15 (D. Vt, May 16, 2025).
963. Phil McCausland, "Who Is Mahmoud Khalil, Palestinian Student Activist Facing US Deportation?" BBC News, June 20, 2025, https://www.bbc.com/news/articles/cgj5nlxz44yo.
964. Rob Picheta and Simone McCarthy, "What Did Israel Know About Hamas' October 7 Attack?," CNN, December 1, 2023, https://www.cnn.com/2023/12/01/middleeast/israel-hamas-gaza-intelligence-intl; Elena Shao and Lazaro Gamio, "Here Are the Statuses of the Hostages Taken into Gaza on Oct. 7," *New York Times,* November 28, 2023.
965. Debora Patta, "Gaza War Has Killed an Estimated 20,000 Kids. CBS News Meets Many More Orphaned, and 'Always Scared,'" CBS News, October 8, 2025, https://www.cbsnews.com/news/gaza-israel-hamas-war-children-deaths-orphans-trauma/.
966. Sam Cabral, "Jewish Students Sue Harvard Over 'Rampant' Anti-Semitism," BBC News, January 11, 2024, https://www.bbc.com/news/world-us-canada-67951434; Bianca Quilantan, "Education Department Dings 2 Schools for Not Protecting Jewish, Muslim Students," *Politico,* June 17, 2024, https://www.politico.com/news/2024/06/17/education-department-antisemitism-university-michigan-cuny-00163665.
967. Jake Offenhartz, "Immigration Agents Arrest Palestinian Activist Who Helped Lead Columbia University Protests," *Associated Press News,* March 9, 2025, https://apnews.com/article/columbia-university-mahmoud-khalil-ice-15014bcbb921f21a9f704d5acdcae7a8.
968. Offenhartz, "Immigration Agents Arrest Palestinian Activist."
969. Offenhartz, "Immigration Agents Arrest Palestinian Activist."
970. Jennifer Peltz, "Trump Administration Cancels $400M in Grants and Contracts with Columbia University," *Associated Press News,* March 7, 2025, https://apnews.com/article/columbia-university-protests-antisemitism-palestine-israel-9c209ce040e4b60d2702b40b9c2fb321.
971. White House (@whitehouse), "SHALOM, MAHMOUD: 'ICE proudly apprehended and detained Mahmoud Khalil, a Radical Foreign Pro-Hamas Student on the campus of @ Columbia University. This is the first arrest of many to come.'–President Donald J. Trump," Instagram, March 10, 2025, https://www.instagram.com/p/DHBzzU9RFLW/.
972. White House, "SHALOM, MAHMOUD: 'ICE proudly apprehended and detained Mahmoud Khalil."
973. McCausland, "Who Is Mahmoud Khalil?"
974. Jonah E. Bromwich, "Mahmoud Khalil's Wife Gives Birth as ICE Bars Him from Being There," *New York Times,* April 21, 2025.
975. Edward Wong, Charlie Savage, Hamed Aleaziz, and Luis Ferré-Sadurní, "Trump Administration Seeks to Expel a Green-Card Holder Over Student Protests," *New York Times,* March 10, 2025.
976. 8 USC § 1227(a)(4)(C)(i) (2025).
977. "ICE Arrests Palestinian Activist Who Helped Lead Columbia University Protests," NPR, March 10, 2025, https://www.npr.org/2025/03/10/g-s1-52923/immigration-agents-arrest-palestinian-activist-columbia-protests.
978. Tim Stelloh and Daniella Silva, "White House Says Pro-Hamas Propaganda Was Handed Out at Rallies Organized by Detained Palestinian Activist," NBC News, March 11, 2025, https://www.nbcnews.com/news/us-news/white-house-says-hamas-propaganda-rallies-palestinian-activist-rcna195947.
979. McCausland, "Who Is Mahmoud Khalil?"
980. Khalil v. Trump, No. 2:25-cv-01963, 2025 WL 1514713, 80–81 (D.N.J. May 28, 2025).

981. Khalil v. Trump, 37.
982. Khalil v. Trump, No. 2:25-cv-01963, 4, 11 (D.N.J. June 11, 2025).
983. Luc Cohen, "Palestinian Student Released on Bail As He Challenges Deportation from US," *Reuters*, May 1, 2025, https://www.reuters.com/world/us/us-immigration-release-detained-palestinian-student-following-judges-order-cbs-2025-04-30/.
984. Cohen, "Palestinian Student Released on Bail."
985. Jake Offenhartz, Kathy McCormack, and Michael Casey, "Turkish Student at Tufts University Detained, Video Shows Masked People Handcuffing Her," *Associated Press News*, March 26, 2025, https://apnews.com/article/tufts-student-detained-massachusetts-immigration-6c3978da98a8d0f39ab311e092ffd892.
986. Offenhartz, McCormack, and Casey, "Turkish Student at Tufts University Detained."
987. Ozturk v. Trump, No. 2:25-cv-00374, 2025 WL 1420540 (D. Vt. May 16, 2025).
988. Ozturk v. Trump, 19.
989. Offenhartz, McCormack, and Casey, "Turkish Student at Tufts University Detained."
990. Michael Kransz, "ICE Officers Could Face Jail Time Under Michigan Bill to Ban Masked Police," *MLive*, July 25, 2025, https://www.mlive.com/politics/2025/07/ice-officers-could-face-jail-time-under-michigan-bill-to-ban-masked-police.html.
991. Deepti Hajela, "In American Life, a Growing and Forbidding Visual Rises: The Law-Enforcement Officer in a Mask," *Associated Press News*, July 18, 2025, https://apnews.com/article/ice-masks-immigration-enforcement-policing-aacbb45b9eca804c2295f52a33a2a0fd.
992. Hajela, "In American Life, a Growing and Forbidding Visual."
993. Hajela, "In American Life, a Growing and Forbidding Visual."
994. Hajela, "In American Life, a Growing and Forbidding Visual."
995. Ozturk v. Trump, 19.
996. Ozturk v. Hyde, First Amended Petition for Writ of Habeas Corpus and Complaint, No. 1:25-cv-10695 (D. Mass. March 28, 2025).
997. Lexi Lonas Cochran, "Student Protesters Face Potential Trump Crackdown," *The Hill*, November 17, 2024, https://thehill.com/homenews/education/4993239-student-protesters-palestinians-israel-gaza-trump-crackdown/.
998. Kyle Cheney and Josh Gerstein, "Judge Excoriates Trump in Blistering Decision Calling Efforts to Deport Pro-Palestinian Academics Illegal," *Politico*, September 30, 2025, https://www.politico.com/news/2025/09/30/judge-young-ruling-trump-deportation-free-speech-00588114.
999. Kinsey Crowley, "Recent Blitz of Anti-Trans Ads Attacks Harris. Advocates Question Their Effectiveness, Call Them Harmful," *USA Today*, October 26, 2024, https://www.usatoday.com/story/news/politics/elections/2024/10/26/trans-ads-trump-harris/75791374007/.
1000. Crowley, "Recent Blitz of Anti-Trans Ads Attacks Harris."
1001. Jordan Liles, "Trump Falsely Claimed Kids Go to School and Come Back with 'Sex-Change Operations,'" *Snopes*, September 13, 2024, https://www.snopes.com/fact-check/trump-children-surgeries-school/.
1002. Kat Tenbarge, "LBGTQ People Face "Groomer' Accusations and Trolling as Culture War Rages On," NBC News, April 19, 2022, https://www.nbcnews.com/tech/internet/lgbtq-abuse-spikes-online-fueled-intensifying-culture-war-rcna24904.
1003. "Defending Women from Gender Ideology Extremism and Restoring Biological Truth to the Federal Government," executive order, White House, January 20, 2025, https://www.whitehouse.gov/presidential-actions/2025/01/defending-women-from-gender-ideology-extremism-and-restoring-biological-truth-to-the-federal-government/.
1004. Evan Perez and Hanna Rabinowitz, "Trump DOJ Is Looking At Ways to Ban Transgender Americans from Owning Guns, Sources Say," CNN, September 4, 2025, https://www.cnn.com/2025/09/04/politics/transgender-firearms-justice-department-second-amendment.
1005. "Prioritizing Military Excellence and Readiness," executive order, White House, January 27, 2025, https://www.whitehouse.gov/presidential-actions/2025/01/prioritizing-military-excellence-and-readiness/.
1006. "Prioritizing Military Excellence and Readiness."
1007. Scott Neuman, "Pentagon Plans to Begin Removing Trans Service Members from the Military Next Month," NPR, March 1, 2025, https://www.npr.org/2025/02/27/g-s1-51057/transgender-soldiers-military-ban-trump.

1008. "GLAAD, Transgender Service Advocates Respond to Discriminatory Executive Order Regarding Transgender People in the Military," press release, GLAAD, January 28, 2025, https://glaad.org/releases/glaad-transgender-service-advocates-respond-to-discriminatory-executive-order-regarding-transgender-people-in-the-military/.
1009. Konstantin Toropin, "'Open Cruelty': Transgender Troops Describe Indignities as They're Kicked Out of the Military," Military.com, July 29, 2025, https://www.military.com/daily-news/investigations-and-features/2025/07/29/open-cruelty-transgender-troops-describe-indignities-theyre-kicked-out-of-military.html.
1010. Toropin, "'Open Cruelty': Transgender Troops Describe Indignities."
1011. Toropin, "'Open Cruelty': Transgender Troops Describe Indignities."
1012. Toropin, "'Open Cruelty': Transgender Troops Describe Indignities."
1013. Natasha Bertrand, "Hegseth Orders Renaming of Ship Named After Gay Rights Icon Harvey Milk," CNN, June 3, 2025, https://www.cnn.com/2025/06/03/politics/hegseth-orders-renaming-ship-named-harvey-milk.
1014. Bertrand, "Hegseth Orders Renaming of Ship."
1015. Bertrand, "Hegseth Orders Renaming of Ship."
1016. Bertrand, "Hegseth Orders Renaming of Ship."
1017. Bertrand, "Hegseth Orders Renaming of Ship."
1018. "Hegseth Reveals New Name for USNS Harvey Milk," *Navy CRF*, June 27, 2025, https://www.navycrf.com/2025/06/27/hegseth-reveals-new-name-for-usns-harvey-milk/.
1019. Jill Lawrence, "The Transgender 'Issue' Is Not a Distraction for Democrats," *The Bulwark*, June 30, 2025, https://www.thebulwark.com/p/transgender-issue-is-not-a-distraction-for-democrats-facts-golden-rule.
1020. "Intersex," Cleveland Clinic, last reviewed July 19, 2022, https://my.clevelandclinic.org/health/articles/16324-intersex.
1021. "Donald Trump OK with Caitlyn Jenner Using Any Bathroom in His Tower," ABC News, April 21, 2016, https://abcnews.go.com/Politics/donald-trump-caitlyn-jenner-bathroom-tower/story?id=38566263.
1022. "Defending Women from Gender Ideology Extremism."
1023. "'They're Chasing Us Away from Sport': Human Rights Violations in Sex Testing of Elite Women Athletes," Human Rights Watch, https://www.hrw.org/report/2020/12/04/theyre-chasing-us-away-sport/human-rights-violations-sex-testing-elite-women.
1024. Lawrence, "The Transgender 'Issue' Is Not a Distraction."
1025. Isabel Lohman and Ron French, "Michigan Transgender Youths to Continue High School Sports, Despite Trump Order," *Bridge Michigan*, February 6, 2025, https://bridgemi.com/talent-education/michigan-transgender-youths-continue-high-school-sports-despite-trump-order/.
1026. Jill Lawrence, "The Transgender 'Issue' Is Not a Distraction."
1027. Tyler Pager, "'I Hate My Opponent': Trump's Remarks at Kirk Memorial Distill His Politics," *New York Times*, September 16, 2025.
1028. Pager, "'I Hate My Opponent.'"
1029. Zolan Kanno-Youngs, Andrew Duehren, Kenneth P. Vogel, and Katie Rogers, "Trump Invokes Kirk's Killing in Justifying Measures to Silence Opponents," *New York Times*, September 16, 2025.
1030. Kanno-Youngs, Duehren, Vogel, and Rogers, "Trump Invokes Kirk's Killing."
1031. Elena Moore and Luke Garrett, "Trump Calls Charlie Kirk 'Martyr Now for American Freedom' at Memorial Service," NPR, September 21, 2025, https://www.npr.org/2025/09/21/nx-s1-5545613/charlie-kirk-funeral.
1032. Amy Sherman, "In Blaming Left for Political Violence, JD Vance Ignores Long-Term Trends," *PolitiFact*, October 20, 2025, https://www.politifact.com/factchecks/2025/oct/20/jd-vance/Trump-Charlie-Kirk-political-violence-left-right/.
1033. Sherman, "In Blaming Left for Political Violence."
1034. Moore and Garrett, "Trump Calls Charlie Kirk 'Martyr.'"
1035. Jonathan Chait, "Stephen Miller Is Going for Broke," *The Atlantic*, October 6, 2025.

1036. "Designating Antifa as a Domestic Terrorist Organization," executive order, White House, September 22, 2025, https://www.whitehouse.gov/presidential-actions/2025/09/designating-antifa-as-a-domestic-terrorist-organization/.
1037. Lisa N. Sacco, "Are Antifa Members Domestic Terrorists? Background on Antifa and Federal Classification of Their Actions," Congressional Research Service, June 9, 2020, https://www.congress.gov/crs-product/IF10839.
1038. Sacco, "Are Antifa Members Domestic Terrorists?"
1039. "Terrorist Designation of the Terrorgram Collective and Three Leaders," fact sheet, Office of the Spokesperson, US Department of State, January 13, 2025, https://2021-2025.state.gov/office-of-the-spokesperson/releases/2025/01/terrorist-designations-of-the-terrorgram-collective-and-three-leaders/.
1040. Eric Tucker and Ben Fox, "FBI Director Says Antifa Is an Ideology, Not an Organization," *Associated Press News*, September 17, 2020, https://apnews.com/article/donald-trump-ap-top-news-elections-james-comey-politics-bdd3b6078e9efadcfcd0be4b65f2362e.
1041. "Designating Antifa as a Domestic Terrorist Organization."
1042. "Countering Domestic Terrorism and Organized Political Violence," presidential memorandum, White House, September 25, 2025, https://www.whitehouse.gov/presidential-actions/2025/09/countering-domestic-terrorism-and-organized-political-violence/.
1043. "Countering Domestic Terrorism and Organized Political Violence."
1044. "Countering Domestic Terrorism and Organized Political Violence."
1045. Devlin Barrett, "Justice Dept. Official Pushes Prosecutors to Investigate Soros's Foundation," *New York Times*, September 25, 2025.
1046. "'We're Not Afraid': George Soros's Foundation on Being Trump's Next Target," transcript, Binaifer Nowrojee interview by Steve Inskeep, NPR News, September 29, 2025, https://www.npr.org/2025/09/29/nx-s1-5554232/george-soros-foundations-investigation-doj-trump.
1047. Fred Shapiro, "Quotes Uncovered: Who Said No Crisis Should Go to Waste?," *Freakonomics*, August 13, 2009, https://freakonomics.com/2009/08/quotes-uncovered-who-said-no-crisis-should-go-to-waste/.
1048. United States v. Castro, No. 19-2300 (6th Cir. 2020).
1049. Asher Stockler, "Texas Woman Sentenced for Role in Nationwide Home Invasion Racket Targeting Indians, Asians," *Newsweek*, October 29, 2019, https://www.newsweek.com/chaka-castro-home-invasion-rico-1468502.
1050. West Virginia State Board of Education v. Barnette, 319 US 624 (1943).

9. Separation of Parties

1051. Sonari Glinton, "How a Little Lab in West Virginia Caught Volkswagen's Big Cheat," NPR, September 24, 2015, https://www.npr.org/2015/09/24/443053672/how-a-little-lab-in-west-virginia-caught-volkswagens-big-cheat.
1052. "Volkswagen AG Agrees to Plead Guilty and Pay $4.3 Billion in Criminal and Civil Penalties; Six Volkswagen Executives and Employees are Indicted in Connection with Conspiracy to Cheat US Emissions Tests," press release, US Attorney's Office, Eastern District of Michigan, January 11, 2017, https://www.justice.gov/usao-edmi/pr/volkswagen-ag-agrees-plead-guilty-and-pay-43-billion-criminal-and-civil-penalties-and.
1053. "Volkswagen AG Agrees to Plead Guilty."
1054. "Volkswagen AG Agrees to Plead Guilty."
1055. Erin Dooley, "Volkswagen Ex-CEO Indicted in Emissions Defeat Device Scandal," ABC News, May 3, 2018, https://abcnews.go.com/US/volkswagen-ceo-indicted-emissions-defeat-device-scandal/story?id=54922971; "German Court Convicts 4 Ex-Volkswagen Managers of Fraud in Emissions Scandal," *Associated Press News*, May 26, 2025, https://apnews.com/article/volkswagen-germany-diesel-emissions-court-fraud-3878fcf6c06c9574bf5bff8d31029f90.
1056. "German Court Convicts 4 Ex-Volkswagen Managers."
1057. "Federalist Nos. 51-60," Federalist Papers: Primary Documents in American History, Research Guides, Library of Congress, https://guides.loc.gov/federalist-papers/text-51-60.
1058. Carl Hulse, "The Senate, Once Insulated from Trump, Has Remade Itself in His Image," *New York Times*, July 25, 2025.

1059. US Const. art. II, § 3.
1060. Sarah Fortinsky, "Trump Executive Orders and Actions: By the Numbers," *The Hill*, January 21, 2025, https://thehill.com/homenews/administration/5098445-trump-executive-orders-first-day/.
1061. Fatma Tanis and Frank Langfitt, "The Trump Administration Kills Nearly All USAID Programs," NPR, February 26, 2025, https://www.npr.org/sections/goats-and-soda/2025/02/26/nx-s1-5310673/usaid-trump-administration-global-health; Julia Shapero, "'We're About to Get Annihilated': Musk, DOGE Descend on Consumer Bureau," *The Hill*, February 11, 2025, https://thehill.com/business/5136827-trump-administration-targets-cfpb/.
1062. Beth Reinhard, Aaron Schaffer, and Laura Meckler, "Trump's Education Pick Once Incorrectly Claimed to Have Education Degree," *Washington Post*, November 20, 2024.
1063. Mackenzie Wilkes, "Linda McMahon Lays Out Education Department's 'Final Mission,'" *Politico*, March 4, 2025, https://www.politico.com/news/2025/03/04/linda-mcmahon-education-department-final-mission-00210057.
1064. Zeke Miller, Eric Tucker, and Will Weissert, "Trump Uses Mass Firing to Remove Independent Inspectors General at a Series of Agencies," *Associated Press News*, January 25, 2025, https://apnews.com/article/trump-inspectors-general-fired-congress-unlawful-4e8bc57e132c3f9a7f1c2a3754359993.
1065. US Const. art. III, § 1.
1066. Matthew Cullen, "The Supreme Court Casts a Skeptical Eye on Trump's Tariffs," *New York Times,* November 5, 2025.
1067. Tony Romm, "Trump Administration Illegally Withheld Head Start Funds, Watchdog Finds," *New York Times*, July 23, 2025; Tony Romm, "Trump Administration Wrongly Impounded Infrastructure Aid, Watchdog Finds," *New York Times*, May 22, 2025.
1068. Miller, Tucker, and Weissert, "Trump Uses Mass Firing to Remove Independent Inspectors General."
1069. Gabriel Sherman, "'They're Scared Shitless': The Threat of Political Violence Informing Trump's Grip on Congress," *Vanity Fair*, February 19, 2025, https://www.vanityfair.com/news/story/trump-congress-political-violence.
1070. Steve Benen, "The Weird Reason Speaker Mike Johnson Claimed Trump Has a '90% Approval Rating,'" *MaddowBlog*, MSNBC, July 18, 2025, https://www.msnbc.com/rachel-maddow-show/maddowblog/weird-reason-speaker-mike-johnson-claimed-trump-90-approval-rating-rcna219651.
1071. Benen, "The Weird Reason Speaker Mike Johnson Claimed."
1072. Kevin Freking, "Budget Office Says Trump's Tax Law Will Add $3.4 Trillion to Deficits, Leave 10 Million Uninsured," *Associated Press News*, July 21, 2025, https://www.msn.com/en-us/news/politics/budget-office-says-trumps-tax-law-will-add-34-trillion-to-deficits-leave-10-million-uninsured/ar-AA1J1yWq.
1073. Catie Edmondson, "The $3 Trillion Question at the Capitol: Will Conservatives Cave (Again)?" *New York Times*, July 2, 2025.
1074. Caitlin Yilek, "Trump Signs Rescissions Bill Clawing Back Foreign Aid, NPR and PBS Funding," CBS News, July 24, 2025, https://www.cbsnews.com/news/trump-signs-rescissions-package-foreign-aid-npr-pbs-funding/; Hulse, "The Senate, Once Insulated From Trump."
1075. Michael Barbaro, host, *The Daily*, podcast, "Congress Just Gave Away Spending Power to Trump," *New York Times*, July 18, 2025, https://www.nytimes.com/2025/07/18/podcasts/the-daily/trump-congress-spending-rescission.html.
1076. Barbaro, "Congress Just Gave Away Spending Power to Trump."
1077. Sadie Gurman, Annie Linsky, Josh Dawsey, and Alex Leary, "Justice Department Told Trump in May That His Name Is Among Many in the Epstein Files," *Wall Street Journal*, July 24, 2025, https://www.wsj.com/politics/justice-department-told-trump-name-in-epstein-files-727a8038.
1078. Stephen Groves and Lisa Mascaro, "House Ending Session Early as Republicans Clash over Epstein Vote," *Associated Press News*, July 22, 2025, https://apnews.com/article/congress-jeffrey-epstein-trump-f2a03eca247268b14a9e38858338eded.
1079. Seung Min Kim, Eric Tucker, and Michael R. Sisak, "After Missing Deadline, DOJ Says It May Need a 'Few More Weeks' To Finish Releasnig Epstein Files," *Associates Press*, December

24, 2025, https://apnews.com/article/senate-epstein-files-trump-justice-department-bipartisan-fe7de7947b4e5b0bd7f8194cdc760f1f.
1080. Sherman, "'They're Scared Shitless.'"
1081. Isabella Murray, "GOP Sen. Tillis Won't Run for Reelection After Trump Primary Threat," ABC News, June 29, 2025, https://abcnews.go.com/Politics/gop-sen-tillis-run-reelection-after-trump-threat/story?id=123322400.
1082. Sherman, "'They're Scared Shitless.'"
1083. Caroline Kelly, "Cheney Says Some GOP Members Voted Against Impeachment Out of Fear for Their Lives," CNN, May 15, 2021, https://www.cnn.com/2021/05/14/politics/liz-cheney-republican-party-cnntv/index.html.
1084. Giselle Ruhiyyih Ewing, "'We Are All Afraid': Murkowski Says Fear of Retaliation from Trump Administration Is 'Real,'" *Politico*, April 17, 2025, https://www.politico.com/news/2025/04/17/lisa-murkowski-trump-retaliation-00295852.
1085. Ewing, "'We Are All Afraid.'"
1086. Isabella Murray, "Murkowski, Peltola Reelected in Alaska's Ranked-Choice Voting, ABC News Reports," ABC News, November 23, 2022, https://abcnews.go.com/Politics/murkowski-peltola-reelected-alaskas-ranked-choice-voting-abc/story?id=93854516.
1087. Jeff Flake, "The Republican Fever Must Break," op ed, *New York Times*, July 6, 2025.
1088. Flake, "The Republican Fever Must Break."
1089. "Congresswoman Charged for Forcibly Impeding and Interfering With Federal Officers," US Department of Justice, District of New Jersey, June 10, 2025, https://www.justice.gov/usao-nj/pr/congresswoman-charged-forcibly-impeding-and-interfering-federal-officers; United States v. McIver, indictment, Crim. No. 25 (D.N.J. May 9, 2025).
1090. United States v. McIver, indictment.
1091. United States v. McIver, indictment.
1092. "DHS Releases Video of Rep. McIver at Delaney Hall Detention Center—Now She Is Being Charged by DOJ," posted May 16, 2025, by Forbes Breaking News, YouTube, 0:26, https://www.youtube.com/watch?v=kqIDzHUixco.
1093. Ry Rivard, "Judge Criticizes DOJ for 'Worrisome' and 'Embarrassing' Blunders in Arrest of New Jersey Mayor at ICE Facility," *Politico*, May 21, 2025, https://www.politico.com/news/2025/05/21/judge-alina-habba-new-jersey-ras-baraka-arrest-00362946.
1094. "Official Statement from US Attorney Alina Habba," press release, US Attorney's Office, District of New Jersey, May 19, 2025, as viewed at Alina Habba (@USAttyHabba), "Today my office has charged Congresswoman McIver with violation of Title 18, United States Code, Section 111(a)(1) for assaulting, impeding and interfering with law enforcement," X, May 18, 2025, https://x.com/USAttyHabba/status/1924615111198576645.
1095. Luis Ferré-Sadurní, "Rep. McIver Charged with Assault over Clash Outside Newark ICE Center," *New York Times*, May 19, 2025.
1096. "Official Statement from US Attorney Alina Habba."
1097. Zach Schonfeld and Rebecca Beitsch, "Habba Announces Criminal Charge Against Rep. McIver over ICE Facility Scuffle," *The Hill*, May 19, 2025, https://thehill.com/homenews/house/5308603-habba-announces-criminal-charge-against-rep-mciver-over-ice-facility-scuffle/.
1098. Tara Suter, "Padilla: 'What Does It Say About' Noem 'to Not Know' a California Senator," *The Hill*, June 15, 2025, https://thehill.com/homenews/senate/5351498-padilla-noem-california-senator-incident/.
1099. Suter, "Padilla: 'What Does It Say About' Noem."
1100. Ivan Pereira, "Padilla Pushes Back Against Noem's Claim He Barged into News Conference," ABC News, June 13, 2025, https://abcnews.go.com/Politics/padilla-pushes-back-noems-claim-barged-news-conference/story?id=122817212.
1101. US Const. art. III.
1102. Judiciary Act of 1789, ch. 20, 1 Stat. 73 (Sept. 24, 1789).
1103. Marbury v. Madison, 5 US 137 (1803).
1104. Suzanne Monyak, "DOJ's No. 2 Official Asks Lawyers to Join 'War' Against Judges," *Bloomberg Law*, November 7, 2025, https://news.bloomberglaw.com/us-law-week/dojs-no-2-official-asks-lawyers-to-join-war-against-judges.

1105. Monyak, "DOJ's No. 2 Official Asks Lawyers."
1106. Monyak, "DOJ's No. 2 Official Asks Lawyers."
1107. Dwight D. Eisenhower, "Address to the Nation on Desegregation in Little Rock, Arkansas," speech, Washington, DC, September 24, 1957, available at American Rhetoric, https://www.americanrhetoric.com/speeches/dwighteisenhowerlittlerock.htm.
1108. Noem v. Abrego Garcia, 604 US ___, 2 (2025).
1109. Noem v. Abrego Garcia, 3.
1110. Noem v. Abrego Garcia, 3.
1111. Noem v. Abrego Garcia, 5.
1112. Devan Cole, "'That Ends Now': Judge Overseeing Abrego Garcia Case Knocks Trump Administration for Repeated Stonewalling," CNN, April 22, 2025, https://www.cnn.com/2025/04/22/politics/abrego-garcia-judge-xinis-justice-that-ends-now.
1113. Cole, "'That Ends Now.'"
1114. Erich Wagner, "Here's How Trump's New Vice Presidential Pick Stacks Up on Federal Workforce Issues," *Government Executive*, July 15, 2024, https://www.govexec.com/management/2024/07/heres-now-trumps-new-vice-presidential-pick-stacks-federal-workforce-issues/398056/.
1115. Steve Vladeck, "Bonus 168: Appointing (and Removing) US Attorneys," *One First*, July 23, 2025, https://www.stevevladeck.com/p/bonus-168-appointing-and-removing.
1116. Samuel A. Alito Jr., "Definition of Vacancy for the Purpose of Interim Appointment of United States Attorneys Pursuant to 28 USC 546, As Amended," Office of Legal Counsel, US Department of Justice, November 13, 1986, https://storage.courtlistener.com/recap/gov.uscourts.njd.578930/gov.uscourts.njd.578930.61.1.pdf.
1117. Gregory Svirnovskiy, "Trump Taps Jeanine Pirro for Interim US Attorney for DC," *Politico*, May 8, 2025, https://www.politico.com/news/2025/05/08/trump-taps-jeanine-pirro-for-interim-us-attorney-for-dc-00337456.
1118. Svirnovskiy, "Trump Taps Jeanine Pirro."
1119. Suzanne Monyak and Justin Wise, "Trump Tests Appointment Power with Pirro Pick for DC US Attorney," *Bloomberg Law*, May 16, 2025, https://news.bloomberglaw.com/white-collar-and-criminal-law/trump-tests-appointment-power-with-pirro-pick-for-dc-us-attorney.
1120. Samantha Waldenberg, "Trump Nominates Jeanine Pirro for Full Term as DC's Top Federal Prosecutor," CNN, June 17, 2025, https://www.cnn.com/2025/06/17/politics/jeanine-pirro-us-attorney-nomination.
1121. Santul Nerkar, "In Rare Move, Judges Reject a Trump Pick for US Attorney," *New York Times*, July 14, 2025.
1122. Mark Weiner, "Federal Judges Oust Trump's Top Prosecutor for Upstate New York," *Syracuse Post-Standard*, July 14, 2025, https://www.newyorkupstate.com/albany/2025/07/federal-judges-oust-trumps-top-prosecutor-for-upstate-new-york.html.
1123. Weiner, "Federal Judges Oust Trump's Top Prosecutor."
1124. Weiner, "Federal Judges Oust Trump's Top Prosecutor."
1125. Weiner, "Federal Judges Oust Trump's Top Prosecutor."
1126. Vladeck, "Bonus 168: Appointing (and Removing) US Attorneys."
1127. Ry Rivard and Madison Fernandez, "Bondi Says Federal Judges' Pick for New Jersey's Top Prosecutor Has Been 'Removed,'" *Politico*, July 22, 2025, https://www.politico.com/news/2025/07/22/bondi-removes-new-jersey-top-prosecutor-replacement-00468833.
1128. Rivard and Fernandez, "Bondi Says Federal Judges' Pick"; Tracey Tully and Jonah E. Bromwich, "Alina Habba Is Named Acting US Attorney in New Jersey," *New York Times*, July 24, 2025; Vladeck, "Bonus 168: Appointing (and Removing) US Attorneys."
1129. Ella Lee, "Judge Disqualifies Trump-Appointed US Attorney in California," *The Hill*, October 29, 2025, https://thehill.com/regulation/court-battles/5578469-bill-essayli-disqualified-los-angeles-trump-nominee/.
1130. Vladeck, "Bonus 168: Appointing (and Removing) US Attorneys."
1131. Donald J. Trump (@realDonaldTrump), "This Radical Left Lunatic of a Judge, a troublemaker and agitator who was sadly appointed by Barack Hussein Obama, was not elected President - He didn't WIN the popular VOTE (by a lot!), he didn't WIN ALL SEVEN SWING STATES, he didn't WIN 2,750 to 525 Counties, HE DIDN'T WIN ANYTHING!

I WON FOR MANY REASONS, IN AN OVERWHELMING MANDATE, BUT FIGHTING ILLEGAL IMMIGRATION MAY HAVE BEEN THE NUMBER ONE REASON FOR THIS HISTORIC VICTORY. I'm just doing what the VOTERS wanted me to do. This judge, like many of the Crooked Judges' I am forced to appear before, should be IMPEACHED!!! WE DON'T WANT VICIOUS, VIOLENT, AND DEMENTED CRIMINALS, MANY OF THEM DERANGED MURDERERS, IN OUR COUNTRY. MAKE AMERICA GREAT AGAIN!!!" Truth Social, March 18, 2025, https://truthsocial.com/@realDonaldTrump/posts/114183576937425149.

1132. Trump, "This Radical Left Lunatic of a Judge."
1133. Chris Megerian, Lindsay Whitehurst, and Mark Sherman, "Roberts Rejects Trump's Call for Impeaching Judge Who Ruled Against His Deportation Plans," *Associated Press News*, March 18, 2025, https://apnews.com/article/donald-trump-federal-judges-impeachment-29da1153a-9f82106748098a6606fec39.
1134. Steph Solis, "President Trump Blasts Federal Judge, Vows to Appeal Harvard Ruling," *Axios*, July 21, 2025, https://www.axios.com/local/boston/2025/07/21/trump-blasts-boston-federal-judge-harvard.
1135. Giulia Carbonaro, "Donald Trump Attacks Judges in All-Caps Memorial Day Message: 'MONSTERS,'" *Newsweek*, May 26, 2025, https://www.newsweek.com/donald-trump-attacks-judges-all-caps-memorial-day-message-monsters-2077023.
1136. Aaron Blake, "The White House Claims a Left-wing Judicial 'Insurrection.' But Many GOP and Trump Nominees Are Rebuking the President, Too," CNN, October 6, 2025, https://www.cnn.com/2025/10/06/politics/republican-federal-judges-trump.
1137. Mattathias Schwartz, "Marshals' Data Shows Spike in Threats Against Federal Judges," *New York Times*, May 27, 2025.
1138. Noem v. Abrego Garcia, 6.
1139. Taylor Romine and Andi Babineau, "Wisconsin Judge Indicted in Federal Court Following Accusations of Obstructing Immigration Agents," CNN, May 13, 2025, https://www.cnn.com/2025/05/13/us/judge-hannah-dugan-indicted.
1140. Ryan J. Reilly and Michael Kosnar, "FBI Arrests Milwaukee Judge, Alleging She Interfered in Immigration Operation," NBC News, April 25, 2025, https://www.nbcnews.com/politics/justice-department/fbi-arrests-milwaukee-judge-alleging-interfered-immigration-operation-rcna203006.
1141. Reilly and Kosnar, "FBI Arrests Milwaukee Judge."
1142. Reilly and Kosnar, "FBI Arrests Milwaukee Judge."
1143. "Trump Administration Sues All of Maryland's Federal Judges over Deportation Order," *Associated Press News*, June 26, 2025, https://www.npr.org/2025/06/26/nx-s1-5445843/justice-department-maryland-judges-deportation.
1144. "Trump Administration Sues All of Maryland's Federal Judges."
1145. Alan Feuer, "Judge Dismisses Trump Administration Suit Against Federal Bench in Maryland," *New York Times*, August 26, 2025.
1146. Feuer, "Judge Dismisses Trump Administration Suit."
1147. Trump v. United States, 603 US ___ (2024), 6.
1148. Trump v. United States, 603 US ___ (2024) (Sotomayor, J., dissenting), 29–30.
1149. Trump v. United States.
1150. McMahon v. New York, 606 U. S. ____ (2025).
1151. National Institutes of Health v. American Public Health Association, 606 US ___ (2025).
1152. Charlie Savage, "The Supreme Court Decision on ICE and Racial Profiling, Explained," *New York Times*, September 8, 2025.
1153. "District Court Reform: Nationwide Injunctions," *Harvard Law Review* 137 (2024): 1701.
1154. Barbara McQuade, "Nationwide Injunctions Are a Problem. Ending Them Isn't the Answer," op ed, *Bloomberg Opinion*, March 26, 2025, https://www.bloomberg.com/opinion/articles/2025-03-26/nationwide-injunctions-are-a-problem-ending-them-isn-t-the-answer.
1155. Trump v. CASA, 605 US ___ (2025).
1156. Trump v. CASA.
1157. "Groups File Nationwide Class-Action Lawsuit over Trump Birthright Citizenship Order," press release, American Civil Liberties Union, June 27, 2025, https://www.aclu.org/press-re-

leases/groups-file-nationwide-class-action-lawsuit-over-trump-birthright-citizenship-order. Fearing that the orders would render babies born in the United States to undocumented mothers stateless, lawyers immediately filed class actions lawsuits on behalf of all plaintiffs similarly situated, thereby again preventing the policies from going into effect.

1158. Abbie VanSickle, "Supreme Court Limits Judges' Ability to Issue Nationwide Injunctions, a Win for Trump," *New York Times*, June 27, 2025.
1159. Ed Pilkington, "The Umpire Who Picked a Side: John Roberts and the Death of the Rule of Law in America," *The Guardian*, August 21, 2025, https://www.theguardian.com/us-news/ng-interactive/2025/aug/21/justice-john-roberts-supreme-court.
1160. Amy Howe, "Supreme Court Clears the Way for Trump Administration to Massively Reduce the Size of the Department of Education," *SCOTUSblog*, July 14, 2025, https://www.scotusblog.com/2025/07/supreme-court-clears-the-way-for-trump-administration-to-massively-reduce-the-size-of-the-department-of-education/.
1161. "Improving Education Outcomes by Empowering Parents, States, and Communities," executive order, White House, March 20, 2025, https://www.whitehouse.gov/presidential-actions/2025/03/improving-education-outcomes-by-empowering-parents-states-and-communities/.
1162. McMahon v. New York, 606 US ____ (2025).
1163. McMahon v. New York, 2.
1164. Pilkington, "The Umpire Who Picked a Side."
1165. Kevin Miller, "Maine Faces Federal Investigation After Gov. Janet Mills Tells Trump, 'See You in Court,'" NPR, March 2, 2025, https://www.npr.org/transcripts/nx-s1-5310653.
1166. NPR, "Maine Faces Federal Investigation."
1167. NPR, "Maine Faces Federal Investigation."
1168. NPR, "Maine Faces Federal Investigation."
1169. 10 USC § 12406.
1170. April Rubin, "Newsom Denies Trump Spoke to Him before Deploying More National Guard Troops," *Axios*, June 10, 2025, https://www.axios.com/2025/06/10/trump-gavin-newsom-call-protests-los-angeles-law-enforcement.
1171. Julie Sharp, "Mayor Karen Bass Continues to Call for an End to National Guard Troops' Deployment in Los Angeles," CBS News, July 21, 2025, https://www.cbsnews.com/losangeles/news/mayor-karen-bass-end-national-guard-troops-deployment-los-angeles/.
1172. Brett Samuels, "Trump Supports Tom Homan Arresting Newsom over California Protests," *The Hill*, June 9, 2025, https://thehill.com/homenews/administration/5340464-trump-arrest-gavin-newsom/.
1173. Sharp, "Mayor Karen Bass Continues to Call for an End to National Guard Troops' Deployment."
1174. Santul Nerkar and Luis Ferré-Sadurní, "Trump Administration Sues Adams and New York City over Sanctuary Laws," *New York Times*, July 24, 2025.
1175. United States v. City of New York, No. 1:25-cv-4084 (E.D.N.Y. July 24, 2025) (complaint).
1176. Nerkar and Ferré-Sadurní, "Trump Administration Sues Adams."
1177. Nerkar and Ferré-Sadurní, "Trump Administration Sues Adams."
1178. National Institutes of Health v. American Public Health Association.

10. Strongmen and Soft Power

1179. United States v. Abdulmutallab, 737 F.3d 891 (6th Cir. 2014).
1180. "NATO's Purpose," NATO, updated May 29, 2024, https://www.nato.int/cps/en/natohq/topics_68144.htm.
1181. "NATO's Purpose."
1182. Daniel Dale, "Fact Check: Trump's Ukraine War Claims," CNN, April 25, 2025, https://www.cnn.com/2025/04/25/politics/fact-check-trump-ukraine-war.
1183. Andrew E. Kramer and Luke Broadwater, "Ukraine Promises Swift Deal for Minerals as Trump Cuts Kyiv Out of Peace Talks," *New York Times,* February 21, 2025.
1184. Andrea Shalal and Joey Roulette, "Exclusive: US Could Cut Ukraine's Access to Starlink Internet Services Over Minerals," *Reuters*, February 22, 2025, https://www.reuters.com/busi-

ness/us-could-cut-ukraines-access-starlink-internet-services-over-minerals-say-2025-02-22/; Kramer and Broadwater, "Ukraine Promises Swift Deal for Minerals."
1185. Kramer and Broadwater, "Ukraine Promises Swift Deal for Minerals."
1186. Shalal and Roulette, "Exclusive: US Could Cut Ukraine's Access to Starlink."
1187. Kramer and Broadwater, "Ukraine Promises Swift Deal for Minerals."
1188. Andrew E. Kramer, Constant Méheut, and Anton Troianovski, "Zelensky Urges More Truth After Trump Suggests Ukraine Started the War," *New York Times*, February 19, 2025.
1189. Kramer, Méheut, and Troianovski, "Zelensky Urges More Truth."
1190. Kramer, Méheut, and Troianovski, "Zelensky Urges More Truth."
1191. Gabriela Pomeroy and George Wright, "Trump Calls Zelensky a 'Dictator' as Rift Between Two Leaders Deepens," BBC News, February 20, 2025, https://www.bbc.com/news/articles/cjev2j70v190.
1192. Jonathan Este, "Trump's Art of the Deal Horrifies Ukraine and Its Allies," *The Conversation*, February 21, 2025, https://theconversation.com/trumps-art-of-the-deal-horrifies-ukraine-and-its-allies-250461.
1193. Pomeroy and Wright, "Trump Calls Zelensky a 'Dictator.'"
1194. Kramer and Broadwater, "Ukraine Promises Swift Deal for Minerals."
1195. Kramer and Broadwater, "Ukraine Promises Swift Deal for Minerals."
1196. Derek Guy, "The Real Reason Zelenskyy Doesn't Wear a Suit," *Politico Magazine*, March 8, 2025, https://www.politico.com/news/magazine/2025/03/08/zelenskyy-suit-ukraine-fashion-style-00219275.
1197. Jonathan Chait, "The Real Reason Trump Berated Zelensky," *The Atlantic*, February 28, 2025.
1198. Peter Baker, "Trump Berates Zelensky in Fiery Exchange at the White House," *New York Times*, February 28, 2025.
1199. Baker, "Trump Berates Zelensky in Fiery Exchange."
1200. Baker, "Trump Berates Zelensky in Fiery Exchange."
1201. Dale, "Fact Check: Trump's Ukraine War Claims."
1202. Adriana Gomez Licon, "Transcript of Trump and Zelenskyy's Oval Office Argument," *Associated Press News*, February 28, 2025, https://apnews.com/article/trump-zelenskyy-vance-transcript-oval-office-80685f5727628c64065da81525f8f0cf.
1203. Veronika Melkozerova, "Fact-checking JD Vance's Statements on Ukraine," *Politico Europe*, July 16, 2024, https://www.politico.eu/article/jd-vance-europe-russia-ukraine-donald-trump-kyiv-vp-pick-policy-us-elections-ohio-aid-war/.
1204. Baker, "Trump Berates Zelensky in Fiery Exchange."
1205. Jeff Cercone, Amy Sherman, and Sara Swann, "Fact-Checking Trump and Vance's Attacks on Ukrainian President Zelenskyy," PBS News, March 2, 2025, https://www.pbs.org/newshour/politics/fact-checking-trump-and-vances-attacks-on-ukrainian-president-zelenskyy.
1206. "'I Would Like You to Do Us a Favor': The 30-Minute Phone Call That Changed Trump's Presidency," CNBC, October 12, 2019, https://www.cnbc.com/2019/10/12/i-would-like-you-to-do-us-a-favor-the-30-minute-phone-call-that-changed-trumps-presidency.html.
1207. Jill L. Colvin and Michelle Price, "Trump's Red Carpet Reception in Alaska Ends Without Deal to End War in Ukraine," PBS News, August 15, 2025, https://www.pbs.org/newshour/politics/trumps-red-carpet-reception-for-putin-in-alaska-ends-without-deal-to-end-war-in-ukraine.
1208. "What Is Democracy?" US Department of State, January 20, 2017, https://2009-2017.state.gov/j/drl/democ.
1209. Molly O'Toole, "A Brief History of Donald Trump's Love Affair with Saddam Hussein," *Foreign Policy*, July 6, 2016, https://foreignpolicy.com/2016/07/06/a-brief-history-of-donald-trumps-love-affair-with-saddam-hussein/.
1210. O'Toole, "A Brief History of Donald Trump's Love Affair."
1211. Kurt Bardella, "Trump Says He and North Korea's Kim Jong Un 'Fell in Love,'" NBC News, October 1, 2018, https://www.nbcnews.com/think/opinion/trump-says-he-north-korea-s-kim-jong-un-fell-ncna915436.
1212. "World Report 2025: China," Human Rights Watch, 2025, https://www.hrw.org/world-report/2025/country-chapters/china.
1213. "World Report 2025: China."

1214. "World Report 2025: China."
1215. Josh Meyer, "Trump Loves Populists and Strongmen. Here's Who He's Invited to the Inauguration," *USA Today*, January 9, 2025, https://www.usatoday.com/story/news/politics/2025/01/09/trump-right-wing-populists-inauguration/77551719007/.
1216. Michael D. Shear, "'A Great Emboldening': Trump Inspires Wannabe Authoritarians Everywhere," *New York Times*, March 29, 2025.
1217. Shear, "'A Great Emboldening.'"
1218. Burcu Cevik-Compiegne, "How the 20-Year Rule of Recep Tayyip Erdoğan Has Transformed Turkey," *The Conversation*, December 18, 2022, https://theconversation.com/how-the-20-year-rule-of-recep-tayyip-erdogan-has-transformed-turkey-188211.
1219. Leila Fadel, Arezou Rezvani, and Milton Guevara, "Former US Ambassador to Hungary Discusses Democratic Decay Under Viktor Orbán," NPR, February 25, 2025, https://www.npr.org/2025/02/25/nx-s1-5294699/former-u-s-ambassador-to-hungary-discusses-democratic-decay-under-pm-orban.
1220. Fadel, Rezvani, and Guevara, "Former US Ambassador to Hungary Discusses Democratic Decay."
1221. Fadel, Rezvani, and Guevara, "Former US Ambassador to Hungary Discusses Democratic Decay."
1222. Nicholas Riccardi and Justin Spike, "Trump Meets with Hungary's Leader, Viktor Orbán, Continuing His Embrace of Autocrats," *Associated Press News*, March 8, 2024, https://apnews.com/article/trump-orban-hungary-conservatives-autocrats-biden-97d6998f747d3543f2f1d-f069b0f9165.
1223. Fadel, Rezvani, and Guevara, "Former US Ambassador to Hungary Discusses Democratic Decay."
1224. Fadel, Rezvani, and Guevara, "Former US Ambassador to Hungary Discusses Democratic Decay."
1225. Fadel, Rezvani, and Guevara, "Former US Ambassador to Hungary Discusses Democratic Decay."
1226. Riccardi and Spike, "Trump Meets with Hungary's Leader."
1227. Ruth Ben-Ghiat, "Trump's War on America," *Lucid* (blog), *Substack*, August 27, 2025, https://lucid.substack.com/p/trumps-war-on-america.
1228. "Restoring Names That Honor American Greatness," executive order, White House, January 20, 2025, https://www.whitehouse.gov/presidential-actions/2025/01/restoring-names-that-honor-american-greatness/; Asma Khalid, "Why Trump Loves Former President McKinley So Much," NPR, February 3, 2025, https://www.npr.org/2025/02/03/nx-s1-5272753/why-trump-loves-former-president-mckinley-so-much.
1229. Khalid, "Why Trump Loves Former President McKinley."
1230. Jill Colvin and Rob Gillies, "Trump, the 'America First' Candidate, Has a New Preoccupation: Imperialism," *Associated Press News*, January 9, 2025, https://apnews.com/article/trump-imperialism-canada-panama-greenland-b4b53445dee97398b498b79eab54d49b.
1231. Dave Roos, "Why the US Returned the Panama Canal," History, January 28, 2025, https://www.history.com/articles/panama-canal-return-panama-treaties-carter.
1232. Eli Stokols and Daniella Cheslow, "After Venezuela Operation, Trump Says the Whole Hemisphere is in Play," *Politico*, January 3, 2026, https://www.politico.com/news/2026/01/03/trump-venezela-mexico-00710063.
1233. Stokols and Cheslow, "After Venezuela Operation, Trump Says Whole Hemisphere is in Play."
1234. Jack Nicas, "The 'Donroe Doctrine': Trump's Bid to Control the Western Hemisphere," *New York Times*, November 17, 2025.
1235. Nicas, "The 'Donroe Doctrine.'"
1236. "What Trump Left Out of His Manifest Destiny Inaugural Address," *The Bulwark*, January 21, 2025, https://www.thebulwark.com/p/trump-left-out-of-his-manifest-destiny-inaugural-address.
1237. Franco Ordoñez and Deepa Shivaram, "Trump Says He Wants the US to Take Ownership of the Gaza Strip," NPR, February 4, 2025, https://www.npr.org/2025/02/04/nx-s1-5287012/trump-netanyahu-ceasefire-gaza.

1238. "Donald Trump Shares Bizarre AI-Generated Video of 'Trump Gaza,'" *The Guardian*, February 26, 2025, https://www.theguardian.com/us-news/video/2025/feb/26/donald-trump-shares-bizarre-ai-generated-video-of-trump-gaza-video.
1239. Gustaf Kilander, "What Greenlanders Really Think About Trump's Desire to Acquire Their Island," *The Independent*, January 15, 2025, https://www.independent.co.uk/news/world/americas/us-politics/greenland-donald-trump-arctic-b2680374.html.
1240. Colvin and Gillies, "Trump, the 'America First' Candidate."
1241. David Goldman, "What Trump Actually Wants from Tariffs," CNN, March 11, 2025, https://www.cnn.com/2025/03/11/business/tariffs-trump-explainer.
1242. Aimee Picchi, "Here's Why Trump Thinks Tariffs Are Good for the US—and What the Experts Say," CBS News, November 26, 2024, https://www.cbsnews.com/news/trump-tariffs-mexico-canada-china-truth-social/.
1243. Picchi, "Here's Why Trump Thinks Tariffs."
1244. Josh Boak, "Trump Signs a Plan for Reciprocal Tariffs on US Trading Partners, Ushering in Economic Uncertainty," *Associated Press News*, February 13, 2025, https://apnews.com/article/trump-tariffs-reciprocal-imports-tax-trade-economy-54c0a26687dc96157d96229068894720.
1245. Boak, "Trump Signs a Plan for Reciprocal Tariffs."
1246. "The Dumbest Trade War in History," editorial, *Wall Street Journal*, January 31, 2025, https://www.wsj.com/opinion/donald-trump-tariffs-25-percent-mexico-canada-trade-economy-84476fb2.
1247. Phil Gramm and Donald J. Boudreaux, "Trump's Tariffs Are as Bad as Bidenomics," *Wall Street Journal*, April 14, 2025, https://www.wsj.com/opinion/trumps-tariffs-are-as-bad-as-bidenomics-d8a0d92b.
1248. Gramm and Boudreaux, "Trump's Tariffs Are as Bad as Bidenomics."
1249. Goldman, "What Trump Actually Wants from Tariffs."
1250. Louise Radnofsky, Jess Bravin, and Gavin Bade, "Appeals Court Rejects Trump's Global Tariffs," *Wall Street Journal*, August 29, 2025, https://www.wsj.com/politics/policy/appeals-court-rejects-trumps-global-tariffs-aae2dc99; Learning Resources, Inc. v. Trump, 607 US ___ (2026).
1251. Josh Boak, "Trump's Tariffs May Mean Walmart Shoppers Pay More, His Treasury Chief Acknowledges," *Associated Press News*, May 17, 2025, https://apnews.com/article/trump-tariffs-walmart-inflation-import-taxes-e2012e0d9e242b0be0b9474aa58d41fd.
1252. Paul Kane, "Trump's Tariffs Remain Unpopular, a Warning Sign for Republicans," *Washington Post*, August 28, 2025.
1253. Goldman, "What Trump Actually Wants from Tariffs."
1254. "Trump Targets Russia via India," editorial, *Wall Street Journal*, August 7, 2025, https://www.wsj.com/public/resources/documents/e3nmpymJpO50ZWvNOXUk-WSJNewsPaper-8-7-2025.pdf.
1255. Danielle Kurtzleben, "Trump Unveils Sweeping 10% Tariff and 'Reciprocal' Tariffs on Dozens of Nations," NPR, April 2, 2025, https://www.npr.org/2025/04/02/nx-s1-5345802/trump-tariffs-liberation-day.
1256. Alan Rappeport, "Trump's Demand to Trading Partners: Pledge Money or Get Higher Tariffs," *New York Times*, August 4, 2025.
1257. Kurtzleben, "Trump Unveils Sweeping 10% Tariff."
1258. Wyatte Grantham-Philips, "Trump Has Dubbed April 2 'Liberation Day' for His Tariffs. Here's What to Expect," *Associated Press News*, March 31, 2025, https://apnews.com/article/trump-reciprocal-tariffs-liberation-day-april-2-86639b7b6358af65e2cbad31f8c8ae2b.
1259. Rappeport, "Trump's Demand to Trading Partners."
1260. Steven Rattner, "Our President Is Economically Illiterate," op ed, *New York Times*, August 4, 2025.
1261. Ben Casselman and Tony Romm, "Trump, Claiming Weak Jobs Numbers Were 'Rigged,' Fires Labor Official," *New York Times*, August 1, 2025.
1262. Rappeport, "Trump's Demand to Trading Partners."
1263. Joseph J. Thorndike, "Ronald Reagan Would Have Hated Trump's Tariffs," *Forbes*, August 4, 2025, https://www.forbes.com/sites/taxnotes/2025/08/04/ronald-reagan-would-have-hated-trumps-tariffs/.

1264. Lynsey Chutel and Ana Swanson, "Trump Called a Canadian Ad Fake. It Faithfully Reproduces Reagan's Words," *New York Times*, October 24, 2025.
1265. Michael Waldman, "Will Tariffs Awaken a Sleeping Congress?" Brennan Center for Justice, April 8, 2025, https://www.brennancenter.org/our-work/analysis-opinion/will-tariffs-awaken-sleeping-congress.
1266. Waldman, "Will Tariffs Awaken a Sleeping Congress?"
1267. Christopher A. Casey, Jennifer K. Elsea, and Liana W. Rosen, *The International Emergency Economic Powers Act: Origins, Evolution, and Use*, Congressional Research Service, September 1, 2025, https://sgp.fas.org/crs/natsec/R45618.pdf.
1268. Casey, Elsea, and Rosen, "The International Emergency Economic Powers Act."
1269. Casey, Elsea, and Rosen, "The International Emergency Economic Powers Act."
1270. Waldman, "Will Tariffs Awaken a Sleeping Congress?"
1271. Casey, Elsea, and Rosen, "The International Emergency Economic Powers Act."
1272. Adam Liptak, "Trump Declares Dubious Emergencies to Amass Power, Scholars Say," *New York Times*, June 10, 2025.
1273. Liptak, "Trump Declares Dubious Emergencies."
1274. Youngstown Sheet & Tube Co. v. Sawyer, 343 US 579 (1952).
1275. Liptak, "Trump Declares Dubious Emergencies"; Youngstown Sheet & Tube Co. v. Sawyer.
1276. Tony Romm and Ana Swanson, "Trump Tariffs Ruled Illegal by Federal Judicial Panel," *New York Times*, May 28, 2025.
1277. Romm and Swanson, "Trump Tariffs Ruled Illegal."
1278. Romm and Swanson, "Trump Tariffs Ruled Illegal."
1279. Kyle Cheney and Doug Palmer, "Trump's Tariffs Get Frosty Reception at Federal Appeals Court," *Politico*, July 31, 2025, https://www.politico.com/news/2025/07/31/trump-tariff-arguments-appeals-court-00486972.
1280. Cheney and Palmer, "Trump's Tariffs Get Frosty Reception."
1281. "Hard Power vs. Soft Power: How Nations Really Influence Each Other," GovFacts, last updated December 6, 2025, https://govfacts.org/explainer/hard-power-vs-soft-power-how-nations-really-influence-each-other/.
1282. "Hard Power vs. Soft Power."
1283. "Hard Power vs. Soft Power."
1284. "Hard Power vs. Soft Power."
1285. "Hard Power vs. Soft Power."
1286. "Hard Power vs. Soft Power."
1287. "Hard Power vs. Soft Power."
1288. Giorgio Leali, "Trump's Move to Silence Pro-Democracy Media Sparks Outrage," *Politico Europe*, March 16, 2025, https://www.politico.eu/article/donald-trump-move-silence-pro-democracy-media-voice-of-america-radio-free/.
1289. Leali, "Trump's Move to Silence Pro-Democracy Media."
1290. "Hard Power vs. Soft Power."
1291. "The Dumbest Trade War in History."
1292. Matina Stevis-Gridneff and Jeanna Smialek, "Trump Is Pushing Allies Away and Closer to Each Other," *New York Times*, June 11, 2025.
1293. Stevis-Gridneff and Smialek, "Trump Is Pushing Allies Away."
1294. Andrew E. Kramer and Luke Broadwater, "US and Ukraine Appear to Move Closer to Deal for Minerals Amid Leaders' Public Feud," *New York Times*, February 21, 2025.
1295. Stevis-Gridneff and Smialek, "Trump Is Pushing Allies Away."
1296. Stevis-Gridneff and Smialek, "Trump Is Pushing Allies Away."
1297. Stevis-Gridneff and Smialek, "Trump Is Pushing Allies Away."
1298. Stevis-Gridneff and Smialek, "Trump Is Pushing Allies Away."
1299. Stevis-Gridneff and Smialek, "Trump Is Pushing Allies Away."

11. Lessons from History

1300. "Our History," Mothers Against Drunk Driving, accessed December 14, 2025, https://madd.org/our-history/.

1301. "Our History."
1302. "Our History."
1303. "Our History."
1304. "2023 State Alcohol-Impaired-Driving Estimates Traffic Safety Facts," National Highway Traffic Safety Administration, https://crashstats.nhtsa.dot.gov/#!/PublicationList/7.
1305. Chrisopher Klein, "How Gilded Age Corruption Led to the Progressive Era," History, July 10, 2025, https://www.history.com/articles/gilded-age-progressive-era-reforms.
1306. Klein, "How Gilded Age Corruption Led to the Progressive Era."
1307. Klein, "How Gilded Age Corruption Led to the Progressive Era."
1308. Jonathan Chang and Meghna Chakrabarti, "America's New Gilded Age," *On Point* (WBUR), March 14, 2025, https://www.wbur.org/onpoint/2025/03/14/america-gilded-age-trump-2024-president.
1309. Chang and Chakrabarti, "America's New Gilded Age."
1310. Chang and Chakrabarti, "America's New Gilded Age."
1311. Klein, "How Gilded Age Corruption Led to the Progressive Era."
1312. Klein, "How Gilded Age Corruption Led to the Progressive Era."
1313. Klein, "How Gilded Age Corruption Led to the Progressive Era."
1314. Barak Orbach and Grace Campbell Rebling, "The Antitrust Curse of Bigness," *Southern California Law Review* 85 (2012): 605, https://southerncalifornialawreview.com/wp-content/uploads/2018/01/85_605.pdf.
1315. Klein, "How Gilded Age Corruption Led to the Progressive Era"; Kat Long, "History Vs. Episode 6: Theodore Roosevelt vs. Corruption," *Mental Floss*, November 25, 2019, https://www.mentalfloss.com/columns/history-vs/history-vs-episode-6-theodore-roosevelt-vs-corruption.
1316. "Theodore Roosevelt and the National Park System," National Park Service, March 9, 2025, https://www.nps.gov/thrb/learn/historyculture/trandthenpsystem.htm.
1317. Theodore Roosevelt, "Remarks at the Laying of the Cornerstone of the Gateway to Yellowstone National Park in Gardiner, Montana," April 24, 1903, online by Gerhard Peters and John T. Woolley, The American Presidency Project, https://www.presidency.ucsb.edu/node/343416.
1318. Klein, "How Gilded Age Corruption Led to the Progressive Era."
1319. Klein, "How Gilded Age Corruption Led to the Progressive Era."
1320. Ellen Terrell, "Ida Tarbell, Author of 'History of the Standard Oil Company,' Was Born," This Month in Business History, Library of Congress, last updated October 2024, https://guides.loc.gov/this-month-in-business-history/november/ida-tarbell-born.
1321. Terrell, "Ida Tarbell."
1322. Klein, "How Gilded Age Corruption Led to the Progressive Era."
1323. Jacob Riis, *How the Other Half Lives: Studies Among the Tenements of New York* (Charles Scribner's Sons, 1890); "How the Other Half Lives," Theodore Roosevelt Center, accessed December 16, 2025, https://www.theodorerooseveltcenter.org/Learn-About-TR/TR-Encyclopedia/Culture%20and%20Society/How%20the%20Other%20Half%20Lives.
1324. "How the Other Half Lives," Theodore Roosevelt Center.
1325. David Brooks, "America Needs a Mass Movement—Now," *The Atlantic*, October 14, 2025.
1326. "Research Starters: Worldwide Deaths in World War II," The National World War II Museum, accessed January 7, 2026, https://www.nationalww2museum.org/students-teachers/student-resources/research-starters/research-starters-worldwide-deaths-world-war.
1327. "How Many People Died During World War I," *Britannica*, accessed January 7, 2025, https://www.britannica.com/question/How-many-people-died-during-World-War-I.
1328. "The War to End All Wars," BBC News, November 10, 1998, http://news.bbc.co.uk/2/hi/special_report/1998/10/98/world_war_i/198172.stm.
1329. United Nations Charter, Art. II, https://www.un.org/en/about-us/un-charter/full-text.
1330. David French, "Trump Is Unleashing Forces Beyond His Control," *New York Times*, January 5, 2026.
1331. French, "Trump is Unleashing Forces."
1332. French, "Trump is Unleashing Forces."
1333. Edward Wong and Julian E. Barnes, "Rubio Helped Oust Maduro. Running Venezuela May Prove Trickier," *New York Times*, January 6, 2026.

1334. Collin Makamson, "'The Grave Responsibility of Justice': Justice Robert H. Jackson's Opening Statement at Nuremberg," National World War II Museum, November 20, 2020, https://www.nationalww2museum.org/war/articles/robert-jackson-opening-statement-nuremberg.
1335. Makamson, "'The Grave Responsibility of Justice.'"
1336. Robert H. Jackson, "Nuremberg Trials: Opening Statement," speech delivered to the International Military Tribunal, Nuremberg, Germany, November 21, 1945, Genius, https://genius.com/Robert-h-jackson-nuremburg-trials-opening-statement-before-the-international-military-tribunal-annotated.
1337. Gerald R. Ford, "Remarks on Taking the Oath of Office," August 9, 1974, online by Gerhard Peters and John T. Woolley, The American Presidency Project, https://www.presidency.ucsb.edu/node/255838.
1338. United States v. Trump, superseding indictment, No. 1:23-cr-00257-TSC (D.D.C. Aug. 27, 2024).
1339. "Reconstruction in America," Equal Justice Initiative, accessed September 9, 2025, https://eji.org/report/reconstruction-in-america/.
1340. "Reconstruction in America."
1341. "Jim Crow Laws," *Freedom Riders*, American Experience, PBS, accessed September 9, 2025, https://www.pbs.org/wgbh/americanexperience/features/freedom-riders-jim-crow-laws/.
1342. "Jim Crow Laws."
1343. "Nonviolence," Martin Luther King Jr. Research and Education Institute, Stanford University, accessed September 9, 2025, https://kinginstitute.stanford.edu/nonviolence.
1344. "Nonviolence."
1345. "Nonviolence."
1346. "Watergate Explained," Richard Nixon Foundation, accessed September 9, 2025, https://www.nixonfoundation.org/watergate-explained/.
1347. "Watergate Explained."
1348. "Watergate Explained."
1349. "Watergate Explained."
1350. "40 Years On, Woodward and Bernstein Recall Reporting on Watergate," *Morning Edition*, NPR, June 13, 2014, https://www.npr.org/2014/06/13/321316118/40-years-on-woodward-and-bernstein-recall-reporting-on-watergate.
1351. "40 Years On, Woodward and Bernstein Recall Reporting on Watergate."
1352. Meghan M. Stuessy, "The Presidential Records Act: An Overview," Congressional Research Service, R46129, last updated December 18, 2023, https://www.congress.gov/crs-product/R46129.
1353. Ethics in Government Act of 1978, Pub. L. No. 95-521, 92 Stat. 1824.
1354. *Intelligence Activities and the Rights of Americans*, S. Rep. No. 94-755, 2d Sess. (1976), 14.
1355. *Intelligence Activities and the Rights of Americans*, 65–66.
1356. *Intelligence Activities and the Rights of Americans*, 66.
1357. "Attorney General's Guidelines for Domestic FBI Operations," US Department of Justice, September 29, 2008, https://www.justice.gov/archive/opa/docs/guidelines.pdf.
1358. *Domestic Investigations and Operations Guide*, US Federal Bureau of Investigation, FBI Records: The Vault, last updated September 17, 2021, https://vault.fbi.gov/FBI%20Domestic%20Investigations%20and%20Operations%20Guide%20%28DIOG%29/FBI%20Domestic%20Investigations%20and%20Operations%20Guide%20%28DIOG%29%202016%20Version/FBI%20Domestic%20Investigations%20and%20Operations%20Guide%20%28DIOG%29%202016%20Version%20Part%2001/view.
1359. *Domestic Investigations and Operations Guide*, 1–2.
1360. *Domestic Investigations and Operations Guide*, 3–3.
1361. "Watergate-Era Reforms, 50 Years Later," *Harvard Law Today*, June 8, 2022, https://hls.harvard.edu/today/watergate-era-reforms-50-years-later/.
1362. Roni Dori, "Bringing Down Dictators: 'Contrary to Myth, Tyrants Are Fragile. Most Fall in the End,'" *Calcalistech*, October 21, 2024, https://www.calcalistech.com/ctechnews/article/b042vy8rf.
1363. Dori, "Bringing Down Dictators."
1364. Dori, "Bringing Down Dictators."

1365. Erica Chenoweth and Maria J. Stephan, *Why Civil Resistance Works: The Strategic Logic of Nonviolent Conflict* (Columbia University Press, 2011), 192.
1366. Chenoweth and Stephan, *Why Civil Resistance Works*, 192.
1367. Marci Shore, Timothy Snyder, and Jason Stanley, "We Study Fascism, and We're Leaving the United States," *New York Times*, May 14, 2025.
1368. Adi Guajardo, "Rutgers Professor Flees US for Spain, Claims He Received Death Threats," CBS News, October 11, 2025, https://www.cbsnews.com/newyork/news/rutgers-professor-mark-bray-antifa-turning-point-usa/.
1369. Chenoweth and Stephan, *Why Civil Resistance Works*, 192.
1370. Chenoweth and Stephan, *Why Civil Resistance Works*, 192.
1371. Chenoweth and Stephan, *Why Civil Resistance Works*, 193.
1372. Ruth Ben-Ghiat, "How Chile Won Back Its Democracy," *The Atlantic*, September 11, 2023.
1373. Dori, "Bringing Down Dictators."
1374. Marcel Dirsus, *How Tyrants Fall: And How Nations Survive* (John Murray, 2024), 211; Jack F. Matlock Jr., "Russia Votes: Will Democracy Win?" op ed, *New York Times*, March 26, 2000.
1375. Joe Conason, "Donald Trump's Dirty Self-Dealing: The Audacity of His Rapacity," *New Republic*, June 11, 2025, https://newrepublic.com/article/196187/trump-corruption-self-dealing-audacity-rapacity.
1376. Mark John Sanchez, "The People Power Revolution, Philippines, 1986," *Origins: Current Events in Historical Perspective*, Oregon State University,February 2021, https://origins.osu.edu/milestones/people-power-revolution-philippines-1986.
1377. Sanchez, "The People Power Revolution."
1378. Sanchez, "The People Power Revolution."
1379. Sanchez, "The People Power Revolution."
1380. Sanchez, "The People Power Revolution."
1381. Neil H. Buchanan, "How the Tide Might Turn: The Inevitable End of Trumpism," *Verdict* (blog), Justia, February 14, 2025, https://verdict.justia.com/2025/02/14/how-the-tide-might-turn-the-inevitable-end-of-trumpism.
1382. Buchanan, "How the Tide Might Turn."
1383. John Austin, Lucas Kreuzer, and Kamil Lungu, "Poland Shows That Democracy Can Triumph. Here's How," *Washington Monthly*, April 24, 2024, https://washingtonmonthly.com/2024/04/24/poland-shows-that-democracy-can-triumph-heres-how/.
1384. Adam Easton, "Conservative Historian Wins Polish Presidential Vote," BBC News, June 2, 2025, https://www.bbc.com/news/articles/cx27897vedno.
1385. Austin, Kreuzer, and Lungu, "Poland Shows That Democracy Can Triumph."
1386. Austin, Kreuzer, and Lungu, "Poland Shows That Democracy Can Triumph."
1387. Austin, Kreuzer, and Lungu, "Poland Shows That Democracy Can Triumph."
1388. "Voter Turnout, 2020–2024," Pew Research Center, June 20, 2025, https://www.pewresearch.org/politics/2025/06/26/voter-turnout-2020-2024/pp-2025-6-26_validated-voters_1-07/.
1389. Tonya Mosley, "As Young Male Voters Shift Right, Can the Left Compete in the 'Battle for the Bros'?" NPR, March 20, 2025, https://www.npr.org/2025/03/20/nx-s1-5333321/as-young-male-voters-shift-right-can-the-left-compete-in-the-battle-for-the-bros.
1390. Barack Obama, "Remarks by the President at the 50th Anniversary of the Selma to Montgomery Marches," speech delivered at the Edmund Pettus Bridge, Selma, Alabama, March 7, 2015, White House, https://obamawhitehouse.archives.gov/the-press-office/2015/03/07/remarks-president-50th-anniversary-selma-montgomery-marches.
1391. Obama, "Remarks by the President at the 50th Anniversary."

12. Building Guardrails

1392. Elisha Anderson, "Detroit Settles Case of 7-Year-Old Girl Shot During Police Raid for $8.25 Million," *Detroit Free Press*, April 4, 2019, https://www.freep.com/story/news/local/michigan/detroit/2019/04/04/aiyana-stanley-jones-settlement-civil/3365796002/.
1393. "Detroit Police Accidentally Shoot, Kill Sleeping 7-Year-Old During Home Raid," *MLive.com*, May 17, 2010, https://www.mlive.com/news/detroit/2010/05/detroit_police_say_7-year-old.html.

1394. Kate Abbey-Lambertz, "How a Police Officer Shot a Sleeping 7-Year-Old to Death," *Huffington Post*, September 17, 2014, https://www.huffpost.com/entry/aiyana-stanley-jones-joseph-weekley-trial_n_5824684.html.
1395. Elisha Anderson, "Weekley Jury Deadlocks in Aiyana Stanley-Jones Death," *Detroit Free Press*, October 10, 2014, https://www.freep.com/story/news/local/michigan/detroit/2014/10/10/weekley-police-shooting/17035877/.
1396. Abbey-Lambertz, "How a Police Officer Shot a Sleeping 7-Year-Old to Death."
1397. Anthony Cuthbertson, "'It Won't Be Boring': SpaceX Starship Launch May End in Explosion, Elon Musk Hints," *The Independent*, April 17, 2023, https://www.the-independent.com/space/spacex-starship-launch-date-elon-musk-b2297482.html.
1398. Megan Garber, "Trump Is Breaking the Fourth Wall," *The Atlantic*, March 6, 2025.
1399. Garber, "Trump Is Breaking the Fourth Wall."
1400. Garber, "Trump Is Breaking the Fourth Wall."
1401. Garber, "Trump Is Breaking the Fourth Wall."
1402. Ben Rhodes, "How Short-Term Thinking Is Destroying America," op ed, *New York Times*, August 11, 2025.
1403. Kristen Welker and Megan Lebowitz, "Trump Won't Rule Out Seeking a Third Term in the White House, Tells NBC News 'There Are Methods' For Doing So," NBC News, March 30, 2025, https://www.nbcnews.com/politics/donald-trump/trump-third-term-white-house-methods-rcna198752.
1404. Bob Bauer and Jack Goldsmith, *After Trump: Reconstructing the Presidency* (Lawfare Press, 2020), 160.
1405. Bauer and Goldsmith, *After Trump*, 161.
1406. Rebecca Beitsch, "Trump Nominates Paul Ingrassia to Lead Office of Special Counsel," *The Hill*, May 30, 2025, https://thehill.com/homenews/administration/5325901-trump-nominates-ingrassia-office-special-counsel/; Paul Ingrassia, LinkedIn profile, accessed September 9, 2025, https://www.linkedin.com/in/paul-ingrassia-22b05810b.
1407. Zach Schonfeld and Ella Lee, "Todd Blanche Takes the Helm of Ghislaine Maxwell Talks," *The Hill*, July 23, 2025, https://thehill.com/newsletters/the-gavel/5414355-todd-blanche-ghislane-maxwell-epstein-files/.
1408. Amanda Becker, "Trump Says Acting Cabinet Members Give Him 'More Flexibility,'" *Reuters*, January 6, 2019, https://www.reuters.com/article/world/trump-says-acting-cabinet-members-give-him-more-flexibility-idUSKCN1P00KW/.
1409. Bauer and Goldsmith, *After Trump*, 327.
1410. Bauer and Goldsmith, *After Trump*, 328.
1411. Bauer and Goldsmith, *After Trump*, 328.
1412. "Section 9-27.000: Principles of Federal Prosecution," *Justice Manual*, US Department of Justice, 2018, https://www.justice.gov/jm/jm-9-27000-principles-federal-prosecution.
1413. "Section 9-27.260 - Initiating and Declining Charges—Impermissible Considerations," *Justice Manual*, US Department of Justice, 2018, accessed December 3, 2025, https://www.justice.gov/jm/jm-9-27000-principles-federal-prosecution#9-27.260.
1414. Michael Wilner, "A Trump Donor, Now a Regulator, Leads Effort to Accuse President's Foes of Mortgage Fraud," *Los Angeles Times*, August 26, 2025, https://www.latimes.com/politics/story/2025-08-26/william-pulte-leads-effort-to-accuse-trump-foes-of-mortgage-fraud.
1415. "Restoring Integrity and Independence at the US Justice Department," Center for American Progress, August 13, 2020, https://www.americanprogress.org/article/restoring-integrity-independence-u-s-justice-department/.
1416. 10 USC § 837(b)(5)(B).US.
1417. Bauer and Goldsmith, *After Trump*, 146–147.
1418. Bauer and Goldsmith, *After Trump*, 147.
1419. Morrison v. Olson, 487 US 654, 699 (1988) (Scalia, J. dissenting).
1420. Billal Rahman and Dan Gooding, "House Democrats Move to Ban ICE Agents From Wearing Masks," *Newsweek*, July 1, 2025, https://www.newsweek.com/democrats-ice-agents-mask-ban-bill-2093186.

1421. Billal Rahman, "Map Shows States Trying to Ban ICE Agents Wearing Masks," *Newsweek*, July 24, 2025, https://www.newsweek.com/map-shows-states-trying-ban-ice-agents-wearing-masks-2103502.
1422. Michael Waldman, "Will Tariffs Awaken a Sleeping Congress?" Brennan Center for Justice, September 9, 2025, https://www.brennancenter.org/our-work/analysis-opinion/will-tariffs-awaken-sleeping-congress.
1423. 10 USC §12406(5)(B).
1424. Gavin Newsom v. Donald J. Trump, No. 25-cv-04870-CRB, Order Granting Plaintiffs' Application for Temporary Restraining Order (N.D. Cal. June 12, 2025), 19.
1425. Gavin Newsom v. Donald J. Trump, 24.
1426. Larry Kaplow, "Judge Rules Against National Guard in LA, and Trump Vows to Send Them to Chicago," NPR, September 2, 2025, https://www.npr.org/2025/09/02/nx-s1-5525647/a-california-judge-rules-that-trumps-deployment-of-the-guard-to-la-was-illegal.
1427. Kaplow, "Judge Rules Against National Guard in LA."
1428. Ann E. Marimow, "Supreme Court Refuses to Allow Trump to Deploy National Guard in Chicago," *New York Times*, December 23, 2025.
1429. Bob Bauer and Jack Goldsmith, "Here's What Trump Could Unleash by Invoking the Insurrection Act," op ed, *New York Times*, October 18, 2025.
1430. Bauer and Goldsmith, "Here's What Trump Could Unleash."
1431. Lindsay Whitehurst, "Trump Takes Over DC Police to Fight Crime. Here's What the Law Says," *Associated Press News*, August 11, 2025, https://apnews.com/article/trump-washington-crime-national-guard-police-13ba96454031352665e59ee67f678482.
1432. Josh Meyer, "DC's Highest Crime Neighborhoods Have Yet to See Trump Crackdown," *USA Today*, August 14, 2025, https://www.usatoday.com/story/news/politics/2025/08/14/dc-high-crime-neighborhoods-no-trump-surge/85654858007/.
1433. US Const. art. I, §9, cl. 8, 10.
1434. US Const. art. II, §1, cl. 7.
1435. Detroit City Charter (2012).
1436. 40 C.F.R. § 4.130.
1437. "AG Brown Statement on Federal Court Temporarily Blocking Unconstitutional Order on Birthright Citizenship Nationwide," press release, Office of the Attorney General, Washington State, January 23, 2025, https://www.atg.wa.gov/news/news-releases/ag-brown-challenges-unconstitutional-order-birthright-citizenship.
1438. "California National Guard Fire Crews Operating at Just 40% Capacity Due to Trump's Illegal Guard Deployment," press release, Office of Governor Gavin Newsom, June 24, 2025, https://www.gov.ca.gov/2025/06/24/california-national-guard-fire-crews-operating-at-just-40-capacity-due-to-trumps-illegal-guard-deployment/.
1439. Chris Hippensteel, "Massachusetts Governor Proposes $400 Million for Colleges, Citing Federal 'Uncertainty,'" *New York Times*, July 31, 2025.
1440. Samantha Cheney, "Massachusetts Announces Vaccine Access Plans, Governor Slams Trump Administration and RFK Jr.," WBZ News, September 5, 2025, https://www.msn.com/en-us/health/other/massachusetts-announces-vaccine-access-plans-governor-slams-trump-administration-and-rfk-jr/ar-AA1LTpAV.
1441. Emily Baumgaertner Nunn, "States Go Their Own (and Contradictory) Ways on Vaccine Policy," *New York Times*, September 3, 2025.
1442. Nunn, "States Go Their Own (and Contradictory) Ways."
1443. "A New Immigration System to Safeguard America's Security, Expand Economic Growth, and Make Us Stronger," NPR, February 12, 2005, https://www.npr.org/2025/02/12/g-s1-48347/steve-bannon-pleads-guilty-border-fraud.
1444. Thomas Jefferson, letter to Edward Carrington, January 16, 1787, A to Z Quotes, accessed November 2, 2025, https://www.azquotes.com/quote/145792.
1445. Jenn White, "In Case You Missed It: Civic Education 101," 1A (NPR/WAMU), March 28, 2022, https://www.npr.org/2022/03/29/1089467750/in-case-you-missed-it-civic-education-101.
1446. "The Comptroller General of the United States," US Government Accountability Office, accessed September 5, 2025, https://www.gao.gov/about/comptroller-general.

1447. Tessa Wong, Leehyun Choi, and Yuna Ku, "'Are We About to Repeat History?' Martial Law's Traumatic Legacy in South Korea," BBC, December 6, 2024, https://www.bbc.com/news/articles/c1el7xxp0gyo.
1448. Maxine Joselow, "Park Service is Ordered to Take Down Some Materials on Slavery and Tribes," *New York Times*, September 16, 2025.
1449. Joselow, "Park Service Is Ordered to Take Down Some Materials."
1450. Citizens United v. Federal Election Commission, 558 US 310 (2010).
1451. Zephyr Teachout, *Corruption in America: From Benjamin Franklin's Snuffbox to Citizens United* (Harvard University Press, 2014), 209; Buckley v. Valeo, 424 US 1, 143 (1976).
1452. Buckley v. Valeo, 143.
1453. Teachout, *Corruption in America*, 209; Buckley v. Valeo, 143.
1454. Teachout, *Corruption in America*, 210.
1455. Teachout, *Corruption in America*, 210.
1456. Citizens United v. FEC, 365.
1457. Daniel I. Weiner, "Citizens United Explained," Brennan Center for Justice, December 12, 2019, https://www.brennancenter.org/our-work/research-reports/citizens-united-explained.
1458. Teachout, *Corruption in America*, 232.
1459. Teachout, *Corruption in America*, 232.
1460. "2024 Outside Spending, by Super PAC," Open Secrets, https://www.opensecrets.org/outside-spending/super_pacs.
1461. Bryan Metzger, "Elon Musk Spent At Least $277 Million Backing Trump and the GOP. Here's Where All That Money Went," *Business Insider*, December 6, 2024, https://www.businessinsider.com/elon-musk-260-million-spending-trump-republican-party-2024-12.
1462. Metzger, "Elon Musk Spent At Least $277 Million."
1463. Charles Duhigg, "Silicon Valley, the New Lobbying Monster," *New Yorker*, October 7, 2024.
1464. Duhigg, "Silicon Valley, the New Lobbying Monster."
1465. Disclose Act of 2021, S. 443, 117th Cong. (2022).
1466. Disclose Act of 2021, S. 443, 117th Cong. (2022).
1467. Amy B. Wang, "Senate Republicans Block Bill to Require Disclosure of 'Dark Money' Donors," *Washington Post*, September 22, 2022.
1468. "Shaheen Renews Push to Overturn Citizens United Ruling, Rid American Elections of Dark Money and Excessive Corporate Campaign Spending," press release, Office of Senator Jeanne Shaheen, March 27, 2025, https://www.shaheen.senate.gov/news/press/shaheen-renews-push-to-overturn-citizens-united-ruling-rid-american-elections-of-dark-money-and-excessive-corporate-campaign-spending.
1469. Ashley Balcerzak, The Center for Public Integrity, "Study: Most Americans Want To Kill 'Citizens United' with Constitutional Amendment," May 10, 2018, https://publicintegrity.org/politics/study-most-americans-want-to-kill-citizens-united-with-constitutional-amendment/.
1470. Robert Reich, "How to Get Rid of 'Citizens United,'" Substack Newsletter, November 24, 2025, https://substack.com/home/post/p-177418904.
1471. James Romoser, "The Friday Read: How Trump Could Snatch a Third Term—Despite the 22nd Amendment," *Politico*, January 31, 2025; https://www.politico.com/news/magazine/2025/01/31/trump-defy-constitution-third-term-00200239.
1472. Scott Bomboy, "How the 22nd Amendment Came into Existence," *Constitution Daily* (blog), National Constitution Center, April 5, 2019, https://constitutioncenter.org/blog/how-the-22nd-amendment-came-into-existence.
1473. US Const. amend. XXII.
1474. Romoser, "The Friday Read: How Trump Could Snatch a Third Term."
1475. Romoser, "The Friday Read: How Trump Could Snatch a Third Term."
1476. Romoser, "The Friday Read: How Trump Could Snatch a Third Term."
1477. Romoser, "The Friday Read: How Trump Could Snatch a Third Term."
1478. Romoser, "The Friday Read: How Trump Could Snatch a Third Term."
1479. Romoser, "The Friday Read: How Trump Could Snatch a Third Term."
1480. Perez v. United States, 402 US 146 (1971).
1481. Lorance v. United States, No. 20-3055 (10th Cir. 2021).

1482. Yunior Rivas, "Texas Republicans Vote to Advance Extreme Gerrymander," *Democracy Docket*, August 18, 2025, https://www.democracydocket.com/news-alerts/texas-republicans-vote-to-advance-extreme-gerrymander/.
1483. Eric Bradner, Arit John, Arlette Saenz, and Steve Contorno, "Texas GOP Now Faces Clear Path to Redraw Congressional Maps in Trump-Backed Push," MSN, August 2025, https://www.msn.com/en-us/politics/government/texas-gop-now-faces-clear-path-to-redraw-congressional-maps-in-trump-backed-push/ar-AA1KMXWw.
1484. Giselle Ruhiyyih Ewing, "Trump on Texas Redistricting: 'We Are Entitled to Five More Seats,'" *Politico*, August 5, 2025, https://www.politico.com/news/2025/08/05/trump-texas-redistricting-00493624.
1485. J. David Goodman, "Texas Democrats Will Return Home, Allowing Vote on Congressional Map," *New York Times*, August 14, 2025.
1486. Patrick Marley, "North Carolina Lawmakers Vote to Add GOP House Seat, in Win for Trump," *New York Times*, October 21, 2025.
1487. Kellen Browning, "California Voters Approved a New Map That Helps Democrats. Now What?" *New York Times*, November 5, 2025.
1488. Steven Levitsky and Daniel Ziblatt, *How Democracies Die* (Crown, 2018), 9.
1489. Michigan Independent Citizens Redistricting Commission, "Frequently Asked Questions (FAQ)," accessed August 18, 2023, https://www.michigan.gov/micrc/about/archives/faq.
1490. Gabrielle Franklin, "Colorado Among the States with an Independent Redistricting Commission," MSN, August 5, 2025, https://www.msn.com/en-us/politics/government/colorado-among-the-states-with-an-independent-redistricting-commission/ar-AA1JYCjT.
1491. Mitch Smith, "Indiana Lawmakers Reject Trump's New Political Map," *New York Times*, December 11, 2025.
1492. "Letter to Congress on Ending Single Member Congressional Districts and Adopting Proportional Representation," Scholars for Redistricting Reform, Medium, September 19, 2022, https://medium.com/@scholars-redistricting-reform/open-letter-to-congress-to-end-single-member-congressional-districts-and-adopt-proportional-97ad1cf6aa2e.
1493. Blake Hounshell, "Scholars Ask Congress to Scrap Winner-Take-All Political System," *New York Times*, September 19, 2022.
1494. Lee Drutman and Jesse Wegman, "To Escape Our Two-Party Trap, We Need a Better System of Electing People to Congress: Proportional Representation," *New York Times*, January 14, 2025.
1495. "Letter to Congress on Ending Single Member Congressional Districts."
1496. "Letter to Congress on Ending Single Member Congressional Districts."
1497. Drutman and Wegman, "To Escape Our Two-Party Trap."
1498. Drutman and Wegman, "To Escape Our Two-Party Trap."
1499. Hounshell, "Scholars Ask Congress to Scrap Winner-Take-All Political System."
1500. Kaitlyn Radde and Connie Hanzhang Jin, "The Next Round of Counting Begins in Alaska. Here's How Ranked-Choice Voting Works," NPR, November 22, 2022, https://www.npr.org/2022/11/22/1138422560/the-next-round-of-counting-begins-in-alaska-heres-how-ranked-choice-voting-works.
1501. Radde and Jin, "The Next Round of Counting."
1502. Jennifer Horton and Dr. Dakota Thomas, "Ranked Choice Voting: What, Where, Why & Why Not," Council on State Governments, March 21, 2023, https://www.csg.org/2023/03/21/ranked-choice-voting-what-where-why-why-not/.
1503. Horton and Thomas, "Ranked Choice Voting: What, Where."
1504. Sam Oliker-Friedland, "Mamdani Won, But Ranked-Choice Voting Lost," *The Hill*, July 25, 2025, https://thehill.com/opinion/campaign/5412702-mamdani-won-but-ranked-choice-voting-lost/.
1505. Darragh Roche, "How Sarah Palin Was Thwarted in Alaska Election by Ranked-Choice Voting," *Newsweek*, September 1, 2022, https://www.newsweek.com/how-sarah-palin-was-thwarted-alaska-election-ranked-choice-voting-1738792.
1506. Patrick Whittle and David Sharpe, "Democratic Rep. Jared Golden Wins Through Maine's Ranked Choice Voting," *Associated Press News*, November 15, 2024, https://apnews.com/article/maine-house-congress-golden-theriault-bb072ca55aaab2ebae3fb8b6339cb545.

1507. Alex Cohen, "The National Popular Vote, Explained," Brennan Center for Justice, December 8, 2020, https://www.brennancenter.org/our-work/research-reports/national-popular-vote-explained.
1508. Denise Lu, "The Electoral College Misrepresents Every State, But Not As Much as You May Think," *Washington Post*, December 6, 2016.
1509. Cohen, "The National Popular Vote, Explained."
1510. Steven Levitsky and Daniel Ziblatt, *Tyranny of the Minority: Why American Democracy Reached Its Breaking Point* (Crown Publishing Group, 2023), 233.
1511. Anderson, "Detroit Settles Case of 7-Year-Old Girl Shot During Police Raid."

13. Vision for the Future

1512. Tresa Baldas, "Troy Restaurant Owner Gets Prison for Hiring Illegal Workers after Fire," *Detroit Free Press*, February 1, 2017, https://www.freep.com/story/news/local/michigan/oakland/2017/02/01/roger-tam-illegal-workers-fire/97351752/.
1513. Ben Rhodes, "How Short-Term Thinking Is Destroying America," op ed, *New York Times*, August 11, 2025.
1514. Rhodes, "How Short-Term Thinking Is Destroying America."
1515. Kaitlyn McInnis, "The Countries Where You Can 'Buy Happiness,' According to New Data," *Forbes*, June 24, 2025, https://www.forbes.com/sites/kaitlynmcinnis/2025/06/24/the-countries-where-you-can-buy-happiness-according-to-new-data/.
1516. McInnis, "The Countries Where You Can 'Buy Happiness.'"
1517. Amie Parnes, "Mamdani Defeats Cuomo: Here are 5 Reasons Why," *The Hill*, November 4, 2025, https://thehill.com/homenews/campaign/5589877-affordability-mamdani-new-york/.
1518. David Marchese, "The Interview: Robert Reich Thinks the Baby-Boomers Blew It," *New York Times*, July 26, 2025.
1519. "National Poverty in America Awareness Month: January 2025," US Census Bureau, January, 2025, https://www.census.gov/newsroom/stories/poverty-awareness-month.html.
1520. Eleanor Pringle, "Trump Said Foreign Countries Would 'Eat' Tariffs—But US Consumers and Businesses Will Actually Pay 75% at Best," *Fortune*, August 11, 2025, https://fortune.com/2025/08/11/trump-foreign-countries-eat-tariffs-pass-through-consumers/.
1521. "Exclusions from Federal Labor-Management Relations Programs," executive order, White House, March 27, 2025, https://www.whitehouse.gov/presidential-actions/2025/03/exclusions-from-federal-labor-management-relations-programs/.
1522. "Exclusions from Federal Labor-Management-Relations Programs."
1523. Chris Cameron, "Appeals Court Allows Trump Order that Ends Union Protections for Federal Workers," *New York Times*, August 1, 2025.
1524. Cameron, "Appeals Court Allows Trump Order."
1525. Eileen Sullivan, "Trump Orders Have Stripped Nearly Half a Million Federal Workers of Union Rights," *New York Times*, September 1, 2025.
1526. Sam M. Huisache, "First-Time Home Buyer Statistics: Age, Income, & Trends," *Today's Homeowner*, May 14, 2025, https://todayshomeowner.com/home-finances/first-time-home-buyer-statistics/.
1527. Huisache, "First-Time Home Buyer Statistics."
1528. Jordan Weissmann, "Trump Officials Plan to Fire 95% of CFPB Staff, Cancel Its Lease, Union Lawsuit Says," MSN, February 14, 2025, https://www.msn.com/en-us/money/human-resources/trump-officials-plan-to-fire-95-of-cfpb-staff-cancel-its-lease-union-lawsuit-says/ar-AA1z40DU.
1529. Weissmann, "Trump Officials Plan to Fire95% of CFPB Staff."
1530. Weissmann, "Trump Officials Plan to Fire95% of CFPB Staff."
1531. Weissmann, "Trump Officials Plan to Fire95% of CFPB Staff."
1532. John Authers, "Why Google's Monopoly Is Outlasting Rockefeller's," *Bloomberg*, September 5, 2025, https://www.bloomberg.com/opinion/articles/2025-09-05/why-google-s-monopoly-is-outlasting-rockefeller-s.
1533. Authers, "Why Google's Monopoly Is Outlasting Rockefeller's."
1534. Authers, "Why Google's Monopoly Is Outlasting Rockefeller's."

1535. Authers, "Why Google's Monopoly Is Outlasting Rockefeller's."
1536. Authers, "Why Google's Monopoly Is Outlasting Rockefeller's."
1537. Neera Tanden and Debu Gandhi,"A New Immigration System to Safeguard America's Security, Expand Economic Growth, and Make Us Stronger," Center for American Progress, July 6, 2025, https://www.americanprogress.org/article/a-new-immigration-system-to-safeguard-americas-security-expand-economic-growth-and-make-us-stronger/.
1538. Jesse Humpal, "The Labor Shortage Is Worsening. 'Iron Cards' Are the Answer," op ed, *Washington Post*, September 4, 2025.
1539. Humpal, "The Labor Shortage Is Worsening."
1540. 8 USC § 1158.
1541. 8 USC § 1158.
1542. "What Does USAID Do," USAFacts, https://usafacts.org/explainers/what-does-the-us-government-do/agency/us-agency-for-international-development/.
1543. Andorra Bruno, "Frequently Asked Questions on Deferred Action for Childhood Arrivals (DACA)," Congressional Research Service, R48590, June 29, 2025, https://www.congress.gov/crs-product/R48590.
1544. Tim Arango, "Trump Crime Strategy May Work for Now, But Not for Long, Experts Say," *New York Times*, August 31, 2025.
1545. Arne Duncan, "Trump's Crackdown Will Make Crime Worse," *New York Times*, August 22, 2025.
1546. Alia Harvey-Quinn, "No, Mayor Duggan, Trump Gets No Credit for Detroit Violent Crime Reduction," *Detroit Free Press*, August 21, 2025, https://www.freep.com/story/opinion/contributors/2025/08/21/trump-detroit-duggan-violence-crime-cvi-shotstoppers-michigan/85748517007/.
1547. Duncan, "Trump's Crackdown Will Make Crime Worse."
1548. Duncan, "Trump's Crackdown Will Make Crime Worse."
1549. Melina Walling and Seth Borenstein, "Trump Called Climate Change a 'Con Job' at the United Nations. Here are the Facts and Context," PBS News, September 25, 2025, https://www.pbs.org/newshour/politics/trump-called-climate-change-a-con-job-at-the-united-nations-here-are-the-facts-and-context.
1550. Max Bearak, "'China is the Engine' Driving Nations Away from Fossil Fuels," *New York Times*, September 8, 2025.

14. Civic Awakening

1551. Michael Barbaro, "Buying a Trump Property, Or So They Thought," *New York Times*, May 12, 2011; Aaron Katersky and M. L. Nestel, "Judge Finalizes $25 Million Settlement for 'Victims of Donald Trump's Fraudulent University,'" ABC News, April 9, 2018, https://www.congress.gov/119/meeting/house/118342/documents/HHRG-119-JU05-20250604-SD020-U20.pdf.
1552. Barbaro, "Buying a Trump Property, Or So They Thought."
1553. Barbaro, "Buying a Trump Property, Or So They Thought."
1554. Barbaro, "Buying a Trump Property, Or So They Thought."
1555. Michael Barbaro and Steve Eder, "Former Trump University Workers Call the School a 'Lie' and a 'Scheme' in Testimony," *New York Times*, May 31, 2016.
1556. Donald Trump with Tony Schwartz, *Trump: The Art of the Deal*, reissue (Ballantine Books, 2015), 60.
1557. Jane Fritsch, "A DAY OF TERROR: THE RESPONSE; Rescue Workers Rush In, And Many Do Not Return," *New York Times*, September 12, 2001.
1558. Michael Scherer, "The Anti-Trump Strategy That's Actually Working," *The Atlantic*, September 2, 2025.
1559. "Litigation Tracker: Legal Challenges to Trump Administration Actions," *Just Security*, accessed November 2, 2025, https://www.justsecurity.org/107087/tracker-litigation-legal-challenges-trump-administration/.
1560. Scherer, "The Anti-Trump Strategy That's Actually Working."
1561. Scherer, "The Anti-Trump Strategy That's Actually Working."
1562. Scherer, "The Anti-Trump Strategy That's Actually Working."

1563. "Read Conservative Judge's Full Opinion Rebuking Trump Administration Over Abrego Garcia Case," *Time*, April 18, 2025, https://time.com/7278774/judge-harvie-wilkinson-opinion-read-full-text-trump-abrego-garcia/.
1564. American Association of University Professors v. Rubio, 1:25-cv-10685-WGY, Findings of Fact and Rulings of Law, September 30, 2025, https://storage.courtlistener.com/recap/gov.uscourts.mad.282460/gov.uscourts.mad.282460.261.0.pdf.
1565. Scherer, "The Anti-Trump Strategy That's Actually Working."
1566. Scherer, "The Anti-Trump Strategy That's Actually Working."
1567. Jim Clark, "Collective Action: The Ultimate Force Multiplier," *Forbes*, February 7, 2025, https://www.forbes.com/councils/forbesnonprofitcouncil/2025/02/07/collective-action-the-ultimate-force-multiplier/.
1568. Ruth Ben-Ghiat, "What Trump and Hegseth Really Fear," *Lucid* (blog), Substack, June 8, 2025,https://lucid.substack.com/p/what-trump-and-hegseth-really-fear.
1569. Ben-Ghiat, "What Trump and Hegseth Really Fear."
1570. Peter Nicholas, "'NATO for Nonprofits': Groups Organize to Band Together If Targeted by Trump," NBC News, October 2, 2025, https://www.nbcnews.com/politics/donald-trump/nato-nonprofits-groups-band-together-trump-rcna234954.
1571. Nicholas, "NATO for Nonprofits."
1572. "Countering Domestic Terrorism and Organized Political Violence," executive order, White House, September 25, 2025, https://www.whitehouse.gov/presidential-actions/2025/09/countering-domestic-terrorism-and-organized-political-violence/.
1573. Nicholas, "NATO for Nonprofits."
1574. "Civil Society Solidarity Letter & Signatories: An Open Letter Rejecting Presidential Attacks on Nonprofit Organizations," press release, Democracy Defenders Fund, October 1, 2025, https://www.democracydefendersfund.org/prs/10.1.25-pr.
1575. "Civil Society Solidarity Letter & Signatories."
1576. "Civil Society Solidarity Letter & Signatories."
1577. Nicholas, "NATO for Nonprofits."
1578. Home page, League of Women Voters, accessed September 11, 2025, https://www.lwv.org/.
1579. David A. Graham, "Why the 'No Kings' Protests Matter," *The Atlantic*, October 2025.
1580. Aaron Blake, "The GOP's Extraordinary Rhetoric About the 'No Kings' Rallies," CNN, October 18, 2025, https://www.cnn.com/2025/10/18/politics/gop-rhetoric-no-kings-protests-analysis.
1581. Blake, "The GOP's Extraordinary Rhetoric."
1582. Brooks Barnes, "Disney+ Cancellations Jump After Kimmel Cancellation," *New York Times*, October 20, 2025.
1583. Barnes, "Disney+ Cancellations Jump."
1584. Kellie Carter Jackson and Nicole Hemmer, "Why We're Holding a Teach-In About American History at the Smithsonian," *The Guardian*, October 24, 2025, https://www.theguardian.com/commentisfree/2025/oct/24/smithsonian-teach-in-trump-war-on-history.
1585. Jackson and Hemmer, "Why We're Holding a Teach-In."
1586. Jackson and Hemmer, "Why We're Holding a Teach-In."
1587. Jackson and Hemmer, "Why We're Holding a Teach-In."
1588. Jackson and Hemmer, "Why We're Holding a Teach-In."
1589. Jessi Hempel, "Social Media Made the Arab Spring, But Couldn't Save It," *Wired*, January 14, 2016, https://www.wired.com/2016/01/social-media-made-the-arab-spring-but-couldnt-save-it/.
1590. Hempel, "Social Media Made the Arab Spring."
1591. Hempel, "Social Media Made the Arab Spring."
1592. "Quote Origin: The Only Thing Necessary for the Triumph of Evil Is That Good Men Do Nothing," Quote Investigator, December 4, 2010, https://quoteinvestigator.com/2010/12/04/good-men-do.
1593. "A Pastoral Note to Migrants from the Catholic Bishops of Michigan," Michigan Catholic Conference, February 2025, https://www.micatholic.org/advocacy/news-room/news-releases/2025/a-pastoral-note-to-migrants/.

1594. Judith Orloff, "The Secret to Empathic Listening," *Psychology Today*, September 11, 2024, https://www.psychologytoday.com/us/blog/the-genius-of-empathy/202409/the-secret-to-empathic-listening.
1595. Michael S. Schmidt, "When Silence Speaks Volumes," *New York Times*, July 11, 2025.
1596. Scott Nover, "Media Including Fox News Overwhelmingly Reject Pentagon Press Policy," *Washington Post*, October 14, 2025.
1597. Alan Blinder, "All But Two Universities Decline a Trump Offer of Preferential Funding," *New York Times*, October 20, 2025.
1598. Erica Orden and Kyle Cheney, "Maurene Comey Warns Her Former Colleagues: 'Fear Is the Tool of the Tyrant,'" *Politico*, July 17, 2025, https://www.politico.com/news/2025/07/17/maurene-comey-letter-firing-00459560.
1599. John Cassidy, "James Comey and Donald Trump Go to War," *New Yorker*, April 13, 2018.
1600. "7c. The Trial of John Peter Zenger," US History, accessed September 12, 2025, https://www.ushistory.org/us/7c.asp.
1601. "The Trial of John Peter Zenger."
1602. Alan Feuer, "Grand Juries in D.C. Reject Wave of Charges Under Trump's Crackdown," *New York Times*, September 6, 2025.
1603. Ruth Ben-Ghiat, "How Artists Use Humor to Mock Tyrants," *Lucid* (blog), September 7, 2025, https://lucid.substack.com/p/my-op-comic-wivan-ehlers-on-autocracys.
1604. Andy Rose, "Trump Says 'It's Anarchy' in Portland. Here's Why Locals Say That's Far from Reality," CNN, September 30, 2025, https://www.cnn.com/2025/09/30/us/portland-residents-trump-troops.
1605. Claire Rush and Jonathan Matisse, "How Inflatable Costumes Ballooned at Anti-Trump Rallies Due to Portland Protester's Frog Outfit," MSN, October 23, 2025, https://www.msn.com/en-us/news/other/how-inflatable-costumes-ballooned-at-anti-trump-rallies-due-to-a-portland-protesters-frog-outfit/ar-AA1PoPFs.
1606. Rush and Matisse, "How Inflatable Costumes Ballooned."
1607. David Marchese, "The Interview: Robert Reich Thinks the Baby-Boomers Blew It," *New York Times*, July 26, 2025.
1608. Nadine Smith, "Laughter, Not Obedience: The Power of Mockery Against Authoritarianism," *Wide Awake America* (blog), Substack, February 9, 2025, https://1nadinesmith.substack.com/p/laughter-not-obedience-the-power.
1609. Dave Roos, "The Political Cartoonist Who Helped Lead to 'Boss' Tweed's Downfall," History, last updated January 31, 2025, https://www.history.com/articles/thomas-nast-boss-tweed-cartoons.
1610. David Folkenflik, "A Pulitzer Prize Winner Quits 'Washington Post' After a Cartoon on Bezos Is Killed," NPR, January 4, 2025, https://www.npr.org/2025/01/04/nx-s1-5248299/cartoonist-quits-wapo-over-bezos-trump-cartoon-washingtonpost.
1611. Alan Feuer, Devlin Barrett, and William K. Rashbaum, "Prosecutors Fail to Obtain Indictment Against Man Who Threw Sandwich at Federal Agent," *New York Times*, August 27, 2025.
1612. Salvador Rizzo, "Jury Finds D.C. 'Sandwich Guy' Not Guilty," *Washington Post*, November 6, 2025.
1613. Rizzo, "Jury Finds D.C. 'Sandwich Guy' Not Guilty."
1614. Guy, @GP Swenson, "I think I like 'A salt with a deli weapon' better. He really is a salt. And Pirro's ham-fisted prosecution was deli-ciously sub-standard," Bluesky, November 7, 2025, 9:47 a.m., https://bsky.app/profile/gpswenson.bsky.social/post/3m52d3zyjyc2w; Josh Meyer (@JoshMeyerDC), "The Reuben Missile Crisis," X, November 7, 2025, https://x.com/joshmeyerdc/status/1986814266926633088?s=43&t=raD4W2T39C6Eynh8HjRUgw.
1615. Rizzo, "Jury Finds D.C. 'Sandwich Guy' Not Guilty."
1616. Tom Dreisbach and Tim Mak, "Yes, Capital Rioters Were Armed. Here Are the Weapons Prosecutors Say They Used," NPR, March 19, 2021, https://www.npr.org/2021/03/19/977879589/yes-capitol-rioters-were-armed-here-are-the-weapons-prosecutors-say-they-used.
1617. John Koblin, "'South Park' Takes On Trump and Wins Bigly," *New York Times*, November 8, 2025.

1618. Samantha Vincenty, "Amy Poehler and Tina Fey Teamed Up as Pam Bondi and Kristi Noem in SNL's Cold Open," NBC, October 12, 2025, https://www.nbc.com/nbc-insider/amy-poehler-tina-fey-snl-cold-open-pam-bondi-kristi-noem.
1619. Heather Hollingsworth, "Politicians and Dog Experts Vilify South Dakota Governor After She Writes About Killing Her Dog, "*Associated Press News*, April 30, 2024, https://apnews.com/article/kristi-noem-book-dog-killing-5710b302e33f61c697f20ab3b227a19b.
1620. Home page, Run For Something, accessed December 17, 2025, https://runforsomething.net/; Home page, Emily's List, accessed December 17, 2025, https://emilyslist.org/.
1621. David Jesse, "Washtenaw County Commissioner Candidate Wins by One Vote," *The Ann Arbor News*, August 3, 2010, https://www.annarbor.com/news/county-commissioner-candidate-projecting-a-one-vote-win/.
1622. Robert A. Caro, *The Power Broker: Robert Moses and the Fall of New York* (Alfred A. Knopf, 1974).
1623. Caro, *The Power Broker*, 14.
1624. Caro, *The Power Broker*, 15.
1625. Caro, *The Power Broker*, 15.
1626. Caro, *The Power Broker*, 18.
1627. Caro, *The Power Broker*, 15.
1628. Caro, *The Power Broker*, 19.
1629. Caro, *The Power Broker*, 19.
1630. Caro, *The Power Broker*, 19.
1631. Caro, *The Power Broker*, 17.
1632. Caro, *The Power Broker*, 19.
1633. Caro, *The Power Broker*, 19.
1634. Katersky and Nestel, "Judge Finalizes $25 Million Settlement."
1635. David Brooks, "America Needs a Mass Movement—Now," *The Atlantic*, October 14, 2025.
1636. Susie Allen, "How Autocracies Unravel," *Kellogg Insight*, August 10, 2023, https://insight.kellogg.northwestern.edu/article/how-autocracies-unravel.
1637. Allen, "How Autocracies Unravel."
1638. Catherine Kim, "Marjorie Taylor Greene's Populist Rebellion," *Politico*, October 9, 2025, https://www.politico.com/newsletters/politico-nightly/2025/10/09/marjorie-taylor-greenes-populist-rebellion-00601061.
1639. Chad de Guzman, "Marjorie Taylor Greene Is a Thorn in the GOP's Side, But on Its Left or Right?" *Time*, October 13, 2025, https://time.com/7325308/marjorie-taylor-greene-georgia-republican-independence-shutdown-gaza-epstein-trump/.
1640. AZ Quotes, Shirley Chisholm, accessed October 19, 2025, https://www.azquotes.com/quote/55041.
1641. Lisa Mascaro, "Democratic Leader Jeffries Says Trump's 100 Days Filled with 'Chaos, Cruelty and Corruption,'" *Associated Press News*, April 30, 2025, https://apnews.com/article/trump-100-days-jeffries-schumer-democratic-leaders-587b5dc7ea0d525e9ebae28a6dcf355e.

INDEX

S

T

U

V

Z

ABOUT THE AUTHOR

University of Michigan law professor **BARBARA MCQUADE** is a legal analyst for NBC News and MS NOW, as well as co-host of the podcast #SistersInLaw. Her 2024 book *Attack from Within: How Disinformation Is Sabotaging America* was a *New York Times* bestseller. McQuade was appointed by President Barack Obama as US Attorney for the Eastern District of Michigan, the first woman to be so appointed, serving in that position from 2010 to 2017. She has received many awards and honors, including *The Detroit News*'s Michiganian of the Year Award and the Arab-American Civil Rights League's Tribute to Justice Award. She and her husband have four children and live in Ann Arbor.